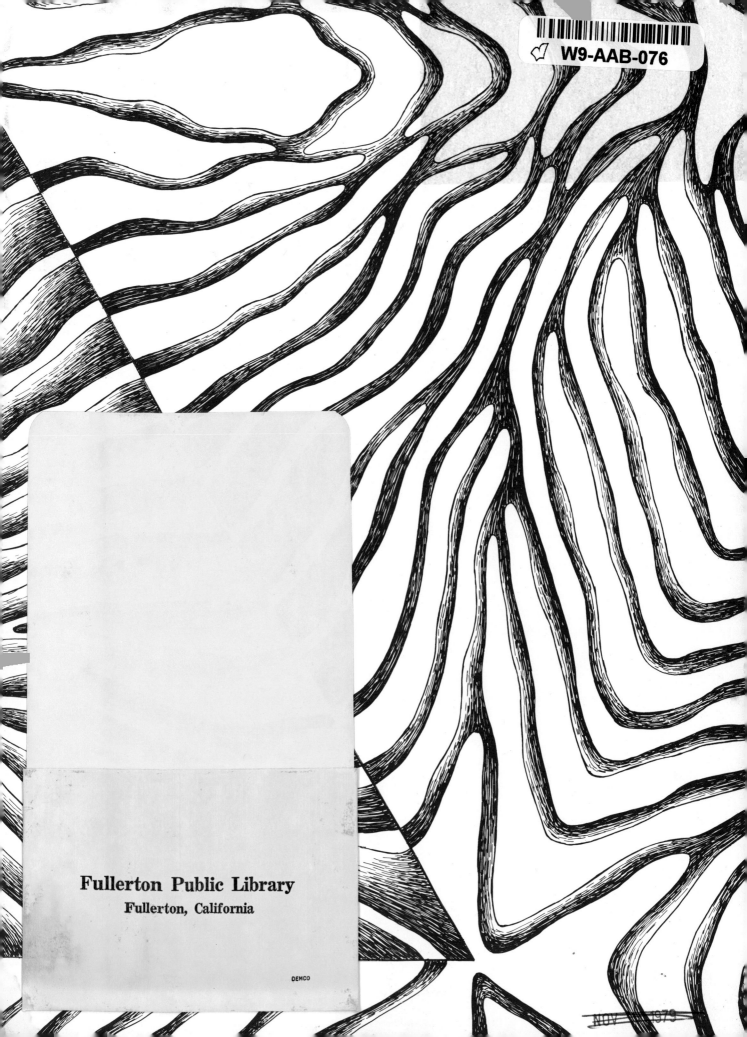

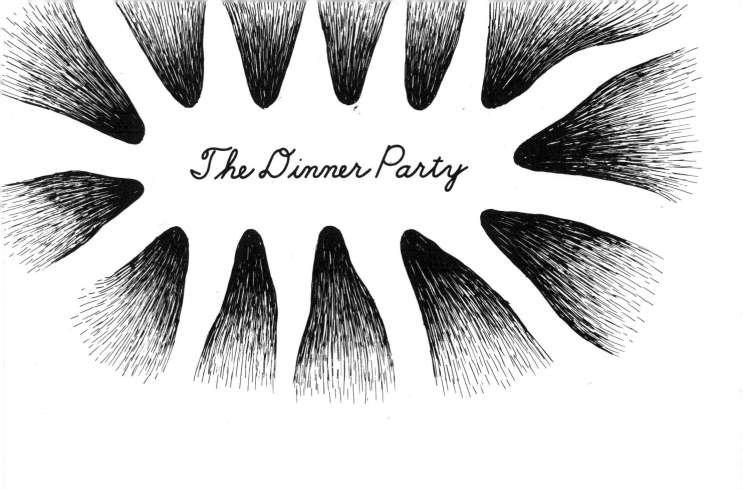

The Dinner Party

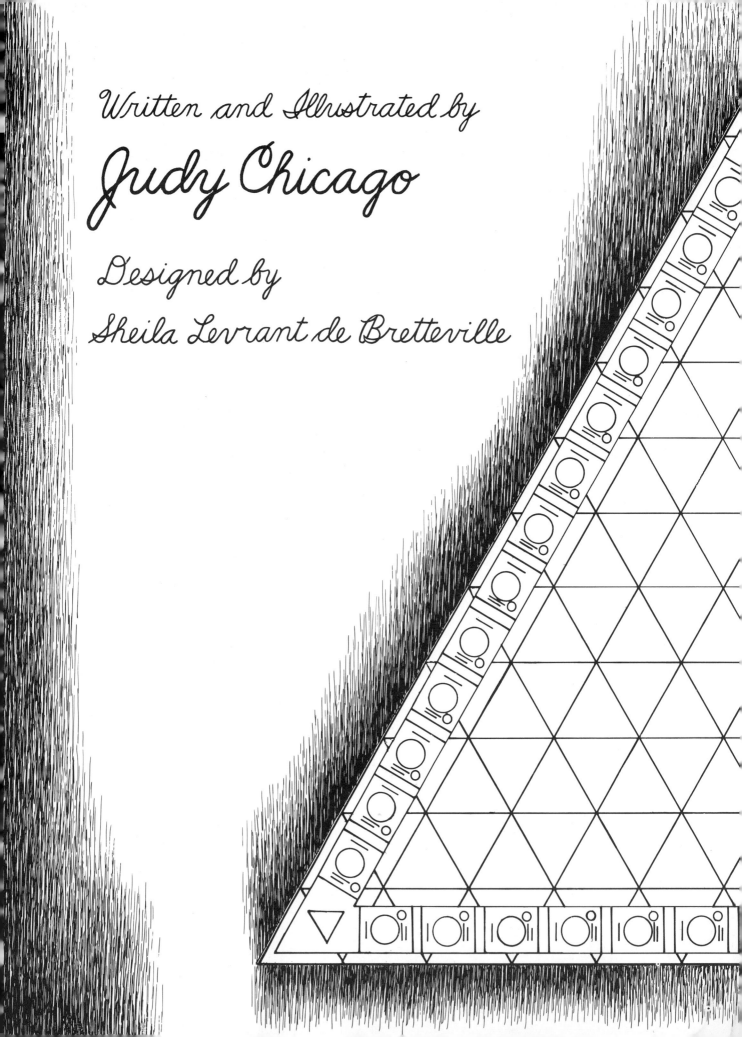

Written and Illustrated by

Judy Chicago

Designed by

Sheila Levrant de Bretteville

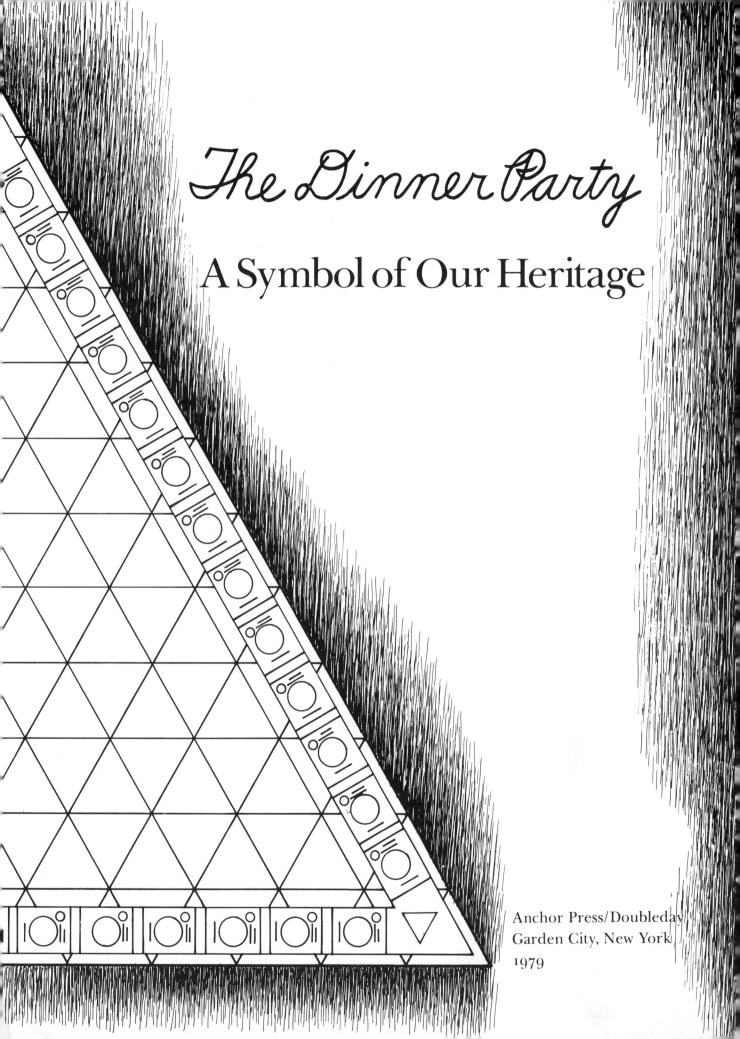

The Dinner Party

A Symbol of Our Heritage

Anchor Press/Doubleday
Garden City, New York
1979

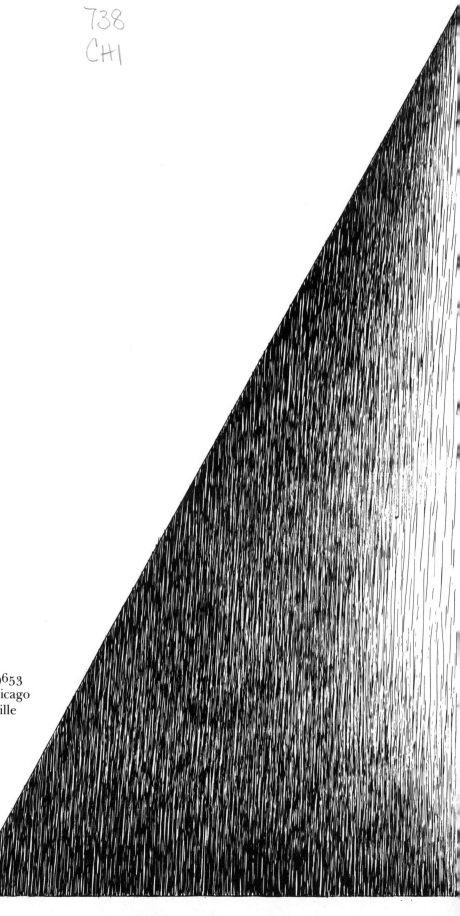

The Dinner Party is published
simultaneously in hardcover
and paperback editions.
Anchor Press Edition 1979

Library of Congress Cataloging in
Publication Data

Chicago, Judy, 1939 –
The Dinner Party.

Includes index.
1. China painting – Exhibitions.
2. Needlework – Exhibitions.
3. Women in art – Exhibitions.
I. Title.
NK4605.C45   738   78-69653
ISBN: 0-385-14566-7

Library of Congress
Catalog Card Number   78-69653
Copyright © 1979 by Judy Chicago
Designed by Sheila de Bretteville
Set in Baskerville type.
All rights reserved.
Printed in the
United States of America
First editions

Contents

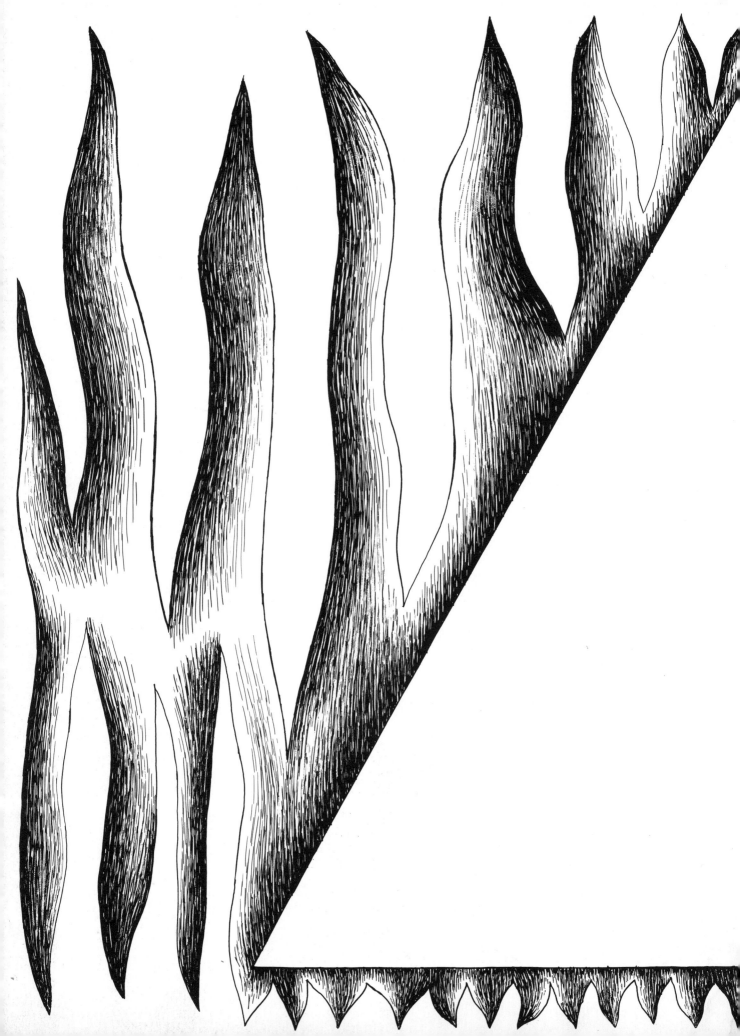

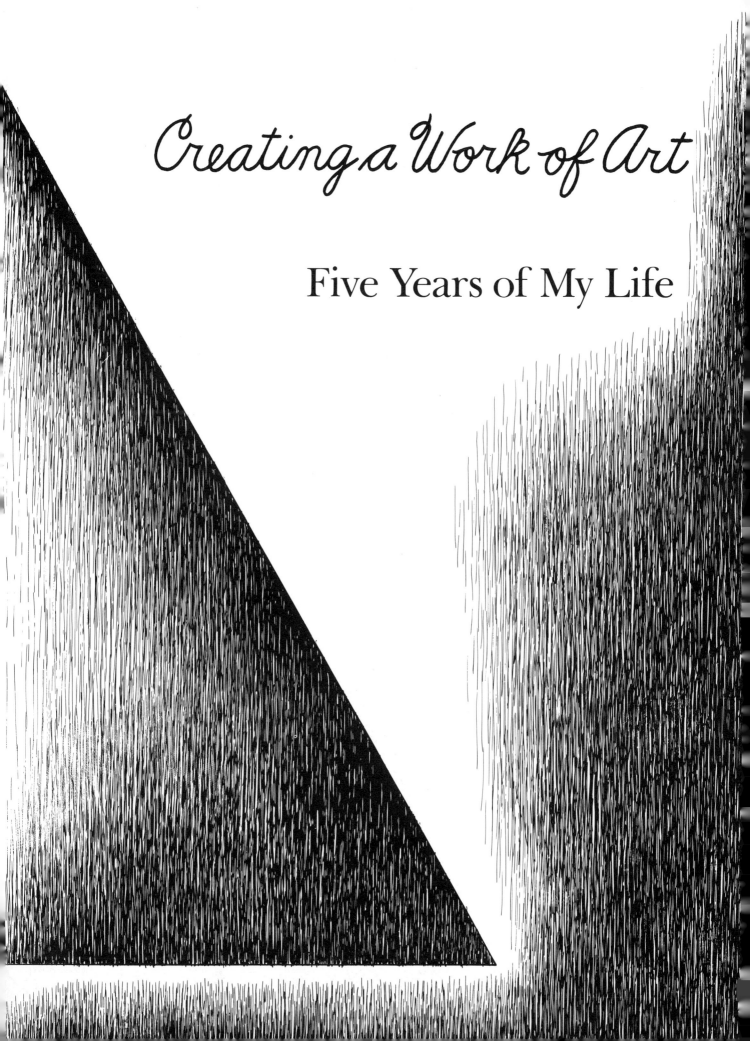

Creating a Work of Art

Five Years of My Life

In the beginning, the feminine principle

During a trip up the northwest coast in the summer of 1971, I stumbled onto a small antique shop in Oregon and went in. There, in a locked cabinet, sitting on velvet, was a beautiful hand-painted plate. The shopkeeper took it out of the case, and I stared at the gentle color fades and soft hues of the roses, which seemed to be part of the porcelain on which they were painted. I became enormously curious as to how it had been done. The next year I went to Europe for the first time and found myself almost more interested in cases of painted porcelain than in the endless rows of paintings hanging on musty museum walls.

Classically trained as a fine artist, I felt somewhat uneasy with my interest in decorative arts. But I was sufficiently fascinated by the china-painting I had seen in Europe to enroll in a class given at a small shop in Los Angeles in the fall of 1972. The first class consisted of learning to mix pigments with what seemed like very exotic oils and then practicing to make dots, dashes, and commas, which, I was told, were the basic components of china-painting brushwork. We also learned how to thin down our paint so it would flow through a crow-quill pen point for line work. We then traced some forget-me-nots onto gleaming white porcelain plates and proceeded to do the pen work we had learned.

I soon realized that this hobbyist approach was not what I had in mind. I wanted to learn the basic components of the china-painting medium and use it for a new work – a series of painted plates that related to the series of paintings I had been doing, entitled "Great Ladies." These abstract portraits of women of the past were part of my personal search for a historical context for my art. After having worked on plexiglass for a number of years, I was now spraying paint on canvas. But I was dissatisfied with the way the color sat on top of the canvas surface instead of merging with it, as it had done on the plastic. I also wanted to use a brush again, thus allowing a contact with the paint surface that cannot be achieved by spraying.

The rose plate I had seen in Oregon suggested not only another painting technique, but also another format for my "Great Ladies." Since plates are associated with eating, I thought images on plates would convey the fact that the women I planned to represent had been swallowed up and obscured by history instead of being recognized and honored. I originally conceived of one hundred plates, which would hang on the wall as paintings normally do; the idea of setting the plates on a table came later.

Although the china-painting class left much to be desired, something else was beginning to unfold. I had been a "serious" art student from the time I was young, and later I became deeply involved in the art world. The women in this class were primarily housewives interested in filling their spare time. However, they also genuinely wanted to find a way to create something of value, and, as I learned more about the china-painting world, I realized that a number of these women were dedicated professionals as well. Shortly after I left the class, a sculptor friend of mine, Bruria, introduced me to Miriam Halpern, a china-painter who was sophisticated about art. Mim agreed to teach me, with the understanding that I didn't want to learn to paint forget-me-nots, but rather to develop an overall knowledge of china-painting techniques.

Under Mim's supervision, I undertook a series of test plates that allowed me to explore the various aspects of the medium. She also introduced me to the world of the china-painter – the magazines, the organizations, and the exhibitions. The first time I attended a china-painting exhibition I was flabbergasted both by the quality of some of the work and by the size of the crowds. I was used to small art-world audiences, not to hundreds – and, at the international show, thousands – of viewers.

At these exhibitions, the painters worked at booths and demonstrated their techniques in classes. Hundreds of women watched attentively, made notes, bought supplies, and exchanged information. I was struck by everyone's seriousness and was somewhat puzzled that the painters, seemingly oblivious to the people around them, could work even while they were being asked questions. I, in contrast, could work only if I were alone, had gone through my morning ritual (which required at least an hour of quiet), and had an entirely uninterrupted day.

During the year and a half I studied china-painting, I attended exhibitions, met painters, visited their houses, and asked questions about the history of china-painting. I learned that for the last thirty or forty years, china-painting had been entirely in the hands of these women and they had been responsible for preserving this historic technique. In the 1950's, a number of china-painters began to organize classes, shows, and publications. Before that, one could only learn the technique through one's mother or grandmother. Many women worked full-time in their home studios – painting, teaching, and showing. Despite the fact that some of them had been painting for as long as forty years, they didn't know how, nor did they have the resources, to present their work properly; it was poorly exhibited, improperly installed, and inadequately lighted, and it sold for outrageously low prices. Many china-painters had gone to art school when they were young and had soon married and had

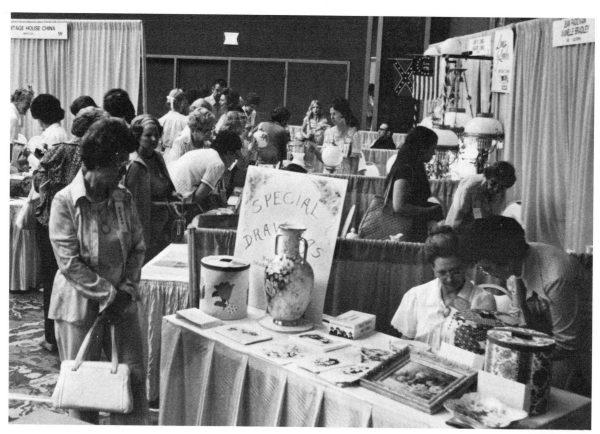

A china-painting exhibition.

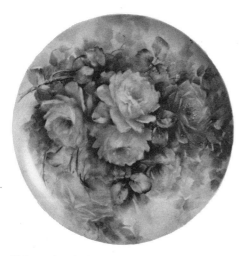

China-painted plate by Rosemarie Radmaker.

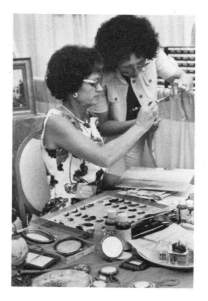

Rosemarie Radmaker and Judy Chicago at a china-painting show.

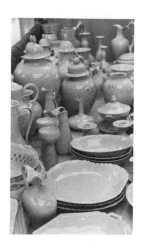

Imported porcelain pieces typical of those decorated by china-painters.

children. They later looked for a way to express themselves that did not require – as it did for so many professional artists – a choice between their family life and their work.

I remember one particularly poignant experience of visiting a china-painter's house and seeing, as Virginia Woolf once said, that the very bricks were permeated with her creative energy. All the chairs had needlepoint cushions; all the beds were covered with quilts; all the pillowcases were hand-embroidered; all the walls were covered with oil paintings; all the plates were painted with flowers; and the garden was planted with the kinds of flowers that were painted on the plates. This woman had done all that work, trying as best she could to fit her creative drive – which could probably have expanded into mural-size paintings or monumental sculptures – into the confined space of her house, which could hardly have held another piece of work.

The china-painting world, and the household objects the women painted, seemed to be a perfect metaphor for women's domesticated and trivialized circumstances. It was an excruciating experience to watch enormously gifted women squander their creative talents on teacups. I wanted to honor the women who had preserved this technique, and, by making china-painting visible through my work, I hoped to stimulate interest in theirs.

I finished my studies by 1974, and by that time my plan had changed. I had discarded the idea of painting a hundred abstract portraits on plates, each paying tribute to a different historic female figure. Instead, I was thinking about a series called "Twenty-five Women Who Were Eaten Alive." In my research I realized over and over again that women's achievements had been left out of history and the records of their lives had apparently disappeared. My new idea was to try to symbolize this. I had seen a traditional dinnerware set that had taken its creator, Ellie Stern, three years to paint. It made me think about putting the plates on a table with silver, glasses, napkins, and tablecloths, and over the next year and a half the concept of *The Dinner Party* slowly evolved. I began to think about the piece as a reinterpretation of the Last Supper from the point of view of women, who, throughout history, had prepared the meals and set the table. In my "Last Supper," however, the women would be the honored guests. Their representation in the form of plates set on the table would express the way women had been confined, and the piece would thus reflect both women's achievements and their oppression.

There were thirteen men present at the Last Supper. There were also thirteen members in a witches' coven, and witches were always associated with feminine evil. The fact that the same number had both a positive and a negative connotation seemed perfect for the dual meaning of the piece; the idea of twenty-five plates therefore gave way to thirteen.

But the Last Supper existed within the context of the Bible, which was a history of a people. So my *Dinner Party* would also be a people's history – the history of women in Western civilization. As I explained in my autobiography, *Through the Flower,* I had been personally strengthened by discovering my rich heritage as a woman and the enormous amount of information that existed about women's contributions to society. This information, however, was totally outside the mainstream of historical thought and was certainly unknown to most people. And as long as women's achievements were excluded from our understanding of the past, we would continue to feel as if we had *never* done anything worthwhile. This absence of any sense of our tradition as women seemed to cripple us psychologically. I wanted to change that, and I wanted to do it through art.

My goal with *The Dinner Party* was consistent with all my efforts in the previous decade. I had been trying to establish a respect for women and women's art; to forge a new kind of art expressing women's experience; and to find a way to make that art accessible to a large audience. I firmly believed that if art speaks clearly about something relevant to people's lives, it can change the way they perceive reality. In a similar way medieval art had been used to teach the Bible to illiterate people. Since most of the world is illiterate in terms of women's history and contributions to culture, it seemed appropriate to relate our history through art, particularly through techniques traditionally associated with women – china-painting and needlework.

I was planning thirteen plate settings, with the name of each woman embroidered on the tablecloth along with a phrase indicating what she had achieved. It became evident, however, that thirteen plates were not enough to represent the various stages of Western civilization, and therefore the number tripled. I arrived at the idea of an open triangular table, equilateral in structure, which would reflect the goal of feminism – an equalized world. (Also, the triangle was one of the earliest symbols of the feminine.) But there was something wrong with the image of this large table without a context: The concept of an isolated woman "pulling herself up by her bootstraps" simply did not stand up to the evidence of history. Rather, women's achievements took place against a background of societies in which women either had equal rights or were predominant to begin with or, later, enjoyed expanded opportunities, agitated for their rights, or built support networks among themselves.

To convey this idea, I decided to place the triangular table on a floor inscribed with the names of additional women of achievement besides those represented by place settings. This would suggest that the women at the table had risen from a foundation provided by other women's accomplishments, and each plate would then symbolize not only a particular woman but also the tradition from which she emerged. The floor would be porcelain, like the plates, and the women's names would be painted on triangular tiles in gold china-paint with a luster overglaze. This would make the names appear and disappear as the viewer walked around the table – a fitting metaphor for women's history.

By March 1975, the conceptual work on the piece was completed. The only changes that would take place later would be the decision to make the goblets and flatware out of clay and the decision to put the women's names on individual runners rather than on the tablecloth itself. I planned to embroider the name and a phrase around the plate in a circle as a way of making the identity of the woman clear. I had obtained a sewing machine, and I now began trying to learn how to embroider the names. At this point I believed that I could do the china-painting in the morning, the needlework in the afternoon, and the research in the evenings!

I had begun work on the plates for the piece the preceding summer. As I was familiar with porcelain imported from Japan, which is used by many contemporary china-painters, I naturally started out using Japanese plates in my first test series. The exact composition of this porcelain is a highly guarded secret, but one of its attributes is that it doesn't break, no matter how many times it's fired. Some china-painters build up color very slowly, and I've heard of a piece being fired as many as forty-two times.

I chose fourteen-inch plates because everything was going to be slightly oversized in order to emphasize that this was not a normal dinner party table. With thirteen place settings on each of three wings of the table, shaped in a triangle, it seemed that the outside dimension of the piece would be about thirty feet on a side and would fit in a standard museum gallery, which is where I wanted to exhibit it. In order to reach a large audience, I thought *The Dinner Party* should travel to a number of museums, but I was worried about the difficulty of getting them to show feminist art.

The plates were going well and a number were completed, most of them incorporating a butterfly image, which I had used in my work for some time. In *The Dinner Party,* I intended to make the butterfly a symbol of liberation and create the impression through the imagery that the butterfly became increasingly active in her efforts to escape from the plate. I soon found myself thinking about having the forms literally rise, which meant making the plates dimensional. Although I had worked in clay in college and exhibited painted clay sculptures in my graduate show, I had never studied ceramics. Deciding that I would have to develop ceramic skills in order to make certain images, in the fall of 1975 I took a bus to UCLA and – eighteen years after I started undergraduate school there – walked onto the campus to take a ceramics class. But to create the plates I envisioned would mean two years of study; I decided to try to find a technical assistant instead. Leonard Skuro, a graduate student with eight years' experience in porcelain, agreed to work with me for the few months he thought would be required to make the remaining plates.

At about the same time I received a letter from a woman named Susan Hill, who had read *Through the Flower,* had heard me lecture, and wanted to work with me. I didn't know what her abilities were, but I happily accepted her assistance and asked her to do some historical research. Shortly thereafter, I ran into Diane Gelon, an art history graduate I had met several years before when she purchased one of my drawings. I discovered that she had some free time and asked if she'd like to help with the research also. Diane agreed, and soon the Project had four workers.

One day Susan mentioned that she came from a family of needleworkers. I asked her if she'd be interested in doing some needlework investigation, as I'd been having trouble solving the problems of embroidering the names. She spent the next six months doing research on embroidery and needlework history. She also enrolled in an ecclesiastical embroidery class at the Episcopal Diocesan Altar Guild of Los Angeles; this class was taught by a woman named Marjorie Biggs, who eventually made a major contribution to the needlework of *The Dinner Party.*

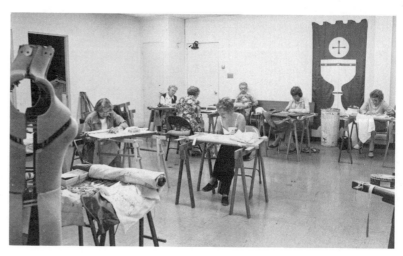

Susan Hill at Ecclesiastical Embroidery Class.

Susan had been showing me the information she was uncovering in her research, and this made me see the richness of yet another neglected area of women's work. She took me to her class, where the women were working on church needlework, and later we went to a show of ecclesiastical embroidery, which both excited and depressed us. Like china-painters, needleworkers receive very little recognition. During the Middle Ages needlework was considered a high art, and the garments women embroidered were worn as emblems of power by church officials and rulers. By the time of the Industrial Revolution, however, needlework had declined and become a domestic art: Women were taught patience and "ladylike" behavior through the discipline of stitchery.

Susan and I thought it would be fitting to turn all this around and use embroidery to aggrandize women, relating our history through the varieties of needlework women have traditionally used. Giving needlework a more significant role in *The Dinner Party* would expand the piece and honor yet another female tradition. Susan had by now informed me that my idea of embroidering circular phrases on the tablecloths was impossible; thirty feet of fabric could not be manipulated through a sewing machine in circles, nor could it be put onto a hoop to do hand-embroidery. She suggested, as an alternative, the idea of individual runners modeled on the "fair linen" that covers the plate during the Eucharist. The runner concept gradually developed from there: We decided to embroider each woman's name on the front of her runner, which would drop over the viewers' side of the table. Instead of using a phrase to describe the woman's achievements, we would design needlework to visually express something about her and the time in which she lived. We also decided to let the runner extend over the back of the table and repeat or expand the imagery on the plate. Specific needlework techniques common to the woman's lifetime would be used, and, additionally, we would illuminate the first letter of her name. Neither of us knew much about embroidery, so we had no idea of the amount of work we were about to undertake.

Since I'd never embroidered and could barely sew, I approached designing for needlework entirely in terms of a visual medium. A number of skilled needleworkers had joined the Project, intrigued by the prospect of using their techniques in new ways. (They were very patient with me, never mentioning that one or another of my runner designs could take as long as a year to complete.) The first time I saw the painted mockup runners translated into stitching, I was ecstatic. The

created parthenogenetically.

color fades and surface quality achieved with silk thread were even more dazzling than those on the china-painted plates. After we had designed the first third of the runners, Susan and I made a trip east to study historic needlework; we returned with the realization that our first designs had only scratched the surface of the potential of embroidery.

In order to accommodate all the needlework we planned, the size of the piece had to expand. Each side of the floor would now be forty-eight feet long and each wing of the table forty-six feet, six inches. The runners were to be thirty inches wide and the table twenty-six inches deep. We decided to cover the corners of the tables with three sumptuous runners embellished with triangular patterns that I designed. The triangle, which symbolizes the feminine, is also the Goddess' sign, and the patterns on these altar cloths are intended to honor the female principle embodied in the concept of the Goddess. Each cloth was done in a different needlework technique. The first, embroidered in white silk by Marjorie Biggs, demonstrates many different stitch patterns. The second was crocheted by Stephanie Martin and Pauline Schwartz, and the last – incorporating shadow-work, needlepoint, and French knots – was a cooperative work supervised by L. A. Olson. All three cloths commemorate the endless hours women have spent trying to create something beautiful by crocheting, making lace, or doing other intricate needlework – labor that has been used for decorations on clothing or in the home and has gone largely unnoticed, never seen or appreciated as art.

Meanwhile, Leonard had been developing the ceramic technology for the plates and, working with a designer friend of his, Ken Gilliam, had produced a jigger machine for us to use in the plate-making process. Leonard and I had decided to make the goblets and flatware in clay. Ken began by designing the flatware and eventually designed the entire installation of *The Dinner Party,* along with the numerous objects, tools, and machines the piece required. The plate-making process, which ultimately took three years, was slowly developed by Leonard. It involved making the plaster molds that formed the interior shape of the plate – as well as the plates themselves – on the jigger machine (a converted potter's wheel). The clay was placed on the mold and compressed by the arm of the machine, which contained a metal template fashioned to cut the exterior of the plate. The plate was left to dry in specially designed drying racks, then trimmed and carved. Later we began to build up the surface of the plate in order to emphasize the rising of the image.

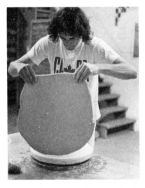

Skuro throwing out a slab of clay.

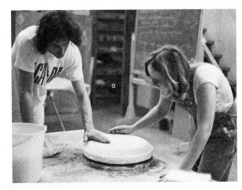

Skuro and Keyes preparing the mold.

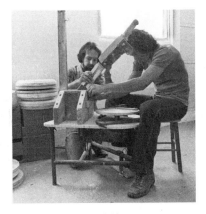

Gilliam and Leonard Skuro building the jigger machine.

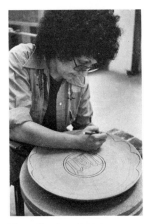

Judye Keyes jiggering a plate.

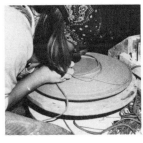

Keyes trimming a plate.

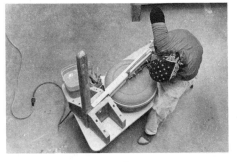

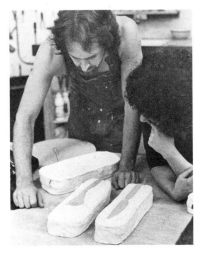

Ken Gilliam and Chicago conferring on flatware design.

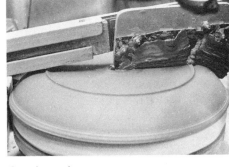

Jiggering a plate.

Transferring the image.

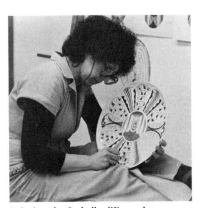

Painting the Isabella d'Este plate.

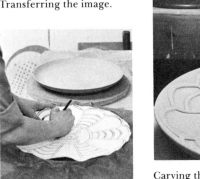

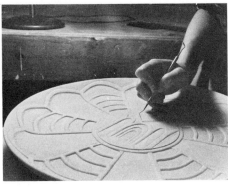

Carving the Isabella d'Este plate.

Transferring the image.

17

connected with coitus, and it was

It required three years to produce the plates, as the ceramic problems we encountered were incredibly difficult. First, there is no porcelain body in America which is comparable to that used for the Japanese plates. Second, the stress placed on a plate that has different thicknesses is enormous and makes it subject to cracking. Carving into the plate or adding onto it creates great variation in thickness, and firing the plate repeatedly puts additional strain on it. In order to achieve a painted surface comparable to the surface of the already finished Japanese plates, the dimensional plates had to be fired at least five times. We had difficulty even making a perfect *flat* fourteen-inch plate and matching the beautiful glaze quality of the plates from Japan. For months Leonard lost every plate he made, and he made hundreds. But these struggles are best described in the journal entries and plate descriptions that appear later in the book.

From the time Gelon joined the Project, my own workload was greatly eased. My initial idea of doing this piece alone was rapidly changing, and I felt staggered by what needed to be done. In addition to carving plates, painting, and designing runners, I was raising money by lecturing and by selling my art. The influx of more people into the *Dinner Party* crew meant integrating them into the studio and, if they came from out of town, helping them get settled as well. Diane began by doing research, then became my personal assistant, and eventually took over all the administrative work of the Project.

The research, like everything else, grew far beyond my original conception. Gelon and I had listed all the women we thought should be on the floor, and it totaled about three hundred. I had determined that there should be nine hundred and ninety-nine – a nice Biblical number, I thought. I had already done a good deal of research for the women on the table, which Gelon completed; she then began the research for the floor. I had previously discovered that there were a great many books dealing with women's history, but the information they provided was fragmented and needed to be unified. We thought we should collect enough research on women of the past so that we could make choices based on an overall historic view. We therefore formed a team – headed by a painter, Ann Isolde – to carry out this work. With no research skills and little scholarly background, team members plundered the libraries for books about women. They learned to cut through the biases of history which usually described, not the woman's achievements, but her physical attributes and the men in her life.

Every Friday afternoon, Ann and the team met at her house to discuss the information they were uncovering and to exchange ideas. Slowly the files grew. Cataloging the material alphabetically and by country, century, and profession, we began to assemble the fractured pieces of our heritage which would eventually appear on the 2,300 twelve-inch, triangular porcelain tiles that make up the Heritage Floor. The research team gradually developed its skills, and new people joined who had sophisticated historical and academic backgrounds. I watched them all undergo a process very similar to my own: As they learned about their history as women, their sense of themselves changed. Their initial lack of confidence was replaced by an understanding of their historic circumstances and a determination to share the information they were finding with other women.

I was already planning a book documenting the creation of *The Dinner Party,* and I decided to expand the section on the Heritage Floor to include short biographies of all the women represented. The book, like everything else in the Project, evolved. This first volume will be followed by a second, which will deal with the needlework in the piece.

As the Project grew and expanded, my isolation as an artist slowly gave way to a studio environment in which many people worked together. At first working with others was extremely difficult for me, and it sometimes still is. But "opening" my studio actually led me to the fulfillment of some earlier goals. I had taught women in Fresno and Los Angeles and encouraged them to work together, openly using their own subject matter, but then I had gone back to my studio and worked alone, making veiled art. I had helped establish alternative exhibition spaces for women and rarely showed in them myself. I had co-founded the Woman's Building and the Feminist Studio Workshop – an alternative educational program – and left within a year because I had not been able to integrate my own art-making life with my need for a support community. When I began working on *The Dinner Party,* I had no idea that it would take five years and so many people to realize my conception. By the time the Project was completed, some of those people had been working for two or three years. The struggle to bring this piece into fruition has given birth to a community – one which is centered on creating art that can affect the world and help change its values.

Several of us have formed a nonprofit corporation which owns *The Dinner Party,* and we hope to house the piece permanently after it has traveled. In order to ensure that women's history will never be lost, I want to design a porcelain room to contain *The Dinner Party*. We also intend to establish an institute to facilitate work in art and design that perpetuates those values which the Project and its process represent.

I am writing this in a house in Bolinas Beach, five months before *The Dinner Party* opens. The studio, which is five hundred miles away, is operating without me for several weeks – an indication that we've built a structure which is independent of me. But none of us knows what will happen after the piece opens, and I admit that I am terrified.

Now, I invite you to read selections from my journals, written over the past five years of the Project. I don't think I could ever recapture the raw feelings you will encounter there. Though it made me anxious to expose the difficulties I've had, I decided to share my struggle, as I have done before in *Through the Flower*. I hope that others will find my experiences useful and will be able to build upon what I have tried to do.

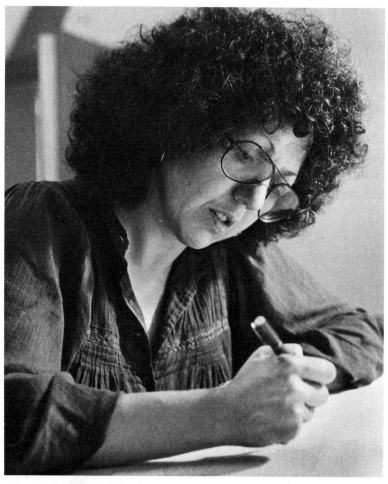

Chicago writing in journal.

Tuesday
MARCH 6, 1973

China-painting is going well –
I'm still learning techniques,
but by the summer I should be
ready to start a real series. I
want to make twenty "Great
Ladies," "Famous Women"
plates, with writing around the
outside edge describing the accomplishments of each woman.
I'm quite excited about that.

Sunday
MAY 13, 1973

I'm planning to make a big
change in my work – to start
the butterflies or papillons, as
they'll be called. I have a lot of
ideas for the butterflies – plates,
porcelain, embroidery, vacuum-
formed, large, small, etc. I want
to work across a variety of
media – some from male culture, some from female culture.
I want the butterfly forms to
allow me to express a variety
of emotional stances and to
be free, liberated forms. They
are slowly taking shape in
my head, and it looks like
they'll occupy me for some time
to come – perhaps for the next
five years. I'm setting up my
new studio to accommodate
them. We have found one at
last, a nice industrial building in
Santa Monica . . .

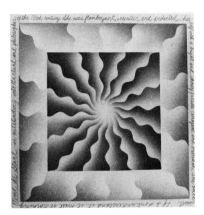

"Madame de Staël" from
Reincarnation Triptych, 1973.

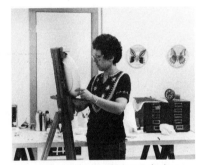

Judy Chicago in the China-Painting
Studio, 1974.

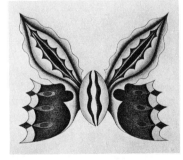

Study for early plate.

Wednesday
MAY 16, 1973

I feel strongly about being a
part of life, rather than separate from it. I have a feeling
that, at this moment in history,
artists have been narrowed into
a remote position outside of
life, and thus are only able to
make art about art about art –
out of contact with themselves
or their community. Maybe artists have to be like congress-
people – representatives of the
needs, feelings, and aspirations
of a group of people. At least
that's what I want to be – to
speak of the longings and yearn-
ings and aspirations of women.

Monday
DECEMBER 10, 1973

I'll let the ideas for the plates
and the embroideries just per-
colate for awhile. I'm not yet
sure exactly what I want. I have
to learn how to fire my kilns,
how to use the embroidery machine. I have to do tests and
maybe even drawings. I might
give myself a few months to
dream. I no longer want to box
myself into long-term decisions.
Rather, I'd like to just give myself lots of time to think about
the ideas and then let them
lead me where they will.

Sunday
APRIL 28, 1974

I've changed my plans. I'm going to work on smaller projects – the first one will be called *The Dinner Party.* It will consist of painted plates presented in the context of a table setting – either a long or round table – cloth, napkins, silver, water glasses, etc. I don't know about chairs yet. In fact, there are a few aspects of the idea that are still unresolved and I'm struggling with them.

The women represented will range from very famous and accomplished women who have been obscured by history to wives of famous men who gave up their careers to unknown women who somehow got lost in their lives. I've been jotting down names on this trip. Hopefully, by the time I go to Bellingham, I'll have worked out the details. Then I'll do small drawings, and when I return to L. A. I will start the china – which I still don't have. I want to work on fourteen-inch plates.

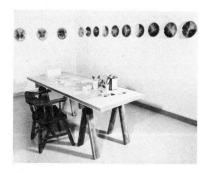

China-Painting Studio, 1974.

Thursday
MAY 9, 1974

I will have Susan B. Anthony at the head of the table, with Elizabeth Cady Stanton at her right, and an array of other women who are not as well known. I want to find a way to make the history of women china-painters become a metaphor for women's history in general. I'm planning to combine images of *traditional* women (symbolized by china-painters) with *radical* women (represented by those who were politically active) at each place setting. My idea at the moment is to write the traditional women's historical information on the backs of their plates. Then the descriptions of the radical women will form a circle around that historical info so that each woman creator will be put into a political context, both women will be contained within a larger set of circumstances, and neither will have escaped the confinement of the female role. All will ultimately be offered up in the *Dinner Party* metaphor – contained within domesticity, served, and ready to be consumed. However, the plates will not be set flat. They sit up on plate racks – rising up, so to speak, from their confinement, but not off the table yet.

Sunday
JUNE 2, 1974

I can't write on the backs of the plates, as I'd planned, and I don't want to write on the fronts. My china-painting teacher, Mim, came over and suggested I have a menu, where I could list each woman and describe her. I decided to do that…I intend to do two drawings a day, allowing myself no more than four hours a drawing – as a way of forcing myself to work more loosely and directly. I want to try to trust my impulses more and push myself to go with what might seem dumb or clumsy images. I want to *be myself* now and get over being worried that it's not enough. But I feel very insecure about what I am going to do next – although I'm ready to do it.

I want to make butterfly images that are hard, strong, soft, passive, opaque, transparent – all different states – and I want them all to have vaginas so they'll be female butterflies and at the same time be shells, flowers, flesh, forest – all kinds of things simultaneously.

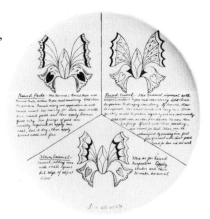

Test plate for china-painting techniques: Raised Paste, Raised Enamel, and Flown Enamel.

Whose body became the symbol of birth

Some drawings go quickly, others slowly. One may take five or six hours, but another ended up taking two days. I've abandoned that arbitrary structure I established and just go along at my own pace. At this point I've done ten drawings. Now I'm working on five more. I want to do each as a monochrome, one hue per drawing. There will be a yellow, red, blue, green, and purple. There's not enough range in orange unless I want to go toward flesh tones, and the first ten drawings include several that are very fleshy. I'll try to do these five before I leave next Thursday. If I can't, I'll continue when I return to L. A. Sometimes I'm very happy with the drawings. Then the next minute I'm very insecure. After these five, I'm thinking of trying to work with specific feeling states – making the images grow out of a feeling. One thing is clear: Unless I'm connected while I'm working, the images go flat and decorative. The only way they work is if they're infused with emotion, and that means I have to be "inside" and not wandering off thinking of something else. It's definitely hard to do. The drawings are more developed than I thought they'd be – but as long as they're going well, I don't want to stop the flow.

Tuesday
JULY 9, 1974

The first few days on the plates were horrendous and frustrating. It's slow, tedious, and I was having a lot of technical difficulties. I finally got over those, but the drawing on two of them is not really good, so I want to do them over. If I hadn't gone to the gym and worked out at the end of the day, I never could have handled the frustration.

Tuesday
OCTOBER 8, 1974

I have been having trouble finalizing the concept of *The Dinner Party*. First I was going to subtitle it "Twenty-five Women Who Were Eaten Alive." Then my concept changed from women who were consumed by history to women who could be models for the future. Then I got into a whole Last Supper thing, thinking I'd do a Last Supper. But then Deena asked me, "Who'd be Judas?", and I realized I didn't want to deal with that. So now I'm somewhat confused, and I want to work it all out and know the limits of the piece. I want it to be multi-layered in meaning, but I think I was getting too complicated. Now I'm thinking again about just *The Dinner Party* with a menu. Each of the women would be on the menu, and they would be women to whom we could look as a panoply of models for the development of a whole new woman. Perhaps I need to outline what facets a truly independent woman would have and then choose women who represent all those facets.

Tuesday
DECEMBER 3, 1974

I'm having a rough time hanging in there lately. Probably because the last group of five plates I fired didn't come out as well as I expected. None of them were right. I felt very frustrated, as if I didn't know enough to do what I wanted to do.

I've asked a number of women for suggested lists of the most important women in history. I'm thinking about making each plate a double woman – one from the past, the other from the present. For example, a goddess and a modern embodiment. The best example would be Margaret Sanger. I discovered that there is a blood-red butterfly called Sangaris. If I can, I'd like to make Sanger all red and have her be a sacrificial figure and herself simultaneously (or a goddess connected to blood sacrifice). What I want to try to do is to make each image layered like that so it compresses history and unites present-day feminist struggle (the last four centuries, that is) with matriarchal times.

and rebirth. Woman's creative power

My mind obsesses constantly about the D. P. I just worked out the installation problem – which a friend, Dextra Frankel, pointed out would present difficulties. She made me realize that the piece would have to be protected from people touching it. So I will have to install it within a viewing area – four white walls, waist-high, with wood tops – which people can walk around to see the piece, which will be just out of arm's reach but readily visible.

Saturday
DECEMBER 7, 1974

I can't seem to stay in there lately, to keep going. I've hit some huge pocket of fear, insecurity, terror, something. It started after I told Lloyd that I was trying to create a masterpiece. I thought he would scoff at me. He didn't, but it made him uncomfortable. I could see my own discomfort with my level of ambition in his eyes.

Since then, it's been heavy social activity, drinking, a hard time working. I feel like I am all thumbs in my studio – feel foolish and inadequate, starting to lose control.

Admitting my ambition to Lloyd freaked me out – admitting it to a man, even him, made me feel dumb and foolish and made me hate him too. I hate men. Yes, I do – at least right this minute. They have made me feel so stupid and so evil for my ambitiousness.

TOMORROW – I WILL START MY SCHEDULE AGAIN – I WILL PUT ONE FOOT IN FRONT OF THE OTHER AND GO FORWARD.

Friday
FEBRUARY 21, 1975

What I'm doing is a sort of *Genesis* – starting with early Mother Goddess figures and working through the change from matriarchy to patriarchy – then on through the centuries, trying to make a link-up between women and their efforts, aspirations, and situations. This can bring me to the twentieth century, where I've decided to end with Woolf and O'Keeffe and the first steps in reestablishing the feminine through imagery.

I'm searching through all this material for women whose lives and efforts allow them to be somehow linked into a larger history of women and of the feminine. I want a curve, I guess – a historical curve – which starts with the origins of human society, the development of matriarchy and its concomitant woman-worship, the

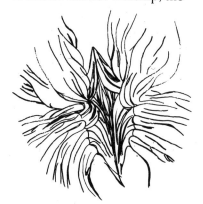

Study for Mary Wollstonecraft's plate – first ceramic version done in 1975.

changeover from mother-right to father-right, the continuing efforts of women to wrest back some power or dignity, the progressive stages of women's situation, the growth of women's rights movements, the reemergence of the female creator and hence the possibility of reintroducing the feminine into the male-dominated and destructive society.

It's really tough and very challenging. I'm very deeply into it, delirious almost, at times. I am up to about the sixteenth century, but I have one or two missing links – a powerful religious woman of the Middle Ages and a Renaissance woman. Then I have to finish the last three centuries, but that's much easier, as I know there are a lot of people who would work. It's more a matter of making choices by then. The later images will require a more active, struggling form. For example, Mary Wollstonecraft struggled against her circumstances a lot more than earlier women. As to the finished plates, some were easy to attribute, some I'm not so sure about.

It's amazing what's happened to me. My art life is infinitely more real than anything else. Everything else is like a dream, or an oasis from the struggle, or a preparation for the struggle, or, in some way, a support system for the work – getting it shown, finished, financed, etc.

Monday
MARCH 17, 1975

After I last wrote in here, I stumbled onto a whole body of information, particularly concerned with the convent, and the changeover from matriarchy to patriarchy, and the way the older images of women were transposed into the Christian structure. This provided me with a view of the origins of the various stereotypes that are still laid on women. It's actually very fascinating and directly connected to the imposition of masculine primacy on the world. Everything is connected with that changeover – all the things we are forever battling. I found more material than I ever dreamed of, and my concept of *The Dinner Party* is expanding to accommodate it.

The plan is complete, I think, but large chunks still have to be put together. First, the table structure will be simple and linear, starting with the early forms of feminine worship, moving through matriarchy, then the changeover (which has to be explained in a sensible way, and I hope to do that), then Christianity and what it provided to women, Feudalism, Chivalry, the Renaissance, the Reformation, and then into modern times – traced both in an imaginative history and in a history of particular women. The whole thing has become a two-part project: a visual piece and a book. Yes, a book, which will contain reproductions of all the plates, technical material on how each was painted, and a historical essay by me.

I don't know yet how many women there will be. I keep feeling that I'd like to structure the number in terms of the witches' covens, which had thirteen. I don't think I can get it into twenty-six, and the next number is thirty-nine. We'll see. There's Gaea, Venus of Willendorf, Ishtar, Snake Goddess, Kali, Sophia, Hatshepsut, Judith, Sappho, Aspasia, Hypatia, Marcella, St. Bridget, Theodora, Herrad, Eleanor of Aquitaine – that's sixteen, and it's only the twelfth century. In addition, I know there'll be Christine de Pisan, a witch, a Renaissance woman, Queen Elizabeth I, Anne Hutchinson, Mary Wollstonecraft, Charlotte Brontë, Emma Willard or Catherine Beecher, Emily Dickinson, Elizabeth Blackwell, Marie Curie, Margaret Sanger, Virgina Woolf, Georgia O'Keeffe, and maybe more. I guess I'll shoot for thirty-nine. Maybe I'll use a triangular table, three sides of thirteen each, which would allow me to use the fact that the triangle is one of the basic forms associated with matriarchal cultures.

Monday
APRIL 14, 1975

I've been working on the drawings for the next group. I have thirteen plates done, and I've got nine new drawings. (I already sold the first set of drawings, and I'd better sell some more work soon, as our money won't last that much longer.) Three more drawings will bring the piece up to the end of the eighteenth century, which is where I'll stop for now.

Friday
JULY 25, 1975

I love to be in my studio now. I just want to be there all the time. Will it be the same after I finish *The Dinner Party*? I worry about the D. P. Are my choices right? Will the piece work when it's all put together? Will I find the money it will take to finish it? Will the last section work? I plan to make sixteen plates in which the image slowly begins to rise up. But can I work it out technically? I've made arrangements to audit ceramics classes at UCLA next year and to work in the studio there, as I have neither the technical skill nor the proper studio facilities to make the plates. And I worry about whether all the museums we're asking will accept the proposal for showing the piece. So far, the San Francisco Museum is tentatively scheduled to be the host museum… But maybe no one else will want it. Then I worry that I won't be able to finish it on time or that I'll get sick or die and never be able to finish it…and I worry and worry, and all this on top of the struggle to do the plates.

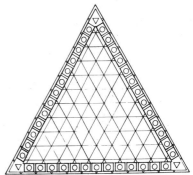

Schematic drawing for *The Dinner Party*.

I have to guard my energy every day so that I'll have it the next. I go to the health club to keep myself fit and work off accumulated frustration so I can handle the next day's effort. I don't talk much, not even to Lloyd, when I'm working hard. This is what I aspired to and this is what I want, no matter what its price. But it is a high price, no question. It costs everything, and the only reward is having done it. That's all.

I just had my thirty-sixth birthday, I cut my hair short, and I somehow am shedding my girlhood. I can feel some womanly part of me developing and growing, and I don't feel like a child anymore. And yet it's hard to have courage to face the struggle every day, knowing one is vulnerable in so many ways – to catastrophe, to illness, to death, to the many things that can happen. I think that is the hardest – living with the reality of human vulnerability and acting and trying and reaching and risking in the face of it.

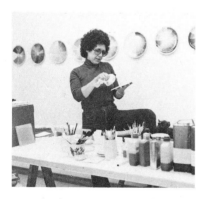

Chicago padding a painted tile.

Tuesday
SEPTEMBER 9, 1975

It is certainly risky investing three years' work in a piece I can only see in my head as a whole. In reality, there are only the parts. I suppose there's a possibility that when it's all put together it will look wrong, but I can't let myself worry about that right now or I'll get more depressed than I already am.

Tuesday
OCTOBER 7, 1975

I finished twenty-three plates – but I want to redo three, two that are not technically solid and one that I'm not happy with esthetically, though I've already done it twice. But I've decided to relief the surface, so it's just as well that I want to do it again.

I am very upset tonight and overwhelmed. I have completed the main part of the D. P. that I can do myself. I've started working at UCLA in ceramics, and the ceramics teacher, Adrian Sachs, has been very helpful. But I thought I would learn all the various ceramics techniques and make the last sixteen plates myself. After one day of trying to make a clay pot, it became clear to me that I don't want to be a potter. Rather, I need a skilled assistant to help me. It looks like Leonard Skuro, a graduate student, will get involved in the ceramics problems. He's very skilled, but I'm not sure whether I'll really be able to work it out. It's going to take a lot of money to finish the piece.

I have to set up the studio to do the ceramics and buy equipment. In order to make the plates I need to do experiments. I don't know what I'll do for money. I guess it means I just go ahead, experimenting, with no guarantee that I'll have either enough money or the facilities to finish.

What it boils down to is that I need the help of society – the help, the support, the resources to finish something that challenges the values of society. Crazy? I really have doubts as to whether I can pull it off this time. Right now I'm in bed. I'm terribly tired. I'm full of anxiety – having bad dreams. I'm tense, frustrated, uptight. I want to get hold of myself and go back to working on what I have some control over... I'm utterly overwhelmed by work, as a matter of fact – so much so that I can't think clearly. So I took to the bed. Tomorrow I'll get up early and start in again, and hopefully that will help . . .

I need some help and support to realize my concept. I must try and trust that it will come forth, but it's very hard for me. Something about this situation brings up some deep mistrust – something connected to my father's death, some sense that he failed me when I needed him. He failed totally: He died, disappeared, abandoned me. I keep thinking that the same thing will happen now – money will not come through, help will not

Her breasts, belly, hips, and vagina.

come through. People say they'll do these things and I am afraid they won't. I'm really up against an internal problem, and I don't want to be immobilized by it. But my knowledge of history and women's defeats, especially combined with my own experiences, can't help but make me worried. My struggle this time is with myself: Can I go forward in the face of all the risks, the probable debts, the uncertainty, the shaky support? Can I just go forward? Can I just keep on plugging away, no matter how frustrating or unsure or shaky the whole project might seem some days? Just continue writing, go back to the research, start the clay tests, make money whenever I can? Can I do it? I don't know. I'm committed to trying, that's all I can say. At this point I'm not sure if it will work out or if it will be successful. But I'm going to try. Will that be enough?

Thursday
OCTOBER 30, 1975

I am on the plane – on my way to San Francisco. I've been at the University of Indiana; in Chicago, where I saw my family and spoke at the Art Institute; and in Carbondale at the college there, where I had an awfully good time and found an apprentice, Judye Keyes. She'll come to L.A. in May. She's a ceramics student with some experience in fibers – which means she knows how to sew. Thus, she can work on the tablecloth and also help with the porcelain…And then I'm

going forward with my plans with Leonard. He'll be my technical assistant. We will do a series of tests over the next six months that will get me ready to make twenty plates. Hopefully, a few will get made during the test period.

Thursday
NOVEMBER 6, 1975

Leonard and I have a big task ahead of us: solving all the technical problems and making the plates, the silver, etc. I still haven't worked out how I'm gonna come up with the $25,000 I need to finish the piece. We haven't sold the book yet, and there's no firm museum schedule. It's all making me nervous – it feels so out of control. I want to go back into my studio, not because there's something I really want to make but rather to provide myself with that feeling of being in control. I'm trying to stay out here, put one foot in front of the other, and do as much as I can.

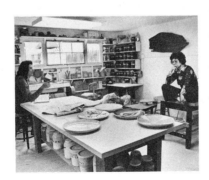

Skuro and Chicago in Skuro's studio, 1975.

Friday
NOVEMBER 21, 1975

Diane Gelon called. She's an art history graduate, sort of undirected. She's bought some art from me, hung around the Woman's Building. I saw her at the art preview for the poster I did for NOW. Suddenly I thought about asking her to work on research for the floor, and she said she'd like to. That made me happy, as another woman – Susan Hill – had written and asked to be my helper; I had put her to work on research, but she wasn't good, and I felt the need for someone more skilled. Suddenly there was Diane. That seems to be happening quite a lot lately. Like that young woman in Carbondale who said she wanted to apprentice herself to me, and then another woman last night who asked about becoming an apprentice. I must be sending out a lot of messages about being accessible and needy, 'cause people just keep cropping up…

We've started plates. I lost two, and we're putting the other six through various underglaze and glaze tests. We're doing simulations of the plates in order to see how the tests work out, and then we'll decide where to go from there. But first we'll do some research on various porcelain bodies and just nose around to make sure we're going in the best direction. It's slow, but we really can't do more.

Wednesday
DECEMBER 10, 1975

It's late in the day – 6:30 or so. Susan Hill is here. By trial and error, we've arrived at the idea of her beginning to work on my embroidery machine and getting involved in the sewn part of the piece. So at this point I have four people helping – Leonard, Susan, Diane, and Judye Keyes.

I go through periods of upset and then periods of calm. The main thing I'm concerned about, of course, is money. I'm applying for all the grants I can, trying to find private sponsorship through my agent, Peri. It's clear that I cannot finish the piece without a team of people, whom I will have to feed and pay at least a minimal amount of money. I could probably easily go through $50,000 in the next two years. I don't quite know how I got to this place, but there's nothing to do but go forward.

I've been working in my studio for the last few weeks, along with Leonard and the others. The first series of plates we did came out lousy, and we're approaching it another way now. We're going to explore casting instead of throwing. Diane is working on research for the floor and making it much more substantial. She's really opening the way to establishing a very coherent history, one which will cross cultures, centuries, and professions and produce a doc-

ument of great value. Meanwhile, Susan is developing familiarity with my embroidery machine…doing research on fabrics, etc. The tablecloth and napkins have to be elaborately conceived, as they have both functional and esthetic purposes. Everything has to be attached, and some system has to be built into the fabric for that.

The piece has grown in concept, even from the point last March when I finalized its shape. The piece now includes the open triangular table, thirty-nine feet on a side, each side holding thirteen plates – thirty-nine in all – tracing the history of women in Western culture. The images combine the particular woman, the period in which she lived, what we know of her, and my imagery. The plates will be presented on the table at a slight angle, supported by a wooden form bolted through the table. Next to each plate will be a napkin with an embroidered edge. There will be oversized porcelain silverware (oversized to match the scale of the plates) which will be lustered with a rainbow luster over a white glaze. There will be a porcelain cup/chalice modeled on those used for communion; I conceive of this cup as white with rainbow luster on the outside and gold on the inside. The plate will be identified by an embroidered semicircle of writing around it on the tablecloth, which will be white, of course, with an edge corresponding to that on the napkin.

The floor tiles will be lustered, and at the moment I am thinking of writing the names in gold. I have found a place to make the tiles.

Everything has to be planned – the way the piece breaks down, how it's set up, the way it's packed, how it's presented – everything…Additionally, I am thinking of a permanent housing. If that comes to pass, I would like to make a porcelain room. But that's far in the future.

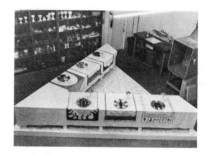

Early mock-up of corner of *Dinner Party* table, July 1976.

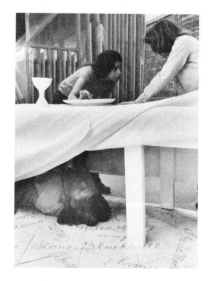

Assembling the mock-up: Diane Gelon and Millie Stein; Kathleen Schneider on floor.

Thursday
DECEMBER 11, 1975

My dream is that I will make a piece so far beyond judgment that it will enter the cultural pool and never be erased from history, as women's work has been erased before. If I am able to do that, I will have achieved the goals I set for myself many years ago. That is my dream – will it become a reality? I don't ultimately care if I'm happy, if I'm sexually satisfied, if I have comfort. This is all that matters to me. It's what I've prepared for all these years. It's what I'm on this earth to do. All the organizing I did, all the reaching out and testing of my resources, everything I've done up till now has prepared the way for this work; to complete it is all I ask from life now.

Friday
DECEMBER 12, 1975

Yesterday Leonard and I went to the County Museum to look at their Italian majolica collection. I saw some in London and was very turned on to it. I think ceramics has lost a lot over the centuries, and I'm interested in retrieving it. I want to incorporate majolica imagery into one of the plates, probably for Isabella d'Este, the Renaissance woman who was involved with a majolica factory. I am now doing some work on glazing, and Leonard is getting ready to work on slip-casting. I also began to investigate making the tablecloth, for which I'll need about two hundred yards of material. Everything's going well in terms of work and help – but no sign yet of where I'll get all the money.

Saturday
DECEMBER 27, 1975

I found a wonderful quote about how God changed sex in the thirteenth century, referring to the widespread worship of Mary then. I want to use it to represent the culmination of Mother Goddess worship and power from the thirteenth to the seventeenth century. I really am weaving a historic viewpoint into this whole piece.

Sunday
JANUARY 4, 1976

I'm realizing that I'm at the outer limits of being able to do any more in terms of *The Dinner Party*. I've got all these people involved, and I'm really going to have to pull back, trust them the best I can, get into the work I can do, and hope for the best. In a way, all these people, with all their ideas about the importance of the piece and their raving about it, make me feel intimidated. Instead of feeling more connected to it, I get afraid of its implications. Perhaps I'll feel better when I'm actually working on it again.

Sunday
JANUARY 18, 1976

Still nothing has firmed up. But on the way down from S.F. with Diane, we decided that she'd work more or less full-time on the D.P. project, not only doing research, but coordinating it. This has begun to be a necessity as the whole project grows, as more and more people come into it (as they are doing). At the moment Diane's living on Unemployment, but that will

only last for three more months – then either she'll have to get a part-time job or I will have to have funding, so that she can have the little bit she needs to live on. The same thing happened when she came into the Project as when Leonard did, and Susan: The area they moved into expanded. Susan has now taken over the sewing section, and she has one helper. Leonard, of course, is in charge of the clay part, and he has two helpers – one here, working two days a week, and Keyes, still in Illinois but coming out here in June.

I've instituted Thursday night sessions for everyone working on the Project. Last Thursday Diane, Leonard, Susan, and I did a consciousness-raising session about expectations, anxieties, and, most of all, money. They all said they'd work till the piece is done whether there's money or not. That took a big load off my mind. Leonard is still dissembling some. It must be difficult for him as the only male, but he's still working and that's something.

I feel, at least most of the time, that the piece will be finished.

Monday
MARCH 1, 1976

Here I am, committed for two years. What an albatross. I can imagine how Michelangelo must have felt – twelve years at that ceiling. Did he do anything else during that time?

29

Sunday
MAY 9, 1976

We are slowly getting organized for the summer. We formed a research team who meet every week and share what they've found. They're slowly compiling the research for the floor. Susan Hill has turned out just great and has been doing marvelously in needlework. We have a team of six or eight women who are starting to do samples of all the various embroidery stitches and techniques, so that I will have a kind of library of reference material in developing the runners underneath the plates. One woman, Pearl Krause, is a needlework designer and came up with a terrific idea for how to do the runners: Just embroider the front piece that drops over the side of the table, letting some of the design move up onto the surface. This eliminates all the problems of the embroidery fighting with the plate and also will allow a more elaborate design on each runner. I'm reconsidering using colored fabric for the runners. I think now they'll be white so that the embroidery and plate will stand out. But I'll wait to make the decision until July, when we do the mockup.

The slowest part is the clay work. Leonard finally found a porcelain body and cast a plate that looked good, but he has virtually stopped working now and is totally engrossed in his Master's show...

The various people are slowly assembling. Judye Keyes is probably bringing a young art student from the Kansas City Art Institute (if her faculty gives her credit) to work for the summer. She, like Judye, is skilled in both fabrics and ceramics; then there's Rachel Seaman, from Irvine, who'll be working three days a week and has already been working with Leonard. Robin Hill (from Kansas) and Keyes will be here at the end of May, and Kathleen Schneider (from Idaho) will be here in mid-June. In June the studio will be reconstructed, and in July we'll do a full-size mockup, a section of the piece, and check the scale and the way the parts come together – making sure we're on the right track with all our decisions. It will probably be the fall, though, before I can really get going on any more plates, as there's still a lot of testing to do.

Monday
JUNE 7, 1976

We're doing some rebuilding in the studio, installing the new kiln, putting in a sink, building shelves and storage cabinets for the molds and plates. Next week Keyes and the others will start casting ceramic tiles for the mockup. Things are going well, though I still have received no grants.

One thing I've been thinking about is the way things seem to go for me. In the past, whenever I tried to *make* things happen, they never did. But if I just put one foot in front of the other, things happen by themselves – I must try and trust that process.

Tuesday
JUNE 15, 1976

I got a National Endowment grant for $5,000, which made me feel TERRIFIC. What a big relief – I managed to round up almost $4,000 to get the studio work done. I guess we'll really pull it off. I need a lot more, though, maybe $3,000, in order to do the floor and still have enough for the materials. But somehow I have confidence that I'll be able to raise enough money. The only problem is not being able to pay people. I have to support Diane, which I'm already doing; eke out a little money for Susan, who is now getting Unemployment; and I'll eventually have to help Keyes. As for Leonard, I'd like to pay him just because I would be able to demand more of him, but for the moment I just have to hope he'll come through. I keep feeling he'll abandon me, which I suppose grows out of my old anxiety about men dying in some way, letting me down. Not helped by the time of year. (Thirteen years now since my first husband, Jerry, was killed. Twenty-three years since my father died. What a long time!)

Thursday
JULY 8, 1976

It's strange. Here I've put this whole project into motion, and instead of feeling good I feel abstracted and disconnected. I got afraid today that there was something wrong with me physically: I was so dizzy and spacy. It's as if it all doesn't matter. I don't know what's with me. It's been so long since I 've been able to paint – maybe that's the problem. I've undertaken this whole big project that involves all sorts of little pieces, which will one day fit together. But in the process of doing everything, I've become so fragmented. Sometimes I wish I'd never gotten into this. I feel tired and depressed and unsatisfied – although everything is going well. I wish I knew what was wrong.

Sunday
AUGUST 1, 1976

We opened the studio and showed the mockup we had built. About thirty or forty people came. I got feedback, which I needed, and learned what aspects of the piece I had overlooked. The calligraphy was one. Since then, I've been working on that (the way the names of the women will be embroidered), the napkin edges, the tablecloth corners and edges, the fastening system. I've begun doing drawings for the next plates. The drawing is very slow and hard. Because so many plates are done, I have to create forms I haven't used already or the images will become repetitive.

I can see when I work how much more focused and conscious I am. Before, I used to give over more to my intuition. Now I have to work within the structure of the piece and use the historic style of the period in some way. I'm thinking more while I work than I used to. I've done the study for Boadaceia, and I did one for Hypatia which I'm going to redo. I didn't do what I had in mind, and though the drawing is beautiful, it is not what I aimed for. So I'm doing it again. I want to fill in all the gaps in the first twenty-six plates and do them first. Leonard is working on the plate problem again After some hassles with him, things seem to be okay. I had had a lot of dreams about his pulling out of the project and, when I returned to L.A. from the china-painting show in New Orleans, he called and said almost word-for-word what he had said in my dream. I confronted him (as I had in my dream) with being scared of the challenge, and finally, after a long and deep conversation, he committed himself. He doesn't function as a member of the team, as the women do, but I'm willing to let him work in the way he wishes. If we ever get any other men on the Project, I am sure it will be easier for Leonard.

As it is, the women are all involved in the process of feminist education. They're in CR, and we have our weekly Thursday nights in which we discuss various subjects. It's nice, though sometimes tedious for me. I try and remind myself that all these people are working with me for nothing, and I try to be responsible to their growth and needs – but sometimes it's hard. And I wonder if I've copped out from the struggle of being alone in the studio. I'll just have to live this all through and then evaluate it.

The work goes on. We're trying to accomplish certain goals by the end of August so that we'll be able to make the first eight runners, start on the napkins, and work out all the details of edges, calligraphy, and fastening. I want to finish the section of drawings I mentioned, work with Leonard, and decide who is going to make the tile floor. Leonard found a tile company outside S.F., run by a woman, and we approached them for sponsorship. So far we've heard nothing. Our alternative is the people in Monrovia who cast the porcelain I've used for china-painting. They want to do it, but it would require more money ($7,500) and more work, as all the two thousand tiles would have to be hand-sanded, and we would have to help. But the floor would be fabulous. I don't know yet how I'm going to come up with the money to finish everything; right now we're only okay till January.

Diane is going to write for grants again, though our last round didn't produce too many results. I realize there is a lot I haven't recorded about the process of the piece. Suffice it to say that it is moving along. I continue to work in the face of anxiety, insecurity, frustration, and lack of the world's support. I realize that only one thing is important – to finish it, no matter what the cost.

Monday
AUGUST 9, 1976

I woke up this morning with the terrors. First thing I thought when I opened my eyes was about *The Dinner Party* – but this time it was negative thoughts – how I was creating the biggest white elephant in the world. I suppose the feelings grow out of having gone to an art opening last night and experiencing the old gap between who I know myself to be and how the powerful people in the world see me (powerful in the sense of having the power to affect my life).

It seems that if I am not with Diane, who sees me as I see myself, or in the process of working on the piece with the other people who believe in me, my own belief falters and I begin to lose my grasp of who I am and what I'm capable of. Then I thought about Mary Cassatt's giant mural and realized that it was because of the support of a large female audience that she painted what was probably one

of the most ambitious paintings ever done by a woman. And it was lost. I can't get over that. Had it not been lost, she would have had to be dealt with in a different way than she has been by art history. It would have been harder for art historians to minimize her; they would be confronted with her power every time they looked at her picture. I really feel low. I wonder if I can sustain myself on my own behalf without the world's reinforcement. And no matter what people say, it is not enough to be supported by those who are powerless. It is in forcing the powerful people to accept one's ideas as significant and important that ultimately one is assured of having those ideas accepted in the world.

So today I am alone, and my self is capsizing. I think there is a growing gulf between my own belief in myself and how I present myself to the world. A crack in the wall, as they say – one that could perhaps lead to despair, madness, suicide. I am not immune, though I have thought myself to be. It is getting harder, not easier.

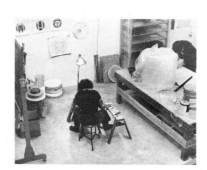

Chicago carving a plate.

I went to an opening last night, and I saw, in the eyes of artists who've been friendly to me, a certain cloud pass over. A cloud that grows from what? A discrepancy between their lack of success and mine? Or their fear of me, perhaps because I've made my position in the world so clear? I saw dealers flee from me, and I even watched another woman artist temper her warmth toward me in front of a hotshot male dealer who was courting her. I woke up this morning with a knot in my stomach and an ache in my throat.

And now many people have heard about the piece, and there is growing curiosity, which certainly increases the pressure on me. I have gotten myself into the hot spot. All my claims are on the line. If I can't pull this piece off, that will be that – at least for the ten years it would take me to retreat, lick my wounds, and slowly create a new body of work that could smooth over the memory of my failure. But the problem is, I'm not at all sure that even if I do pull it off, it will matter one iota. It could be trivialized, or we could fail in our efforts to create a permanent housing, and *The Dinner Party* – like Cassatt's mural – could be lost. It would all come to nothing, and now, as every day brings the piece more into being, I get increasingly anxious. When I'm working on it my anxieties are allayed, and then a day of quiet and they boil up in me.

Tuesday
SEPTEMBER 7, 1976

Here is what has been accomplished: We have designed eight runners, obtained enough linen to begin (having finally found a fabric we like and can afford), built the embroidery frames, done all the necessary translation from painted designs to needlework techniques. The actual runners will soon be underway. In ceramics, we are close to having solved the problems connected with making plates that can be reliefed. As of now, one nicely carved plate is in the kiln, being tested for china-painting problems and process. The silverware and fastening systems are all worked out. We've designed corner pieces for the table, and I even designed a needlework pattern in the shape of a triangle for the Great Goddess that sits on the corners. We got everything accomplished this summer that we set out to do. We haven't yet worked out where we'll do the floor. My porcelain casters in Monrovia want to do it, but they're not set up to do production and they would have to do it piecemeal – seventy-five tiles a week, which we would have to go out to Monrovia and sand every Saturday. At first I was contemplating doing it, but Leonard sort of balked, though he thought the floor would be wonderful. But I felt so overwhelmed by it that I appealed to him, and he's investigating other places where we could produce it all, mount the tiles, and color-code them for setup in four to six weeks.

How, I ask, do men do it – take on huge projects with a lot of risk involved and maintain their belief that all will work out? I worry that my fundamental fear and anxiety will permeate the Project unconsciously – that I will make it fail by not being able to believe deeply enough that it will succeed. But I feel paralyzed to break through. I cannot believe I will really get what I want – it's that simple! Others are going forward with confidence. I am pretending I will accomplish this. If I do, it's only because of others' investment in the Project – because I, who don't believe, have made them believe, and it will be their belief that will pull us through. For example, I cannot go out and sell myself and the scope of the Project to strangers for funding – which we desperately need. Diane has taken on the fund-raising. If she manages to raise money, all will be well. Of course, that brings up my feelings that I need so much from others and my fears that they will never come through – which is why I remain in suspended disbelief even while people *are* coming through.

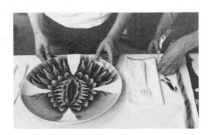

Mock-up place setting.

What is it that I generate that brings people here? Daily or at least weekly, we get a new volunteer – a day here, a month there, the work progresses. I shake and tremble in fear and keep working. To be released from this: to just go into the studio with nothing particular to do, to doze and go where my impulse takes me, to paint what I please. Yet I'd probably not be content and would just take on something else. I am afraid it is my destiny to be in over my head – which is where I am. I feel often as if I'm drowning, as if it will never be over, and the anxiety as to whether it will work out is there every day. As I invest more and more, the anxiety grows. I can feel it and taste it. I wake up with it and go to sleep with it. If I am not hard at it, it overtakes me and threatens to paralyze me.

Still no more museums; enough money only till January, and then only if we don't start the floor; people not staying; new people coming; I'm living on pennies. I don't even know if I can pay the rent next month. The people to be worked with, rewarded, trying to stay focused, work, work, more work – always more to do. My life is consumed by this piece with no guarantee that it will be accomplished. Four years it will be – this is already the third and the hardest so far.

Friday
SEPTEMBER 10, 1976

It's pouring rain this morning, the kitchen is flooded, my nose is running, and the first reliefed plate that made it to the point of being painted cracked the second time it was fired. I am trying to calm down after a heavy Thursday night session in which we discussed the problems that are growing out of having Leonard and other men in the Project. Leonard started working regularly in the studio yesterday and brought with him all the difficulties of dealing with men. I need him and I don't want to have to "accommodate" him, which is what I've been doing, so he won't leave the Project (my fantasy).

Last night I felt the power of what I've created: Fifteen women were there – assertive, eager, committed to the Project. I've built an environment again – like in Fresno. I've threatened it slightly by having Leonard around. I felt like it's taking on too much to pull off this piece, handle all the technical and esthetic problems, and deal simultaneously with integrating men into the situation.

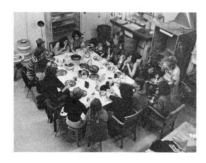

A Thursday night pot luck.

Thursday
SEPTEMBER 30, 1976

I've designed three more runners. That means there are eleven done. They are just now stretching the linen on the absolutely beautiful embroidery frames we designed and built. Leonard is doing better, and we are in the process of integrating several other men into the Project. I have been working on plates, although we have not really gotten all the way through the stages of jiggering, carving, glazing, firing, and china-painting. But we're close. By November first, when I return from my second lecture trip this month, I think we'll be about there. We're moving along on the silverware and goblets – I've been working very long hours, some days 8:00 a.m. to 1:00 a.m., and then back at it the following day. I can't even chronicle the days – I am just in them so deeply, so engrossed in the work.

Thursday
JANUARY 20, 1977

I've worked on plates this week. We're about to fire a couple of early carved ones to see what the glaze does to the surface. After one and a half years, we seem to be on the track of solving the technical problems of making plates. We haven't gotten many out of the kiln, though we certainly had some success with the reliefed surfaces. The next few weeks will tell us a lot.

Tuesday
FEBRUARY 15, 1977

I'm china-painting the first group of plates. Yes, we finally seem to have plates, though I won't believe it till I see some finished, painted, reliefed plates sitting in the cabinets. But I feel better; perhaps it's because I'm back at the activity I love the most.

(Later – same day)

I have been trying to work in the china studio – having terrible trouble – alone with floods of feelings which I don't want to feel but must. It is painting again and getting close to my center that is causing the trouble. It is bringing me into contact with layers and layers of longing, loss, fear, disappointment, anger. Layers and layers, and I don't want to go inside again, but I must – and I'm tired, deeply emotionally tired. I feel the strain of the Project – the endless months, the endless giving out, and now to have to go deep again and pull creation out of the morass of agony –

NO — o — o — o — o!

BUT I MUST...

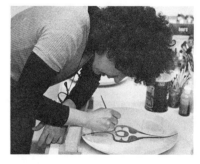

Chicago painting the Boadaceia plate.

Monday
FEBRUARY 21, 1977

Just as we were running out of money, I sold something. I still need lots of money to finish. I'm going back to the Endowment next month to see about the grants we applied for. I'm also going to look at historic needlework in preparation for designing the next round of runners. We're nearing completion of the first group, and soon we'll take them off the frames. I hope they'll be okay.

We're doing tests for the mounting, grouting, and writing for the floor. The studio atmosphere is wonderful. People are growing as a result of the permission the Project and the studio afford. It's great to see. If growth is not stunted and people are allowed some space, they expand and fill it, assuming that their expansion is not seen as a threat by those whose space it is.

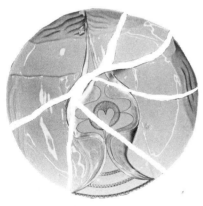

Cracked Boadaceia plate.

Sunday
MARCH 6, 1977

I am beginning to see that in taking on the Project I took on the real nexus of the problem that has prevented women from overcoming their oppression: (1) the enormity of the task of changing attitudes on a large scale; (2) the problems of female role conditioning and how it prevents women from working at all, much less facing the challenge of changing their condition; and (3) the absence of support in society. These three things all loomed up in front of me. Had I been able to get more support from society, the task would have been easier. But it's been such a struggle to eke out what support we've gotten. And the piece is going to take longer than I had thought to finish – and much more money. When I really allowed myself to confront exactly what I had undertaken, I felt it was more than I could handle, at least the way things were going. I felt that people took too much from me, that I had to be artist, organizer, and energy source all at once when I could hardly keep myself together. I brought this all up at our Thursday night meeting because I needed to find out if the other women would want to stop the Project once they knew what was really ahead of us and how hard it would be. If they wanted to go on, I wanted to make it clear that a number of them would

have to take on greater responsibility. Diane and Susan are needed, plus maybe ten or twelve more, all carrying the load of overseeing the many people who will help over the next couple of years.

Yes. They said Yes, we are ready. In a way, I wished they had said no, and I would have been released. On the other hand, I probably knew that they would say yes or I wouldn't have taken the risk. Finally, after seven years, I have begun to build a structure that is solid. By Friday we had begun to shift responsibility and several women had already begun to take greater power. I guess the months of working in my studio, of having the space to grow, of learning about their history, have made a number of women ready to commit themselves as I have. They've seen, like I have, that they have no choice. So we're restructuring the studio, setting up for a long haul, developing a staff, selling things from the Project (posters, etc.), fund-raising, writing for grants, going forward and reaching out for support to our friends, to other women, to those who hear me lecture or write to me after reading *Through the Flower*.

egalitarian, democratic, and peaceful.

Friday
MARCH 25, 1977

There is a transference of power going on in the studio, with people accepting more and more responsibility and taking authority and sharing the burden of the work. But there is, of course, no bloodless change in power, and the strain on me last night was ferocious, particularly after painting all day. People are struggling to emerge from their fantasies and misconceptions about me – from seeing me as "up there," the authority, to allowing me to be a person among them. This is a consequence of their extending themselves into "my arena" – into leadership, consciousness, and commitment.

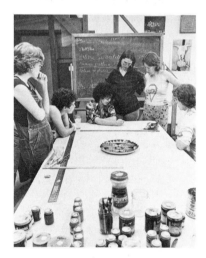

clockwise – Susan Hill, Adrienne Weiss, Chicago, Elaine Ireland, Jan duBois, and Connie von Briesen.

Monday
MARCH 28, 1977

I spent most of the weekend carving plates, losing almost a whole day's work when I carelessly moved the light I was using and it dropped on a plate and cracked it. If I'm not able to focus and concentrate totally, things like that happen, and I must say, it's hard to bring my whole energy to bear day in and day out for such a long haul. I was upset, of course, particularly since I lost several plates in the china-painting kiln this week, including an older one of Eleanor of Aquitaine, whose paint was starting to chip. I refired her, hoping to get the color to settle back into the glaze, only to have the color chip even more. Sometimes I feel as if I take five steps backward for every step forward. A year and a half ago I had twenty plates; now I have eighteen (two having chipped), and no new ones yet. But I have four in process now, at various stages of painting…

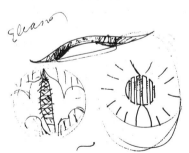

Sketch for Eleanor of Aquitaine.

Last night we met with people who wanted to form a D.P. staff – twenty women showed up, too many of course, but it allowed us to form a core staff (by election) and other various committees, which should spread responsibility around, even if, as one woman said, it seems like we have too many chiefs and not enough Indians. But that will change by the summer, when we are sure to get an influx of new people. I am looking forward to the core group meeting and being able to discuss overall planning for the piece, long-range goals, etc. We have our first meeting Wednesday.

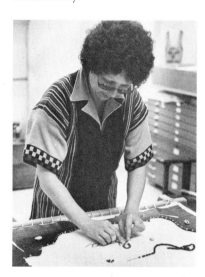

Chicago working on the Primordial Goddess runner.

Wednesday
MARCH 30, 1977

Instead of designing the runners the way we did last time, we're trying to form a small team: Susan, me, and three needleworkers who will supervise the translation of the design into embroidery and be consultants on the inevitable problems. I insisted upon being very up front with them instead of protective. Although it isn't working quite yet (they got somewhat intimidated, especially Susan), we've agreed that a good creative flow requires honesty and direct communication, with people having to take responsibility for themselves and jump in; we'll see what happens. We came up with some great ideas for runners and also with ideas that will begin to affect the creation of the plates themselves. It's interesting how the process of making the piece, which began with me alone, is gradually evolving and growing until even the plates will be shaped by the whole cooperative process.

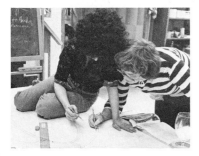

Chicago and von Briesen designing Gothic arch motif for Hildegarde's runner.

Thursday
MARCH 31, 1977

Last night was our first core staff meeting – Susan, Diane, me, plus Helene, Sharon, Ann, and Sandy – all elected at the big meeting last week. It was quite amazing. They really have come to a place of great vision and are prepared to commit themselves to not only finishing the piece but taking it out into the world. We talked about traveling plans, about finances, about our goal of having the piece make an impact, about how to accomplish that.

Friday
APRIL 1, 1977

In the afternoon, we had meetings with several needleworkers in preparation for designing the next runners. We have developed a new method of doing this, based on our experience of the last round, but we have encountered some unexpected problems. We decided to have "runner mistresses," each of whom would be involved in preliminary research and then the design (in conjunction with Susan and me) and supervision of the runner. People have already been doing research, and this week we set up preliminary design meetings between the runner mistresses and the design team we formed, which consists of three of the needleworkers (Connie, Terry, and Natalie) and Susan and me. This team was conceived as developing an overview of the whole table and the range of techniques available, as well as doing problem-solving with the

runner mistresses. All went well till the first day of meetings, at which point one of the runner mistresses (an older woman) got all uptight about Connie, who is also older, projecting her disappointment that we didn't accept all her ideas (which were totally non-contextual, though she had done some valuable research into patterns of the time, which we are using). She also expressed unconscious jealousy of Connie, something that came up with another of the older women. Now that we're expanding the staff and people are taking responsibility, we're beginning to hear things about "bureaucracy" and "hierarchy," words that indicate some of the women are feeling that the new structure will prevent them from having access to me.

Thursday
APRIL 4, 1977

Things are moving along in the studio. The structure is so strong that people hardly even know if I'm there or not, buried as I've been in the china-painting studio or the drawing studio. The core staff is wonderful – it allows me a chance to really talk about studio problems, and it is providing people in the studio with the sense that they can affect things, as they can talk to the staff members in a way they can't with me (because I'm always busy working) or with Diane (as she's so closely identified with me).

Monday
MAY 2, 1977

I got my first finished, painted, carved plate out of the kiln today. At last – after a year and a half!

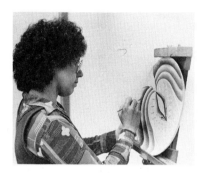

Chicago painting the Hatshepsut plate.

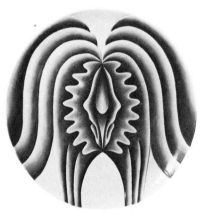

Hatshepsut's plate.

(Same evening)

My pleasure did not last very long, for even though I finally got a finished carved plate painted and out of the kiln, the one on the bottom was totally busted. We have been working and working and working on getting the electric kiln to fire well, and I had just done three or four firings with two test plates that were perfect. Then I put in the real ones and wham! The Boadaceia plate that broke was the second version – the first broke in almost exactly the same way. It really made me depressed – not just because the plate cracked, but also because I just suddenly felt overwhelmed again – by the lack of money, the difficulties, the frustration, the length of time, how hard it is...

But what's bothering me is the plates – the damn plates. We've been working on them a year and a half, and we've only got one. I had really thought we'd solved the technical problems for at least the first eight – which would complete the second wing of the table. I made six; one cracked – the mosaic plate for Theodora, which needs more tests, as the test plates broke in the china-painting kiln, though the real plate is done and ready to be fired. That left five, all in various stages of painting when I left town. Now there are four, one done and three close to being done. It's getting harder to invest the time and the caring, not knowing what will happen to the plates, and, worse, I can't take them as far with painting as I could if they were uncarved; the risk of breakage is always there.

Is it better to abandon the relief image and get more control in the painting? If the rest of these plates break, I think I will have no choice – I won't be able to handle any more and will have to back off from the carving problem. The frustration I feel from the plates, linked up with the frustration of this long haul...I am at the edge of my tolerance.

a male-dominated political state

Thursday
JUNE 2, 1977

Last night at our staff meeting, three people from the Project discussed the summer workshop we're planning. We are setting up a two-month program where, in addition to working on the Project, people will have a focused group process. Several women who have gone through a less structured growth process will be the facilitators. I've let people pretty much function as best they can, but now I feel the time has come to change that and begin to train women as facilitators who can actually instigate feminist education processes.

So far, just providing the environment, the Project, and me as a role model has allowed a lot of growth, but the move toward real education has to take place. I realize that if feminist art education is to develop as a viable alternative tool, I will probably have to train people here in the studio and then send them out in the world. But it's very tiring. I do wish I could just be an artist and that would suffice, but it's just not possible unless I am willing to accept the limits of the present system, which I am not willing or able to do. Of course, I don't have to work with women the way I did in Fresno either – I've come to another place – I'll train women to work with other women, but at what cost to myself, I wonder? I am not sure how much I can do now or if it will have to wait till the Project is over.

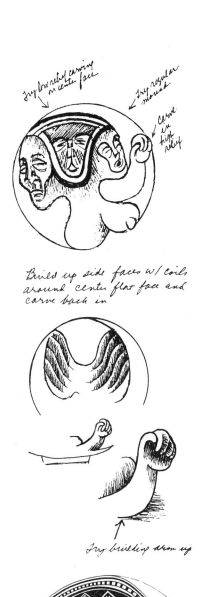

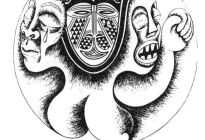

Detail of study for the Sojourner Truth plate.

Wednesday
JUNE 8, 1977

I'm in bed and not feeling too well, though I've been drawing. I think one of the reasons I got so scared by the bleeding from my navel that occurred after I had my tubes tied, apart from the fact that I was terribly overtired (and am still, and need a vacation), was that on some level I knew it had symbolic meaning. I think, after several days of pondering it, that my body was telling me that this project was bleeding me of all my strength and that somehow I had to be relieved of that part which was not essential for me to do. There is a great deal of creative work left – the plates, the drawings, the next round of runners, and a book to write. If I work steadily for the next year without interruption, I will just about get it all done. But in addition to that, there's the training of people to lecture, training some to be facilitators, and staying involved in the organization of the studio, which I don't really have the skills to do (the organizing skills, that is). I have to let go of some of it…

As I worked on these plate drawings, I knew how much I love to make art. I created this whole structure in order to be able to do that, and now I must trust that it's okay if that's what I do: make art. That's all I have to be responsible for – conceiving and making art. Yet as I write this, I find myself not able to accept it.

Sunday
JULY 10, 1977

In the middle of a rather chaotic week, I was able to do nine drawings for illuminated letters for the new runners, but I crave quiet and am sure that I'll need a private studio space in the fall. Tomorrow we start intensive ceramics work, and suddenly I have a ceramics team – Leonard; Keyes; Margaret, from Hawaii; a new woman, Kathy Erteman, who is highly skilled; and perhaps one or two more people. The time has come to focus on the plates and try to finish them. The studio is okay. I've been training certain people as facilitators (Sharon, Susan, Terry, Diane), and they've been attending some of the sessions of the Educator's Workshop at the Woman's Building. Susan, in particular, has grown from it.

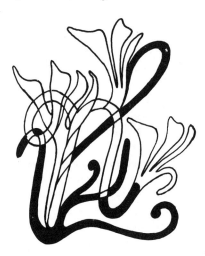

Study for illuminated letter for Natalie Barney's runner.

There have been a lot of people in and out of the studio this week – some women from other parts of the country who were attending the "Feminist Methodologies" course. Everyone really connects to the use of the D.P. as a symbol and a rallying point for women everywhere. It's as if I stand in the center of a great current which I generated, but it is building its own rhythm and direction now. It is getting larger and larger and more and more out of my control. I am still trying to hold onto the connection with the D.P. long enough to finish it before it leaves me and enters the flow of that current, where it will be engulfed. The birth of this piece is terrible and wonderful, and I have another year of holding myself aloof from the community I've generated – of keeping myself separate in the aloneness that is essential to creation. The pressure mounts around me as more and more people learn of the piece and begin to want it. Hands reach out, souls open, the longing hangs in the air, the piece could be all I dream for it – the symbol for a great change.

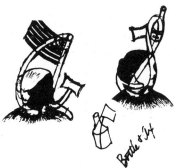

Study for illuminated letter for the Susan B. Anthony runner.

But tomorrow the struggle begins again to produce the rest of the plates – two months of frustration, hope, fear, concentration, anguish, difficulty. I'm ready but I am also afraid. We'll finish and we'll solve the problems, but the hardest part is holding onto the plainness of work while the energy all around is building; the mythology of the D.P. is growing, and my legend is expanding all around me. I still have to stay connected to what is hard and very unglamorous work for another year. I have to get to another space where I can be alone and apart from the mythic "Judy Chicago." I knew when I changed my name that I was setting something in motion and offering myself up as a symbol to other women. Now I have to struggle to keep that symbolic self from destroying my real self.

P.S.: I forgot to mention I got another NEA grant for $4,000 – bringing the total to $21,000 – about which I feel great.

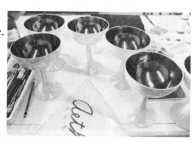

Lustered chalices and floor tile.

Saturday
JULY 16, 1977

In the meantime, the plate problems continue. We lost a lot of plates again, and both Leonard and I got demoralized. He's being absolutely wonderful. I can hardly believe it. We're in the process of changing clay bodies, hoping to find one that is more flexible and won't have such a high percentage of breakage (seven out of eight or nine, thereabouts, maybe more). Both Leonard and I have a high frustration tolerance, but this is more than either of us can bear. There's no question – I'm in the hardest struggle of my life!

Saturday
JULY 23, 1977

Ken and I have been doing a lot of work on the installation of the piece. We've backed off the idea of trying to create a total alternative structure and instead are going to design a system that can be adapted to different spaces. Talking about that with Ken and other people has put a strain on me, especially since I experience intense dialogue as a struggle. Diane pointed this out to me, and I'm trying to change my perception and understand that I'll have to be involved with that level of "discussion." But it's hard for me. As Ken says, I'm used to making decisions, having people either support them or say, "I don't like that," and then making another decision. I am working on that.

Friday
JULY 29, 1977

In ceramics I've been trying to get some plates done that I've worked on before. I think I mentioned that we have changed clay bodies, which seems to have increased the chances of getting plates done. I have some ready to paint and a new slower electric kiln firing schedule that I hope will make a difference. I'm investing more in the plates now, taking longer in the carving. If they continue to break at the previous rate I will not be able to have reliefed plates, and that's all there is to it. But the images are developing every day, and it will be harder to live with flat images – probably impossible. I hardly can allow myself to even think about it, as it gives me terrible cramps.

Thursday
AUGUST 4, 1977

Last night I felt the loss of my space intensely. All but three of us had left by six. I worked till eight. Susan was in the loft, and Keyes was working with me in ceramics. I wanted music on; I was carving and wanted the rhythm of music. I had to negotiate with Susan – she liked this, I didn't – I liked that, she didn't. I suddenly wanted my studio back, all to myself, the peace, the psychic privacy. And yet, hand in hand with that is the powerlessness of the single artist.

Monday
AUGUST 8, 1977

It's early in the morning. I want to go into the studio soon and get some time working while it's quiet. I've been having some trouble concentrating and focusing when a lot of people are there. And it's been quite busy in the studio. Some days I'm good and get "deep in" despite the distractions. Other days I get completely off base and never really connect with myself. I get angry with myself for using the situation to avoid focusing. But day in and day out it's hard – particularly as carving becomes more complex and takes more time.

Tuesday
AUGUST 16, 1977

Friday we went to Monrovia and filmed Evelyn and the whole process of making the tiles. The day before I had to stop carving, as my plate-in-progress cracked (though our success rate is getting higher now that we've switched clay bodies and slowed down the firing); so I did some preparatory work for the china-painting essay for Dextra's show. Saturday I worked all day on a color drawing for the Eleanor of Aquitaine runner that's being woven, and yesterday Leonard and I began working on a new image, which we'll continue today.

Thursday
AUGUST 25, 1977

It is late – the Thursday night session has just ended. It was wonderful! Tonight was the last night of the summer workshop, and they presented a piece made of all their body parts cast in plaster, with an accompanying tape of statements. It was very moving, and it made clear that I have found a way to provide a profound learning experience simultaneously with work on a project. What a long way from Fresno and even from Womanhouse. I see the progress finally – fusing my own artmaking with an educational context that allows me to operate fully (if not with as much private space as I'd like) while providing a context in which women can grow. It's amazing how a part of me goes forward while another part holds back and doubts and worries.

Tonight Stevie (one of the Project women) turned to me and said, "You are one of the finest women I've ever known." It really made me feel good. I need a lot more of that, years of it probably, to make up for the years of hurt done to me by a world that denied my value. Someone tonight mentioned how they liked being in the studio 'cause they felt powerful (and we all know women don't feel like that too often in the world). The thing I'm wondering is whether the world will acknowledge the power in the piece.

Tuesday
SEPTEMBER 13, 1977

Henry Hopkins, the Director of the San Francisco Museum of Modern Art, came down for a meeting Saturday night. It was good; he was supportive, as usual. We discussed all the problems of getting the piece out into the world, where it will have to stand or fall; that time is looming. Henry said something about the phenomenon of the piece and the energy that is building around it – how it could be magnificent or disappointing, which of course I know. And I am scared. It brings up the issue of trust, not only trusting other people but trusting myself – which I am trying to do – trust that I am who I think I am and can do this work and pull it off, and it will be all right. I try to think only about the work at hand. Tomorrow I run, then carve all day – and the next day and the next day until next week, when we go east. I am having my usual separation anxieties.

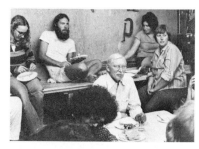

Henry Hopkins visits the studio.

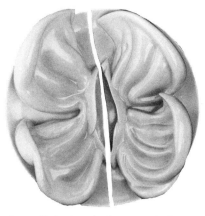

Susan B. Anthony's plate – cracked.

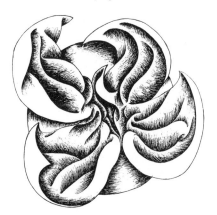

Study for the Susan B. Anthony plate.

42

Monday
SEPTEMBER 19, 1977

I hardly even know what day it is. I've done nothing but work fourteen to eighteen hours a day. I've had a huge burst of energy, partly in response to going away, partly because of the energy in the studio. Leonard and Keyes have been working steadily with me for several weeks, sometimes late into the night. For the first time I've felt part of a working group, and it's fantastic. We've done a whole bunch of plates, which we're all afraid to fire. We'll wait till we get back and then fire them and see where we are. If we get them all, or most of them, we'll have five or six more and we'll plunge in again and try to push even farther than we've gone already – and we've gone pretty far. The images are really rising off the table now.

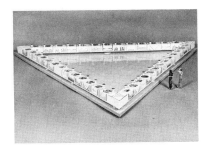

Dinner Party model designed and built by Ken Gilliam.

Adrian Sachs came over Friday. He's really knowledgeable about porcelain and was very encouraging; he made us all feel we could do even more, so we're planning another intensive month. I'll have to give Leonard some money, as he has none to live on, and that will mean I'll have to go out lecturing sooner, which I hate. I feel that I am so "deep in" I can't talk about the piece unless I do it as we're doing it in the East – all five of us. Diane suggested I wing it this year and don't show slides, just answer questions and rap with the audience, which I think I'll do.

The most exciting part of the week is that Ken has built an absolutely wonderful model of the entire installation. It's really terrific, makes the whole concept finally visible, which freaked me out. Now I am out there with all my trembling self and the whole truth of the piece obvious, and the world has just got to support me – really support me – and the systems have to work for me, and a lot of money has to come in, and people – a lot of people – have to come through, or the Project will never get done.

Wednesday
OCTOBER 19, 1977

I had a conversation with a woman who had come to work in the studio for a few days, and I discovered she'd been referred by a ceramicist from S.F. named Daphne Ahlenius. I'd met Daphne last spring on my lecture tour, and she had promised to come down and help with plates. I did not have her number, however, and never heard from her. When I talked with this woman, I realized that fate had interceded again to solve our problems. I called Daphne and asked her to help us finish the plates, which are giving us enormous troubles again – not the least of which is Leonard's recurring resistance.

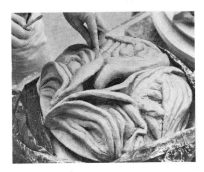

Building Georgia O'Keeffe plate.

43

of the social and political forces,

Friday
OCTOBER 21, 1977

The new plates are forming inside me. Daphne was down on Wednesday – all day. She, Keyes, and I spent the morning looking at plates, then went and met Leonard and Kathy for lunch. We established a working schedule for November and December: two long ten-day sessions, one in each month, with preparatory work in between, for making the last five plates – Blackwell, Anthony, Smyth, Woolf, and O'Keeffe, the women I most identify with. My goal is to individuate them; I'm prepared to invest weeks in each one in order to have them come alive and be realized. Leonard will have the hardest time. It's just so difficult for him to be part of our group, it threatens his sense that he's special, I think. He's already figuring out how to work at home. He'll operate at the level he can, I guess, and the women will take over. It's funny, I know what I want these images to be, and yet I can't make them myself. I'm dependent on my team. Kathy and Keyes already started on developing the Blackwell image from my drawing. Here is how I see these women and what I want them to express:

Anthony: A giant, who stood firm in her values for fifty years. I don't know how she did it. I'm capsizing after a decade. The pressure is bearing down on me. I can't breathe. I wonder if she felt like that.

Blackwell: The first woman doctor in America. She broke into the professions and created an ever-growing effect. Blinded in one eye by an accident, she was jeered at, ridiculed, ignored, and cursed, but she went on. How did she find the strength to face that all-male world of doctors who despised women and all they represented, who lived off controlling and denying the life force?

Smyth: The first woman to try and operate as a composer at the level of the best men. She wanted to do operas, cantatas, symphonies. Her gift was large, her capacity great. She would have needed the support of the musical establishment and the whole system to facilitate her talent. She was quashed, and her own gift, her ear, turned deaf as if to shut out the music she could not actualize.

Woolf: Poor Virginia, a flower of delicacy, a genius, a shaking, trembling leaf. She tottered on the brink of sanity, holding on long enough, often enough to speak with a pure female voice which wedded thought and feeling into a transparent translucent tone whose ring sounds in the air for all of us to build upon.

O'Keeffe: Fiercely guarding her privacy, insisting upon her uniqueness, denying her female identifications while giving birth to a language that provides a foundation for female art. An iron rod up her back to support her. Her will burning fiercely – the will to survive, to do it.

Each of them is me, and I am all of them. My body reels from the task of making their portraits. I do not know if I am good enough. I prepare for the struggle like a warrior going to battle. My troops prepare, they work on the wheel, they make molds, they think. How can I help them? Spend time with them, talk, exchange ideas, let everything else go but the task at hand.

But my body gives out and insists I give it room – room to think, room to breathe, room to dream, room to prepare.

I have to rest a lot and store up energy like a squirrel putting away nuts for a bleak winter.

We originally planned to make the entryway banners here in the studio. Then June Wayne put us in contact with some weavers in S.F. who are trained in Aubusson tapestry techniques. We have worked out a deal with them (finally, yesterday, after a lot of back-and-forth haggling) – and they'll be doing the banners with our people in a workshop program. I'm very excited about it, even if I did have to sell a porcelain miniature I didn't want to part with in order to finance it.

Wednesday
NOVEMBER 30, 1977

Leonard has left the project. He says his internal pressures to work have built up to such a point that he can't deny them. Judye Keyes is dealing with him, and we're both insisting he remain responsible to those few things no one can do but him – jiggering, glazing, and finishing the plates he started.

Tuesday
DECEMBER 6, 1977

Last night we had a meeting to plan the next round of runners. We have the idea of making them somewhat different, more sculptural and less embellished, but I'm worried about that. Stuffed and dimensional fabric work is always so tacky, and I'm not sure we can make it work.

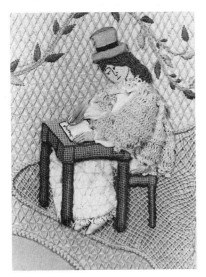

Detail of stump work for Mary Wollstonecraft's runner.

Wednesday
DECEMBER 21, 1977

Today is the last day of the ceramics blitz, and last night, around midnight, we all stood on the balcony overlooking the ceramics area and looked at the plates for Susan B. Anthony, Virginia Woolf, and Georgia O'Keeffe. We decided *not* to try to finish their plates this time, but, rather, to finish all the ones we had started last time. I've made the three images that were the hardest – at least we resolved them in terms of images and technique. These particular plates may not survive firing, etc., but images like them – better constructed – will be worked out in terms of technical flaws. This is the process we've developed – work on prototypes and thereby figure out how plates are going to be built and what they'll look like. Then, by watching them dry, firing them, and seeing what happens, we modify the method of making them until we get them through the kiln – several of them, preferably, so we have a backup if one cracks at any stage.

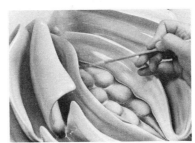

Painting the Virginia Woolf plate.

It was very exciting last night. It is clear that these images came to be only through the evolution of an all-female team. It was hard for us to talk about last night, although we did a little at dinner – the feelings we all had about creating these incredibly powerful images that were struggling to free themselves from the plates . . . We all agreed that Leonard's leaving the Project worked out for the best. These plates had to be made by women alone.

I have never had a more wonderful creative experience with the Project before – six days this time, from waking to sleeping. We've had people cooking for us and running errands, so we've had no interruptions. The energy has been incredible. The plates may still have to be remade, but they're all conceptualized; they're all worked out image-wise and simply have to be worked out technically so they'll survive the firing. We've all agreed we'll do anything – patching, using a lower-fire porcelain, and even going to white earthenware if necessary for those that won't make it in porcelain. It doesn't matter; it only matters that the images exist, though I'd like it best if they were all porcelain.

Saturday
JANUARY 14, 1978

We have to redesign the Primordial and Fertile Goddess runners, as they didn't work before. I have *no* ideas for the Woolf and O'Keeffe runners, although the others have been pouring out of me. The new ones are very powerful and very raw, and I'm having a reaction to that. I'm feeling frightened of what's coming up in the last wing – my rage against women's condition – and the absolute out-front images that only needlework techniques will make into art. They are images that have simply not been seen: Mary Wollstonecraft dying in childbirth, her strength trivialized by flowers and butterflies and scenes from life done in a technique called stump work. It's something like bread-dough sculpture in look and was very popular in the seventeenth century.

We're moving toward closure in the runner design. After Woolf and O'Keeffe we'll go back to Sanger, Blackwell, and Barney, and then we'll be done. And the plate images are done, although we will have to redo some and they'll have to be painted. There's still so much work to be done, I feel staggered, and I am beginning to balk now. I'm getting frightened. I'm not sure I want to finish. I'm afraid of what I've made – afraid that all the work will be for nothing. We still don't have enough money to last to the end of the Project. I don't know what will happen. If nothing happens, no more money, that'll be it. We won't be able to go any farther. And I feel like it's so out of my control. All I can do is pump out the work. It's taking everything I have and more. I can't do the creative work and re-cruit people and raise money and run the studio and write press releases. I can't do it all.

Why don't I have any ideas for the O'Keeffe and Woolf runners? I'm pulling some of the people in the studio into the design session, hoping they'll make some suggestions I can relate to. But I have this fear that I won't like their ideas. What do I want the runners to be? Do I want them flat or raised? If raised, how can they be raised without padding them like soft sculpture, which I hate? If they're not dimen-sional, then do they relate to the change in dimension in the plates? What kind of environ-ment do O'Keeffe and Woolf require? How about relating them to where they lived? It's so easy for O'Keeffe – the New Mexico desert. But Woolf – gray London? I don't know, it's eating away at me. I probably took to my bed because of it. Tomorrow I'm taking off. I don't know what I want to say at the end. What do I believe? That they found our voice – that they broke the silence – that through creative art we will be redeemed? Hopeful, pushing out, the plates almost cease to be plates. The images break free and begin to push off the plates – perhaps something like that should happen in the runners. We've never broken the edge of a runner. With whom? Woll-stonecraft first – then Anthony – then Smyth, Barney, Woolf, O'Keeffe – and Dickinson?

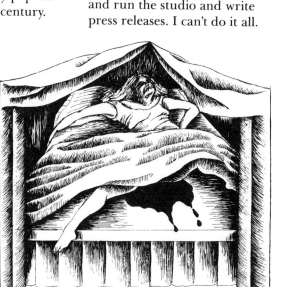

Study for Mary Wollstonecraft's death scene.

That's it: We have to break the runner format in the third wing. The plates were modified long ago: the edges cut and shaped, the forms altered, the women trying to be free. But the historical context didn't provide an occasion for a break until the beginning of the feminist revolution. That's not altogether true. There were often times in history when a break might have suggested itself, but perhaps never a time when it could really happen until this moment in human evolution – Hutchinson is the bottom line, the pits – then with Wollstonecraft the first stirrings...

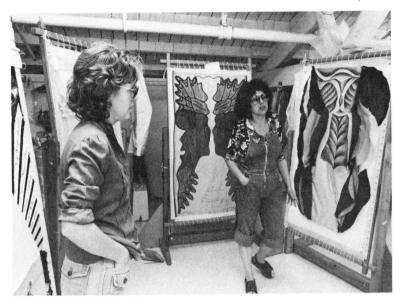

Hill and Chicago discussing runners.

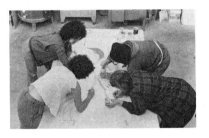

Designing Elizabeth Blackwell runner: clockwise – Sharon Kagan, Chicago, Judye Keyes, L.A. Olson.

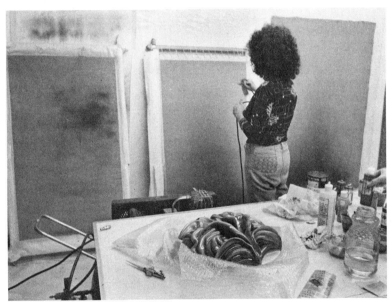

Chicago spraying the O'Keeffe runner; O'Keeffe's plate, foreground.

Wednesday
JANUARY 18, 1978

This design problem – Primordial Goddess, Fertile Goddess, Woolf and O'Keeffe – is the toughest so far. First, never has the esthetic discrepancy between me and the design team been greater nor my dependency on them larger. We're trying to activate the Woolf and O'Keeffe runners, which means fabricating with fabric. Some of the team, particularly Elaine and Terry, are knowledgeable about that – but their esthetic sense is not developed enough to "see" what I see. So all day yesterday we struggled to make a form they could grasp. We finally did make a prototype for one side of the O'Keeffe, which will be raw canvas and a flower/butterfly/cave image. But along the way, there was difficulty. I am actually learning to deal better with conflict, which has always been hard for me. One reason I used to hide away alone in my studio was to avoid the inevitable conflict of more than one ego. But here we have a lot of conflict, and we're surviving it, and we're making good art out of it.

Our reworking of the Primordial and Fertile Goddess runners was really good. Much better than the first time. Today we go at Woolf. I tossed and turned all night last night struggling with it.

Tuesday
JANUARY 24, 1978

Diane left Sunday night for another go at fund-raising and museum approaches. It looks like we may get some money this time. It has a lot to do with persistence, going back at it again and again. The circles of support seem to be growing a little – at least we're still here and still working.

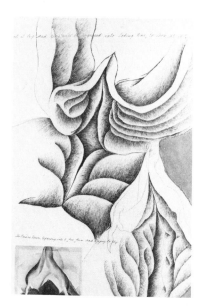

Detail of O'Keeffe drawing.

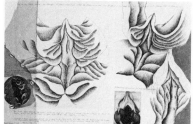

Drawing for Georgia O'Keeffe's plate.

Drawing for Virginia Woolf's plate.

Friday
FEBRUARY 17, 1978

We've been china-painting all week – Sharon Kagan, Rosemarie Radmaker, and I. It thrills me to have Rosemarie, a traditional china-painter, painting with us. It makes a real bridge between worlds. The plates are zipping right along, and I'm hoping we'll get some done. Of course, that depends in part on our breakage staying low. We just fired eight plates and lost only one. I did two plates for Sojourner Truth that are very expressive. If they don't survive I'll be very upset, as I'm not at all sure I could do them again and maintain the same force and directness. At any rate, I love painting, and the energy of my little china-painting team is carrying me past whatever tiredness I might feel if I were alone in there.

Some change is taking place inside me – I can feel it. It's a kind of growing acceptance that I am *in* my life. It won't change a great deal, although I hope new options will emerge – I'll be able to do more of what I want, enrich my life with travel, with building a place of my own.

It's like realizing that I'm not going to walk away after the piece is done (unless it's a failure and I have to run for the hills) – but that I'll probably rest, regroup, tie up the loose ends, and then go on. I still indulge in the idea that it will get easier – more money, less resistance and struggle – but it might not. It might be like this until the end of my life.

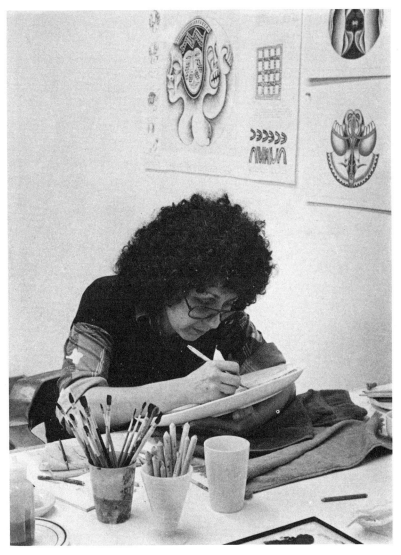

Chicago in the China-Painting Studio.

49

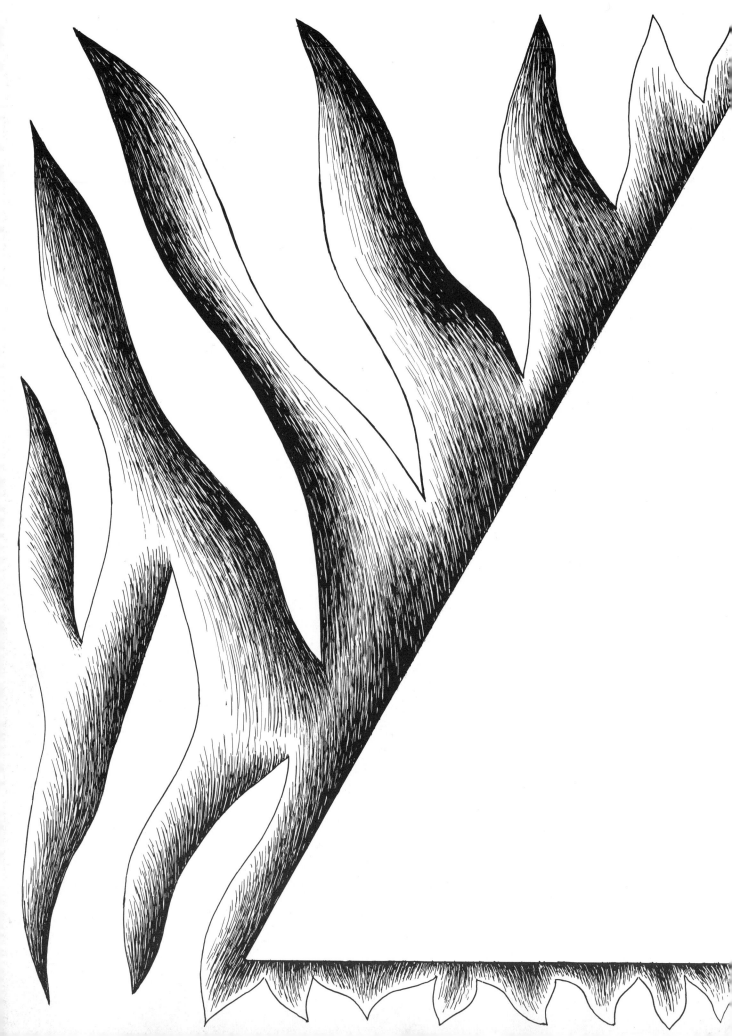

The Dinner Party Table

Thirty-nine Guests

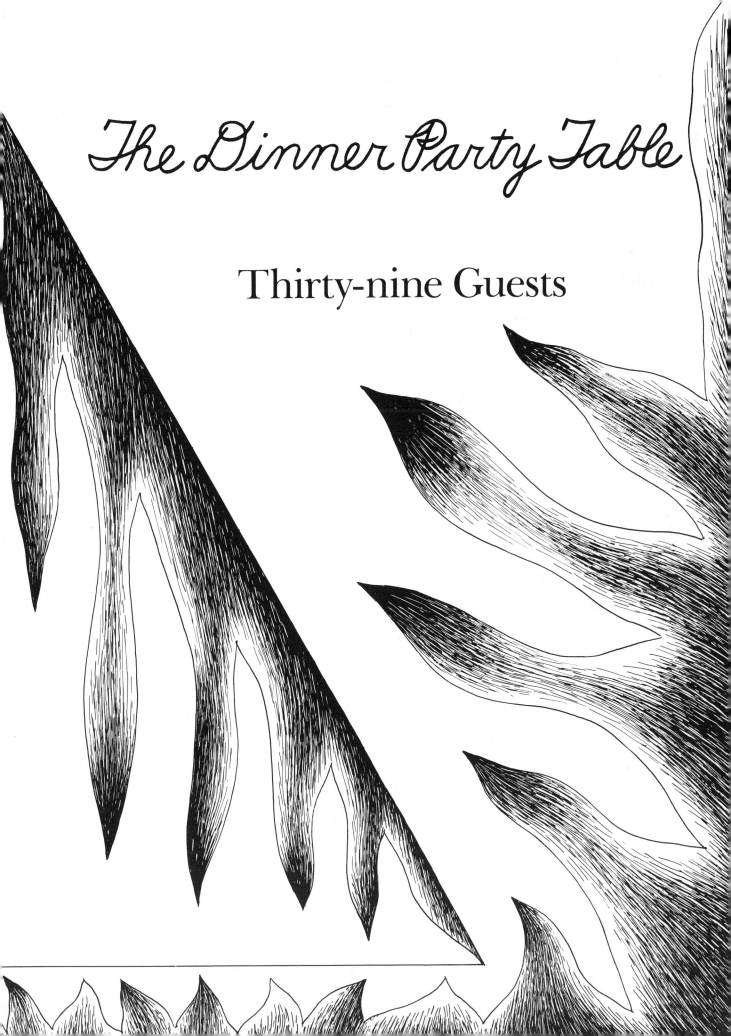

The women represented at the *Dinner Party* table are either historical or mythological figures. I chose them for their actual accomplishments and/or their spiritual or legendary powers. I have brought these women together – invited them to dinner, so to speak – in order that we might hear what they have to say and see the range and beauty of our heritage, a heritage we have not yet had an opportunity to know.

These guests, whether they are real women or goddess figures, have all been transformed in *The Dinner Party* into symbolic images – images that stand for the whole range of women's achievements and yet also embody women's containment. Each woman is herself, but through her can be seen the lives of thousands of other women – some famous, some anonymous, but all struggling, as the women on the table struggled, to have some sense of their own worth through five thousand years of a civilization dominated by men. The images on the plates are not literal, but rather a blending of historical facts, iconographical sources, symbolic meanings, and imagination. I fashioned them from my sense of the woman (or, if a goddess, what she represented); the artistic style of the time (when it interested me or seemed to have a potential to express something about the figure I was portraying); and my own imagery.

When I began working on the *Dinner Party* plates, I developed an iconography using the butterfly to symbolize liberation and the yearning to be free. The butterfly form undergoes various stages of metamorphosis as the piece unfolds. Sometimes she is pinned down; sometimes she is trying to move from a larva to an adult state; sometimes she is nearly unrecognizable as a butterfly; and sometimes she is almost transformed into an unconstrained being. During the earlier stages of the work, I imagined that all the plates would be flat and only the imagery would change. I painted half the plates on imported Japanese porcelain and then decided to alter the dimension of the plates. The ceramic difficulties I describe in the first part of the book were a result of trying to match the quality of the industrially made, imported plates with studio technology. Additionally, the images I had in mind required new ceramic methods and the blending of many peoples' skills. By the time the plates were completed, the ceramic team included seven people, all of whom brought different technical experience to bear on the problems of creating the highly dimensional plates. It took three years and enormous frustration to finish the plates, but the introduction of dimension on the surface allowed me to symbolize another aspect of women's history – the rise and fall of opportunities, and the efforts women have made in the last two hundred years to change their destiny.

from matriarchy to patriarchy

There is a strong narrative aspect to the piece that grew out of the history uncovered in our research and underlying the entire conception of *The Dinner Party*. This historical narrative is divided into three parts, corresponding to the three wings of the table. The first table begins with pre-history and ends with the point in time when Greco-Roman culture was diminishing. The second wing stretches from the beginning of Christianity to the Reformation, and the third table includes the seventeenth to the twentieth centuries. Beginning with pre-patriarchal society, *The Dinner Party* demonstrates the development of goddess worship, which represents a time when women had social and political control (clearly reflected in the goddess imagery common to the early stages of almost every society in the world). The piece then suggests the gradual destruction of these female-oriented societies and the eventual domination of women by men, tracing the institutionalizing of that oppression and women's response to it.

During the Renaissance, the male-dominated Church – built in large part with the help of women – and the newly emerged, male-controlled State joined hands. They began to eliminate all who resisted their power – the heretics who held onto pre-Christian, generally female-oriented religions; the lay healers who continued to practice medicine in the face of increasing restrictions by the emerging medical profession; the political dissenters who challenged the corruption of the Church; the women who refused to submit to their husbands, to their fathers, and to the priests; those who insisted on administering the drug ergot to relieve the suffering of women in labor; those who helped women abort themselves; those who wished to practice sexual freedom; those who wanted to continue preaching or healing or leading social groups and religious groups; and all who resented and resisted the steady but inevitable destruction of what was left of female power. These women were harassed, intimidated, and – worst of all – burned, in a persecution whose real meaning has completely evaded the history taught to us today.

By the time of the Reformation, when the convents were dissolved, women's education – formerly available through the Church – was ended. Women were barred from the universities, the guilds, and the professions; women's property and inheritance rights, slowly eroded over centuries, were totally eliminated; and women's role was restricted to domestic duties. Opportunities were more severely limited than in pre-Renaissance society. The progress we have all been educated to associate with the Renaissance took place for men at the expense of women. By the time of the Industrial Revolution women's lives were so narrow, their options so few, there is little wonder that a new revolution began – a revolution that has remained hidden by a society that has not heard the voices raised in protest by women (as well as by some men) throughout the centuries.

The women represented in *The Dinner Party* tried to make themselves heard, fought to retain their influence, attempted to implement or extend the power that was theirs, and endeavored to do what they wanted. They wanted to exercise the rights to which they were entitled by virtue of their birth, their talent, their genius, and their desire, but they were prohibited from doing so – were ridiculed, ignored, and maligned by historians for attempting to do so – because they were women.

Each plate stands for one or more aspects of women's experience. I chose Caroline Herschel, the eighteenth-century astronomer, for example, to represent the appearance and achievement of women in science in the late seventeenth and early eighteenth centuries. Selecting Herschel also allowed me to denote those women who could gain access to scientific education, equipment, and employment only through a brother, a father, or a husband. (In Herschel's case, it is debatable whether she would have elected to be an astronomer had she not been the unmarried sister of an ambitious man.) Moreover, her life clearly demonstrates the way a woman was both exploited and denied recognition even if she was able to make a place for herself in her chosen field. I tried to consider each of the women who seemed sufficiently accomplished to qualify for the table from this point of view.

If I'd already picked a person of one discipline or period, I would try to find another who reflected a different set of life conditions. There were more women than I could accommodate. There were women whose achievements were greater than those I chose, but whom I rejected because I already had too many writers, or because I had another important woman from Germany, or because it seemed essential to represent this or that period in Western Civilization. Sometimes I did not choose someone because I did not feel I could adequately represent her, either because her life did not offer me information I could use in an image or because she had been represented by history in too negative a way (like Lucrezia Borgia, whom I really wanted to include, feeling there was an untold and important story in her life). It seemed impossible in these situations to create an image that could challenge our previous perceptions of that woman.

Conversely, I sometimes chose someone specifically because – after she had met the basic criteria for the table – something about her or her life experience suggested a visual conception that interested me. This was the case with Isabella d'Este, who not only represented the achievement of female scholars during the Renaissance, the importance of female patronage of the arts, and the political position of Italian women of her century, but also offered me the opportunity of trying to simulate, with china paint, one of my favorite ceramic styles – Urbino majolica, a luster-ware produced in a factory patronized by D'Este. Majolica had intrigued me from the moment I first saw it in European museums. The possibility of recreating it for my own purposes, combined with the significance of D'Este's own achievements, supported her candidacy for the table over that of Vittoria Colonna or Margaret Roper, two other highly distinguished Renaissance women.

Each plate is set on a sewn runner* in a place setting that provides a context for the woman or goddess represented. The plate is aggrandized by and contained within that place setting, which includes a goblet, flatware, and a napkin. The runner in many instances incorporates the needlework of the time in which the woman lived and illuminates another level of women's heritage. The place settings are placed on three long tables – which form an equilateral triangle – covered with linen tablecloths. On the corners of the tables are embroidered altar cloths carrying the triangular sign of the Goddess. The tables rest on a porcelain floor composed of over 2,300 hand-cast tiles, upon which are written the names of 999 women. According to their achievements, their life situations, their places of origin, or their experiences, the women on the Heritage Floor are grouped around one of the women on the table. The plates are the symbols of the long tradition that is shared by all the women in *The Dinner Party.* The floor is the foundation of the piece, a re-creation of the fragmented parts of our heritage, and, like the place settings themselves, a statement about the condition of women. The women we have uncovered, however, still represent merely a part of the heritage we have been denied. If we have found so much information on women in Western civilization during the duration of this project, how much more is there still? Moreover, what about all the other civilizations on Earth?

*The designs and needlework techniques that embellish the runners will be described in the second *Dinner Party* book. Because this book focuses on the plates, I will only briefly describe each runner when I talk about the plate.

primacy gave way to gradual

       The Dinner Party takes us on a tour of Western civilization, a tour that bypasses what we have been taught to think of as the main road. Yet it is not really an adequate representation of feminine history – for that we would require a new world-view, one that acknowledges the history of both the powerful and the powerless peoples of the world. As I worked on research for *The Dinner Party* and then on the piece itself, a nagging voice kept reminding me that the women whose plates I was painting, whose runners we were embroidering, whose names we were firing onto the porcelain floor, were primarily women of the ruling classes. History has been written from the point of view of those who have been in power. It is not an objective record of the human race – we do not know the history of humankind. A true history would allow us to see the mingled efforts of peoples of all colors and sexes, all countries and races, all seeing the universe in their own diverse ways.

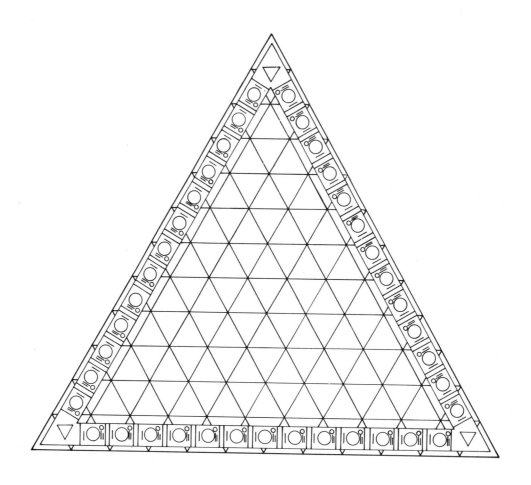

Primordial Goddess

In almost all ancient religions, the feminine principle was seen as the fundamental cosmic force. This female creative energy is embodied in the first plate on the table, that of the Primordial Goddess, who symbolizes the original feminine being from whom all life emerged. She is the Primal Vagina – her center, dark and molten; all her energy emanates from her bloody womb and core. She is the Sacred Vessel, the gateway to existence and the doorway to the abyss. In the beginning, life and death were merged in her body as parts of the endless process of rejuvenation and decay.

There was a time when there was no distinction among this Primordial Goddess, the Earth, and Earth's daughter, Woman. All were one, part of the mysterious female universe. The human race, awed by this nameless force, watched plants grow from the body of the Earth and life spring from the body of Woman, and could only venerate this magical power possessed by the feminine spirit.

I painted this plate at an early point in the Project, when I was still working alone. The image is a relatively undeveloped butterfly form, the wings not yet evolved from the flesh/rock substance of which the Primordial Goddess is made. I originally named her Gaea, after the Greek goddess who embodied the idea of this universal female principle or Earth Mother, but changed the name when I realized that the image on the plate actually refers to a concept that existed before there were words. I looked at the earliest pictographs to see how this Primordial Goddess was represented. They were only primitive markings, holes in rocks, sacred stones. She was too immense to be easily conveyed; her enormous power could only be symbolized. I tried to imagine what it must have felt like to live under the stars with no houses or roads, no words for anything one saw – just a succession of sights and sounds that were frightening and wonderful. I could easily understand making an association between the female body and the Earth; I make it now, between my flesh and that of an animal or the soil or the bark of a tree.

The Primordial Goddess rests on a coiled form, one of the earliest shapes fashioned by female hands. It is the basic shape of a pot and a basket, the objects which allowed our ancestors to store precious water and carry their possessions out of the cave and into the beginnings of civilization. Around the plate are animal skins, stretched over the runner to remind us of the earliest forms of clothing, stitched down with cowry shells, the ancient symbol of women and the earliest form of money.

Fertile Goddess

From a generalized concept of the universe as an amorphous, feminine being with all living creatures merged into one life-force, distinctions began to arise.

People were able to identify themselves as different from the animals, from the plants, and from the Earth itself. Faced with epidemics, famines, and the untamed forces of nature, their survival – and that of their children – was of utmost importance. Women were developing agriculture, pottery, and basket-making. From them emanated all that sustained life, and early peoples began to fashion images of these magical beings. The awe of the universe which once informed all human actions became centered in the awe of Woman herself, whose body was the symbol of birth and rebirth and the source of nourishment, protection, and warmth.

This "fertile woman" or "fertile goddess" has been discovered underneath the remains of civilizations everywhere on Earth. Called Venuses, the small, faceless figures usually have pendulous breasts, large bellies, and rounded buttocks. These little amulets were worshiped by women and men alike, and they were the basis of a Mother Goddess religion that was spread throughout the world by the migrations of people looking for more food, better climate, or a safer place to make their home.

These nameless Venuses, these crude feminine representations, and all they stand for, were the source for the image of the Fertile Goddess. The plate is done with thin washes of color fired on top of one another, and the forms are created with a hatched line called "pen work." In this technique, china-paint pigment, already mixed with oil, is thinned with a special pen oil and used in a crow-quill pen with a hard point. This pen-work method is quite different from the traditional pen-and-ink technique known to most artists. The pen is filled from the side, and the line is begun with a dot that is then pulled along until the ink runs out. It was necessary to unlearn all one's developed ability with a pen in order to do this kind of pen work.

The plate sits on a roughly woven and stitched runner reflecting the early stages of human civilization and the development of weaving and pottery by women. Small clay figurines adorn the runner – little Mother Goddesses that resemble the original effigies made by our ancestors many centuries ago. Several of us made them in the studio, looking at reproductions of those ancient fetishes and feeling connected across time with our foremothers. Following the techniques used by women for centuries, as we did in this runner – making coils, carving amulets, choosing shells and starfish to embellish the woven surfaces – we felt connected to another time, performing acts that were routine to ancient women whose bodies were worshiped, not degraded, by the civilization they were helping to create.

Ishtar

Ishtar, the Great Goddess, the giver and taker of life, was conceived by those who worshiped her as a being whose power was infinite. Revered for thousands of years in Mesopotamia, she expressed the power of the female principle as life-giving, protecting, and nourishing.

The various societies that worshiped Ishtar were highly developed civilizations. Writing, mathematics, legal codes, astronomy, canal-building, and – in some places – weapons characterized their cultures. With weaponry, the identity of the Goddess changed, as she also became responsible for the victory of the warrior-king. But this newfound association was a dubious one. The traditional Goddess had represented a positive force, and, as long as women had ruled the world, wars had been rare. The new, warlike image of the Goddess reflected a profound shift in social structure: Men's power was on the rise, and women's position was changing.

It is Ishtar's positive side that is represented on the plate. Here she is the many-breasted giver of life, the omnipotent female creator, whose presence on the table marks the apogee of women's power in the ancient world. Reverence for the female body and its spiritual powers had been translated into real social and political power. Women had laid the groundwork for the development of a complex civilization, and the great figure of Ishtar acknowledged the potency of our foremothers. Worshiped by men and women alike Ishtar was the supreme symbol of an ancient religion that extolled the feminine, even at a time when women were already beginning to lose their stature in the secular world.

When I was a child, I did theater pieces on my back porch, directing the other children of the neighborhood. I always reserved the role of priestess for myself, beginning each performance with the phrase, "Tomorrow at sunrise, Ishtar will rise." While I was working on Ishtar's plate, I thought of my childhood incantation and wondered how I had happened to utter those words.

The Ishtar plate, which employs pen work over a surface achieved with eight fired layers of liquid-bright gold and rainbow luster, rests on an appliqued and embroidered runner. The motif of the runner is derived from the arch of the Ishtar Gate and the Ziggurat of Ur, both famous architectural monuments of Babylonia.

Kali

My reason for choosing Kali for the table is complicated. Although *The Dinner Party* was not intended to include women outside Western Civilization, Kali, an ancient Indian goddess, provides a rather dramatic representation of what has been considered the destructive aspect of the Mother Goddess. I felt compelled to deal with such a figure because the idea that powerful women are harmful is deeply ingrained in present-day society, and I believe it is a result of the distorted mythology we have inherited. I wanted to represent, explore, and transform an archetypal symbol of the female as devourer/destroyer, and I chose Kali for that purpose. She is always represented as fierce, cruel, and bloodthirsty. A typical mantra used in her worship makes this clear: "Hail Kali, three-eyed goddess of horrid form, around whose neck a string of human skulls a pendant – Salutation to thee with this blood." Depicted as a hideous creature, she was supposed to love strife and rejoice in drinking the blood of those she destroyed.

In most of the ancient myths, female power was considered awesome, but essentially positive. Although the Goddess often possessed the power of death, life and death were considered indivisible and part of the same process. It was that process which was celebrated in the fertility rituals until, gradually, attitudes toward the Goddess – and hence toward women – changed. The "death" aspect of the Mother Goddess ceased to be part of a unified and venerated concept and became instead a separate and terrifying entity.

By the time of Ishtar (who predated Kali), women had begun to lose some of their former status in Mesopotamia as well as in other parts of the world. Kali began to be worshiped during the first millennium B.C. in the Hindu religion. When Hinduism became established, so did a rigidly patriarchal family system. Women were placed under the complete control of men, with such results as infanticide of females, polygamy, child-marriage, and eventually widow-burning, or "suti." Women lost all education and all rights and could only look forward to marriage and children, without which they had no identity.

As the Kali image was among the first plates I painted, my iconography was generally less specific than it became

later. The arms that extend from her dark body are derived from the many-armed representations that are so prevalent in traditional Indian symbols of this supposedly terrifying goddess. The plate rests on a runner translated from my painted design by Connie von Briesen, a painter and needleworker. Working with overlays of transparent materials, she transformed the gaping maw and dancing fingers associated with Kali into a compelling – rather than frightening – image.

Snake Goddess

When I was an art student and studying art history, I saw a small female figure from Crete with snakes coiled around her arms. The professor said that little was known about the origin of this Snake Goddess, but I always preferred it to later, better known Greek statues. Recent research has established that, until 1400 B.C., Crete was matriarchal. Something about that Cretan goddess had spoken to me across the centuries, and now I know it was her spiritual power.

The Snake Goddess in *The Dinner Party* incorporates the colors and symbols of its historic antecedent: Outstretched arms of pale yellow grow from a center form whose egg-like shapes represent the generative force of the goddess. The runner employs Cretan patterns, with two spectacular golden snakes embroidered on the back. Flounces reminiscent of the skirts worn by Cretan women complete this contemporary image of an ancient deity.

The relationship between the snake and the female has its origins in the goddess religions of earliest history. The snake was the embodiment of psychic vision and oracular divination, both of which were traditionally considered to be part of women's magical powers. The snake was connected to a succession of goddesses for thousands of years, even into Greek times. The priestesses of the goddesses served as advisors and counselors to their societies, entering trance states in order to solve the problems that were presented to them. Priestesses achieved these trances through fasting and through snake bites or the administration of snake venom, which produced altered states of consciousness. In such states, the priestesses were considered to be in direct communication with the goddess.

It was in Crete that the snake aspect of the Mother Goddess religion reached its highest development, and there the beautiful remains of a great civilization have been unearthed. The snake in Cretan society represented the wisdom of the goddess and was associated with life, death, and regeneration. Venerated as a protector of the household, the snake was also considered the reincarnation of a dead family member. Special rooms equipped with snake tubes (which enabled snakes to travel through the house) were found in many homes.

Snakes were also associated with fertility and the growth of vegetation. They appeared on statues of the Mother Goddess and were usually green with purple-brown spots, the color of plant life. Later, the male role in procreation became known and the snake came to symbolize the male principle. But the male consort/son was always subordinate to the goddess in Crete, never developing an independent god status. There were no male cult figures or phallic symbols, and most sacred scenes depict the Mother Goddess in conjunction with the tree of life. Crete was organized around a female totem system of clans and was primarily agricultural; for two thousand years, until its invasion by the Myceneans, it remained a peaceful land under matriarchy.

Sophia

Conceived as the highest form of feminine wisdom, Sophia is an abstract symbol in which female power, once actualized in social and religious structures, is transformed into a purely spiritual dimension. The concept of Sophia developed in the centuries after Christ, when early gnostic religions believed in her as an incorporeal entity – the active thought of God – who created the world. She is traditionally portrayed as a single delicate flower, a spiritual whole in which the material world is transcended. In this idea, one can still see the dim outlines of the Primordial Goddess, but the original force of the Goddess concept was steadily diminished as Sophia became an ever less substantial being. The later medieval concept of woman as spiritual intermediary, expressed most clearly in the relationship between Beatrice and Dante, is a result of gradual erosion of the pre-Christian idea of a female deity who was powerful in and of herself.

Sophia is usually represented as nourishing the human spirit and transforming it, as individuals strive for greater understanding of the mystery of life. Her identity merges with that of the Virgin Mary, and both are depicted as having nurturing and regenerative powers. A medieval manuscript drawing presented Mary suckling two Apostles with her milk, and, in a beautiful drawing, Dante rendered Sophia as the supreme flower of light.

Sophia was a very difficult image for me to paint, tending as I do toward strong, earthy forms. Moreover, in china-painting one can only go from light to dark. It is almost impossible to make a form lighter, because white or light colors are generally so transparent that they do not cover previous coats of darker paint. One uses the white of the clay body to work against, allowing the ground to provide the luminosity one could achieve in oil painting by simply bringing the light area back through impasto painting. It was not easy to represent the muting of women's former strength, which is another aspect of Sophia's portrait.

I painted this plate repeatedly, firing each of the three versions seven or more times. In the first two plates, the paint cracked on the last firing because I piled a light tone too heavily while trying to regain the paleness I had lost by applying too much color.

The plate is placed on a runner made of thin pieces of colored chiffon, each one carefully formed into a flower petal. Color shades color to create a richly hued floral wreath whose tones are then concealed by layers of thin white fabric and shrouded by the wedding veil of Karen Valentine, who, with Stephanie Martin, worked on this runner. The netting that covers the surface of the runner renders it as pallid as life became for women as a result of the death of the Goddess.

Amazon

Amazon societies are thought to have existed during the third and second millennia B.C., one on a lost island off the coast of North Africa and another on the southern shore of the Black Sea. Myths characterize these people as living most of the year in all-female societies and mating with men at random in the spring. Girls were taught pride in their sex, learning athletics and the martial arts in order to preserve their independence. Male children were supposedly killed or crippled and made to work as servants.

While little actual evidence has been found to support the reality of entire societies of warrior women, there are many documented instances of women leading battles or fighting side by side with men. The Greeks left us the most extensive information about the Amazon, but research contradicts their mythology, informing us that matriarchal societies were usually communal, clan-based structures and were egalitarian, democratic, and peaceable. It is possible that we have not yet uncovered existing evidence of warrior queendoms or that matriarchal societies fought in battles only when their power was being challenged in a vain effort to turn the tide.

Although the names of many warrior queens are known, I chose to depict a symbolic Amazon rather than a particular woman. Her portrait incorporates some of the most fundamental symbols of the mother cults. The white egg, the red crescent, and the black stone combine to make the body of this Amazon warrior. (The white egg, symbol of fertility, was carried by the women of Anatolia on the helms of their ships. Riding across the vast plains, women strapped the red crescent on their saddles as an homage to the Great Mother, whose worship was tied to the moon. In Sumeria, they carried a black stone – the earliest incarnation of the Goddess – in a cart drawn by oxen.) Wearing metallic breastplates, the Amazon holds a double axe in each hand. (This double axe, part of the worship of the Mother Goddess in Crete, was traditionally used by women to cut down trees and clear the land.)

The iconography of the plate is repeated on the back of the runner. Red lacing borders the top and front of the runner; derived from images of Amazons in Greek sculpture, this lacing joins with a strip of red snakeskin like those which Amazon women from the North wore in battle.

Hatshepsut

1503–1482 B.C.

In ancient Egypt, men and women were equal under the law. Affection and consideration for the woman of the family is one of the most common motifs in tomb art, where husbands and wives are frequently seen embracing and sharing activities together. Women enjoyed economic independence, moving freely about the society. New Kingdom Pharaohs prided themselves on keeping such good order in the country that women could travel anywhere without fear of being molested.

The position of women underwent changes during the three thousand years of Egyptian history, but certain features remained constant. While royal men and women shared the rule of the country equally, the throne was always passed on through the female line, as the principles of matrilineal descent and matrimonial inheritance rights were firmly established. Occasionally a matriarchy developed; four women are known to have ruled as Pharaohs, but little is known of any except Hatshepsut.

63

Hatshepsut, the mighty ruler of the XVIII dynasty, was the daughter of a great warrior-king. She continued her father's policies of strengthening the country's defense, leading military expeditions to achieve this end. She initiated many construction projects, including the building and refurbishing of temples; she bolstered Egypt's economy through trade and achieved peace and prosperity during her reign. Hatshepsut's own words reveal the pride she felt in her accomplishments: "My command stands firm like the mountains and the sun's disk shines and spreads rays over the titulary of my august person, and my falcon rises high above the kingly banner unto all eternity."*

Hatshepsut stands between the mythological and real worlds, as Phar-

*Barbara Lesko, *The Remarkable Women of Ancient Egypt,* Berkeley, Calif: B.C. Scribe Publishers, 1978.

aohs were considered to be the human incarnation of the Deity. Her plate is the first one on the table with any reliefing on the surface; this was accomplished after a year and a half of almost total failure. The center of the plate is slightly raised, which was achieved by carving into the surface of an unbisqued plate. The change in dimension is almost imperceptible, as we wanted to introduce the reliefing gradually. It was important to make a smooth transition between the precision of the Japanese plates and the slightly less exact form of our studio-made versions. Hatshepsut's portrait required three or four china-paint firings; we must have made this plate eight or ten times, trying several different clay bodies. The plate is set on a runner embroidered with hieroglyphs which loosely tell the story of Hatsheput's life.

all deities into a single male godhead.

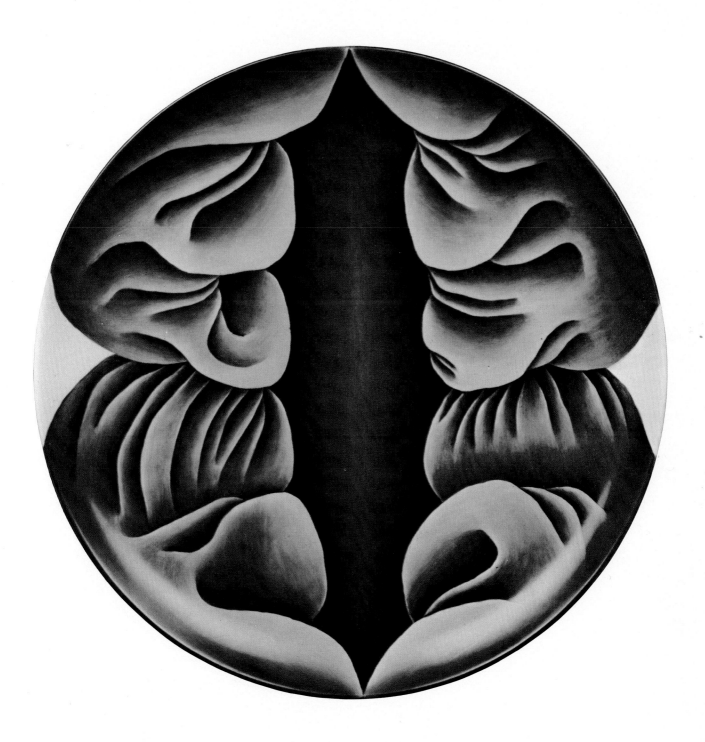

Primordial Goddess

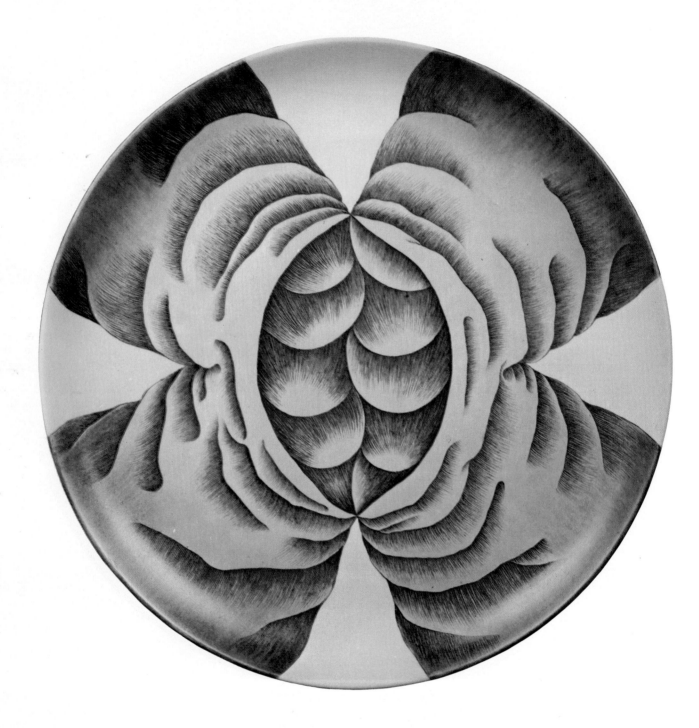

Fertile Goddess

peoples - were matriarchal and worshipped

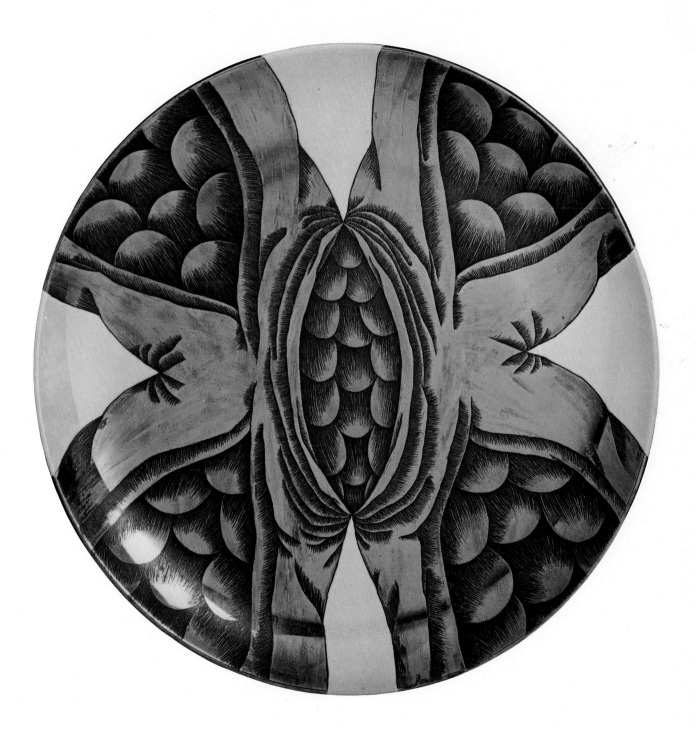

Ishtar

a goddess. It required six centuries for

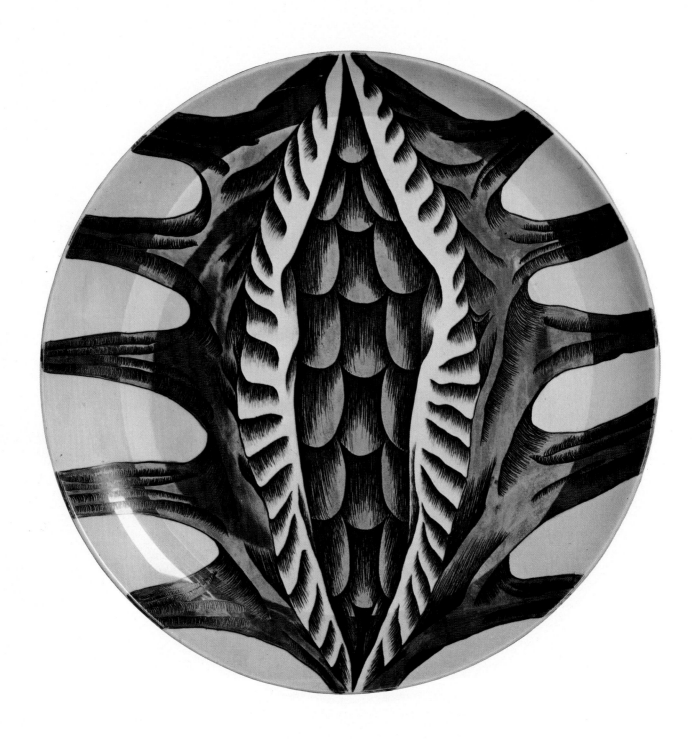

Kali

Yahweh to replace Ashtoreth as the primary

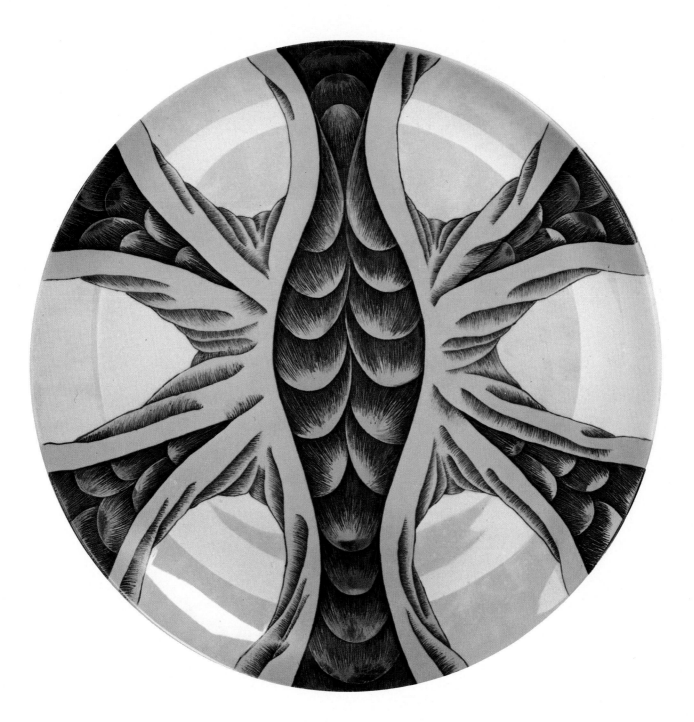

Snake Goddess

deity of the Jews; for a long time their temples

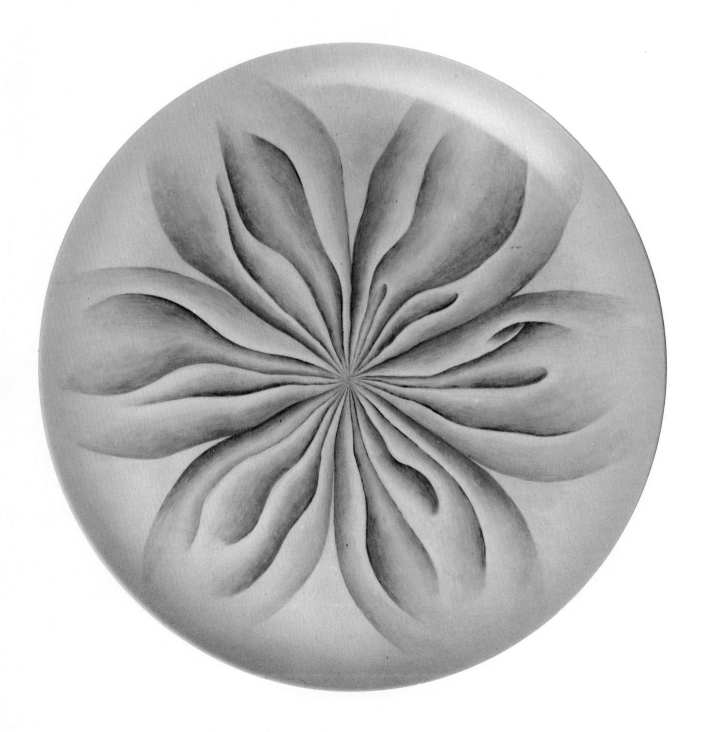

Sophia

were side by side. After the Jewish

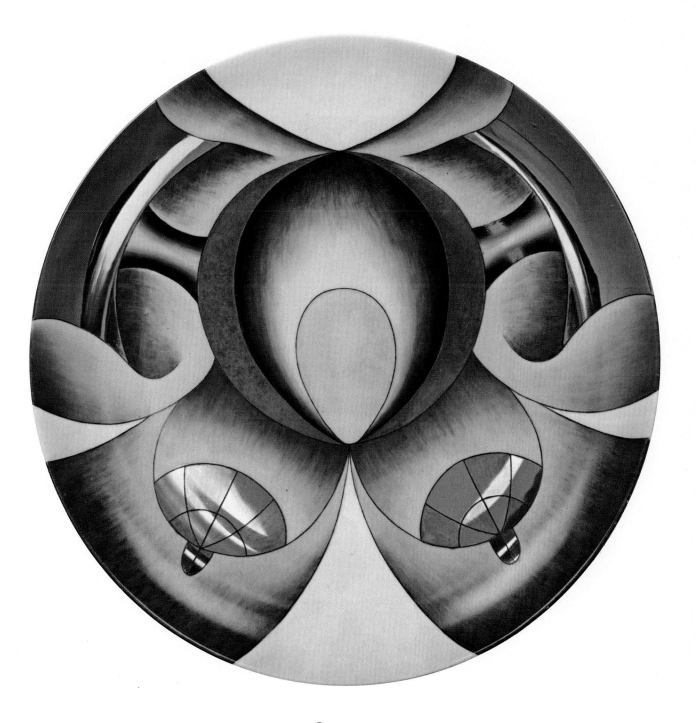

Amazon

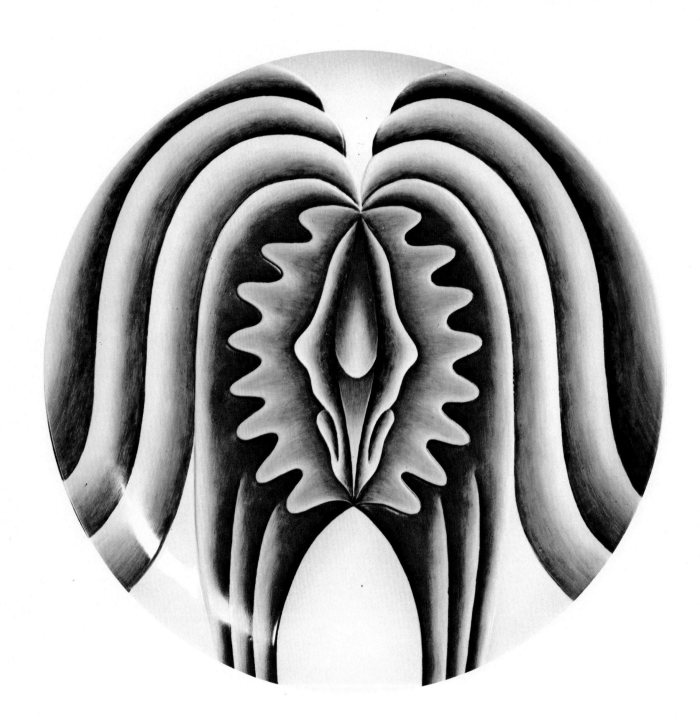

Hatshepsut

Judith

6th c. b.c.

Judith, a Jewish heroine, is a legendary figure whose story is told in the *Book of Judith,* written to inspire the Jews to acts of heroism. Judith lived in the town of Bethulia, which had been conquered by the Assyrian general Holofernes and his troops. Jews were forced into exile, taken into slavery, or persecuted for their refusal to pay tribute to Holofernes' king. Judith, a very devout and learned woman, decided to take action against the enemy while most of her fellow Jews were bemoaning their fate.

She prayed for the strength to take vengeance on those "...who had loosened a maiden's headdress to defile her and stripped her thigh to shame her, and profaned her womb to disgrace her...," an obvious reference to the rape of the women of her town. Putting on festive attire, Judith adorned herself in jewels and – taking along wine, cheese, oil, bread, and figs – entered the camp of Holofernes. She easily passed by his soldiers, who did not suspect that a woman could be a real threat, and was invited to feast with the general. They drank a great deal of the wine, which Judith – skilled in herbs and powders – had carefully prepared. The liquid put Holofernes to sleep, and, silently, Judith went up to his bedpost. Taking Holofernes' sword in her hand, she caught him by the hair and cut off his head with two sharp strokes. She then wrapped the tyrant's head in some cloth and stole from the tent. She reached the gates of the city without detection and placed Holoferne's head on one of the gateposts of the city for all to see. The army – disoriented by the loss of their leader – retreated, and the Jews honored Judith with feasts and praises. The women held a special ceremony in which they sang, played instruments, and danced all day and into the night in honor of their savior.

The Judith plate rests on a runner whose embroidered Hebrew letters identify Judith as a heroine of her people. The iconography of the runner is derived from the headdress traditionally worn by Hebrew women during the marriage ceremony. Encrusted with jewels and spangles, dowry coins were hung directly on the headdress, a rather overt demonstration of some of the Hebraic attitudes toward women.

Sappho

fl. 600 b.c.

Sappho, the greatest lyric poet and one of the finest poets of Western Civilization, was born on the island of Lesbos in 612 b.c. There, where the bright sun filled the air with light and the blue water sparkled, women came and went as they pleased, for they knew nothing of the changes that were taking place in other lands. Women were highly valued in Lesbos, well-educated and free to pursue their interests and develop their talents. Sappho spent most of her life on this island, where she founded a "thiasos" – a sacred society of women who were bound by special ties.

Each year this society participated in religious festivals that were held for women only, as ancient religions were based on the idea that she who gives birth has power over life and death. This power was expressed in music, with singing, dancing, and playing instruments considered divine arts belonging to women. Ancient rock paintings depict female musicians, and there are hundreds of myths and legends about the musical activities of goddesses, priestesses, and musicians. In tribal times, women gathered in the sacred menstrual huts they had built and welcomed their daughters' first menses with celebratory songs. Women sang as they worked in the fields and composed melodies as they wove. They crooned softly to each other to ease the pain of childbirth, and, when death struck, female musicians were summoned to mourn. The basic sound of women's music was the wail, and through women's songs of ecstasy, grief, or joy, the feelings of the community were expressed. But when women's authority waned, their music ceased.

Sappho became a renowned teacher, with many women gathering around her to learn the arts of poetry, music, and dancing. Her fame spread throughout Greece; statues were erected in her honor; her likeness was imprinted on coins; and her poetry was thought to rival Homer's. In addition to developing new poetic structures and meters, Sappho is known for poems expressing her love of women, often in openly erotic terms. Homosexuality was then viewed as a natural impulse for both women and men. Because Sappho came from the island of Lesbos, the word "lesbian" has come to mean a woman who loves women.

This eminent woman, so celebrated in her own time, later became the object of ridicule. She was satirized and maligned by Greeks, and her love of women was distorted by Roman writers into something unfeminine and perverse. The Church made her a criminal for her eroticism and homosexuality. Fanatical monks burned her poems, so that only a few hundred lines still survive.

Sappho's portrait is inspired by the fact that she was known as "the flower of the graces," whose colors were green and lavender. On the back of her runner is a Doric temple, and between its columns can be seen the brilliant blue of the Aegean sky. Sappho's name rests within a burst of color that stands for the last burst of unimpeded female creativity.

Aspasia

470–410 B.C.

Unlike Sappho, Aspasia stood as a lonely woman in an environment which systematically isolated women. Athenian society, as it became progressively more democratic for men, became increasingly repressive for women of all classes, eventually subjecting them to total segregation. Women sat with men only at the marriage feast; afterward they lived in separate quarters and rarely were permitted outside. Girls were kept in ignorance, while boys were required to learn to read and write. Because of the enormous emphasis on intellect in this culture, the fact that most women were virtually illiterate created a deep gap between the sexes.

Aspasia came to Athens from an area of Greece where women were still allowed some independence. She joined the ranks of the "hetaerae" (a word that originally was used by Sappho to refer to her companions, but later took on pejorative meaning), who were the only Athenian women to participate in Greek culture.

Aspasia, a scholar and philosopher, became the companion of the orator and statesman Pericles. They began to live together in 445 B.C., and soon the most learned men of the day frequented their house. Aspasia had created the first known salon, which allowed her – as it would allow women after her – to be part of the intellectual dialogue of the day. She was particularly known for discussing the role of women in society, asserting the right of woman to live as man's equal, not his slave. She urged her male guests to bring their wives to her salon, and for the first time these women were exposed to Greek culture. For such heretical behavior, Aspasia was eventually charged and tried for "impiety." Only Pericles' intervention on her behalf saved her life.

Aspasia's portrait is done in muted tones of the earth colors which the Greeks loved to paint on their sculptures and their buildings. Her plate sits on a runner whose motifs are taken from Greek vases. Draped fabric, formed to resemble the costumes favored by the Athenians, embellishes both the front and the back of the runner. Two embroidered pins hold the drapery to the runner much as a jeweled clasp decorated the Greek toga.

Boadaceia
1st C. A.D.

Boadaceia, whose plate is the twelfth on the table, represents the tradition of warrior-queens extending back into legendary times. The portrait of this British heroine is slightly carved, its surface raised more than any other on the first wing of the table. The plate was remade at least six times, one cracking at the bisque stage, one in the glaze firing, and two more when nearly completed. An image of a stone structure reminiscent of Stonehenge (an ancient British monument whose origin is unknown) cradles a helmet-form decorated with motifs from gold shields of the time. The plate rests on a runner of handmade felt, an old-fashioned fabric made by shearing sheep and compacting the wool. We designed convoluted patterns that resembled the motifs of early British art and stitched them onto the felt, embellishing the forms with jeweled pieces like those Boadaceia might have worn.

Although available information about early Celtic life is sketchy, it is known that women had legal and political rights. Celtic religion had powerful female deities who, much like Ishtar, conferred the right to rule on the king in a ritual mating designed to ensure the fertility of the land and the people. Boadaceia, growing up in such a society, had no difficulty in establishing her right to rule after the death of her husband, the king.

Living during a period when the Romans were spreading their empire into the British Isles, however, Boadaceia's people, the Iceni, were conquered by the Romans and then – though only for a short while – left relatively undisturbed. Boadaceia's husband had willed half his property to the Roman Emperor (this was required of conquered rulers) and the other half to Boadaceia and their two daughters, in the hope that this inheritance would protect his family from the Romans. Instead, the will was used as a pretext for Roman officials to regard the whole kingdom as their spoil. They seized the estate of Boadaceia's relatives, then broke into the queen's quarters. Boadaceia was bound, flogged, and forced to witness the brutal rape of her daughters by Roman soldiers.

Enraged, this great queen called together neighboring tribes, all of whom despised Roman rule. Uniting them in one great army, she said, "Roman lust has gone so far that not even our own persons remain unpolluted. If you weigh well the strengths of our armies, you will see that in this battle we must conquer or die. This is a woman's resolve. As for the men, they may live or be slaves."

With men and women fighting side by side, the British attacked their Roman oppressors and at first seemed successful. But Boadaceia's apparent triumph was of short duration – the Romans were a highly skilled army, while Boadaceia's troops were unaccustomed to single combat. The Roman general, who hated Boadaceia, vented his rage on her people, slaughtering over 80,000 and leading a campaign of annihilation against entire sections of the British community. Boadaceia managed to make her way home, where she took poison rather than accept her defeat.

Hypatia
370–415

Hypatia, a Roman scholar and philosopher who lived in Alexandria, is the last representative at the table of female genius and culture in the classical world. The Coptic imagery of Alexandria is used extensively in both her plate and

68

her runner. Her portrait has indented, scalloped edges, as if the image had broken slightly from its confines. Painted in strong colors, the leaf forms describing Hypatia pull away from the center, suggesting the events of her life. The plate is placed on a runner whose border patterns are drawn directly from Coptic weaving, as is the small goddess whose head illuminates Hypatia's name. The back of the runner, woven by Jan du Bois from my design, emphasizes the horror of this distinguished woman's death.

Unlike most of their Athenian sisters, Roman women were educated, particularly those who lived where Egyptian influence was strong. Hypatia, a child prodigy, was tutored by the most celebrated scholars of her day. She rapidly mastered mathematics, astronomy, and the natural sciences and became famous in these fields. Because she was an outstanding scholar and very popular as well, she was appointed head of the University of Alexandria.

Hypatia attempted to create an intellectual reawakening of reverence for the Greek gods and goddesses. She particularly stressed the importance of goddesses and the feminine aspects of culture, arguing that the Mother Goddess religion conferred dignity, influence, and power on women. When consulted about the unrest in Rome, she stated that Roman men had misused their women – causing the next generations to be born not through love, but through seduction and rape. This had produced violence and turmoil in the empire that could only

be solved, she said, by elevating women to their former status.

Through her eloquent teachings, Hypatia attracted both plain and cultured people to her philosophy and gradually became a political force that threatened the power of the emerging Church. Constantine had already proclaimed Christianity the State religion, but the Church had not yet established sole control. Hypatia was anathema to many Christians; the Bishop of Alexandria despised her, no doubt in part because she dared to preach. Silence and submission were what he expected of women, and Hypatia's stature in Alexandrian society incensed him.

Because she had become an advisor to the government, it was difficult for the Bishop to openly attack Hypatia. Instead, he organized a group of fanatical monks who waylaid her on the way to her weekly lecture at the university. Dragging her from her carriage, they pulled her limbs from their sockets, plucked out her organs, hacked her remains into pieces, and burned them. Years later, when the great library of Alexandria was sacked, Hypatia's writings – like her body – were burned.

Marcella

325–410

Marcella, born of a noble and wealthy family, lived in Rome during the time when the Roman Empire was crumbling. She was forced to marry at an early age, and, although widowed while still quite young, dedicated herself to a religious life instead of following Roman custom and remarrying. She had become interested in Christianity, particularly in the doctrine that "in Christ there is neither male nor female," an idea to which some Christians still suscribed, despite the misogynist teachings of the Church. There were then a number of religious communities where men and women had equal rights: Women taught, baptized, served at the altar, held public office, and generally exercised considerable power. As the Church became more organized, however, women were excluded from many of the activities they had previously been able to perform.

Marcella withdrew from Roman society and made her palace a center for women who were interested in a simple life of purpose. Many women gathered around her – some because they were devoted Christians, some because they desired an alternative to the growing decadence of the classical world, and others because they wished to avoid a forced and loveless marriage. In Marcella's community, called the "Little Church of the Household," women studied religion and the Scriptures and – under her guidance – were educated in the Christian way of life. They traveled and preached, set up religious houses and schools for women, established hospitals, and ministered to the sick and the needy.

In 410, during the Sack of Rome, Marcella was beaten by invading soldiers and her estate destroyed. Although she was able to escape, she died shortly thereafter. But Marcella had planted the seed that flowered into the great monastic system of Christianity which, for centuries, provided women with education and a refuge from their increasingly circumscribed world. Her convent was to be only the first of many communities of religious women.

Marcella's plate is done in luminous but modulated tones. It sits on a runner which is embroidered with a basilica structure, the earliest architectural form of Christian churches. The front of the runner has a rough surface, woven like the hair shirts worn by Marcella and the women in her community. The back of the runner carries Marcella's symbols, a scroll, a boat, and a fish, acquired when she became a saint.

Saint Bridget
453–523

Christianity spread slowly through Europe, and meanwhile the Church absorbed many of the customs and divinities from earlier times. Thus when Christianity came to Ireland, instead of destroying the Celtic traditions, it preserved them. Like many indigenous peoples, the Celts had held to the mores and customs of the age of matriarchy. Mother Goddess worship still existed in Ireland when the early Christian evangelists arrived, and religious leaders encouraged the populace to bring their traditional convictions, deities, rituals, and holidays into the structure of the Christian faith. This process of cultural amalgamation is clearly demonstrated in the story of Saint Bridget.

Bridget, a patron saint of Ireland, founded the first convent there, was important in the development of monasticism, and contributed to the Irish Renaissance. Born in 453, she resolved as a young girl to consecrate her life to religion. Since there were then no religious houses for women, she established a cell in the trunk of a giant oak tree which had formerly been used as a shrine of the Mother Goddess Brigid (with whom Bridget later became identified). There, Bridget gathered a number of other young women around her and founded a sisterhood devoted to teaching and charity. She soon built the first nunnery in Ireland on that site.

Bridget's convent eventually grew to be a great monastery and center of learning; men as well as women worked under her benevolent leadership. Bridget was one of the earliest Christians to make the monastery a kind of settlement house, to which all the neighboring peasants could come for help, advice, and education. Under her inspiration, the arts flourished and a masterpiece of an illuminated manuscript was produced at the monastery. She also established a school of metalwork that became famous for its exquisitely crafted product. Bridget traveled extensively, established new religious houses and monasteries, and was extremely influential in both political and Church affairs. After her death she became extraordinarily popular, and countless churches, monasteries, and villages were named after her.

Through Bridget the Celts maintained their religious ties to Mother Goddess worship, for she came to be associated with all the symbols that had formerly belonged to the Celtic goddess.

Vestal virgins had kept a sacred fire burning for Brigid, and this custom was taken over by nuns who maintained the flame until the convents were dissolved. Fire was holy to the Goddess, who was often depicted with a column of fire – an image of immortality which I incorporated into Saint Bridget's plate, painted in the colors of Ireland.

The plate rests on a runner covered by a bark-colored silk and embellished by an oak cross and a panel carved with Celtic motifs. Christian and Celtic imagery is combined in the plate and the runner to represent the continued tradition of the Mother Goddess as it was incorporated into the worship of this female saint.

Theodora
508–548

Theodora, the famed Byzantine empress, began her life as an actress – a profession that was despised in Byzantine society. After living a rather dissolute early life, she became religious and established herself in Constantinople, living simply and supporting herself by spinning. Shortly thereafter she met Justinian, the Emperor's nephew, and they were married as soon as he was able to have the laws changed to permit union between himself and a women of humble origins. Theodora was crowned with Justinian in 527 and became the Empress of Byzantium. In Ravenna, a cathedral built by them is filled with glittering mosaics that depict the joint rule of the royal couple. Theodora's plate incorporates both the color and the technique of these mosaic walls.

It required months for Judye Keyes to develop this plate, which cracked repeatedly in the kiln. We experimented with several clay bodies and made at least a dozen plates before we succeeded. Keyes first applied individual tiles to the surface of an unfired clay plate; then she decided to lay a slab onto the plate and carefully cut it with a sharp tool to create the illusion of separate tiles, scratching notches even deeper after the plate was bisqued. Five china-painted firings were needed to build up the color and the gold. Theodora's runner, embroidered by Marjorie Biggs, repeats the motifs on the plate. The plate rests on a gold halo, which, like the halo around Theodora's head in the Ravenna mural, honors this great empress for her efforts on behalf of women.

Theodora was, from the beginning of her reign, deeply concerned about the position of women. She never forgot the suffering and humiliation she had seen women endure when she was an actress. Prostitution was rampant in Constantinople, and there were brothels throughout the city. To supply these houses, procurers traveled around the empire seducing poor women with clothes, jewelry, and money. Other women were forced into prostitution through seduction and rape. Once a woman had been brought to a brothel, she was virtually a prisoner. Even if she escaped there was nowhere for her to go, for she was a moral outcast – as were actresses. Often the latter were forced, against their wills, to sign contracts binding them to the theaters for which they worked.

Theodora passed laws nullifying these contracts and broke down barriers that kept actresses in a socially inferior role. She issued an imperial decree making it illegal – and punishable by death – to entice a woman into prostitution, and she turned one of her palaces into an institution where prostitutes could go to start new lives. She helped raise the low status of women in marriage, improved the divorce laws in their favor, passed laws protecting women from mistreatment by their husbands, saw to it that women could inherit property, and instituted the death penalty for rape. Moreover, Theodora personally enforced all these women's rights measures and left a legacy that enhanced Byzantine women's lives for many years.

Hroswitha
935–1002

Hrosvitha, Germany's earliest poet and dramatist, occupies a unique place in literary history, for she was the first playwright in medieval Europe. She was a member of the Saxon tribe, one of the last German tribes to resist conversion until Charlemagne conquered them and they were forcibly Christianized. With the development of feudalism, German women lost their traditional property rights. In an effort to retain their land, countless princesses refused to relinquish their property to their husbands and founded religious houses instead. Aided by the Church, they retreated to the convents they had established and, as abbesses, ruled independently of men; in some cases they were responsible only to the king, not to the Church. If the abbess was related to the ruling family, heading an abbey could make her extremely powerful – the political equal, in fact, of a baron of the land.

Gandersheim, the convent which Hrosvitha entered when she was young, was a free abbey. Her abbess' relationship with the nobility meant that Hrosvitha had the opportunity to associate with the scholars, churchmen, and royalty who visited there. Like most girls who were convent-trained, Hrosvitha was well educated; she studied Latin and Greek and was taught scholastic philosophy, mathematics, astronomy, and music. She proved a gifted student and soon began to write, at first secretly. ("Unknown to others and secretly, I wrote by myself. Sometimes I composed, sometimes I destroyed what I had written.") After working for some years, Hrosvitha collected her poems and dedicated them to her abbess, who encouraged her and brought her work to the attention of the educated world. The poems were well received, and Hrosvitha continued to write.

She wrote sacred legends in verse, historical poems, prose prefaces, and the history of the Ottonian dynasty. But her most important works were her plays. Hrosvitha wrote a series of dramas which dealt with the conflict of virtue and spiritual aspiration versus evil and the temptation of sin. In developing these dramas, she looked to the Roman playwright Terence, whose plays all turned on the frailty of the female sex. Hrosvitha challenged Terence's misogyny, and the keynote of her work was its celebration of women. In her plays, men embodied paganism and lust, while women were shown as strong, steadfast, and representing the purity and gentleness of Christianity.

The story of Hrosvitha's life is recounted on the back of her runner, embroidered by Marny Elliott in a needlework technique called Opus Teutonicum. Commonly employed by German nuns, this type of embroidery utilizes flat patterning and simple drawing. The front of the runner is embellished with four raised, circular forms that resemble the medieval coins minted by abbesses. These padded discs portray popular tales and legends from pre-Christian Germany. Images of an armed Valkyrie and a bloodthirsty Cimbrian princess recall the time when women appeared in armor, fighting and uttering loud shrieks to drive away advancing armies. Hrosvitha's plate, which repeatedly cracked, was remade more than a dozen times and changed its form during the months it took to get it out of the kiln. Deeply reliefed, the plate combines the ivory carvings of Ottonian art with the praying hands and nun's cap typically associated with religious women.

Trotula
d. 1097

In Salerno, as in most of southern Italy, Byzantine influence was strong. Thanks to the laws of Theodora, the position of women was better than in any other civilized society of the time. Against a luxuriant background of terraced vineyards, men and women studied together at the medical school, the first university of the Western world. While most of Europe was still relying on saints' relics, prayers, and poisonous remedies for curing sickness, Salerno doctors were employing the more advanced forms of medical healing. Among them was a group of women doctors, the most prominent of whom was Trotula.

Although she was a renowned physician, author, and professor, it was as a gynecologist that Trotula won lasting fame. Her carved symbol derives from the Aztec goddess of healing, who took the form of a serpent, and is combined with a birth image, pre-Columbian motifs, and a caduceus (a rod entwined with two snakes that has become the modern symbol of medicine). I chose the snake motif because of its historical association with feminine wisdom and powers of healing. The runner incorporates a tree-of-life motif, traditional in women's needlework and appropriate, I thought, to Trotula's profession. We used a quilting technique called Trapunto after discovering an example done in the eleventh century in nearby Sicily.

Trotula's husband and two sons were also physicians, and they worked together on a new medical encyclopedia. At the university in Salerno, where she taught, the curriculum included practical work and bedside instruction based on close observation of the patient. Since doctors were forbidden by the Church to dissect the human body, diagnosis was dependent on symptoms of disease. Trotula excelled at observations of the pulse, urine, facial expression, and "feel" of the skin; using these indices, she could distinguish between diseases whose overt symptoms were the same.

Trotula wrote prolifically on gynecology and obstetrics, and her book *Diseases of Women* was consulted for 700 years after her death. In order to help women by describing the diseases that affected them, Trotula synthesized in this book the information she had gained from her vast practical experience concerning pregnancy, menstruation, sterility, difficulties in labor, emergency procedures for midwives, and abortions. She was the first doctor to give advice on the care of the newborn infant, and throughout her writings she stressed hygiene, cleanliness, and exercise – at a time when people thought disease was cured magically. When she died in 1097, her casket was attended by a procession of mourners two miles long. Centuries later male doctors dismissed Trotula as a witch, and for a time it was believed that her book had been written by a man.

The twelfth century brought with it a general revolution in medical training, but women gradually came to be excluded from the profession. With the exception of those in Italy, the new universities – where medicine was increasingly emphasized – would not accept female students. Medicine slowly became closed to them through civil restrictions, prohibitions, legal actions, and, finally, persecution.

Eleanor of Aquitaine
1122–1204

Eleanor of Aquitaine was one of the most powerful women of the Middle Ages. Born to the ruling family of southern France, she was raised in a court where women had considerable power. Eleanor inherited this rich duchy of Aquitaine and brought her property, as well as the liberal ideas of her childhood, to the court of Louis VII, whom she married when she was fifteen.

In Paris the young queen attempted to find an outlet for her ambitions, but her husband was hostile toward women's authority and thwarted her every move. When the king informed Eleanor of his intention to leave for the Crusades, she insisted on going with him. Louis opposed her, and capitulated only because the nobles of southern France would not support him unless they were led by their queen. Eleanor organized three hundred women and prepared them for the long journey. The Queen's Amazons, dressed in coats of mail and skirts of tinted silk, carried the special insignia of the Amazonian corps on their sleeves. They followed Eleanor to be of service – to attend the sick and to fight when they could. But the Crusade was a disaster and ultimately led to a divorce between France's king and queen.

Eleanor then married Henry of England and helped him gain the crown. She had hoped to expand her power, but was eventually imprisoned by her husband instead. In an effort to regain her ancestral lands, the queen had encouraged her sons to revolt against their father. While the king and the princes were eventually to be reconciled, Eleanor remained sequestered for sixteen years.

Before her imprisonment Eleanor had established the Courts of Love, graced by the troubadour poetry which had been introduced by her grand-father and carried with Eleanor from the French to the English throne. She made this "religion of the gentle heart" the foundation for courtly love throughout the land. By sustaining the troubadours, noblewomen were able to make their courts major cultural and social centers and thereby play a primary role in shaping the mores and values of their class. In feudal castles women heard cases concerning relationships between women and men. Their judgments were then communicated by the minstrels, who spread reverence for women through poetry and song. Although this idealization of women ultimately had negative effects, for a while women's lives were improved and their influence felt as a powerful force.

Eleanor's plate – made by casting a dome, applying it to a greenware plate, and then cutting through the dome to make lattice-work – is done with pen work on top of overlaid lusters. The image, a fleur-de-lis, was a common symbol in the Middle Ages and relates to the iris, the sacred flower of the Virgin Mary. The plate rests on a tapestry woven by Audrey Cowan from my cartoon based on the Unicorn Tapestries. A corral imprisons the plate, containing it as Eleanor was contained. Surrounding the corral are flowers like the ones with which women covered the floors of their castles, where the Courts of Love were held.

Hildegarde of Bingen
1098–1179

Hildegarde of Bingen, the monastic counterpart of Eleanor of Aquitaine, was one of the greatest and most original thinkers of medieval Europe. She was an abbess, a scientist, a leading medical woman, a scholar, a musician and prolific composer, a political and religious figure, and a visionary. Her writings are among the earliest important mystic works of the Middle Ages.

Hildegarde's own illumination of her vision of the universe was the basis of my design for the back of her runner; I wanted to honor her unique view of the world. When I saw her drawings, I felt deeply moved by the beautiful, centered images that reached across eight centuries and united her vision with mine. The top and front of her runner form a Gothic cathedral, embroidered and couched in the gold stitching called Opus Anglicanum, which was used to embellish the vestments of bishops and kings. Her plate, painted like a stained-glass window, rests inside the Gothic arch and forms the rose window – the exalted spiritual focus of every medieval church.

Hildegarde spent almost her entire life in the convent, where she received an excellent education. She later headed a small monastery for women – established after she had a series of visions that told her where to found her religious house. She did this in the face of great opposition from churchmen, who attempted to denounce the authenticity of her revelations and only agreed to her plan when she became gravely ill. She was sufficiently important that they did not want her to die.

The leading medical writer of her day, Hildegarde wrote books on medicine which foreshadowed later ideas on the circulation of the blood and the characteristics of the nervous system. Her remedies for disease revealed a wide knowledge of drugs and herbs, and her medical treatments, despite their emphasis on magic, were quite progressive. Also a natural scientist, she cataloged and described plants, particularly those with medicinal properties.

Hildegarde maintained a voluminous correspondence with leading medieval thinkers and became increasingly involved with the political and religious issues of the day. In her later years, she concentrated on developing a theory of the universe which stressed the relationship between the divine and the human. Like Dante, Hildegarde conceived the universe holistically and emphasized the inseparability of the physical and the spiritual. In her writings she described her revelations and their allegorical meanings, which involved commentary on the Scriptures, the Trinity, and other religious issues. These works became quite popular and helped reinforce the idea that a strong Church was necessary as a source of morality and spiritual regeneration. Unfortunately, as has happened throughout history, the institution Hildegarde supported ultimately betrayed her, but she died before she could witness the way Church-organized witch hunts attacked those of her sex.

Petronilla de Meath
d. 1324

Despite the spread of Christianity throughout Europe, much of the local population clung to the traditional worship of the Mother Goddess. Many rural peoples tacitly accepted Christianity but continued to worship the Goddess, sometimes incorporating their particular female deity into the figure of Mary. The practices and rituals of the ancient doctrines became known as witchcraft – a joyous religion that worshiped the life force and treated women with respect. The Church became steadily more threatened by the power of witchcraft and was particularly incensed that it allowed women to preach.

The extent of the witch-hunting craze was much wider than is commonly thought. Eighty-five percent of those executed for witchcraft were women, and, although they were tried and burned on countless pretexts, their real crime was their attempt to preserve the traditions of the past and to resist the destruction of female power. Witch hunts were prevalent from the thirteenth through seventeenth centuries. According to male scholars, no more than three hundred thousand women were exterminated, but contemporary feminist scholars are beginning to suspect that there were probably between six and nine million killed. The exact figure is difficult to determine because few records were kept, but those that do exist are horrifying: Nine hundred people were accused of witchcraft and executed in a single year in southwestern Germany; in Toulouse, four hundred were put to death in a day; and there were some villages where nearly all the female inhabitants were wiped out.

One of the first documented witchcraft trials took place in Ireland in 1324. Petronilla de Meath, represented on the table a a symbol of all the women sacrificed as witches, worked as a maid for Lady Alice Kyteler. Kyteler was an extremely rich woman who had had three previous husbands. Her fourth claimed that she was bewitching him, and a bishop – inspired in no small part by his desire to confiscate Kyteler's property – pursued the charges. Lady Alice, her son, Petronilla, and several others were accused of denying God and the Church, making animal sacrifices, and concocting secret potions. The noblewoman was also charged with having sexual relations with a man who could supposedly appear as both a black male and a cat. The witch hunters always emphasized sexuality during the witchcraft trials, and through the years the sexual charges brought against women became increasingly preposterous.

Lady Kyteler was able to escape to England, taking Petronilla's child, but Petronilla herself was imprisoned and tortured. Her arrest took place before the Church had devised detailed instructions on the use of torture to procure confessions and denunciations. Later, it became common to strip the accused woman naked, shave off all her body hair, and then subject her to thumbscrews and the rack, spikes and bone-crushing boots, starvation and beatings. Petronilla was merely flogged and burned, refusing to the last to accept the Christian faith.

Petronilla's plate employs the symbols of the witches' covens. A bell, a book, and a candle are combined with the cauldron which traditionally represented the Great Mother and around which witches grouped. The flames that envelop the center of the plate are a terrible inversion of the sacred fire that once burned in honor of the Goddess of the ancient world. The runner engulfs Petronilla in twisted patterns derived from typical Irish-Celtic motifs and is bordered by a red garter that symbolizes a witch's belief.

Christine de Pisan
1363–1431

Despite the terror induced by the witchcraft trials, women continued striving to achieve. But the idea of female inferiority, a theme certainly present in medieval thought, took on new meaning in a society bent on containing female power and enforcing the domination of men. Throughout the Middle Ages, misogynist thinking was moderated by the Christian belief in spiritual equality between women and men. The increasing secularization of society undermined this later attitude and reinforced – in both theory and practice – women's dependency on men.

By the fourteenth century, townships had begun to rival the monasteries as intellectual centers. Although religious houses were open for men near these towns, female orders remained outside the new centers of learning. Women were generally excluded from the developing universities as well; if a male professor believed in education for women, he might allow them to sit in on his classes, but usually they were not permitted to speak. A father might decide to educate his daughters or let them assist him in his work; however, a woman could not be apprenticed to an artist or even to a tradesman. The middle-class woman usually worked with her husband in the profession for which he had been trained, and, upon her husband's death, she could take over the business. Yet while there are many records of widows' success, these women were also a frequent target of the witch hunters' wrath. Meanwhile, in the nunneries, education was steadily deteriorating. The intellectual and artistic excellence of earlier times gave way to stricter confinement of nuns, their increased separation from the intellectual centers, and greater control of female houses by male bishops.

Literature attacking women was becoming both prevalent and popular. In the late fourteenth century, one woman emerged who was dedicated to defending her sex. Christine de Pisan was the first female professional author in France. Educated by her father, a humanist from Italy, she was able to surmount many of the barriers placed before women because he encouraged her talents. Widowed at twenty-five, she supported herself and her three children by writing. She first became prominent when she attacked a popular book, *Le Roman de la Rose,* considered a cornerstone of French literature. This work outraged Christine by its vicious attack on women. She argued for the equality of women, and, because she was by that time one of the few women accepted in the world of letters, her arguments carried considerable weight.

Christine then wrote a book which recorded the achievements of women of the past. Called *La Cité des Dames,* This work described a mythical city peopled by the greatest women of all periods and social classes. Stating that books which degraded women exerted an evil influence on peoples' minds, she offered her "City of Women" as a tribute to the women of her times.

In Christine's plate, one wing is raised in a gesture which defends her own body and, symbolically, other members of her sex. The runner's sharp points – stitched in a needlepoint technique popular in Christine's time – thrust toward the plate, and the angry Bargello patterns begin to encroach ever more severely on the space which surrounds the plate.

Isabella d'Este
1474–1539

In Renaissance Italy, noblewomen exercised far less political power than they had during feudal times. What power they retained was a result of the continued tradition of female inheritance which still allowed women certain rights, but these rights became indirect and provisional. Even the so-called equal education of men and women, often pointed to as a distinct achievement of the Renaissance, was not at all what it was reputed to be. Although they studied much the same subjects as men, Renaissance ladies were ultimately expected to be charming, docile, and pleasing to their fathers, brothers, and husbands, whom they would never dare to oppose.

Isabella d'Este was a perfect example of a Renaissance princess, and as such she symbolizes the countless women who have played this kind of role. Born during the height of the Italian Renaissance to the governing family of Ferrara, she was betrothed at six to the Duke of Mantua. Isabella, educated according to humanist principles, became a more serious scholar than women were expected to be. She studied the classics as well as literature, theology, and languages. She read voraciously, with a particular love for poetry; was a talented musician; and, like other noblewomen, was proficient in embroidery and design. By the time she left her family's court to marry the Duke of Manuta, she was well prepared for her position as a Renaissance wife.

But D'Este was somewhat more ambitious than other women of her class. Although expected to be an art patron, she brought more than the usual taste and intelligence to that role, soon acquiring a collection that was the best in the land. And although she knew that her acquisitions brought glory to her husband, the Duke, she treasured her private museum, where she claimed the best work as her own. While – in contrast to the patronage of women like Eleanor of Aquitaine – Renaissance women's patronage in no way benefited their own sex, Isabella's position as patron allowed her some influence in the shaping of contemporary cultural life.

Like many other Renaissance women, D'Este's correspondence was vast. Two thousand of her letters still exist, many of them written to the leading scholars and statesmen of her day. She became an important political figure and often governed and defended Mantua in her husband's absence. She devoted much of her energy to consolidating her family's position, ensuring the success of her sons' careers. She played a crucial part in Italian history, but, nonetheless, her biography was not written for more than four hundred years – and even then many of her achievements were ignored.

Her plate was inspired by a richly decorated ceramic ware, Urbino majolica, made at a factory Isabella helped support; I was fascinated by its color and surface. The plate incorporates traditional majolica decoration with a reference, in its center, to the famous Renaissance pictorial space. The runner repeats the plate's motifs and uses the kind of Assisi needlework that Isabella herself may have done. The back of the runner carries an image derived from the D'Este crest, but this time in honor of a woman instead of the family in which she was obscured.

Elizabeth R

1533–1605

Elizabeth I's plate is an image of a great queen who said, in response to the counselors who continually pressured her to wed, "I am already bound unto a husband, which is the Kingdom of England, and a marble stone should hereafter declare that a queen, having reigned such a time, lived and died a virgin." (She re-

ferred to herself as a virgin in the traditional, rather than the modern, sense of that word – an independent woman, not dictated by any man.) One of the greatest rulers of the Western world, Elizabeth is honored at the table by a white satin runner encrusted with gold and pearls and embellished by the blackwork embroidery prevalent in her time.

Elizabeth, whose birth had been cursed by her father – Henry VIII – because he wanted a male heir, ascended the throne of England in 1559. Among the most erudite women of the sixteenth century, she continued the tradition of female scholarship advocated by English humanists and first introduced into England by Catherine of Aragon (who brought these ideas from the Spanish court of her mother, Isabella, an ardent supporter of women's rights). Despite the presence of strong and learned women in the English courts, however, arguments against female rulers abounded. Because government was considered a masculine affair, Elizabeth was constantly urged to find a husband and give England a king – but she was determined to retain her autonomy and rule England in her own way. She even manipulated her marital status to forge alliances under the pretense of engagement, then forestalling the actual marriage while she obtained her political goals.

During the forty-five years Elizabeth governed England, the country prospered and grew. There was a vast increase in national power and economic wealth as well as a cultural renaissance that made England an intellectual and artistic center of the world. She was a humane and tolerant ruler and was able to decrease the religious struggles between Protestants and Catholics that threatened the stability of the land. She established religious tolerance, maintained relative peace throughout her reign, modernized the British Navy, and made diplomacy an art.

As one of the earliest heads of state to recognize the sovereignty of the people, Elizabeth built a popular base of support. She established the right to a fair trial and organized governmental relief for the old, the infirm, and the poor. Her death brought with it an end to the respect for intellectual women that had pervaded English culture and politics. Reformation ideas, at first progressive with regard to women, became increasingly conservative – as reflected by the growing acceptance of Luther's dictum that "Women should remain home, sit still, keep house and bear and bring up children."

Artemisia Gentileschi

1590–1652

The end of monasticism brought with it a general decline in opportunities for a woman artist of the seventeenth century. Training became almost impossible to obtain, as apprenticeships – the primary vehicle for learning – were available only to men. Even the artisan guilds, formerly open to women (particularly in textiles), were gradually closed to them. One of

the few ways a woman could acquire training was if her father was an artist and would teach her himself.

Artemisia Gentileschi's father, an Italian painter, recognized his daughter's talent when she was young. He taught her in his own studio, where she was protected from the world's doubts about a woman's ability to achieve. However, the artist her father hired to teach Gentileschi perspective skills raped her in the studio and almost ruined her life. The rapist was brought to trial, but it was Artemisia who was tortured and questioned. She refused to retract her accusation; the man was finally imprisoned but served less than eight months. Because she had openly admitted to being assaulted, Gentileschi became the object of endless gossip. She retained a reputation as a loose woman throughout her life, and this was always extremely painful to her.

In order to protect Artemisia from scandal, her father arranged for her to be married; but the marriage did not last, and she began to move about from town to town. Everywhere Gentileschi went she painted – portraits as well as historical and religious works – and she soon became a well established artist. Though she received a number of commissions, she had to struggle to be paid as much as a man would have been for the same work. However, she was admitted to the Academy of Design in Florence – a rare honor for a young woman.

The twisting, turning forms of Artemisia's plate represent both the baroque style she employed and the extraordinary efforts required of any woman of her time who wanted to make art. The draped velvet of her runner, which almost engulfs her plate, reflects the "protective" environment (her father's studio) which shielded her from much of the world but harbored her rapist as well.

The women in Gentileschi's paintings – primarily heroines of the Bible or mythology – challenged prevailing ideas of the inferiority of the female sex, for she presented them as strong and courageous. One of her favorite themes was the story of Judith, savior of the Jews. From Judith's attack on Holofernes, Artemisia not only created a powerful image, but also expressed her outrage at the violence she had experienced.

Artemisia's canvases exhibit the dramatic use of lights and darks and the sensuous movements characteristic of the Italian baroque school. Her work is at its best, however, when she treats women with a sympathetic view, rendering them as full persons instead of sex objects for male eyes. Her important role in seventeenth-century painting is finally beginning to be understood. Although she was famous and successful in her own time, her art was later obscured – and some was even attributed to men of her era.

Gentileschi died in 1652, the first established woman artist to paint from a woman's point of view. Her work reaches out across the centuries, provides female images that affirm women, and offers solid evidence that women can also be great artists.

Anna van Schurman
1607–1678

Embroidered on Anna van Schurman's runner is an abbreviated version of this poignant statement from a book she wrote advocating female education: "Woman has the same erect countenance as man, the same ideals, the same love of beauty, honor, truth, the same wish for self-development, the same longing after righteousness, and yet she is to be imprisoned in an empty soul of which the very windows are shuttered." The lack of adequate education for women increasingly became the focus of those women who were able to write. Although writing was something women could do quietly, by themselves and out of the sight of a society which really wasn't interested in what they had to say, even Reformation women tried to make themselves heard. One of the most extraordinary women of this period was Anna van Schurman.

Born in Holland, Van Schurman was a genius at a time when female genius was considered an impossibility. Because northern Europe was somewhat more liberal in its attitudes toward women, she was allowed not only to study but also to achieve some recognition for her work. Anna, a child prodigy, and her brothers were educated at home by their father. Although she received a classical education, at first she directed most of her energies toward art, devoting herself to those techniques she could teach herself. She did fine engraving, drawing, modeling in wax, wood-carving, etching on glass, oil painting, and intricate needlework. Most of her work has been destroyed, but some can still be found in European museums and in the area where she lived.

At that time, most intellectual discussions in Holland centered on religious issues. Van Schurman became interested in theological questions and studied Greek, Hebrew, and the ancient languages in order to read and interpret the Bible. As women were not admitted to the university, she had to attend lectures concealed behind the curtains of a box. The unfairness of this situation stimulated her to write a book in which she argued, both by logic and by example, that women's native abilities were not being recognized. This work was followed by another in which she demanded the same educational opportunities for women as for men. These books made her famous and increasingly involved her in the international world of letters. Correspondence with important cultural figures was one way to participate in the intellectual dialogue of the day, and Anna corresponded with those who shaped the values of European society.

As Van Schurman grew older, she withdrew from society, preferring the solitude of work. She became increasingly doubtful of the validity of prevailing religious dogma; she joined a religious community in which women had equal rights and lived there for the rest of her life. Although the community was often persecuted, Anna preferred it to the injustice of secular life.

Van Schurman's plate is modestly colored, but the form tries to fly. It rests on a sampler embroidered in the Dutch needlework popular during Anna's life. At first samplers were done by professional embroiderers to demonstrate their skills, but soon they became a vehicle for confining the activities of little girls. Forced from childhood to learn tiny stitches which taught them patience, forebearance, and how to "think small," girls were thus conditioned to be docile and content with the female role.

Anne Hutchinson

1591–1643

After the death of George Washington, colonial women created an original form of needle painting – the mourning picture. Intended at first to commemorate the President's death, mourning pictures soon became a vehicle to express grief for the death of a loved one or sympathy for a neighbor's loss. These needle paintings were usually done on silk and reflected certain consistent motifs: a weeping willow tree, a tombstone and Grecian urn, and a grieving woman dressed in the then-popular neoclassical style. When Susan Hill and I first saw these unique and authentically female works, we decided to make an image to mourn not only the tragic life of Anne Hutchinson, but also the terrible waste of women's talent that characterized the seventeenth century. The plate, which depicts a shawl-like form that also resembles a shroud, sits beneath a drooping willow tree on the runner. The image grips the edge of the plate, a metaphor for Hutchinson's efforts to escape from an envi-

authority. However, women did not

ronment that "contained" women and expected them to suffer and be still.

Hutchinson arrived in the Massachusetts Bay Colony with her husband and family in 1634. The mother of sixteen children, most of whom survived, she soon became widely known for her knowledge of midwifery and herbal healing. She had been raised in England and educated at home, where she learned about theology and theological argument from her father (a minister), and in the Colony she remained vitally interested in the religious issues of the day. As a follower of John Calvin, she began gathering women in her home to discuss his sermons, since women were not allowed to attend the regular after-sermon debates. Between fifty and a hundred women met weekly, sometimes traveling great distances to hear Anne's commentary and to voice their own thoughts.

Hutchinson's teachings contradicted those of the Church, which required as blind a submission to its doctrine as was then demanded of a wife by her husband. Anne believed that the Holy Spirit dwelt in everyone, and not – as Calvin and other ministers insisted – only in those who had been selected for grace. Encouraged to believe in their own inner powers, her followers grew bold, arguing with clergymen during sermons and even walking out of services when ordered to be silent and remember woman's place.

Frightened by Hutchinson's power, the clergy tried to convince her to modify her views. Because she had so much community support, they felt they

had to move slowly, but she was finally brought to trial for heresy. During the two-day trial, Anne was accused of stepping out of her place – of being a "husband rather than a wife, a preacher rather than a hearer, and a magistrate rather than a subject."

Although no charges were proven against her, Hutchinson was excommunicated by the Church and banished by the Colony. She and her family moved to Rhode Island, but the church elders followed her and forced her to leave again. After her husband died Anne settled near New York, but it was not long before she, six members of her family, and two others of her household met a brutal death at the hands of hostile Indians.

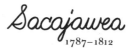

Sacajawea
1787–1812

As the fur trade developed in North America, traders took Native American women as mistresses almost as a matter of course, with or without their consent. Yet because these traders were dependent upon the good will of the Indians in order to move safely through their territory, they were generally far less cruel than the soldiers. By the time the first settlers arrived, attitudes had changed. The new arrivals were determined to be rid of the Native Americans, even if that meant exterminating them. Indians were despised, and native women were regularly hunted like animals and clubbed to death or shot with rifles.

Previously, most Native American women had enjoyed high status in their

passively accept this loss of power, as is

societies, but there were some tribes in which women were less well treated. Sacajawea was born a Shoshone and captured as a child by the Minnataree; neither of these tribes held women in high esteem. While still a child, Sacajawea was acquired as wife and servant by a fur trader, either by barter or in a gambling game. The trader was later hired by Lewis and Clark as an interpreter for their expedition, which had been organized to explore some of the land gained through the Louisiana Purchase and to find a route to the Pacific Ocean. Sacajawea ultimately became both interpreter and guide, although it was her trader husband who had been formally hired. She was only sixteen when the trip began, her baby just six weeks old.

As the only woman on the Lewis and Clark expedition, it fell to Sacajawea to forage and prepare the food, gather herbs and make healing potions, nurse the sick, and mend clothes as well as care for her infant son. Her daily assistance was accepted by the explorers without comment, though her very presence protected them by assuring the Indians they encountered that their mission was peaceful (a war party never traveled with a woman who carried a baby in her arms). Also, while in Shoshone country, she secured the necessary horses and equipment that ensured the expedition's success. When they returned from their long journey, however, she received no pay and her name was almost lost to history, despite her importance to Lewis and Clark. Sadly, Sacajawea had no way of knowing that her help in opening up the

Northwest Territory would eventually lead to the wholesale slaughter of Native American tribes.

Sacajawea's plate stands as a symbol of the efforts she made to bring about peace between Indians and whites, but it also commemorates her tragic error in aiding the conquerors of her people. Carved in low relief and utilizing the straight lines Shoshone women preferred, the iconography of the plate is derived from the parafleche, or rawhide paintings, traditionally done by Sacajawea's tribe. Matte and gloss paints are combined on the surface of the plate by applying two firings of vellum to the glazed porcelain before using the matte color. Attached to the plate is a beaded papoose carrier like that in which Sacajawea might have carried her child, and this elaborate beading, which employs traditional techniques and motifs, is repeated on the back of the runner, on the borders, and in and around her name.

Caroline Herschel
1750–1848

Caroline Herschel, an astronomer and one of the leading women in science in the eighteenth and early nineteenth centuries, composed her own epitaph. Engraved on her tombstone, it reads: "The eyes of her who is glorified here below turned to the starry heavens. Her own discoveries of comets and her participation in the immortal labors of her brother bear witness of this to future eyes."

Herschel's plate and runner pay tribute to a woman who never received the recognition she deserved. Wings lift from the surface of the plate in a gesture that represents the efforts she made to become an independent woman. In the center of the form, there is an eye that looks out upon the embroidered universe which covers Herschel's runner and provides her with an image of the skies at which she gazed. The crewelwork, translated by Marjorie Biggs from my painting, repeats both the color and the pen-work hatching on the plate.

Born in Hanover, Germany, Caroline was tutored in secret by her father. (Mrs. Herschel was opposed to her daughter's being educated, perhaps fearing that erudition would only make her restless with a woman's lot.) As the child grew older she became obsessed with the idea of earning her own living. Gifted in music, she became a solo performer, but, just as she had begun to achieve some measure of success, she was forced to give up her career and go to England. Her brother William, a musician and astronomer, needed an accompanist, someone to help him with his scientific work, and a housekeeper as well.

William's involvement in astronomy soon became his sole preoccupation and he expected his sister to give up her music and spend all her time assisting him. At night she took notes on her brother's observations, and during the morning she recopied the notes, made calculations, and systematized the work. Each day she planned the evening's labor and, in order to accomplish all that was expected of her, taught herself mathematics by sheer force of will. Her brother had too little patience to teach her, and

therefore she gathered information when and as she could. She also helped in the tedious work of constructing William's telescopes, making models and grinding and polishing the reflectors.

In addition to all this, she ran William's household, even after he was married. While her brother and his family vacationed during the summers, Herschel did her own astronomical work. She was the first woman to discover a comet, finding eight in all. In 1798 the Royal Astronomical Society published two catalogs of stars she had compiled, and in 1825 she completed her own (and her brother's) work by presenting a star catalog of 2,500 nebulae and clusters to the Royal Society. The Society made her an "honorary" member, for, of course, women were not admitted to regular membership. The highlight of her life, however, was receiving a small salary from the king; despite the fact that this was only one-fourth the money paid to her brother, she had achieved her modest goal of earning her own keep.

Mary Wollstonecraft
1759–1797

Mary Wollstonecraft, a novelist, pivotal feminist writer, and theoretician, was born in England in 1759. She became acutely aware of the position of women through watching her father constantly bully her submissive mother. As soon as possible Mary left home and opened a girls' school, which she hoped would give her a chance for independence. The school was prestigious during its brief life, but its main importance in Wollstonecraft's development was the exposure it offered her to the radical ideas of this period.

In 1786, after the publication of her book *Thoughts on the Education of Daughters*, Wollstonecraft obtained a job as a magazine reviewer in London and soon became a serious student of the political and social issues of the day. The French Revolution was creating turmoil in the intellectual community with which Mary had become involved. Like many women of her era, she looked to the events in France to bring about the emancipation of women. But she was soon disillusioned and, in a rage, wrote *A Vindication of the Rights of Woman*, which made her famous overnight.

In this book, Wollstonecraft argued that (1) if women failed to become men's equals, the progress of human knowledge and virtue would be halted, and (2) if women were to contribute to the development of the human race, their education would have to prepare them to do so. In order for this to occur, both sexes had to be identically educated. Moreover, Mary insisted that the tyranny of men had to be broken both politically and socially if women were to become free to determine their own destinies. Though Wollstonecraft did not live to see the effect of her arguments, she said on her deathbed, "I have thrown down the gauntlet. It is time to restore women to their lost dignity and to make them part of the human species."

It would be a long time before this vision could be actualized. In the meantime, many women buried their frustrations in the needlework with which they filled their days; they covered their pillowcases with fine stitching, did needlepoint on all their chairs, crocheted doilies for their bureaus, and made lace for the collars and cuffs of their clothes. In England a craze developed for a technique called stump work, which involved stuffing tiny figures, dressing them, and applying them to boxes and lids. Stump work covers Wollstonecraft's runner as a symbol of the "silken fetters" which she proclaimed, held women in chains. The image on her plate is in stark contrast to its trivializing context and struggles to transcend its confines by sheer power and force. The back of the runner depicts Mary's death in childbirth, a gruesome testimony to the loss of female genius and the tragic waste of women's lives.

Sojourner Truth
1797–1883

"Look at me!" demanded Sojourner Truth, an abolitionist and feminist. The audience at the Women's Rights Convention in Akron, Ohio, gasped at the sight of this tall, imposing black woman. "Look at my arm," she continued, "it's plowed and planted and gathered into barns and no man could head me – and ain't I a woman?" She seemed unaffected by the sneers and hisses of some of the men in the audience; as difficult as it must have been to confront a prejudiced and resistant white crowd, it was not unbearable, as slavery had been.

Sojourner's challenge was directed to one of the clergymen who had warned that, if women continued their efforts to obtain "rights," they would lose the consideration and deference with which men treated them. But this former slave knew all too well that the privileges enjoyed by white women were built in part on the exploitation of Blacks and that the "deference" to which this minister referred was not offered to black women.

Sojourner had discarded her slave name (Isabell Hardenburgh) when she finally gained her liberty, choosing *Sojourner* because sojourn meant "to dwell temporarily," which she thought an apt description of one's tenure in this life, and *Truth* as the message that she intended to carry to the world. Traveling around the country on foot, she told her life story as a way of exposing the evils of slavery. She spoke of her brothers and sisters being sold off and she herself sold several times, of being mistreated and raped by her master and deceived with promises of freedom.

On these journeys Sojourner discovered, like many women of her time, that the liberation of Blacks and that of women were actually intertwined. Her anti-slavery lectures soon became infused with arguments for women's rights. In 1850 she published her autobiography and, with the proceeds from the book, supported herself. During the Civil War she visited Union troops and then, after the war was over, spent her time finding jobs and helping the newly freed slaves. She was an inspiration to all who heard her and a proud symbol of black women's struggle to transcend the oppression of both their sex and their race.

Sojourner's image was carved out of a solid two-inch plate jiggered on a specially made mold. Three faces, emanating from a single body form, were inspired by African art. The sad face on the left is painted naturalistically and weeps for the suffering of the slaves. The highly stylized face on the right reflects the rage experienced by black women but expressed only at the risk of harsh punishment – sometimes death. The center face, a highly decorated mask, symbolizes the concealment of the real self required not only of black women, but of their white sisters as well. The upraised arm and clenched fist which complete Sojourner's portrait repeat the angry gesture she made in that Ohio church.

The Sojourner Truth plate sits on a runner made of a pieced quilt combining strip-woven African patterns with triangular sections of printed fabric. This design honors southern slave women, who, in an effort to retain some vestiges of their proud heritage, pieced scraps of weaving from their homelands into large, beautiful quilts.

Susan B. Anthony
1820–1906

Susan B. Anthony's form lifts up from the surface of the plate with great force in a vain effort to escape its confines. Raw and angry, her image was carefully modeled and built from one of my drawings by Daphne Ahlenius, an English-trained ceramicist from northern California who brought thirty years' experience in clay to the problems we confronted in creating the fully dimensional plates. To bring my drawings to life required the combined skills of a whole team of female ceramicists (Leonard Skuro had left the Project) – headed by Judye Keyes – who assembled in my studio for an intensive period during which we did nothing but work, run, sleep, and eat. By this time we had evolved a process of defining the image and then solving the technical problems. Working on the prototypes for the last plates on the table required that everyone involved identify with the yearning of these women of recent history to liberate themselves and their sex. Perhaps that was why only women were on the team by then, for there was an unspoken understanding among us of what I intended these last images to mean.

Anthony's life has become a legend that inspires us all. To me she is the queen of the table, who stood firmly for fifty years. She changed the face of the nation and – with her colleague, Elizabeth Cady Stanton – led the revolution which began in 1848. Addressing themselves to eighteen grievances, the women who gathered in Seneca Falls demanded the right to vote, to be educated, to enter any occupation, to have control over their bodies, to sign legal papers, to manage their own earnings, and to administer their own property.

At first the outcry was enormous, and women were ordered back to their "place." But by the 1860's Anthony and her co-workers had produced some measure of reform. Then, though she and Stanton argued against it, most of the women involved themselves in the Civil War. Afterwards their sacrifice, which

many women thought would earn them the vote, was instead rewarded by the word "man" being entered into the Constitution for the first time. Their work of Seneca Falls had to begin all over again; this time the focus was on suffrage, although no one imagined that it would take over half a century to achieve.

In 1893 Anthony attended the Columbian Exposition, where – partly through her efforts – a Woman's Building had been created. A World Council of Women was held there, and, when Susan B. Anthony appeared at the opening, tens of thousands stood and cheered. An international feminist movement had been built in 50 years, and all around the world women were agitating for their rights. It seemed that no force could stop them and that equality was in sight. But when Anthony was on her deathbed, before the vote was won, she grasped the hand of one of her co-workers as if to communicate to her that their job had only begun. For she and Stanton had always known that only through a fundamental transformation of the world could women's position really be changed.

Elizabeth Blackwell
1821–1910

Elizabeth Blackwell, the first woman in America to graduate from a medical school and become a licensed physician, struggled throughout her lifetime to open the medical profession to women. Deciding early that she would challenge the restrictions which barred women from becoming doctors, she began to both study medicine on her own and save money to attend school. She applied to twenty-nine institutions and was rejected by all but one – where a doctor agreed to let her sit in on his classes provided that she wear male attire. Although she knew there were some women who had done this, Blackwell refused; it was as a woman that she wanted to be accepted.

Finally, Blackwell was admitted to Geneva College, a small school in New York. The dean had asked the male students to decide her fate, and – more as a joke than anything else – they had agreed to let her attend. When Blackwell arrived, however, not only did the students treat her badly, but she was avoided by all the "proper" women of the town. Nonetheless, she graduated with honors in 1849 and went to Paris and London to complete her training.

Blackwell decided to set up her practice in New York City, but the hostility which greeted her made a shambles of her plans. She was denied work at hospitals, was unable to rent office space, went months without any patients, and wrote, in 1851, "I stand alone." She then began to lecture on sex, birth, and health to women. As a result, people followed her down the streets shouting insults and sent her vile anonymous letters.

Eventually, Blackwell established a practice with her sister, Emily, and Marie Zakrzewska, both of whom had – with her help – become doctors. Together they opened the New York Infirmary for Women and Children, the first hospital where female doctors could get training and clinical experience as

well. In 1865, Elizabeth Blackwell founded a medical school for women, after which she went to England to help open the profession there.

Blackwell's plate twists and squirms around the "black well" that is its center. Painted in spectral colors and oversprayed with china-paint, the plate was made by casting a dome, trimming it on the potter's wheel, and then applying it to a jiggered plate. The design team decided that the plate needed to be pierced, and the hole in the center was introduced by Judye Keyes. The latter also worked with me and the design team on the runner, which extends the forms of Blackwell's portrait and is made with reverse appliqué. The brightly colored fabrics shrouded with gray chiffon give the runner a dreary appearance. For me, this reflects the quality of this pioneer doctor's life and emphasizes the difficulties she faced.

"I understand now, " she once said, "why this life has never been lived before. It is hard, with no support but a high purpose, to live against every species of social opposition."

Emily Dickinson
1830–1886

Born in Massachusetts, Emily Dickinson lived an outwardly uneventful life. She remained in her father's house, living as a spinster daughter, and spent most of her time in her room. Her father treated her as a child even after she was grown; she had to beg him for postage stamps and plead for money to buy books. But at least she was able to maintain her personal freedom and had time to read, think, and write.

Dickinson felt that her own poetry was dangerous, for it revealed feelings that society had taught women to repress. "I took my power in my hand, and went out against the world," she wrote, knowing that her intense creativity was hopelessly at odds with the prevailing ideas of what a woman was supposed to be. She produced 1,775 poems, which she bound into booklets with a darning needle and carefully placed in trunks to be found, read, and published after her death. Her subject matter was varied and her poetry filled with passion and rage. "A letter to the world," she called it, but it is only recently that her personal language has begun to be understood.

Whenever I thought about the Victorian lady that a woman like Dickinson was expected to be, I envisioned lace: lace collars and cuffs on her dresses, lace doilies on all the chairs, lace cloths on the tables, and lace edgings on the demure nightgowns she would wear. Imagining a female creative genius imprisoned in all that lace evolved into my concept of Dickinson's runner and plate. We jiggered a plate with a thick center, which I then carved. Its strength is in stark contrast to the surrounding layers of immobile lace, achieved through a process called lace-draping which was originally used in the production of Dresden dolls. Judye Keyes solved the technical problems of draping the lace in porcelain slip. Each piece of lace had to be basted, then carefully shaped around the center form.

Painted by Rosemarie Radmaker, a traditional china-painter from Oregon, the soft but fleshy colors suggest a sensuality that nineteenth-century women were not supposed to have.

Shortly after the plate was completed, a woman gave us a beautiful lace collar that we placed directly beneath it. The runner, made under the supervision of Connie von Briesen, has extraordinary ribbon embroidery utilizing the kind of antique ribbons with which von Briesen's mother worked years ago. Lace borders over netting with ruffles on the back provide an incongruous setting for a poet whose voice was as powerful as her will. The lace also embodies the tragedy of women's past: Endless hours were required to make these beautiful but unappreciated patterns by women who remain unknown.

Ethel Smyth
1858–1944

Ethel Smyth, a gifted young composer raised in an upper-class English family, arrived in Leipzig in 1877 and quickly became involved in its lively musical world. By the time she was twelve she knew that her life would be dedicated to music, and by 1889 her compositions were being performed in Germany and receiving glowing reviews. Upon her return to England, however, she discovered that few conductors would perform her compositions.

Smyth struggled desperately to establish herself, but even when she was able to arrange a concert, something would inevitably go wrong. The orchestra would be inadequately prepared or the conductor unable to attend. If she was invited to participate in a program, male composers would complain. If her work was included anyway, there would rarely be any critical response in the musical journals. Or if she *was* mentioned by a critic, he would accuse her of plagarizing a male composer's work. The little positive critical response she received brought no new offers, none of the opportunities that male composers enjoyed.

While Smyth's early work consisted of orchestral and chamber music, she later became interested in operas and large choral works. She wanted to compose in a scale previously reserved for men and wrote her "Mass in D," one of the most ambitious pieces ever undertaken by a female composer. Its production was possible only because of the support of two influential women; the audience was wildly enthusiastic, but the work was attacked by critics and eclipsed for thirty years. Smyth recorded her struggles as a composer in a series of books. At first her writing brought attention to her music, but it ultimately failed to alter the neglect she endured.

Angry and frustrated at the obstacles she encountered, Smyth became involved in the struggle for women's rights. During the two years she devoted to suffrage work, she wrote "The March of Women" – sung by the suffragists during demonstrations, in prison, and whenever their spirits faltered. Once, while visiting the wife of an influential politician in order to gain her husband's support,

Smyth played some of her music, including her march. After hearing it, the woman said, "How can you, with your gift, touch a thing like politics with a pair of tongs?" "I do it just because of my music," Smyth replied, "for owing to the circumstances of my career as a woman composer, I know more than most people about the dire workings of prejudice."

Smyth's plate is in the shape of a piano whose lid threatens to totally compress the form. On the music stand are notations for one of her operas, *The Boatswain's Mate,* a comic work with a feminist point of view. The plate rests on a runner made from tweed fabric cut and sewn to suggest a tailored suit – the outfit Smyth preferred. Taken in to fit the confines of the runner's dimensions, it is a metaphor for the containment of Smyth's great dream.

Margaret Sanger
1879–1966

Margaret Sanger's life is a testament to her commitment to the idea that women should "look the world in the face with a go-to-hell look in the eyes; have an idea; speak and act in defiance of convention." From the time she opened her first birth-control clinic in 1918, Sanger was repeatedly arrested as she battled to break through the curtain of silence that surrounded all matters of sex and reproduction.

"Who cares whether a woman keeps her Christian name...?" Sanger demanded as she lectured around the country. "Who cares whether she wears her wedding ring? Who cares about her right to work? Hundreds of thousands of laundresses, clockmakers, scrub women, servants, telephone girls, shop workers would gladly change places with the feminists in return for the right to have leisure, to be lazy a little now and then. For without the right to control their own bodies all other rights are meaningless."

When Sanger first began studying nursing, she was confronted with countless pleas by women for some sort of birth control. Determined to find an answer, she renounced nursing and went to Europe and the Orient to investigate contraceptive research being done there. Upon her return to America, Sanger forced the issue of birth control into the public forum through her magazine *The Woman Rebel*, simply ignoring the laws of the time that prohibited the dissemination of any information on contraception. Convinced that the birth-control movement had to be worldwide, she convened the International Birth Control Congress in 1925. The organization formed there was the forerunner of Planned Parenthood, of which Sanger became president in 1953.

A visionary and a feminist theoretician, Sanger believed that once women were freed of involuntary childbearing, they would change the world. "War, famine, poverty, and oppression," she wrote, "will continue while woman makes life cheap. When mother hood is a high privilege…, it will encircle all."

Although Sanger's conception of a new order forged by women has not yet been realized, she made a major con-tribution to the expansion of their choices. Her plate – painted in brilliant reds – proclaims women's bodies as their own. Cast in sections, then attached with slip and carved, the image reaches around the edges of the plate and tries to lift itself off, as a symbol of Sanger's efforts to lift up her sex and thereby the world. The plate sits on a runner, embroidered in pinks and reds by Terry Blecher and L. A. Olson, which extends the gesture on the plate and transforms the female reproductive system into an image of beauty and power.

Natalie Barney
1876–1972

Natalie Barney's richly beaded runner celebrates the life of this "Amazon," as she was frequently called. Shaped like a butterfly, it departs from the geometric format of previous runners and begins to assume a singular identity. Barney, a writer, aphorist, and lesbian feminist, was – like her runner – independent and wildly extravagant. She once prepared her bed for a night of love by covering it entirely with lilies.

The lily, traditionally associated with the feminine, was Barney's trademark as well as a common motif in art nouveau, which her plate and runner incorporate. The plate is dark and edged with gold and was made by first carving the flower form and then making a plaster cast into which the clay was press-molded. After the cast shape had been applied to the plate, it was carved again and sanded. The surface was achieved by firing multiple layers of different colored lusters, over which gold pen work was applied. This image, which we thought would be easily accomplished, cracked at every stage – perhaps, like Barney herself, refusing to be confined.

Barney came from a wealthy Ohio family, but she instinctively rebelled against the social expectations of her class. From the time she was young, she was aware of her homosexuality and the implications of being a woman. When she was seven she was taken on a European tour, and in Belgium she saw a cart pulled by a woman and a dog, both in harness; the woman's husband walked beside them, complacently smoking his pipe, which outraged Barney. She never forgot this sight, and when she was older she often told the story of the poor woman saddled like a horse.

By the time she was twenty, Barney had made a conscious decision to live as she pleased. She reveled in her lesbianism and wore it as a badge of pride, an unusual and courageous attitude at a time when strictures against homosexuality ranged from religious prohibitions to legal restraints.

Barney settled in Paris in 1899. Shortly after her arrival, she became involved with the lesbian feminist poet Renée Vivien. The two women were drawn together by their shared vision of a society where women were free and lesbianism was revered. In an unsuccessful effort to resurrect the Sapphic tradition, they went to Greece to found a poetic colony for women, but their affair ended somewhat unpleasantly. Barney had numerous relationships, the longest of which was her fifty-year friendship with the painter Romaine Brooks.

Every Friday night for almost sixty years, women gathered at Barney's salon at 20 rue Jacob to see each other, to hear concerts, and to read poems and essays exploring their own attitudes and sexuality. Barney's commitment to living as she chose and providing support for other women is clearly reflected in her suggested epitaph: "She was the friend of men and the lover of women, which, for people full of ardor and drive, is better than the other way around."

Virginia Woolf

1882–1941

Virginia Woolf was born in England and – because she was "delicate" – educated primarily at home by her father. She was intimidated by his tyrannical ways and later commented that had he not died when he did, she would have written no books. While still young, she was raped by her half-brother, which permanently affected her sexuality and contributed to the first of the mental breakdowns that tormented her throughout her life.

In 1904 Woolf moved to Bloomsbury, the center of London's bohemian intellectual world. She had decided to become a writer, and her work developed against the background of the violent English suffrage fight. The mere thought of being discriminated against made Woolf physically ill; she often left parties when an anti-female remark was made.

Generally she shied away from social protest, however, and addressed herself to the deeper issues of women's plight. In 1912 she married Leonard Woolf, despite her preoccupying concern – manifested both personally and in her writing – with the question of whether a woman's intellectual and creative needs could be satisfied within the framework of married life.

When Virginia Woolf's first novel was published she had another breakdown, terrified that the book would be rejected. Her mental condition is usually ascribed to her childhood experiences and "failure" at sex and motherhood, but there is another view which relates to her philosophy and her work: Woolf had studied the lives and writings of the women before her and knew that they had been consistently misunderstood; she feared that the female point of view put forth in her work would cause it to be belittled by critics, and whenever she completed a manuscript she was in danger of another breakdown because of this anxiety.

According to Woolf's philosophy, the subjugation of women was the key to most of the social and psychological disorders of Western Civilization. She believed that only by wedding masculine and feminine traits on personal, social, and esthetic levels could the world become sane. But her struggle to build an integrated language and to affect the world seemed hopeless in the face of fascism, which she saw as the values of patriarchy gone mad. She believed that the rise of Nazism was an infantile reaction to women's demands for equal rights.

Unable to maintain her sanity, in 1941 she deliberately submerged herself in a river and drowned.

Although women have been writing about their experience for centuries, they have not had their own language; this is the problem Woolf addressed. Her work, like the beacon emanating from the lighthouse in her most famous book, illuminated the path to a woman-formed language in literature.

Woolf's image breaks away from the basic plate shape and – though still contained within its place setting – is the most liberated form on the table. The "breaking open" of the plate's structure symbolizes the breaking of the historic silence about women's lives, which can only be fully understood if women possess their own forms of expression. The luminous petals spread open to reveal the bursting center, an image of Woolf's fecund genius.

Georgia O'Keeffe
b. 1887

Originally from Wisconsin and later Virginia, Georgia O'Keeffe studied at the Chicago Art Institute and the Art Students League in New York. For the next few years she worked at commercial art until, frustrated because her painting seemed to be at a standstill, she returned to her family's home with the idea of giving up her art career.

She eventually took a teaching position in Texas, however, and there – among the "terrible winds and wonderful emptiness" and far from debates on women's rights – she began to find a per-

95

sonal visual language that could express her perception of the world.

One day O'Keeffe assembled all the painting she had done and, seeing that her work was mostly derived from other artists, destroyed it. She then did a new series of drawings and sent them to a friend in New York. Although O'Keeffe had asked that she show the work to no one, her friend took it to the small but famous gallery called "291." Alfred Stieglitz, the photographer and owner of the gallery, looked at the drawings intently and said, "Finally a woman on paper," commenting on the fact that the work was not only by a woman artist but by one who "gives something of a 'woman' feeling; and a woman isn't a man."

Stieglitz decided that O'Keeffe's work should be given a chance and exhibited. In addition, he offered to do for her what he had done numerous times for men of talent – support her financially while she painted. This brought her to New York and made her part of the art scene that centered around Stieglitz and his gallery. His support allowed her to work freely for the first time; he also gave her work exposure, as he exhibited it regularly for over twenty years. In 1924 O'Keeffe and Stieglitz were married, but O'Keeffe kept her own name. "Why should I take on someone else's famous name?" she asked.

When Stieglitz died O'Keeffe moved permanently to New Mexico, where she had gone for some part of every year since 1929 – drawn by the landscape, which she painted again and again. Her life became increasingly centered on painting, and she refused to allow anything to distract her from the well-ordered pattern of her existence. In the late 1960's people developed great interest in her work, although her style had not really changed. "It is just that what I do seems to move people today in a way that I don't understand at all."

I – like many other women artists – see O'Keeffe as "the mother of us all." Her work provides a foundation upon which we can build a universal language to express our own point of view as women. Her plate is derived from one of her paintings and is a sculptural translation in which her forms merge with mine. Built on a dome whose center is punctured to become a mysterious, internal space, O'Keeffe's image rises higher than any other on the table. Though it tries to force itself further upward, it is prevented from doing so by its firm connection to the plate. Thus, despite their heroic efforts, all the women represented are still contained within their place setting at *The Dinner Party* table.

much freer. Although they were considered

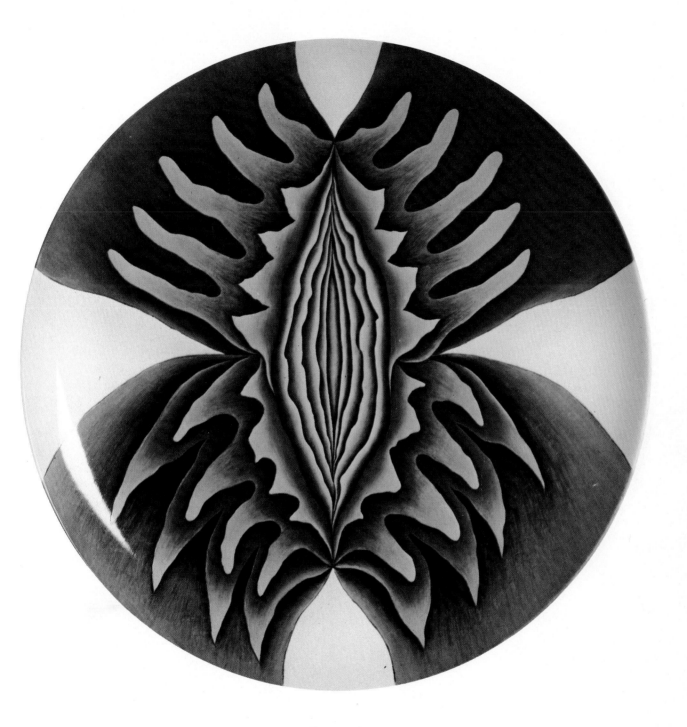

Judith

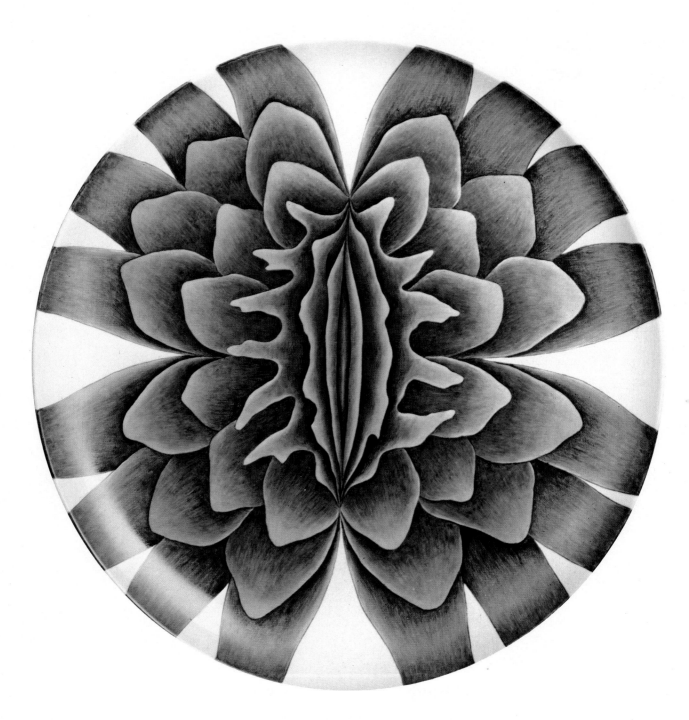

Sappho

fathers' and husbands' jurisdiction, public

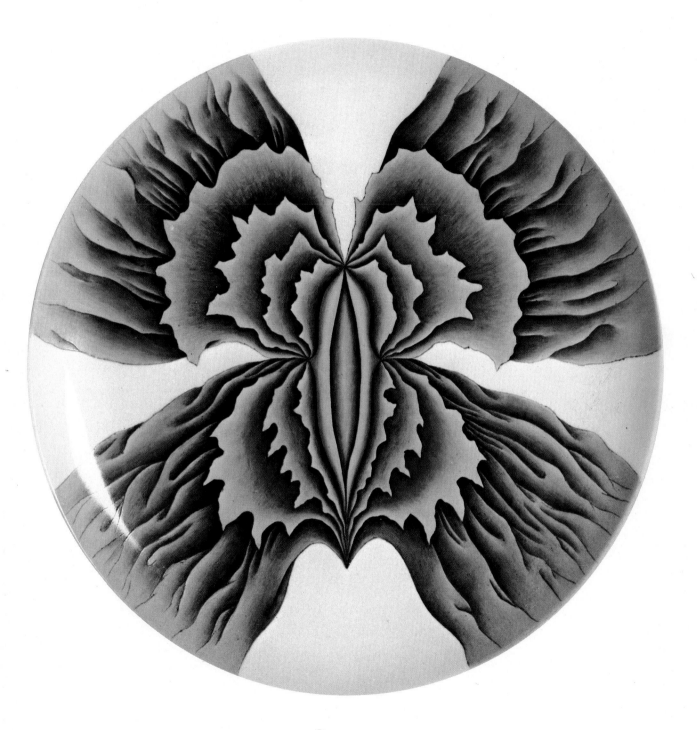

Aspasia

sentiment was at odds with the laws.

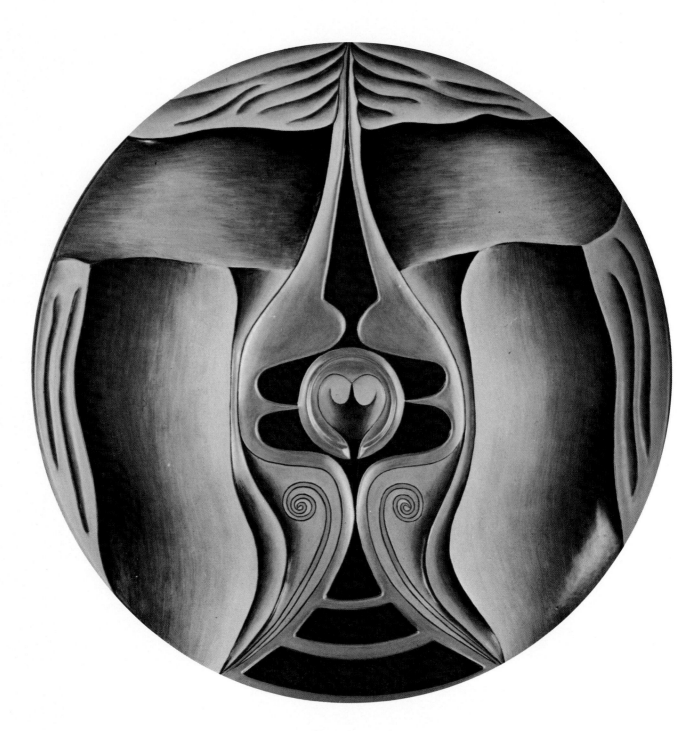

Boadaceia

These laws improved for a while as the result

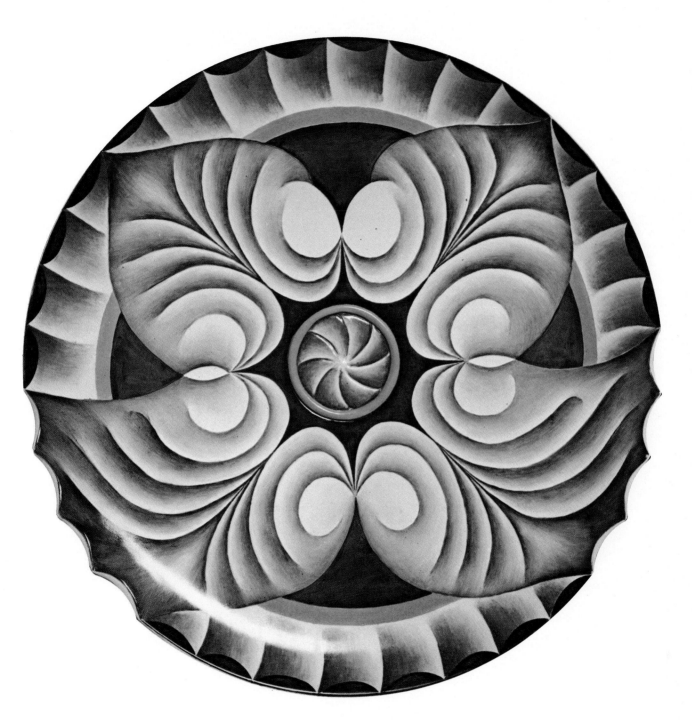

Hypatia

of a protest organized by Roman women,

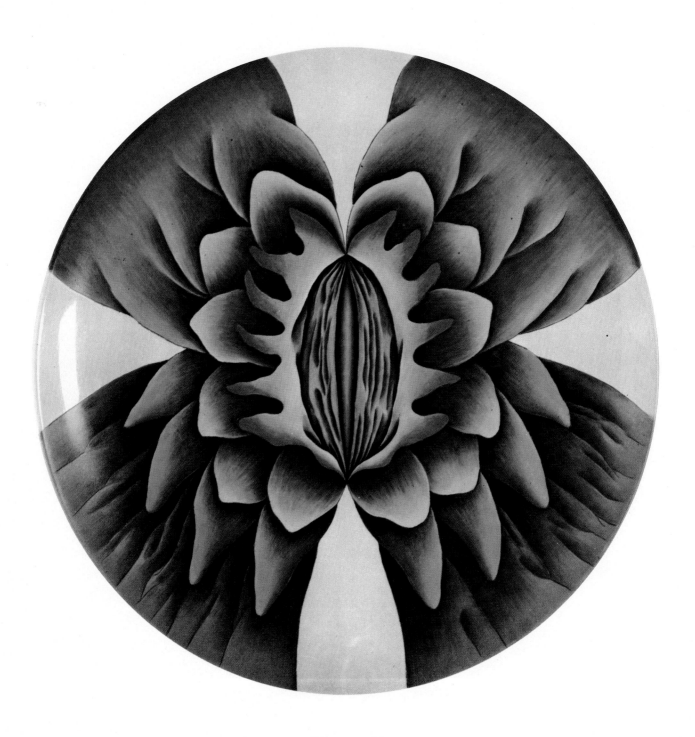

Marcella

but their gains were later eroded.

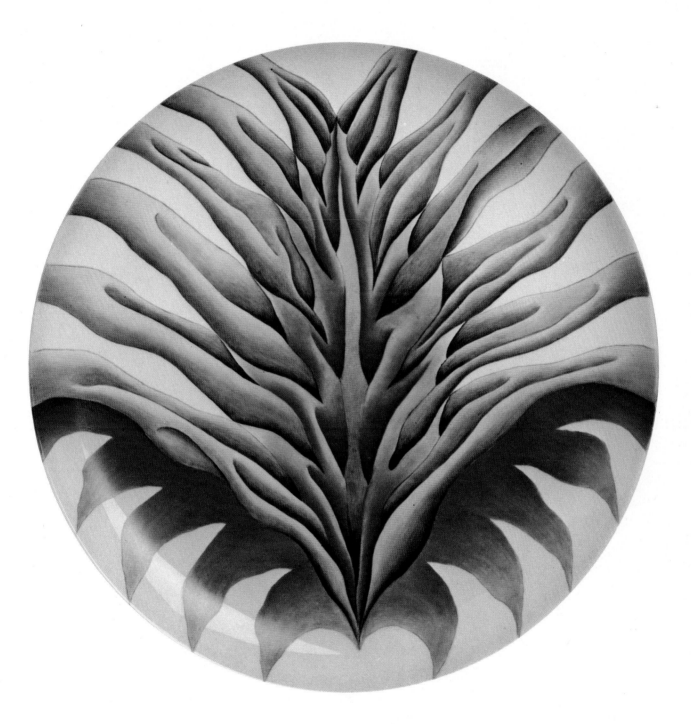

Saint Bridget

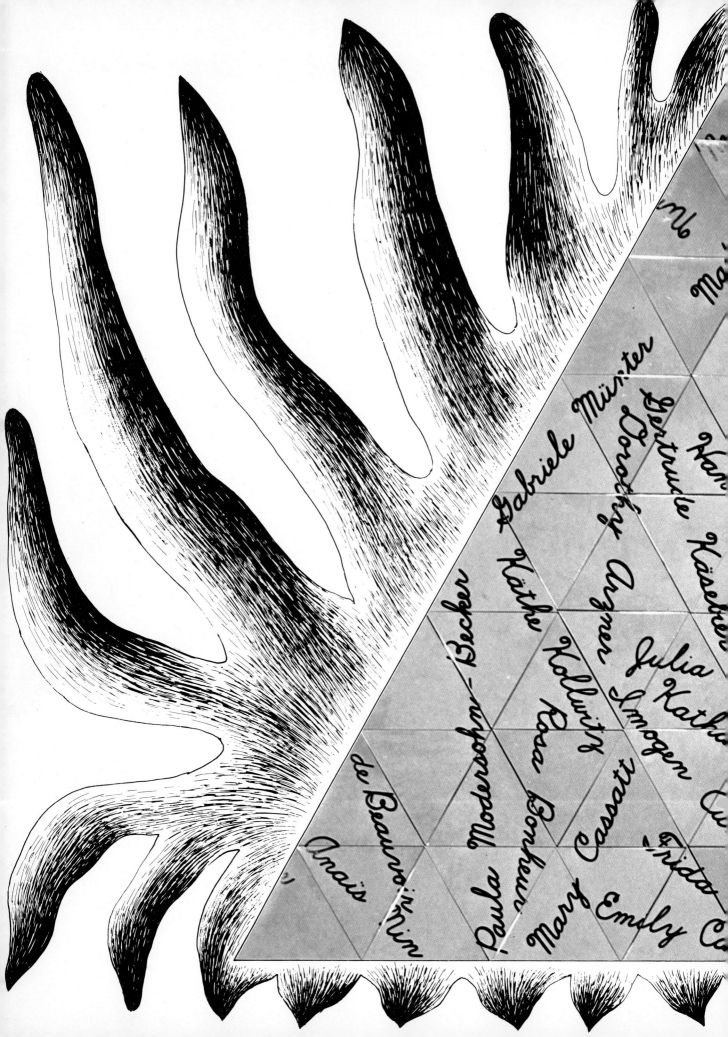

The Heritage Floor

Nine Hundred and Ninety-nine Women of Achievement

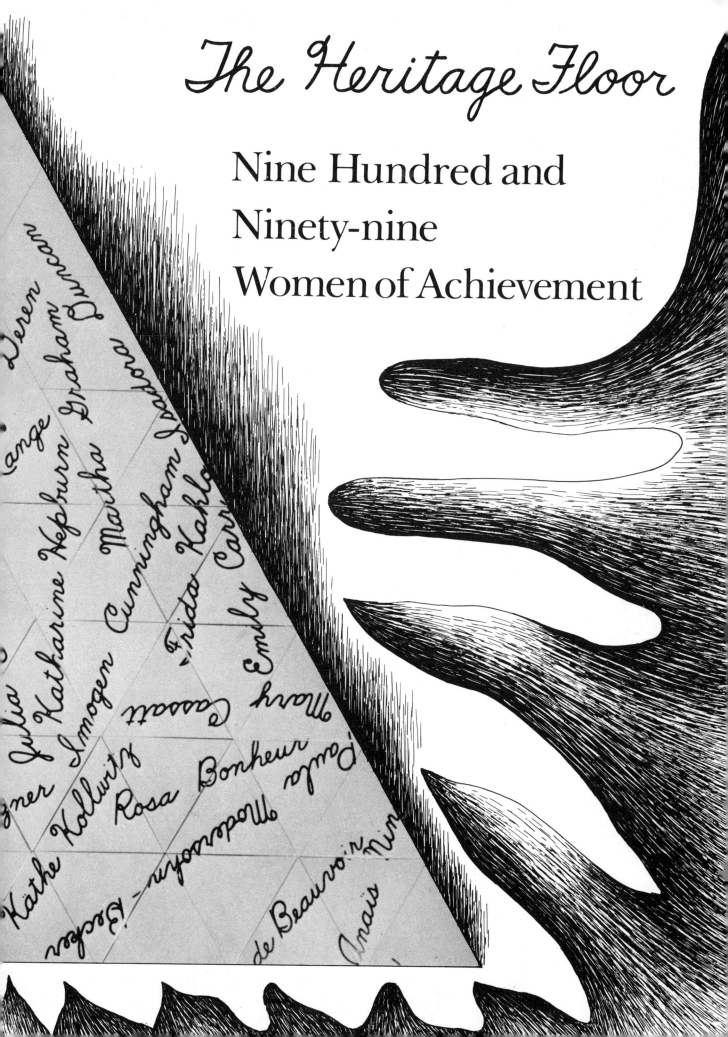

It required over two years and a team of more than twenty researchers to compile the information about the women represented on the Heritage Floor. The research team, headed by Ann Isolde, learned to "read through" the biased way women are usually presented in history books. Painstakingly, the researchers ferreted out the important facts about each woman which were buried in material focusing on her physical attributes or the achievements of her husband or son. These facts were then typed onto cards and cross-filed alphabetically by country, century, and profession. Slowly the cards accumulated until the accomplishments of almost three thousand women emerged.

Then we began to make choices based on three criteria: (1) Did the woman make a significant contribution to society? (2) Did she attempt to improve conditions for women? (3) Did her life illuminate an aspect of women's experience or provide a model for the future? We selected 999 women who, we believed, represented a range of nationalities, experiences, and contributions. Our choices were limited by language barriers, fragmented information, and our own inexperience and biases. Our intention, however, was not to *define* women's history but to symbolize it – to say that there have been many women who have done many things, and they deserve to be known.

All the women represented on the floor are grouped around the women included at the table. These groupings are based on common experiences, achievements, historic periods, or places of origin and are symbolized by the plate drawing that identifies each section. The bibliography of source material for *The Dinner Party* is extensive; close to a thousand books were consulted. Because of space limitations the bibliography could not be included in this book, but it will be published separately.

The Heritage Floor, which commemorates women's achievements, is dedicated to those who did the major part of the research:

Katie Amend	Laure McKinnon
Ruth Askey	Juliet Myers
Diane Gelon	Anne Marie Pois
Ann Isolde	Karen Schmidt

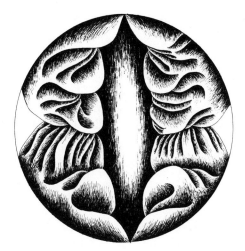

Primordial Goddess

The Primordial Goddess was originally referred to by primitive markings, triangular shapes that stood for the vulva, and sacred holes in rocks, the presence of which on or near animal images was thought to cause animals to multiply. It was not until much later in history that the concept of the Primordial Goddess was expressed in sophisticated myths, visual representations, and specific goddess figures. By that time, the original creative power attributed to this feminine being had been greatly diminished and/or transferred to male gods.

As expressed in these later myths, female creators were conceived as having brought the universe into being either alone or in conjunction with a male partner, and the female spirit was generally predominant. It was not until men gained control of the social and political forces that the idea of life originating entirely from a male – rather than a female – source arose. It is possible to trace this slow changeover from matriarchal to patriarchal views of the origin of life through the surviving mythology.

The goddesses represented on the Heritage Floor illustrate this historical transformation. Beginning with those who were seen as sole creators of the universe, the goddess images gradually changed, becoming co-creators with – and then subordinate to – the male gods; if the goddesses continued to have power, their power was seen as evil. Finally, the Judeo-Christian tradition absorbed all deities into a single, male godhead.

Ajysyt

Mythic; Siberia

Ajysyt, whose name means "birth giver" or "procreator," was the Siberian Goddess of Birth. She also appeared in many prayers as the Milk Lake Mother, a reference to the mythical divine lake, the life source that exists beside the tree of life in the center of the Earth. Ajysyt's antecedent may be found in ancient Iranian Paradise myths, in which she was viewed as the Great Mother who administers a white elixir to the dying to aid them in their journey back to her.

Atira

Mythic; North America

Atira – Mother Earth and Universal Mother – was held in deep veneration by the Plains Indians. It was she who brought forth all life and into whose body all life would return at the end of its appointed time. Her symbol was the ear of corn, for as the kernel was planted in Mother Earth and she brought forth the ear of corn, so the child was begotten and born of woman.

Gaea

Mythic; Greece

Gaea, a Greek version of the Earth Mother, sent up fruits from the soil to nourish the human race and was the principle be-hind the life/death cycle, to whom all creatures eventually returned. She was descended from the deities of ancient religions which viewed the feminine Earth as the source of all life and the home of the dead.

According to Greek creation myths, Gaea originally emerged from chaos and gave birth to her husband, Uranus (or Heaven), the mountains, and the sea. Every aspect of the natural world was thus part of her. As Greek religion developed, however, Gaea's ascendancy was diminished, derivative goddesses taking over her specific roles, and she was gradually displaced by the Sky God introduced by the patriarchal Doric invaders.

Ilmatar

Mythic; Finland

The Virgin Daughter of the Air, Ilmatar, was a primary creation goddess who was responsible for all creation, including that of the first human. Myths say that because she became tired of floating alone in space, Ilmatar flew down to the bottom of the ocean, where she remained for 700 years, creating Heaven and Earth from the seven eggs of a wild duck. At the end of this time she gave birth to a son parthenogenetically.

99

Nammu

Mythic; Sumeria
Nammu, Controller of the Primeval Waters, was the early creation goddess of Sumeria. Also described as She Who Gives Birth to Heaven and Earth and as Mother of the Deities, she existed at a time when all life was conceived as proceeding from the union of the Goddesses of Water, Air, and Earth. Nammu, the primordial sea, gave birth to other gods and goddesses and, with their help, created human beings from the clay which hung over the abyss.

Neith

Mythic; Egypt
Neith was a local divinity of Sais, the capital city of Egypt in the seventh century B.C. A virgin goddess, she was self-created and self-sustaining, personifying the female principle from very early times. Neith was called the Great Weaver, who wove the world on her loom as a woman weaves cloth, and she had various incarnations. At one time she was represented as a goddess of hunting and was worshiped in the form of a fetish made of two crossed arrows on an animal-skin shield, which was carried on the standard of a prehistoric clan. Later Neith was depicted as a woman with bow and arrows in her hand, and she also appeared as a cow goddess with the head of a lioness. Under the name of Mehuert, she was said to be the celestial cow who gave birth to the sky when nothing existed. After the fall of the dynasty at Sais in 525 B.C., Neith lost her position of prominence.

Omeciuatl

Mythic; Meso-America
Omeciuatl, the Lady of Our Subsistence, was considered the direct creator of the spirit of human life and the source of all nourishment. The most ancient Mexican creation myth states that the original goddess Omeciuatl gave birth to a sacrificial knife made of obsidian; this knife fell upon the northern plains, and as it fell it gave birth to sixteen hundred goddesses and gods. A later myth diminishes her creative power and asserts that goddesses, gods, women, and men were the daughters and sons of an original divine couple. This second myth probably reflects the recognition of the male role in procreation.

Nut

Mythic; Egypt
The Goddess of the Sky, as recorded in the Pyramid texts during the third millennium B.C., Nut was often represented as a woman having an elongated body arching to vault the Earth with her fingertips and toes. Sometimes represented as a woman along whose body the Sun traveled, her star-studded belly held all the constellations and formed the curved dome of Heaven. She gave birth each morning to the Sun and every evening to the stars, and she was believed to have been present at the creation of the Universe. In another aspect, as the night sky, she became the protectress of the dead.

Siva

Mythic: Russia
Siva – worshiped as the Great Goddess of Life – was represented seated, with an ornamental headdress suggestive of the sun's rays. Shoulders and chest bared and wearing flowing skirts, Siva held in her left hand a sheaf of wheat and in her right a pomegranate, both symbols of the fertility of the Earth as embodied in the female.

Some goddesses were thought to have created the universe in conjunction with a male god or other female deities. There were others about whom there were conflicting myths, some identifying the goddess as sole creator and others asserting her relationship with another god.

Aruru

Mythic; Babylonia
The Earth Goddess Aruru was known as The Potter and The Shaper in Babylonian mythology. When the god Marduk wanted to create the Earth, he called on the goddess Aruru to help him create the human race out of clay. In a fragmentary myth used as an introduction to a childbirth incantation, Aruru is described as fashioning the first humans herself by mixing clay with the blood and flesh of another deity killed in a great battle.

Eurynome

Mythic; Greece
Eurynome, Goddess of All Things, was a Pelasgian creation goddess who resembled, yet preceded, the Greek Gaea. The Pelasgians were an agricultural people who populated the mainland and islands of Greece before 1900 B.C. Their creation myth describes how the virgin goddess Eurynome originally rose naked out of chaos, divided the sea from the sky, began to dance on the waters, and – by her wild and ecstatic dancing – created the North Wind. Grabbing the wind, she rubbed it between her hands, thus producing the great serpent Ophion, who coupled with her. Then the goddess assumed the form of a dove above the waters and laid the universal egg; at her command, Ophion coiled around the egg seven times until it hatched and split in two. Out of this egg came the Sun, Moon, planets, stars, and the Earth with all its vegetation and living creatures. Ophion became jealous and claimed to be the creator of the universe. In response, Eurynome bruised his head with her heel, kicked out his teeth, and imprisoned him in the dark cave underneath the Earth.

Gebjon

Mythic; Sweden
A fertility goddess, Gebjon was identified as The Giver, who gave the king so much pleasure through her knowledge of magical arts that he offered her as much land as she could mark out in a day and a night. She dug the plowshare so deeply that it tore away the entire crust of the Earth, leaving a lake and an island.

Ninhursaga

Mythic; Sumeria
Ninhursaga, the ancient Earth Goddess of Sumeria, was originally called Mother of the Land. Her life-giving powers were symbolized by twigs sprouting from a "horn-crown" (ears of corn over her shoulders) and a cluster of dates from the Tree of Life in her hand. Ninhursaga was considered to be the fertile soil which gave birth to all vegetation and – with her son/lover – to have produced all plant and animal life on the Earth. Ninhursaga was also known as Lady of the Mountain, Pure Lady, and as Nintu-ama-Kalamma, Lady Who Gave Birth. Under the name Ninmah, she aided other deities in creating the human race.

Tefnut

Mythic; Egypt

Tefnut was one of the nine deities who formed the divine pantheon in Egypt. She was worshiped in the form of a lioness or as a woman with the head of a lioness. According to one myth, she came into being when Re-Atum, the Sun God, united with his shadow or, according to another account, when he coupled with the Cow Goddess, Hathor. As a result of one of these acts, Tefnut, the wet atmosphere, and her brother/husband Shu, the dry atmosphere, were born. Tefnut was the Goddess of Dew and Rain, and as the offspring of Re, she was considered to be the left eye of the Sun or its reflective aspect as represented by the Moon. She and her brother symbolized the two opposite forces which had to unite, according to Egyptian beliefs, to produce life. Together they created the Heaven and the Earth.

Tiamat

Mythic; Babylonia

Tiamat, like her predecessor Nammu, personified the primordial sea. In the beginning there existed only Tiamat, who represented the blind forces of primitive chaos against which the male gods struggled. She was eventually killed by one of her descendants, the god Marduk – who, although he claimed to be the creator of Heaven and Earth, had to use the body of Tiamat in the creation process. The myth relates that he trampled on her body and broke her as if she were a reed. From one half of her body he made a covering for the sky; with the other half he made the Earth. Tiamat held a primary place in the creation myths of Sumeria, for all the later principal gods issued from her.

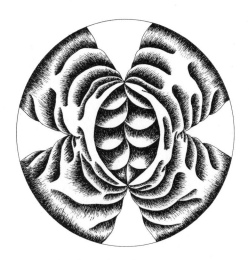

Fertile Goddess

The concept of the Primordial Goddess preceded that of the Fertile Goddess. The idea of an original female presence predated most of the image-making which expressed awe of the female body and its capacity to produce life. Procreation was not understood to be connected to coitus, and it was thought that women brought forth life alone and unaided. The worship of women's creative power was manifested in the multitude of female figurines that emphasized women's breasts, bellies, hips, and vaginas.

The Fertile Goddess represents the holiness of women's bodies as expressed in images that had no contemporary names (like the icon that eventually came to be called the Venus of Willendorf). Later in history, there were also a number of named goddesses who embodied attributes of the original Fertile Goddess concept, but whose power was diminished or destroyed as female-oriented agricultural societies gave way to a male-dominated political state in which occupational specialization, commerce, social stratification, and militarism flourished.

This group of Fertile Goddesses lost their original status, were diminished by later myths, or were dominated by the male gods over whom they or their predecessors had once ruled. In some cases, the goddesses tried to regain their earlier status or punish those who had denied them.

Bona-Dea

Mythic; Rome

Bona Dea, also known as Fauna (one of the names of the Earth), was an agricultural divinity representing the maternal, procreative principle in nature. A festival to ensure prosperity and well-being was held in honor of Bona Dea every year in December. Men were excluded from this celebration, at which the most respected women of Rome – including the chaste state priestesses, the Vestal Virgins – came to pay homage to the goddess. The feast chamber was decorated with vines, and the women drank wine, ate pork (the flesh of the sacrificial sow, sacred as a symbol of fertility), and sang and danced. Bona Dea was also a goddess of the feminine power of healing and was associated with health and longevity; in her temple there was a cave filled with sacred snakes and herbs to cure sterility and the diseases of women. Later, Bona Dea, or Fauna, came to be considered only the wife/daughter of an agricultural fertility god, which totally diminished her earlier stature.

"in Christ there was neither male nor female."

Brigid

Mythic; Celtic Ireland
Brigid was an ancient Irish fertility goddess whose mythology was incorporated into the figure of St. Bridget. Frequently represented as a triple goddess, she was the Goddess of Plenty and was associated with the fruits of the Earth as well as with the fire and the hearth. She later evolved into the patron of culture, skills, and learning. Although reverence for the Mother Goddess never entirely died out in Celtic Ireland, the mythology gradually became dominated by male gods who glorified the warrior/aristocratic society of the day.

Hera

Mythic; Greece
Hera, the Greek goddess who presided over all phases of feminine existence, was originally a queen of the sky and a celestial virgin. After her marriage to Zeus, however, she lost her cosmic attributes and her procreative function was primarily viewed in relation to marriage and maternity. She was the chief feminine deity of Olympus, sitting on a golden throne next to her husband and jointly receiving the honor of all the other deities, but her power was severely restricted. She was seen as the ideal woman and wife, particularly in Rome, where she was known as Juno. Although she was faithful to Zeus, the same was certainly not true of him. Proud of her virtue, Hera consistently protested his infidelity, but was severely punished by Zeus for her attempts to revolt.

Freya

Mythic; Norway
The Goddess of Love, Marriage, and Fecundity, Freya was the Scandinavian counterpart of Venus and Aphrodite and the daughter of the great Earth Mother Nerthus. When the Mother Goddess religion moved north to the more patriarchal society of Norway, Nerthus was replaced by the god Nord, who, in a peculiar reversal of biology, became the sole creator of Nerthus' children, Freya and her brother Frey. The feminine side of the religion continually struggled to reassert itself, however, and – through the figure of Freya, who was very popular – the Earth Mother regained her ancient position.

Later, Freya became identified with the goddess Frig, losing her original status but achieving a limited role as the Goddess of the Atmosphere and Clouds and the wife of the Sky God, Odin.

Frija

Mythic; Germany
Goddesses did not play as primary a role in Teutonic mythology as they did in other cultures, essentially because Teutonic society was predominantly male-oriented. There were numerous goddesses, but little is known about them save for their names; the wives of the gods remained in the background. Frija is the one goddess who seems to have been revered by all the tribes. As the Goddess of Marriage, Love, and the Home, everything was known to her and Nature was under her control.

Juno

Mythic; Rome
As a moon goddess and the feminine principal of celestial light, Juno was venerated earlier by the Etruscan, Sabine, and Umbrian tribes. With time, she became associated with childbirth, since the newborn infant is brought out of the dark womb into the light of day. Also the symbol of the Roman matron, Juno was honored in cult rituals celebrated exclusively by women. Her worship was carried on until after the time of Christ, although in her other form – as the sister and consort of Jupiter (identified with the Greek Zeus) – she gradually suffered the same reduction in status as her Greek counterpart, Hera.

Macha

Mythic; Celtic Ireland
A fertility goddess, Macha was the patron of the capital city of Ulster, then known as Emain Macha. She presided over the fertility of the earth, animals, and humankind and was probably descended from an earlier Mother Goddess figure who was worshiped in parts of Ireland prior to the arrival of the Celts. Also represented as a fearful warrior queen, she was sometimes associated with two other goddesses, and together they formed a triad of warrior goddesses who presided over battles with supernatural powers. The shifting of identity from fertility goddess to warrior queen was common to Celtic goddesses, who underwent multiple transformations.

According to legend, Macha met her death after being forced to race against a team of horses despite the fact that she was pregnant. She won, but died soon after giving birth to twins. At her death she imposed a curse on the warriors of Ulster that incapacitated them for nine generations. Whenever they attempted to fight they were stricken with childbirth pains, which made them experience the same agony Macha had suffered before she died.

Madderakka

Mythic; Lapland
It was said of Madderakka, a birth deity, that she created the body of the child and rendered both women and cattle fruitful. She was originally regarded as the mother of all deities, but her power diminished as time passed.

Ninti

Mythic; Sumeria
The prototype for Eve, Ninti translates as "Female Ruler of Life" (the original Hebrew designation for Eve was "She Who Creates Life"). According to legend the goddess Ninhursaga allowed eight lovely plants to sprout in Paradise, which were eaten by Enki, the Water God. As this was forbidden, Ninhursaga, angry at Enki's defiance, condemned him to death. He fell ill, his strength failed him, and eight of his organs were afflicted. The goddess took pity on him and created eight special healing deities, one for each of his sick organs. Ninti was created to cure his rib; her original role was a positive one as "mother" and "ruler of life," but when her image was incorporated into the Bible, the Hebrews distorted her healing of Enki's rib into Eve's birth from Adam's rib.

Tellus Mater

Mythic; Rome
In ancient times, Tellus Mater was a goddess of fecundity who was similar to the Greek Gaea. She was seen as Mother Earth, presiding over the common grave of all living things, and represented the parallel between the fruitfulness of woman and of the soil – a common theme in early religion. Her domain became more and more usurped over time, and she was eventually associated with Jupiter, the principal male deity of the state.

A number of Fertile Goddesses were eventually transformed into male deities.

Cardea

Mythic; Rome

Although her origins are shadowy, Cardea was considered to be the Goddess of the Four Winds and to rule over the "celestial hinge" at the back of the North Wind, where the universe revolved. As Queen of the Circling Universe, she lived at the axle of the cosmos and held the keys to the underworld. Cardea was associated with the bean plant, which grows in an upward spiral and suggested resurrection to the ancients. It was believed that ghosts tried to be reborn by entering into beans and being eaten by women. In primitive times only priestesses could plant and cook these beans, while in classical times they were used as a charm against witches and an offering to the souls of the dead. In her personification as Earth Goddess, Cardea was connected with wooded groves and to the Moon. Messages from the goddess came through the wind, and inspirational trances were induced by listening to the wind in the trees of a sacred grove.

Legend says that Cardea was captured by the ancient Latin god Janus, an early form of Jupiter, and that she then became his mistress. Once he married the goddess and put her under his subjection, he gradually assumed her characteristics. Cardea was given the menial job of keeping witches away from the nursery door. The reduced goddess of a superseded religion, she was relegated to a subordinate position and portrayed as a demon which she herself had to guard against.

Danu

Mythic; Celtic Ireland

Danu, the Goddess of Plenty, was the universal mother who represented the Earth. She also was associated with the Moon, watched over crops and cattle, and gave birth to the Irish deities who presided over the Tuatha dé Danaan – a confederacy of tribes in which kingship descended through matrilinear succession. Eventually the name Danu was masculinized to Dôn, and the goddess was thus transformed into a god. By the time of the Roman records Dôn had become Donnus, the divine father of a sacred king.

Nerthus

Mythic; Old England

Worship of the Earth Mother Nerthus was brought from the Near East and the eastern Mediterranean to old England, southern Denmark, and northern Germany. Her cult was extremely popular and included specifically feminine rites. On a Danish cauldron from the first century B.C., she was represented as a woman with a gold collar around her neck, flanked by two oxen. This was a reference to the annual ritual in which an image of Nerthus was taken around the countryside in a wagon pulled by oxen, stopping frequently for prayers and feasting, which was thought to ensure good crops. Transported to the patriarchal society of Norway, Nerthus was transformed into the god Niord, and some of her fertility attributes were taken on by his son, Frey.

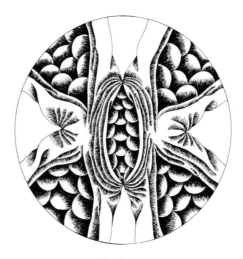

Ishtar

Ishtar, the Great Goddess of Babylonia, represents a period in history when a goddess was thought to possess ultimate and omnipotent power. She was seen as a medium between Nature and people, between divine forces and human ones, as expressed in the "sacred marriage" rituals. All earthly authority was derived from the goddess, and the women who served as her priestesses were considered her incarnation. The priest or king mated with the priestess in a symbolic act of union with the Earth and the Universe. This fertility rite infused sexuality with profound religious meaning and also determined power and authority in the society. If the male "pleased" the goddess through this sexual union with her priestess, he maintained his kingship or priesthood.

By this time, the role of men in procreation was known and acknowledged in myths and religious rites. Vegetation rituals embodied and celebrated various forms of goddess/god relationships. Sometimes these relationships were equal, sometimes the goddess predominated, and, in a few cases, she was reduced to the role of consort to a male god. There were myths in which the goddess held power with a male god who was not her lover, and legends about castes of male priests began to appear. Previously, only priestesses had served the female deity, and it seems possible that the advent of priests implied increased political and religious power for men.

The goddesses who appear in conjunction with Ishtar reflect the differing relationships between the female deity and a male companion or order. Additionally, there is a group of historical figures who represent upper-class women and their connection with the goddess; they were generally priestesses in religious ceremonies, although they often had secular functions or actual professions.

Arinitti

Mythic; Anatolia

Arinitti was a Mother Goddess who became the principal deity of the Hittite pantheon after Indo-European tribes invaded the area and established the Hittite Empire about 1900 B.C. She was called "Queen of the land of Hatti, Heaven and Earth, Mistress of the Kings and Queens of the land of Hatti, directing the government of the King and Queen of Hatti." There is some mystery surrounding Arinitti's origin. The center of her cult was only 125 miles south of Catal Huyuk in Turkey, the site of a female-dominated, agricultural society that is the earliest goddess-worshiping people uncovered to date (ca. 7th millennium B.C.). Arinitti may have been related to or derived from that culture. She was worshiped along with her two daughters and granddaughters, an indication of matriarchal descent.

Aphrodite

Mythic; Phoenicia/ Greece

Aphrodite, the Greek Goddess of Love and Beauty, was of Phoenician derivation. Like her predecessors, Ishtar and Astarte, she was originally a complex goddess who ruled over all of Nature. Her Phoenician genesis and her connection with the fertility cults are reflected in the myth of Aphrodite and Adonis, which was based on an earlier legend of Adonis and Astarte. In the Greek legend, the goddess Aphrodite gave birth to Adonis, then placed him in a chest and gave him to the Goddess of the Underworld to protect. Enamored of Adonis, she refused to give him up until Zeus decreed that Adonis should spend half the year on Earth and half in the underworld, a death-and-resurrection myth that came to be celebrated in a festival every year.

In comparison to the strength and generative power of Ishtar and Astarte, Aphrodite was a rather passive figure, and even her function as a love goddess became fragmented and degraded. The holistic view of sexuality was divided into the two aspects of Aphrodite – one spiritual, the other earthly. As Aphrodite Urania, the goddess represented what was considered the "highest" form of love, particularly wedded love and fruitfulness. As Aphrodite Paudemus, she was a goddess of "lust" and the patron saint of courtesans (who were probably descendants of the hereditary priestess class, once the representatives of the goddess but later reduced to temple prostitutes by the developing patriarchal society).

Astarte

Mythic; Phoenicia

Astarte, the Phoenician version of Ishtar, associated with the planet Venus, was the Goddess of Fertility. She was often represented standing naked on a lion, and her fertility aspect was depicted in the many figures representing Astarte and her priestesses which were unearthed in Biblical Canaan. The sacred marriage ceremony was practiced extensively in connection with the worship of Astarte, who was one of the three goddesses mentioned in the Ugareitic texts of Canaan. It has been suggested that these goddesses represented the three aspects of womanhood: Asherah, mother and protector; Astarte, mistress and lover; and Anath, virgin and warrior. She is often associated with Adonis, an agricultural divinity who replaced the vegetation gods Baal and Mot (closely related to Asherah and Anath in the Ugareitic poems). Sup-

posedly Adonis, still a youth and Astarte's lover, died in a hunting accident in a forest grotto. His death and resurrection were celebrated by the Phoenicians every year at a natural woodland sanctuary dedicated to Astarte. This myth was borrowed by the Greeks as a basis for their similar account of Aphrodite and Adonis.

Blodeuwedd

Mythic; Wales

Blodeuwedd, Goddess of the White Flower, was often imaged as a "fragrant, seductive blossom which is pollinated by the bee." A moon and love goddess, she was part of a trinity which included Cerridwen and the Underworld Goddess, Arianrhod, who conceived the Sun God, Llew Llaw Gyffes. Arianrhod then adopted the form of Blodeuwedd and persuaded Llew Llaw Gyffes to be her partner in a sacred marriage. After consummating the marriage, the god was sacrificed in honor of the summer harvest; then his soul took the form of an eagle and he was restored to life. Arianrhod assumed her original identity, and a new child developed in her dark womb – maintaining the goddess' prominence in the life process. Thus, in this cycle, the son issued from her, united with her, reached maturity, and died, only to be reborn.

Cerridwen

Mythic; Wales

Cerridwen was a barley goddess and a moon goddess who represented the continuous cycle of life and death in the progression of the seasons. She was also called the White Sow because pigs have crescent-moon-shaped tusks, are very prolific, and were generally associated with the goddess and frequently sacrificed in her honor.

Cerridwen, sister deity of both Arianrhod and Blodeuwedd, possessed a magic liquid that gave the gift of inspiration to anyone who drank it. In one of the myths about this goddess, a servant boy mistakenly drank from her magic cauldron. Cerridwen, enraged, pursued him, both of them going through shapeshifting transformations in imitation of the seasonal cycles. The boy ultimately turned into a kernel of grain, which Cerridwen – in the form of a hen – swallowed. The seed impregnated her, and she gave birth to a son. In this myth the goddess used her servant/lover as an instrument of fertility, resurrecting him from her own womb just as she nourished and brought forth the grain from her own body.

Hathor

Mythic; Egypt

As a primary goddess, Hathor was the mother of the Sun God, Re, whose human incarnation, the Pharaoh, she suckled and protected, passing to him the right of kingship as her son. Hathor was one of the oldest deities of Egypt and was worshiped as a cow, an animal with great fertility significance since prehistoric times. Often depicted as a celestial cow whose body was covered with stars, Hathor was honored also as a sky goddess, a mistress of the stars, and a goddess of love, music, and sacred dance. A nourisher of the living, Hathor later also came to be regarded as a protector of the dead, giving sustenance to those who appealed to her for a happy life in the hereafter.

Inanna

Mythic; Sumeria

The Queen of Heaven in the Sumerian pantheon, Inanna was an earlier version of the Babylonian Ishtar. As Goddess of Love and Fertility, she represented the life-producing mother who extended her enormous reproductive power to all plants and animals on the Earth. She played the dominant role in the life process, her son/consort being of secondary importance; it was only after her son Dumuzi proved himself in her bed, then I in turn will show my love for the lord. I shall make him a shepherd of the land." In Mesopotamia the Mother Goddess remained the ultimate source of regenerative power, with the young god always subordinate to her as the instrument of her fertility.

These goddesses had equal status with the male gods with whom they were associated.

Asherah

Mythic; Canaan

Asherah, Goddess of Sexuality and Procreation, was one of the two principal Earth Goddesses described in the ancient myths of Canaan before the Hebrew tribes invaded that area around 1250 B.C. They borrowed the worship of Asherah, renaming her Ashtoreth. Before Biblical times, Asherah, mother of the deities, ruled jointly with her male consort, El, with whom she had a son, the Weather God Baal. His power gradually increased until it eclipsed that of El.

Asherah tried to retain her own position, and in later myths she attempted to become Baal's consort. Although Asherah's power was never entirely diminished, it was Anath – sometimes considered an aspect of Asherah and at other times her daughter – who became Baal's lover. There is archaeological evidence that Asherah was still worshiped as late as the sixth century B.C.

Ashtoreth

Mythic; Hebrew

The Hebrew equivalent of Ishtar and Astarte, Ashtoreth was the Goddess of Fertility and Reproduction. The widespread worship of Ashtoreth, from 1150 to 586 B.C., is attested to by strong archeological and literary evidence; originally, temples to Yahweh (God) and Ashtoreth existed side by side. This goddess was venerated in the royal household of Solomon and became part of the temple worship during the time of Jezebel. For this practice, Jezebel was greatly maligned by the Levite prophets in the Bible. As part of their anti-polytheistic teachings, they denounced the Mother Goddess and what they called "temple prostitution," a reference to the continued practice of sacred marriage.

Isis

Mythic; Egypt

In Egypt the royal family's lineage was matrilineal during most periods, and daughters, not sons, inherited the rulers' titles at birth. In addition, there was a preference for property to pass through the female line, and as a result the Pharaoh usually gained his title on coronation day

through marriage to his sister. Isis, whose name means "the throne," personified the sacred coronation stool which represented the power of kingship, and she was often depicted as wearing a throne on her head. The extent of her power was great, for she ruled in Heaven, Earth, the Sea, and the underworld. Known as Mother of Heaven and Queen of All Gods and Goddesses, she was one of the most widely worshiped deities of Egypt. The earthly queen, as Isis' representative, symbolized the continuing female vitality inherent in the throne.

According to legend, Isis exerted great influence in the development of civilization. She taught women the arts of grinding corn and weaving cloth, was associated with magical charms, and bestowed the knowledge of healing. She also dispensed wisdom and justice and acted as regent when her brother/husband, Osiris, was away (as the queen did in the Pharaoh's absence). Because Isis was regarded as the goddess who "gives birth to gods and men, suckles kings and bestows life and fecundity on the Earth," she was often represented with her son, Horus – the resurrected image of Osiris – seated on her lap. In this maternal aspect, Isis became identified with the Cow Goddess (Hathor or Neith). Her cult became so popular that it spread to Western Asia, Greece, and Rome.

Tanith

Mythic; Carthage

A winged goddess of Heaven, Tanith was the Mother Goddess worshiped at the Phoenician colony of Carthage in Africa. She was depicted on numerous stelae used to commemorate various celebrations and was frequently represented standing beneath the vault of Heaven and the zodiac. Tanith was associated with Ba'al-Hammon, a fertility god. The word Ba'al means "god" or "lord," and Tanith was frequently referred to as the "face of Ba'al," which suggests that either Tanith herself was regarded as a god (a term for which the word "goddess" is not an adequate parallel), or that she ruled interchangeably with Ba'al Hammon.

Some goddesses were either identified/ connected with male gods who were not their lovers or had priests dedicated to their service who derived their power from the goddess.

Anahita

Mythic; Persia

Anahita, Goddess of Sacred Waters, is closely identified with Ishtar. As Queen of Heaven, her dwelling place was said to be among the stars, and she was sometimes associated with the planet Venus. As Earth Mother, she was the Goddess of Springs and Rivers, and her life-giving waters ensured fertility. Anahita was usually shown richly arrayed in a crown of gold adorned with stars, wearing earrings, bracelets, a gold collar and shoes, and an otter-skin cloak embroidered in gold. (But, like Ishtar, Anahita had a fearful as well as a beneficent aspect). Although Iranian texts as late as the fourth century A.D. state that she was in charge of the universe, she was supposedly "given" this task by the god who created her. This suggests that her power, as one of the few goddesses in this male-dominated Persian religion, was somewhat less than that of Ishtar, whose power was inherent rather than given to her.

Cybele

Mythic; Phrygia

Cybele personified the Earth in its primitive state. Called the Mountain Mother, she was worshiped on the tops of mountains and was often depicted in a turreted crown, seated on a throne flanked by lions. As a Nature goddess, she was associated with such fertility symbols as the pine tree, the pine cone, the pomegranate, and the bee. Around 1000 B.C. worship of Cybele and her son/consort, Attis, began to predominate. Of early origin, it followed in the vegetation-cycle tradition, with the young god dying and being resurrected at the spring festival.

The cult of Cybele became associated with a group of eunuch priests, who considered themselves impersonators of Attis. Their goal was to attain immortality through mystical identification with the goddess as the source of life. This was accomplished in an altered state of consciousness, which was arrived at through ecstatic dancing to wild music of flutes, drums, and cymbals, sometimes resulting in voluntary castration. This perverted form of the sacred marriage ceremony was a distortion of the earlier Mesopotamian tradition.

Many goddesses were intimately involved with complex myths that focused on male gods.

Anath

Mythic; Canaan

Anath was a goddess of fertility and love as well as of war, and she shared her position with Asherah, Goddess of Sexuality and Procreation. Both goddesses played a part in the account of the Rain God Baal's mythic struggles against his adversary, Mot, the God of Sterility and Draught. The scope of Anath's influence was described in the Anath/ Baal myths recorded around 1400 B.C., which recounted two major battles between Baal and Mot, with Anath functioning as the continuing thread that linked up those struggles. Baal lost the first battle, and when Anath found his dead body, she killed Mot in revenge. That night she had a dream in which she saw Baal alive again. He then revived and reappeared, joining Anath in a sacred marriage. Finally Baal engaged in and won a second battle with Mot who had also revived. This myth symbolized the reassertion of the life-force, and – although Anath was prominent – the glorification of Baal was its central theme.

Hannahanna

Mythic; Hittite Empire

Hannahanna, known as The Grandmother, played an important role in one of the vegetation rituals of the people of Hatti, whose legends were incorporated into Hittite mythology. According to these legends, a young fertility god became angry with the queen and stormed off, causing the crops to die and the life process to stop. Hannahanna sent a bee to recover him, and upon his return she used magic spells to soothe him until he was reconciled with the queen and life regenerated. Thus, Hannahanna guarded and protected the fertility of the Earth and ensured the perpetuation of the human race.

There are some records of women who lived during the time Ishtar's worship was prevalent.

Amat-Mamu

*fl. 1750 B.C.; Babylonia

Since early temples were also storehouses for surplus food supplies, writing probably developed out of account-keeping, and it is quite probable that priestesses as well as priests recorded the inventories. Thus, although Hammurabi's dynasty in the eighteenth century B.C. greatly limited opportunities for women, it appears that some were still able to practice the profession of scribe within the temple. Amat-Mamu was one such official scribe in the convent community of 140 priestesses at Sippar. She was named again and again in their documents, which attests to her importance as a scribe and to the prominent role she played in the religious institution where she lived and worked.

Baranamtarra

fl. 2500 B.C.; Sumeria

Baranamtarra, called by the honorable title "The Woman," ruled the city of Lagash with her husband. Lagash and other important cities such as Ur and Mari were temple and palace communities that evolved during the early dynasties in Sumeria. Baranamtarra had her own court, called The House of the Woman, which was separate from The House of the Man, which was occupied by her husband (a "patesi," or high priest). As one of the earliest woman philanthropists, Baranamtarra is recorded as having donated money to religious cults, primarily those which worshiped the Mother Goddess.

*fl. – flourished

Encheduanna

fl. 2050 B.C.; Sumeria
The earliest recorded poet, Encheduanna wrote hymns to the ancient Great Goddess. She was both a high priestess and a member of the ruling class, a combination that was common when power existed through a close relationship between palace and temple.

Encheduanna, like all priestesses, performed ritual sacrifices in the temple as well as fulfilling the role of the bride in sacred marriage. The priestess prepared for that ceremony by taking a luxurious bath, applying fragrant oils, and adorning herself with jewelry. Some priestesses wrote special poetry for the love ritual, and Encheduanna is famous for a long poem of her own. This selection from a later sacred-marriage text (ca. 2050 B.C.) expresses the sensual as well as the sacred delights enjoyed by a priestess and her consort:

Bridegroom let me caress you,
My precious caress is more
savory than honey.
In the bed-chamber honey-filled,
Let me enjoy your goodly beauty.

Iltani

fl. 1685 B.C.; Babylonia
Iltani, a wealthy priestess from the royal family, enjoyed an influential position during the First Dynasty of Babylon. Her vast estates included eleven hundred head of cattle and were administered by her own officials. She belonged to a special class of priestess called "nadiatum," most of whom did not marry and were connected with a convent community such as the one at Sippar, where the scribe Amat-Mamu lived.

Kubaba

fl. 2573 B.C.; Sumeria
Originally an innkeeper and beer seller, Kubaba rose to power during a volatile political situation, attained the throne, and founded the Third Dynasty of the city-state of Kish. She became one of the few independently reigning queens in the ancient Near East. Her dynasty retained power for about a hundred years, and she became a legendary figure in Sumerian history.

Shibtu

fl. 1700 B.C.; Babylonia
The official correspondence of Shibtu, queen of the kingdom of Mari, demonstrates that she played a significant administrative role in the affairs of state. She was kept informed of political and military matters by the high officials of the court, engaged in diplomatic relations, and is known to have secured the release of some women from debtors' prison. When the king was away on military campaigns or inspection tours, Queen Shibtu conducted the royal business affairs.

Shub-Ad of Ur

fl. 2500 B.C.; Sumeria
Queen Shub-Ad lived during the first dynasty of Ur, when city-states had replaced female-dominated kinship groups based on communal ownership of land. Although the kings had gradually gained control over the temples, the Sumerian queen still fulfilled the triple role of queen, priestess, and musician. She and her women carried out religious ceremonies that incorporated elaborate music and incantations based on the "wail," the most basic form of women's music.

The extent of Shub-Ad's influence was revealed by the discovery of her royal tomb, which contained staggering wealth; it is probable that this wealth was hers, because her tomb bears an inscription while her consort/king's does not.

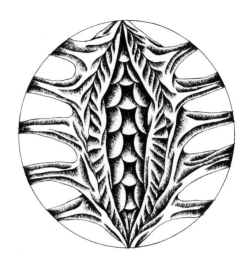

Kali

Kali, the Indian goddess who represents the idea of female power as a destructive spirit, had a dual nature. In Indian culture, however, the fearful rather than the generative aspect of this goddess was emphasized. Because Kali gave life, blood was thought to be her due, and therefore human sacrifices were made to her. (In recent centuries, goats were slaughtered instead.) The blood sacrifice was perversely believed to give birth to new living forms, and the temple often resembled a slaughterhouse more than a house of devotion. Worship of Kali was centered around Calcutta, a city named in her honor which grew in importance as the *saktis* (or female counterparts of the gods) became established as the base of a separate women's religion.

The Kali figure had a number of counterparts in other cultures. Rarely, however, except perhaps in the South Americas, was she so clearly depicted as a demonic figure. In addition to single destructive goddesses, there have also been groupings of female figures, such as the Furies, who represent this so-called devouring female energy. A close reading of the myths surrounding most of these figures allows one to see, again and again, how the former power of the goddess in matriarchal societies came to be distorted and represented as a negative force.

There were a number of goddesses who were described as harmful and as figures guarding the doorway to death.

Alukah

Mythic; Canaan
Alukah represented the darker side of the Mother Goddess in Canaan culture, which flourished between the Jordan, the Dead Sea, and the Mediterranean around 1400 B.C. Alukah was depicted as a succuba or vampire, and her two daughters were Sheve and The Womb, or Death and Life.

Arianrhod

Mythic; Wales
Arianrhod was the Death Goddess who turned the "Wheel of Heaven." She was also the destructive aspect of the Moon Goddess and Earth Mother, Cerridwen, and another form of Blodeuwedd. Symbolized by the curved sliver of both the new and the waning Moon, she ruled over the double spiral in the tomb beneath Cerridwen's castle-fortress. This double spiral, which represented the continuous cycle of death and rebirth, had the head of a second spiral coiled in reverse direction at the center to allow an exit from the maze. Although the dead went to live in Arianrhod's castle, they went with hopes of resurrection, because Arianrhod was also characterized as a Virgin Mother Goddess who gave birth to new life as the great "Wheel of Heaven" continued to revolve.

Coatlicue

Mythic; Meso-America
Coatlicue, the Aztec Earth Goddess, represented the negative aspect of the Great Mother. She was often depicted with a death's head and the serpent-woven skirt from which her name is derived, and her hands were raised in an awe-inspiring gesture. Her image reflects the way life and death were believed to be profoundly interconnected: She who gives life is also the life-taker.

Ereshkigal

Mythic; Sumeria
Ereshkigal, or Allatu, the Sumerian Goddess of Death, originally reigned over the subterranean world. No one entering her realm except her sister Inanna was allowed to leave it. Then Nergal, the God of War and Hunting, invaded her domain in answer to Ereshkigal's demand for his death (he had failed to honor her properly at a banquet of the deities). With 14 demons to help him, Nergal dragged Ereshkigal from her throne by the hair and threatened to cut off her head. To save her life and to obtain peace, she offered to share her throne with him. By the time of the later Greek myth, the sole ruler of the netherworld had become the male god Hades.

Hecate

Mythic; Greece
Hecate, known as the Invincible Queen of the Underworld, was the triple-headed Goddess of the Moon who ruled in the infernal regions along with Persephone and Hades. She was personified by the three phases of the new, full, and waning Moon. Her three heads represented the three phases of a woman's life – young girl, mature woman, and old hag. As the old hag of the subterranean depths, she was worshiped by witches, who in her day were women who practiced healing by means of medicinal herbs and incantations. Images of the three-headed Hecate were often placed at crossroads, and offerings were made to her when the Moon was full.

Hel

Mythic; Norway
Hel was the name applied to both the territory of the underworld and its presiding goddess. The latter was a vague and shadowy figure, represented by a face that was half human and half obscured by darkness, or the black void. She had a vast palace where she received the heroes and deities who descended to the netherworld.

Irkalla

Mythic; Babylonia
Irkalla, the Babylonian Goddess of the Underworld, a sister of Ishtar, represented the destructive, death-related aspect of the Mother Goddess. Irkalla had the head of a lioness (Ishtar's sacred animal) and the body of a woman, and she grasped a serpent in her hands. The dead existed in her dark realm by eating dust and mud. Her kingdom was known as the Land of No Return, but Ishtar – like Inanna – did return. Ishtar and Irkalla were the connecting links between life and death; although Ishtar was thought to possess the power over death as well as life, the darkest side of female potency was embodied in her sister.

Nephthys

Mythic; Egypt
The sister and companion of Isis, Nephthys was the Goddess of the Dead and one of the nine deities of the divine pantheon of Egypt. The daughter of the Earth and the sky, she represented the twilight, and – like Isis – she had a place in the "Boat of the Sun" at the creation. According to legend, together with Isis, she performed ministrations to the dead. Although she was a death goddess, Nephthys was not a negative deity, probably because the Egyptians did not fear death itself but only decay.

Rhiannon

Mythic; Britain
Rhiannon, called the Great Queen, ruled the underworld jointly with her husband, the god Pwyll. She was depicted as a mare-headed goddess who fed on raw flesh. The horse symbolized the Mother Goddess, and Rhiannon's horse-like appearance represented the terrifying aspect of the Great Mother.

Tuchulcha

Mythic; Etruria
Of Etruscan origin, Tuchulcha was the principal female demon who inhabited the Roman underworld. She had ferocious eyes, a beak instead of a mouth, the ears of a donkey, two serpents wound around her head, and another snake around her arm. The

Romans had no significant indigenous underworld deities, and terrifying, primitive creatures such as Tuchulcha were derived from Etruscan mythology.

The idea of female power as frightening is expressed in similar myths about groups of awesome women.

The Furies

Mythic; Greece

The Furies (Erynines), winged women with snakes entwining their bodies, played a prominent role in the debate concerning the supremacy of mother-right over father-right in the myth of Orestes. Orestes was pursued by the Furies for killing his mother, Clytemnestra, in order to avenge the murder of his father, Agamemnon. As supporters of the matriarchy, the Furies did not consider Agamemnon's death a crime because he was not a direct blood relation to Clytemnestra. But Orestes' act was unforgivable, and his acquittal by Athene enraged the Furies, who decided to hide in the subterranean depths in order to destroy the fertility of the Earth if any further crime against women were committed. (When angered, the Furies had the power to inflict sterility, crop failure, and disease. In their more benevolent underworld aspect, they were the forces which worked to generate life and send it upward; in death everything returned to them.)

Morrigan

Mythic; Celtic Ireland

Morrigan, known as the Great Queen, was actually a trinity of three warrior goddesses sharing one name: Macha, who took the form of a raven; Badb Catha, "The Cauldron"; and the old hag Anu. Accompanied by her pro-

phetic raven of death, and watching over her boiling kettle – wherein bubbled the everchanging faces of life and death – Anu constituted the supernatural power of Morrigan. Warriors invoked this triple goddess by blowing on their war horns in imitation of a raven's croaking.

The Norns

Mythic; Norway

The three Goddesses of Fate, the Norns, were female giants. Urda, Verdandi, and Skuld represented the past, the present, and the future, and their job was to sew the web of fate and water the sacred ash whose roots reached down into the subterranean depths of the Earth. Urda and Verdandi were kind, but Skuld was cruel; she would often tear up her sisters' work as they sewed the web of fate. The Norns also guarded the third root of the ash tree, which was continuously gnawed by a serpent demon. Because of their efforts, the tree continued to sprout green leaves and to maintain the indestructible strength of its trunk at the center of the Earth. The Norns balanced the forces of life and death which were constantly at work in the weaving of destiny.

The Valkyries

Mythic; Germany

The Valkyries, thirteen armored Amazon maidens, were the dispensers of destiny within a male-dominated mythology who watched the progress of battles and chose the winners. Their benevolent function was to lead the souls of dead war heroes back to the kingdom of Valhalla. The appearance of female warriors in Teutonic mythology reflects the fact that early Teutonic women often participated in battles.

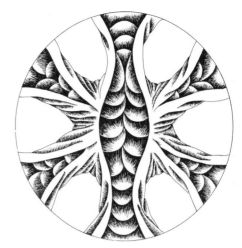

Snake Goddess

Between 1700 and 1650 B.C. an earthquake occurred in central Crete, accompanied by fires which caused extensive damage to several cities and partially destroyed the Palace of Knossos, the religious center of Crete. This disruption of Cretan society made the island vulnerable to colonization, which occurred when a group from the mainland of Greece invaded the country. They were, however, sympathetic to the Mother Goddess religion there, and because of this their arrival did not greatly affect Cretan practices. Unfortunately, this was not true of the next invasion.

Around 1450 B.C. a volcano erupted at nearby Thera, and tidal waves, earthquakes, and fires devastated much of Crete. Shortly thereafter the Myceneans, a patriarchal tribe from the Greek mainland, invaded Crete. The tradition of matriarchy and the predominance of the goddesses was too strong, however, for the invaders to be able to simply impose their religions and social practices

wished to devote themselves to scholarship

on the Cretes. They were forced into intermarriage with the Cretan aristocracy, accomplished through sacred marriage rites in which the Cretan queen married the Mycenean king. This process is reflected in the myths which explain the dynasty of Minos, the later legendary king of Crete.

As a result of these successive Greek invasions, the powerful goddesses and queens of Crete were incorporated into Greek myths. This transition from Cretan to Greek mythology clearly reflects the changeover from matriarchal to patriarchal values – a transformation which can be seen in other goddesses, many of whom had a snake aspect.

Ariadne

Mythic; Crete

Ariadne, the daughter of Pasiphae, was identified with an early Cretan moon goddess. Ancient legends of the Greek islands describe Ariadne's cult as an orgiastic one which continued to practice the periodic sacrifice of the young king as part of its fertility and vegetation rituals. In an attempt to prolong his rule, King Minos brought men and women over from the Greek mainland – the men to be sacrificed in Minos' place and the women to act as priestesses in the cult of Ariadne. Theseus, a Greek, volunteered to go to Crete and participate in this ritual sacrifice as a ruse; his real purpose was to end the

oppression of Greek mainlanders by the Cretan overlord. Legend tells how Ariadne helped Theseus to overthrow the Minoan king. Theseus then married Ariadne in order to maintain peace, but instead of establishing a new reign in Crete, he tried to convince Ariadne to leave with him. She refused, and Theseus abandoned her on an island near her homeland. The matrilineal tradition was thus broken, and the government of Crete was weakened in the process. This situation paved the way for the final destruction of traditional Cretan culture.

The Dorians eventually invaded Crete, Zeus was established as the supreme deity, and the Mother Goddess religion was finally overthrown.

Britomartis

Mythic; Crete

Britomartis was among the few Cretan goddesses besides Rhea who were documented in Greek legends. One of Crete's most ancient goddesses, she was associated with the Moon, which in gynocracies controlled planting, harvesting, festivals, and religious rituals. Representations of Britomartis depict her as a huntress, suggesting that goddess worship existed in the hunting stage of early society and reached its peak during the agricultural phase.

Buto

Mythic; Egypt

Buto, the Great Serpent, was a Snake Goddess usually represented in the form of a cobra and sometimes as a cobra with the head of a woman. She was often depicted as the protectress of lower Egypt and was associated with Nekhebet, the Vulture Goddess of the South. The Neolithic cultures of Egypt venerated these two goddesses as supreme deities, but, with the beginning of the Egyptian dynasties around 3000 B.C., the Cobra Goddess and the Vulture Goddess lost prominence. Their previous power survived to the extent that their symbols were both worn in the center of the Pharoah's crown and appeared on official documents. There is evidence that Cretan Snake Goddess worship was derived from Egyptian Cobra Goddess worship.

Chicomecoatl

Mythic; Meso-America

Chicomecoatl, known as Seven Snake, had the double ear of corn for a symbol. She was the ancient and indigenous Mexican Maize Goddess, the agricultural personification of the Earth Mother who was related to the fruitful and fallow cycles of vegetation. She resembles the figure of Demeter, symbolizing the complex rhythm of life, growth, and death in nature.

Europa

Mythic; Crete

The myth of Europa is somewhat unclear. She was probably a real Cretan queen who, in a sacred marriage, was joined with the Mycenean king at the beginning of the dynasty of Minos. In the myth, Europa is raped by Zeus (whose presence might be a later addition to the myth) and

gives birth to Minos, the legendary founder of the Minoan dynasty. This rape, although presented in mythical form, has its source in the real rape of Cretan culture by the Myceneans. The myth could have been created to legitimize the origin of King Minos.

Pasiphae

Mythic; Crete

Described as a Cretan Moon Goddess and "She Who Shines for All," Pasiphae was the daughter of Europa and the mother of Ariadne. According to Greek myth, she married Minos; however, as Minos means "king" and does not refer to a particular man, she may possibly have married the heir to the Minoan throne. The myth of Pasiphae recounts how she fell in love with a white bull and hid inside a wooden cow in order to mate with him. This story indicates that the sacred marriage rites continued in Crete after the matriarchy came under the domination of the Myceneans and suggests that it required many generations to alter the traditional worship of the Mother Goddess.

Python

Mythic; Greece

According to Greek legend, Python was a female serpent who had a lair in the wooded hills near Delphi. This snake derived from the earliest days of the temple there. Originally established by Cretan priestesses, this temple was built in Mycenean times in honor of the Mother Goddess. A real python was kept in one of its underground chambers to act as the guardian of the dead and a symbol of resurrection. The temple at Delphi became famous as a center of oracular divination, and the python, as a symbol of women's psychic power, was kept there even after that power was dead.

Rhea

Mythic; Crete

Rhea was the powerful Earth Mother of Crete, comparable to Gaea or Cybele. Representing fertility and the fruits of the soil, she was originally considered the ruler of the heavens, the Earth, and the underworld. By the time her existence was recorded by the Greeks, her identity had been altered and she was described merely as the mother of Zeus. She was further fragmented into Demeter, Artemis, and Athene, each of whom assumed some of Rhea's original attributes.

It is possible to trace the gradual transformation of earlier goddesses into fragmented shadows of their former selves.

Artemis

Mythic; Greece

The continued transition of the goddesses from Cretan to Greek to Roman culture can be traced through the figure of Artemis, which takes several forms. The earliest is the famous Ar-

temis of Ephesus at the temple in Ionia in the western part of Anatolia. Artemis was originally a Mother Goddess figure whose fertility cult followed in the Ishtar tradition. Her worship may have been transported to Ionia during the establishment of the Hittite Empire, when many goddess-worshiping people fled westward. By the time Artemis appeared in the Greek pantheon of Olympus, she was viewed as an agricultural deity and Moon Goddess connected with the chase and the forests. The Greek Artemis watched over the forest and its inhabitants, but she had become a cool, chaste huntress instead of a vital symbol of the teeming life of all Nature. Artemis was identified with the Roman goddess Diana, and these two goddesses shared certain attributes – they were connected with the Moon and the hunt and were both seen as protective figures. The goddess Diana was eventually incorporated into the Roman Vesta, whose role as a virgin priestess was only a trivial reflection of her predecessors.

Athene

Mythic; Greece

The destruction of Mother Goddess religion can clearly be seen in the figure of Athene. Although few known descriptions of her earlier forms exist, it is possible that she was derived from the similar Egyptian goddess, Neith. By the time Athene became part of the Greek pantheon, she had been transformed into the daughter of Zeus and was described as springing full-grown from his head. When Athene acquits Orestes in Aeschylus' play *The Eumenides,* she decides against the whole tradition of mother-right and the taboo against matricide. Her action symbolically

announces that the old matriarchal order has been replaced by the law and moral authority of the patriarchy. Athene was a virgin goddess who was both a warrior and a patron of culture; she was also a deity of architects, artists, and weavers, the protector of Athens, and the Goddess of Wisdom and Healing. She is traditionally associated with the snake – probably in connection with her role as Goddess of Wisdom – and numerous images of her contain serpents.

Demeter

Mythic; Greece

Derived from Cretan religion, Demeter was the daughter of Rhea, the ancient Cretan Mother Goddess. She symbolized fecundity, fruitfulness, and rebirth and, as the Goddess of Agriculture, was responsible for the cultivation of the soil. In her primitive form, she was associated with snakes. Demeter also represented the underground where the seeds were planted; this subterranean aspect was transferred to her daughter Persephone when the Demeter figure was fragmented by the Greeks. In the Eleusinian mystery rites which occurred at harvest time, Demeter and Persephone were symbolically reunited and the fruitfulness of the Earth was ensured.

Fortuna

Mythic; Rome

By Roman times, the sacred oracular golden wheel of divination was remembered only in facetious references to Fortuna as the Goddess of the Turning Wheel. She represented fate with "all its unknown factors," a far cry from the omnipotent god-

dess who once knew all. Fortuna was known under many names, each connected with her various functions. Eventually she became a good-luck charm, and small statues of her were placed in the Emperor's bedroom to protect him from misfortune.

Kore

Mythic; Greece

Persephone, the daughter of Demeter, was called Kore before she was abducted. In a rewriting of the Babylonian myth in which Ishtar descended into the underworld in pursuit of her consort, the Greek legend recounts how Demeter goes to retrieve her daughter. There are several accounts of Kore's kidnaping – one states that she was abducted by Zeus' brother Hades, and another myth suggests that Kore was raped by Zeus, who was her father. The introduction of rape as a prominent theme in Greek myths seems to be connected to the takeover of culture by the patriarchy in either a literal or symbolic way. After Kore disappeared, Demeter searched the world for her daughter for nine days. She finally returned to her temple and threatened to make the Earth barren if her daughter were not returned to her. Kore was returned, but only for two thirds of the year. For the other third of each year she lived with Hades, whom she had been tricked into marrying by Zeus' messenger. Kore is symbolically connected to seasonal change, for during the winter when she stays with Hades in the underworld, the Earth sleeps in sadness and mourning; the flowering of spring occurs upon Kore's return to her mother, Demeter.

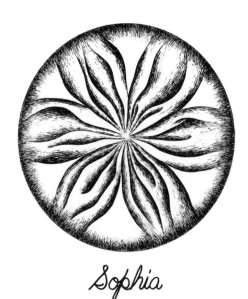

Sophia

Sophia was a unique figure in the goddess tradition. Grouped around her are later goddesses, legendary figures, heroines of Greek tragedies, and a few real women who tried to resist becoming the victims of the developing patriarchy. The nature of the traditional goddess changed considerably in Greece and Rome; no longer was she a strong figure, but rather a somewhat impotent, evil, or limited character.

The most powerful images of women probably existed in Greek epic poems and tragedies – but in these, women were generally manipulated, tricked, or punished by men or by male gods. There were, of course, legendary and mythic women who were involved in a later version of the sacred marriage ceremony, or possessed powers of divination, or represented the growing idea that female power was evil.

Arachne

Legendary; Greece
The discovery of woven cloth and the art of net-making is attributed in Greek mythology to Arachne. Her weaving was so perfect that she challenged Athene to a contest. Athene destroyed Arachne's work because of its perfect beauty, and Arachne hanged herself. Athene, taking pity on her, turned her into a spider and her noose into a web.

Cassandra

Legendary; Greece
Legend has it that Apollo fell in love with Cassandra and taught her the art of prophecy to win her love, but after she had acquired this knowledge Cassandra rejected him. In revenge, Apollo condemned her to always tell truthful prophecies but never be believed.

Cassandra warned the Trojans of the impending war, predicted that Paris' trip to Greece would bring the downfall of Troy, and insisted that armed men were in the Trojan Horse, but no one responded. During the sack of Troy she took refuge in the Temple of Athene, where she was found clinging to Athene's statue. A Greek soldier toppled the statue and raped Cassandra, who was then taken prisoner by Agamemnon. After Agamemnon was murdered by his wife, Clytemnestra, Cassandra announced the king's death; no one listened to her, however, and she herself was soon killed by Clytemnestra.

Because her prophecies were preceded by ecstatic trances, Cassandra was believed to be mad. Her name has become synonymous with one whose wisdom is impotent because it is unheeded until too late.

Circe

Legendary; Greece
According to legend, in some parts of archaic Greece only women's bodies were buried, while men's were wrapped in oxhides, suspended from trees, and eaten by birds. Originally Circe tended the men's cemetery. In later legend she was an enchantress who lived alone on an island, where she transformed anyone who tried to invade her territory into an animal. According to Homer, when Odysseus' men attempted to land on her island she turned them into swine. Then Odysseus arrived and – with the aid of the god Hermes – was able to convince Circe to return his men to human form. Enchanted by her, he remained on the island for three years, during which time Circe bore three sons. Upon Odysseus' departure she used her psychic powers to predict the trials that lay in store for him, and he survived by heeding her warnings. Circe embodies the continued tradition of the female powers of divination and prophecy.

Pandora

Legendary; Greece
Originally a bestower of good upon Earth, later Pandora came to personify the belief that women were the greatest evil inflicted on men. According to Hesiod, she was given a great jar as a dowry, but was instructed not to open it. She did, however, and supposedly unleashed all the evils of the world. Because the Greeks buried their dead in such jars as well as stored their food in them, Pandora's act symbolically associated women – and the Earth – with the giving of life and death.

Pythia

Legendary; Greece
The temple where Pythia was consulted was an oracular center at Delphi dedicated to the Cretan Earth Goddess and used by Greeks and Romans for approximately 1000 years. The priestesses of Pythia had full freedom and were considered to be in direct communication with the Great Goddess, having been selected for their occult powers rather than their social status, lineage, or training. The Pythian Oracle was sought for advice on religious procedures, politics, law, and everyday affairs; its influence was considerable,

since the entire country considered this temple the center of spiritual authority. By Homeric times, however, the Oracle at Delphi had been taken over by patriarchal invaders, who turned it into a shrine to Apollo. The Pythia priestesses were then considered instruments of Apollo who supposedly received oracles from Zeus through their mouths.

Rhea Silva

Legendary; Rome
Rhea Silva, a priestess of Vesta, participated in the sacred marriage festival of the Oak Queen and King, at which time she conceived the twins Romulus and Remus. Silent group couplings took place during these festivals in the darkness of a sacred cave, and Rhea Silva claimed that Mars had fathered her children in one such coupling (which may refer to the participation of a priest acting the role of a god in the sexual ritual). Rhea Silva was thrown into prison by her brother, who ordered her sons drowned because – as the children of a Vestal Virgin – they would have had a claim to the throne, since kinship still passed through the female line. Romulus and Remus survived, however, and are said to have founded Rome.

Sibyl of Cumae

(Amalthea)
fl. 500 B.C.; Rome
Sibyls were prophetic women in ancient history who, by direct inspiration possessed knowledge of the future and how evil could be averted. Sibyls are found in the histories of Egypt, Persia, Greece, Babylonia, and Italy. The most celebrated of these was Amalthea, to whom was attributed the writing of the nine Sibylline books which played a prominent part in the history of Rome and are said to have predicted the Trojan Wars, the rise and

fall of the Empire, and the coming of Christ. The Sibylline books became highly esteemed by Roman priests, who consulted them frequently until their destruction in the fire that devastated Rome during Nero's reign.

Vesta

Legendary; Rome
In early Rome, during the midsummer and midwinter festivals of the Oak King and Queen, there was a marriage feast for the purpose of conceiving – by a Vestal Virgin – a new heir to the throne. The women who participated in this ceremony were the priestesses of the goddess Vesta, whose worship was the exclusive duty of women. Vesta was similar to the Greek goddess Hestia, though held in much higher honor. A flame was kept perpetually lit in Vesta's honor by young girls who entered into the service of the goddess at between six and ten years of age. These priestesses were greatly respected and were free of the guardianship by male relatives to which all other Roman women were subject. By the time of the Republic, the Vestals had been stripped of their royal privileges, however, and were no longer responsible for producing an heir to the throne. In fact, the later Vestal Virgins were required to take a vow of absolute chastity, the violation of which was punishable by death.

A number of women in plays or legends were the victims of male guile, manipulation, or anger.

Antigone

Legendary; Greece
Antigone, the leading character in a play by Sophocles, represents the

rebellious woman who flaunts masculine authority. She defied the edict of the king which denied burial to her brother. Saying that she would not have disregarded the king's decree for a husband or children, Antigone sacrificed herself in order to honor the uterine relationship that was the basis of the matriarchal kinship line: "And yet what greater glory could I find than giving my own brother [a] funeral...When was it shameful to serve the children of my mother's womb?" To punish her, the king had Antigone walled up in a cave; she committed suicide in order to avert a long, painful death there.

Atalanta

Legendary; Greece
Rejected by her father, who desired a son, Atalanta was raised in the woods by a she-bear sent by Artemis and became a formidable hunter, warrior, and sportswoman. Although Atalanta was warned against marriage by the Oracle at Delphi, she challenged all suitors to a foot-race in which she would marry the winner and those who lost would be killed. Aphrodite gave Hippomenes three golden apples with which to tempt Atalanta, and, because she stopped to retrieve them, he won.

Camilla

Legendary; Rome
Camilla was the daughter of Metabus, King of the Volscians, who was driven out of his kingdom, taking the infant Camilla with him. He prayed to Diana for their safe passage and, when it was granted, dedicated Camilla to Diana's service. She was raised in the woods, became a hunter and warrior, and was killed by an Etruscan, who was supposedly aided by Apollo. Diana avenged Camilla's death by sending a nymph to slay her killer.

Clytemnestra

Legendary; Greece
A Greek queen, Clytemnestra was the wife of Agamemnon and the sister of Helen. Agamemnon sacrificed their daughter Iphigenia at the outset of the Trojan War; upon his return, Clytemnestra asserted her mother-right and avenged her daughter by killing Agamemnon. She was then slain by her remaining children, Orestes and Electra, who were acquitted of the crime of matricide, thus symbolically illustrating the shift from matriarchal to patriarchal power.

Daphne

Legendary; Greece
Daphne was a nymph and hunter and the daughter of the River Peneuis. Determined to remain chaste, she rejected all suitors, including the god Apollo. Apollo chased her to the river, where she entreated her father's aid and, he turned her into a laurel tree just as Apollo reached her. Apollo declared that henceforth laurel leaves would serve as wreaths for musicians and as a sign of victory. In earlier legends, however, Daphne was a priestess of Mother Earth, and when Apollo pursued her it was Mother Earth to whom she cried out. Mother Earth spirited her away to Crete, where she became Pasiphae, and left a laurel tree in her place; from its leaves Apollo made a wreath for consolation.

Hecuba

Legendary; Greece
In Homer's *Iliad*, Hecuba, Queen of Troy, was the second wife of Priam and the mother of nineteen children,

113

including Hektor, Paris, and Cassandra. Hecuba saw her husband and all her children slain or made slaves by the enemy, and she herself became the slave of Odysseus. After blinding a Greek soldier and killing his two sons, Hecuba supposedly was metamorphosed into a dog and swam to the Hellespont, a strait near the Aegean Sea.

Helen of Troy

Legendary; Greece
Helen – daughter of Zeus and the mortal, Leda, and a favorite of Aphrodite, is the prototypical heroine of male literature, the pivot around whom action takes place but never the central actor herself. The most beautiful woman of her time, Helen fled to Troy with her lover, Paris, abandoning her husband, Menelaus. The latter's attempts to reclaim her resulted in the ten-year Trojan War. Although later writers blamed the devastating war on Helen's infidelity, Homer portrayed her as a helpless victim of Aphrodite, loved and idolized by Greeks and Trojans alike.

Virginia

Legendary; Rome
A plebian of great beauty, Virginia was killed by her father so she would not be taken as the slave of a Roman. Although Virginia did not act directly in her death it was a symbolic event which inspired a political revolt in Rome.

Some women tried to resist the loss of their power by trying to take political action or promote peace in order to keep family ties intact.

Hersilia

fl. 800 B.C.; Rome
The "Rape of the Sabine Women," an important event in Roman legend, has been glorified by history, with emphasis on the male figures at the expense of their victims. Hersilia was a heroine of the Sabine women, who were abducted by the Romans to bear their children. By the time the Sabine men returned to free the women, they had established bonds with their new husbands and children and were reluctant to break with them. Hersilia voiced a plea for peace, asking that original families be rejoined but that the newer family ties be recognized as well. She averted bloodshed, a truce was declared, and the "Festival of the Matronalia" came to be celebrated by Roman women to commemorate the pact.

Lysistrata

Legendary; Greece
Lysistrata is the heroine of Aristophane's bawdy comedy about women who take over the Treasury and then refuse to have sex with their husbands until the men bring a halt to the Pelopennesian War. Her character was based upon certain actual, prominent women of Athens who were determined to alter the status of women in society and public affairs.

Praxagora

Legendary; Greece
A heroine in the *Ecclesiazuoe,* by Aristophanes (ca. 400 B.C.), Praxagora was the leader of a group of women who disguised themselves as men, entered a public assembly, and – by a majority vote – overturned the government and proclaimed the supremacy of women.

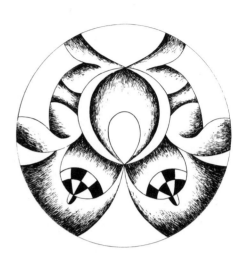

Amazon

It is not known for certain whether women participated in warfare among themselves during the thousands of years of gynocracy, but all archaeological evidence suggests that matriarchal societies were peaceful. Much of what we know of the Amazons comes from the Greeks, who were particularly fascinated by these warrior women and represented them in art, mythology, and history. Our earliest actual record is of the Amazon queendom of Eurypyle (ca. 1750 B.C.). Since this period corresponds to the documented rise of a male-dominated society, it is possible to speculate that the development of female warrior societies, as expressed in the myths of the Amazons, was a response to the growing threat to the matriarchate.

114

Antiope

13th c. b.c.; Scythia

Antiope was one of a long line of Amazon warrior-queens from the region of Themiscyra, now a part of Greece. She is said to have fought Hercules and to have been taken prisoner along with her two sisters. She succeeded in freeing herself and one sister, with whom she continued to rule.

Hiera

fl. 1184 b.c.; Asia Minor

Hiera was the general of an army of Mysian women who fought in the Trojan War. She was one of Greece's most famous warriors and is mentioned in the *Heroicus* by Philostratus, who suggested that Homer chose to exclude her from the *Iliad* because she would have outshone Helen!

Hippolyte

13th c. b.c.; Scythia

Hippolyte, Antiope, and Orithya were sister-rulers at the time of the invasion of the Amazon capital of Themiscyra by Greek adventurers. Hippolyte was either killed or captured, and in retaliation the Amazons invaded Athens, leading to the eventual fall of the Amazonian empire.

Lampedo

13th c. b.c.; Greece

Lampedo and her sister Martesia, who called themselves the Daughters of Mars, were queens of an Amazon tribe. Because the majority of their males were killed by Scythian princes, the women of this tribe coupled with men from neighboring communities. As soon as they became pregnant they returned home, where, it is said, their male offspring were killed at birth. Female children were spared for education in the military arts; their right breasts were supposedly caused to wither so they would not interfere with the use of bow and arrow, while the left breasts were left unharmed for the nurturing of future children.

Martesia

13th c. b.c.; Greece

Martesia ruled in conjunction with her sister Lampedo as a queen of the Amazon nation in the region of Themiscyra; while one consolidated the empire and attended to domestic government, the other enlarged the empire by conquest. After Martesia was killed during an invasion by neighbors, her daughters – Antiope, Hippolyte, and Orithya – succeeded their mother and Lampedo as sister-queens.

Orithya

13th c. b.c.; Scythia

Martesia's daughter Orithya ruled with her sisters, Antiope and Hippolyte, as virgin queens of Themiscyra, and together they brought great military honor to the Amazons. According to myth, they were finally defeated by the Athenians Hercules and Theseus.

Medusa

fl. 1290 b.c.; Greece

According to legend, Medusa was the leader of the Gorgons, an Amazon tribe. The prevailing myth states that Perseus, King of Mycenae, killed her, after which the main shrines of the Mother Goddess were destroyed in a major defeat for the matriarchal order.

There were Amazon queens with empires in other parts of the ancient world.

Egee

12th c. b.c.; Libya

Egee is thought to have commanded a vast army of women who marched from Libya into Asia, conquering all they encountered. Opposed by the King of Troy, whose power she challenged and overcame, Egee and her troops were said to have acquired a great booty from him.

Eurpyle

fl. 1760 b.c.; Near East

Eurpyle was the leader of a women's expedition against Babylon, and it is said that they conquered the capital of an area inhabited by a Semitic people living west of Mesopotamia who had themselves invaded Babylonia around 1950 b.c. This dates Amazon queendoms as early as the 1750's b.c.

Myrine

13th c. b.c.; Libya

Myrine led 30,000 Libyan horsewomen in battle against the Gorgons, another Amazon culture. She then mounted a campaign in which she and her army conquered parts of Syria, Phrygia, and the islands of Samos, Lesbos, Pathmos, and Samothrace. Myrine died at Samothrace in a battle against the invading patriarchal Thracian and Scythian forces.

Penthesilea

d. 1187 b.c.; North Africa

According to legend, Penthesilea – the last in the dynasty of great Amazon queens – went to Troy with twelve of her warrior women to help defend the city against the Greeks in the Trojan War. She and her troops fought valiantly and bravely, but they were defeated by Achilles.

Thalestris

fl. 325 b.c.; Asia Minor

Thalestris, an Amazon queen, led an expedition of over three hundred armed women across Asia. It is said that her purpose was to meet and mate with Alexander, whom she considered sufficiently courageous to be the father of her child. The outcome of her voyage is unknown.

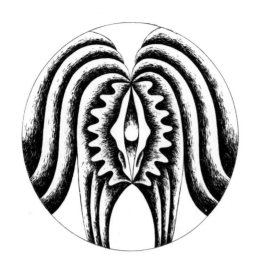

Hatshepsut

d. 1479 B.C.

Although women were rapidly losing power in Greece, the women of Egypt continued to have control over their lives. All landed property went through the female line, with the result that a husband enjoyed his wife's property until her death, after which it passed to their daughter. Men and women worked side by side and were paid in proportion to their work. The same standard of dress was applied to both sexes; men as well as women used eye paint, jewelry, and perfume. Divorce was easily obtained, and alimony was allocated based on which partner left the marriage. Women in ancient Egypt generally had more rights than do many women in the world today.

Hashop

fl. 2420 B.C.; Egypt
Little is known of the Egyptian queen Hashop other than the fact that she was an architect as well as a ruler.

Khuwyt

fl. 1950 B.C.; Egypt
Khuwyt, a singer and harpist, was portrayed in two paintings in the household of the Minister of State and was also depicted as a female effigy adorning the top of a harp. She is one of the first women musicians in recorded history.

Mentuhetop

fl. 2300 B.C.; Egypt
Queen of the XI Dynasty at Thebes, Mentuhetop was a skilled medical doctor as well as a ruler. Her medical bag is on exhibit at the Berlin Museum. (Among the educated Egyptians, it was common for the queen to be the leading authority on medical matters.)

Nefertiti

fl. 1300 B.C.; Egypt
Nefertiti was the daughter of Queen Tiy and Amenhotep III and the wife of Akhenaton. Unfortunately, she is remembered primarily because of a sculpture that reveals her as a great beauty. Religious texts of the period, however, indicate that she probably shared the reign of Egypt equally with her pharaoh husband, and contemporary iconography represented her as wearing a pharaoh's crown. It is possible that it was Nefertiti who was responsible for the religious revolution in Egypt attributed to Akhenaton and that she assumed the leadership of Egypt upon his death.

Nofret

fl. 1900 B.C.; Egypt
Nofret, a queen who ruled in conjunction with her husband, Sesostris II, was a woman of great power and distinction. She was called "the ruler of all women" because she was responsible for then-current laws and practices concerning Egyptian women.

Rahonem

Old Kingdom; Egypt
In Egypt the queen, as the female leader, was followed by an independent group of women including a prophetess, a spiritual teacher, a priestess-musician, and choirs of dancing, singing attendants. Rahonem was a director of female players and singers, a position equivalent to that of the priestess-musician.

Phantasia

12th c. B.C.; Egypt
Phantasia is said to have gone to Greece from Egypt in pre-Homeric times. A skilled story teller, musician, and poet, she and another poet were reputed to have invented the heroic meter – the hexameter.

Tetisheri

fl. 1650 B.C.; Egypt
Tetisheri was the first of six great queens, mothers of the 17th Dynasty of Egypt. For six generations this royal family was a matriarchy.

Tiy

fl. 1400 B.C.; Egypt
Queen Tiy, wife of the Pharaoh Amenhotep III, was the mother of Nefertiti and Aknaton. Amenhotep, who was very fond of Tiy, issued a commemorative scarab throughout Egypt in an effort to induce the people to accept her, despite the fact that she was a

commoner. Tiy corresponded with many foreign rulers in an effort to maintain peace.

Many women outside of Egypt still enjoyed the privileges inherited from antiquity and the traditional power of women.

Bel-Shalti-Narrar

fl. 540 B.C.; Babylonia
Because the priestess tradition was well established in Bel-Shalti-Narrar's family, her father – the last King of Babylon – dedicated her as High Priestess to the Moon God at Ur. Historical records give evidence that high priestesses of the time were revered as wise women and consulted in vital political, governmental, and military matters.

Dido

fl. 850 B.C.; North Africa
Dido was a Phoenician princess who fled her home when her brother murdered her husband while attempting to seize the husband's treasures. After long wanderings, she settled on the African coast of the Mediterranean, where she founded the great city of Carthage. Dido later killed herself rather than submit to a forced marriage with a neighboring chief, who threatened war with the city if she refused him. Carthage grew and prospered for 600 years, however, until it was finally destroyed by the Romans in 45 B.C.

Lucretia

fl. 600 B.C.; Etruria
According to legend, a group of young nobles, in an effort to test the character of their wives, surprised them in their quarters. Some were feasting and others were sleeping, but Lucretia was found sitting with her handmaidens,

weaving at her loom. One of the king's sons returned secretly later that night and threatened to kill Lucretia and one of her slaves if she didn't submit to his sexual advances. After the rape, she sent for her husband and father, told them what had happened, and killed herself, fearing that her rapist would accuse her of adultry. When Lucretia's story became known, the citizens rose against their king and insisted on an end to such abuses of royal power.

Makeda

(Queen of Sheba)
fl. 950 B.C.; North Africa
In an effort to improve trade between her country and Israel, the Queen of Sheba traveled twelve hundred miles to meet with King Solomon. Makeda was a scholar as well as a ruling queen, and in her country women were involved equally with men in civil, religious, and military functions. She was probably also the Queen of Abyssinia, and there is some evidence that she reigned over Egypt and/or Ethiopia as well. Her personal accomplishments, however, have been obscured by her reputed relationship with Solomon, who supposedly was responsible for her conversion to Judaism.

Mama Oclo

fl. 800 B.C.; Peru
It is said that Mama Oclo taught the women of ancient Peru to sew, weave cotton and wool, and make clothes.

Naqi'a

704–626 B.C.; Assyria
Naqi'a was a great and energetic ruler who played

an outstanding role in both the internal and the general politics of the court. During the reigns of her son and grandson, she occupied the post of king mother – a position more active and revered than the later post of regent. Naqi'a was officially represented with her son on a bronze tablet, a sign of the high esteem in which she was held.

Nicaula

fl. 980 B.C.; Ethiopia
A learned woman and one of the wealthiest queens of the ancient world, Nicaula may have ruled over Arabia as well as Ethiopia and Egypt. At a time when knowledge was generally scorned, she traveled widely in order to study with the greatest teachers of the time.

Nitocris

6th c. B.C.; Assyria
Queen Nitocris was said to have been a woman of extraordinary abilities who helped sustain the Babylonian Empire through her public works. She built a bridge over the Euphrates to connect the two parts of Babylon, thus improving commerce and trade. Upon her death she left a vast sum of money to be used by the city in the case of dire need.

Puduchepa

fl. 1280–1250 B.C.;
Hittite Empire
Queen Puduchepa, the daughter of a priest, had once been a priestess herself. She played an active role in the affairs of state, and nearly all the royal documents of the time were signed jointly by her and her husband, Hattusilis III. She continued her religious duties throughout his life, carrying out the traditional role of priestess-queen.

Semiramis

fl. 650 B.C.; Assyria
As Queen of Assyria, Semiramis was responsible for making Babylon one of the most magnificent cities in the world. In order to bring irrigation to its deserts and plains, she leveled mountains, filled valleys, and constructed dikes and aqueducts. She also conquered nations in military campaigns which took her as far as India. During these expeditions she invented and wore trousers so she could move about more freely. An outstanding testimony to her importance as an energetic queen is the fact that she was the only female ruler represented in a row of stelae of the Great Assyrian Kings at Ashur. Semiramis reigned for forty-two years, but her son plotted against her and may have been responsible for her death. Legend says, however, that she turned into a dove and became a deity.

Tanaquil

fl. 570 B.C.; Etruria
Tanaquil became Queen of Rome and, when her husband died, managed to preserve the crown for her daughter's husband. Historians do not describe her role as queen dowager in detail, although it is known that she was very well regarded by the Romans. They renamed her Gaia Cyrilla, which means "the good spinner," a reference to her marvelous needlework and weaving. Women were urged to emulate Queen Tanaquil, and a law was passed that required newly married women to mention her Roman name (Gaia) upon first entering their houses in order to bring good fortune upon themselves.

117

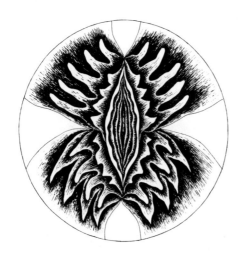

Judith

6th c. B.C.

According to prevailing thought, Jewish society was always patriarchal, but careful reading of the ancient texts calls this idea into question. The Jews, like all early peoples, were matriarchal and worshiped a goddess. It required six centuries for Yahweh (God) to replace the goddess Astoreth as the primary deity of the Jews. Thereafter, Hebrew women gradually came to be treated like chattel, so that eventually they were subject to the total control of their fathers and then their husbands, who could divorce them at will. They lost all their legal rights and could neither own property nor engage in business on their own. Girls were raised with only the goal of marriage and procreation in mind. Once married, they were required to do all the household work and manual labor while their husbands taught or studied or worked. However, Jewish women were educated in order to teach their sons about Jewish law. This resulted in a somewhat inconsistent doctrine – women were encour-

aged to be intelligent and assertive, but their intellectual power was seen as positive only if it was directed toward the family rather than toward personal fulfillment.

Nonetheless, Judith was not the only heroic woman in Hebrew history. Jewish matriarchs were hardly all passive and repressed; many were scholars and leaders. There were certainly those who were submissive, but generally the stronger figures were more respected – unless they openly rebelled against patriarchal authority, in which case they were denigrated or punished.

Abigail

fl. 1060 B.C.; Hebrew
Abigail has been called the earliest female pacifist on record and the wisest woman in the Old Testament. David – the shepherd who would become king – asked Abigail's husband, Nebal, for provisions. He drunkenly refused, but Abigail generously prepared food for David and his men. Her husband died soon thereafter; she then married David, her gentle character moderating his tempestuous and willful personality.

Beruriah

n.d.; Hebrew
Beruriah, a scholar and legal expert, was one of the few women in Jewish history to write commentaries on the law and is the only woman mentioned in the *Talmud*. She often contradicted the judgments of her rabbi husband, which greatly threatened him. In an effort to discredit her, he ordered a student to attempt to seduce her. After numerous efforts, he finally succeeded, and, as a result, Beruriah committed suicide.

Deborah

fl. 1351 B.C.; Hebrew
Deborah, the only woman of her time to possess political power by common consent of the people, is the sole female judge mentioned in the Scriptures. Her position was rare in that she was a prophetess, and prophetic functions were given to no judges before Samuel. When the Jews were being intolerably oppressed, Deborah developed a plan to overthrow the enemy with a military man named Barah. The latter, sensing the spiritual insight Deborah possessed, said, "If thou will go with me, then I will go; but if thou will not go with me, then I will not go." This is one of the most unusual passages in the Bible, spoken by a man to a woman. Deborah assured him that God would deliver the enemy into the hands of a woman, and her prophecy was fulfilled when a woman slew the leader of the enemy army. To celebrate the victory, the *Ode to Deborah* was composed (in which she is referred to as the Mother of Israel). She then governed the Hebrews in peace for forty years.

Esther

fl. 475 B.C.; Hebrew
When the King of Persia selected Esther from a group of the most beautiful virgins in the land, he did not know she was Jewish. He married her, and, after he had issued a decree ordering the massacre of the Jews, his wife told him she was Jewish. She then convinced him to reverse the order and pass a law which allowed the Jewish people the right to defend themselves against their enemies. The holiday of Purim is celebrated in Esther's honor.

Huldah

fl. 624 B.C.; Hebrew
Huldah, one of the wisest and most pious members of the Jewish nation, was often consulted by kings and religious leaders. Jewish tradition reveres her as a teacher and prophetess.

Miriam

fl. 1575 B.C.; Hebrew
Known primarily as the sister of Moses, who guarded him (though still a child herself) until he was saved by the Pharaoh's daughter, Miriam has been reduced to a minor figure by historians. It is clear in reading the Bible, however, that she was as much a leader of the Jewish people as Moses. As a grown woman, she was a prophetess and teacher. While Moses led the men of Israel, Miriam led the women to freedom, walking on the dry sea bottom after a strong wind had backed up the waters.

Zipporah

fl. 1500 B.C.; Hebrew
Zipporah, a learned woman, studied medicine alongside her husband Moses at the medical school in Heliopolis, Egypt. Her resistance to the religious beliefs of her husband was manifested in her refusal to allow the circumcision of her two sons. Only the violent illness of Moses, which she viewed as a sign of God's anger toward her, persuaded her to worship Jehovah. She finally circumcised one of her sons, which might signify a shift in her beliefs, simple fear, or submission to Moses' request.

There were a number of mythical and real women in Jewish history who attempted to carry on the matriarchal tradition or to reinstate Goddess worship. Several either openly rebelled or simply went on practicing prophecy and healing.

Athaliah

fl. 842 B.C.; Hebrew
Athaliah, the daughter of Queen Jezebel, claimed the throne of Judah as her own despite the fact that Hebrew law forbade women to reign alone. Much to the distress of the Hebrew patriarchs, she reinstated the ancient Mother Goddess religion during her six-year reign. Athaliah was so popular that it required a violent revolution to dethrone her.

Jezebel

9th c. B.C.; Hebrew
Married to King Ahab, leader of the Jews, Jezebel converted him to her belief in the Goddess, but the men of the society were very hostile to her beliefs and her influence over the king. After ruling the northern kingdom of Israel for over three decades, Jezebel was killed by fanatical worshipers of Jehovah.

Lilith

Apochryphal
According to Hebrew legend, Lilith was created by God at the same time and in the same manner as Adam. She was Adam's first wife and his equal, but they were in conflict over the recumbant posture he demanded of her in sex. She fled when Adam tried to compel her to obedience. According to myth, Yahweh then sent three angels to retrieve her. They threatened that if she did not return, she would, as the mother of the human race, lose a hundred of her children every day. When Lilith still refused to submit the angels tried to drown her, but Lilith pleaded her cause so eloquently that she was allowed to live. However, she was then given to Satan as his wife and was henceforth seen as a heartless, devouring, tempting, and destructive force.

Maacah

fl. 915 B.C.; Hebrew
Queen Maacah attempted to reinstate the Mother Goddess religion within the Hebrew state, by then one of the strongest patriarchal structures in the ancient Middle East. She erected an image to Asherah (Biblical name for the Goddess), which was destroyed by her son. He dethroned Maacah and suppressed Goddess worship.

Vashti

fl. 475 B.C.; Persia
Queen Vashti, Esther's predecessor, was dethroned for disobeying her husband, the king. He and some of his princes were drunkenly bragging about whose wife was the more beautiful. The king wanted Vashti to "display her beauty to them," but she refused. Because of this, she lost her royal position and may have been beheaded. The King then decreed "that all the wives will give to their husbands honor, both to great and small...and that every man should bear rule in his own house."

Witch of Endor

fl. 1060 B.C.; Biblical
A wise old person (described as having gnarled hands, coarse leathery skin, and dark hair falling over stooped shoulders), the Witch of Endor – as she became known – told fortunes, prophesied, and practiced witchcraft. Many, including King Saul, went to her cave seeking counsel, for she had a reputation for making accurate prophecies. The Witch of Endor represents the continued tradition of female witches, seers, and prophetesses who, by Hebraic times, were continually being denounced as evil.

Other women mentioned in the Bible are discussed in relation to their roles as mothers – either like Eve, the mother of the human race who is considered responsible for its downfall, or like the mothers of those men who would rule the Jewish nation.

Eve

Biblical
Derived from earlier myths, the original Eve story was altered to make her appear secondary to Adam and responsible for all the evil that befalls humankind. That familiar story relates how Eve was created from the rib of Adam and transgressed against the wishes of God by eating the forbidden fruit of knowledge. But it would be hard to imagine human existence without a quest for knowledge, so Eve's act might actually be seen as that which defined human existence – i.e., the

119

reaching for the knowledge of life. Her punishment was endless pain in childbirth, a punishment enforced with increasing severity by the Church as it developed.

Leah

fl. 1700 B.C.; Hebrew
Niece of Rebekah, sister of Rachel, and mother of Dinah, Leah was the first daughter to be named in the Bible. She is representative of the passive role created by men for women; her father duped her into intercourse with Jacob, after which she married him and bore seven children – with no recourse and no protest. Her sons were among the major figures in the development of Judaism.

Naomi

fl. 1000 B.C.; Hebrew
During the famine of Judah, Naomi migrated with her family to Moab, a fertile area east of the Dead Sea, where she lost her husband and both her sons. After ten years she returned to Bethlehem penniless, accompanied by her daughter-in-law Ruth, who pledged her devotion in these immortal words; "…for whither thou goest, I will go; and where thou lodgest, I will lodge; thy people shall be my people, and thy god my god; where thou diest, will I die, and there will I be buried." This tale indicates the deep love, loyalty, and friendship that must have existed among women in Biblical times.

Rachel

fl. 1753 B.C.; Hebrew
Rachel and Leah, along with their two maids, mothered the twelve sons designated to head the twelve tribes of Israel. Rachel also had the dubious distinction of being the first woman in the Bible to die in childbirth.

Rebekah

fl. 1860 B.C.; Hebrew
After twenty years of childlessness, Rebekah conceived and then learned that she would bear twins. She asked God why this had happened, and He answered that "two nations were within her and two manner of people, and…the elder should serve the younger." She bore two sons, Esau and Jacob. Jacob was her favorite, and she convinced her husband Isaac to give his blessing to Jacob as his successor. When Esau threatened to kill his brother, Rebekah interceded. She sent Jacob away and never saw her favorite child again.

Ruth

fl. 1000 B.C.; Hebrew
Ruth was the daughter-in-law of Naomi and the central figure in the "Book of Ruth." She was living in her native land of Moab when Naomi, her husband, and her sons sought refuge there from a famine in Judah. Ruth married one of Naomi's sons; but when Naomi's sons and husband died, Ruth chose to follow Naomi back to Bethlehem rather than stay with her own people. Her loyalty to Naomi gained her acceptance by the Jews. In Jewish history Ruth represents the heroic woman of devotion.

Sarah

fl. 1900 B.C.; Hebrew
The story of Sarah is a didactic one, for her life was one continuous trial of her faith in God's promise that she was to be the mother of nations. After years of waiting, Sarah gave birth to Isaac when she was beyond childbearing age.

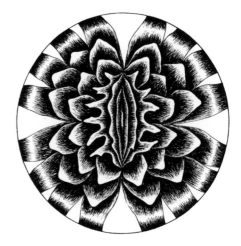

Sappho

fl. 600 B.C.

The island of Lesbos, where Sappho lived, remained conducive to women's creativity for some time after the Greek mainland had become repressive. The women who studied with Sappho maintained Goddess worship and enjoyed great freedom. It was not long after Sappho's death, however, that the lives of these women also began to be restricted: The religious festivals of women were taken over by men, who altered them to fit their needs; the men imposed limitations on women writers, excluding them from competitions; the men even tried to appropriate the ancient art of healing, which, like magic and music, had always been evidence of women's supernatural power. In the group of women surrounding Sappho on the Heritage Floor, it is possible to see various trends. The women who worked closely with her were able to participate in the rich heritage of female culture. Those in other parts of Greece had greater or lesser independence, depending on the laws governing women.

Amyte

3rd c. B.C.; Greece
A poet and healer, Amyte was represented in *The Greek Anthology* as having introduced pastoral poetry, which influenced Virgil. She was committed to a philosophy of equality, often asserting that in death the slave is equal to the king.

Carmenta

8th c. B.C.; Etruria
Carmenta, revered as a poet, a prophetess, and a queen, led her people into the area which would later become Rome. There she established her son as king and brought agriculture to the native inhabitants of the region. She also introduced them to music and poetry and was responsible for the building of the first temple.

Cleobuline

5th c. B.C.; Greece
Influenced by Sappho, Cleobuline collaborated with her father, Cleobulus, in the writing of *Griphor* (Riddles in Verse).

Corinna of Tanagro

fl. 490 B.C.; Greece
Corinna, called the Lyric Muse, left five books of poems and was the friend and critic of the great lyric poet Pindar. (It is a mystery why her work – which was greatly esteemed – has not survived, while Pindar's has.) Corinna was thought to be second only to Sappho in poetic ability.

Erinna

6th c. B.C.; Greece
Sappho's most gifted student, Erinna composed the 300-verse poem "The Distaff" before her nineteenth year, the year of her death. Her verses were considered as good as Homer's. Unfortunately, only fragments of her work are extant.

Manto

fl. 850 B.C.; Greece
According to Greek legend, Manto was the daughter of a Theban seer. Sent to Delphi to become a priestess of Apollo, she became famous for the inspiration and wisdom of her prophecies and it was said that Homer included many of her verses in his work.

Moero of Byzantium

3rd c. B.C.; Greece
Moero wrote a heroic poem, "Mnemosyne," plus numerous epigrams and elegies. Only two of her works are known.

Myrtis of Anthedon

6th c. B.C.; Greece
Myrtis was a member of a group of women poets who were referred to as the "Nine Earthly Muses." She was the teacher of Pindar of Thebes and also instructed Corinna, another of the nine famous poets.

Neobule

8th c. B.C.; Greece
Neobule was a poet whose engagement to another poet was broken off by her father. Enraged, her former lover blamed her, attacking her in a poetic form that was the basis for the creation of satiric verse.

Nossis

3rd c. B.C.; Greece
Well represented in *The Greek Anthology,* Nossis is one of the few female lyric poets whose work has survived. Only fragments remain, however, because most of it was destroyed by Christian monks. Many of Nossis' poems dealt with themes of special interest to women.

Very little information exists about women artists of the Greek period.

Anasandra

5th c. B.C.; Greece
Anasandra, the daughter of a well-known artist, Neacles, studied painting with her father. She eventually became an eminent painter.

Cresilla

5th c. B.C.; Greece
Cresilla took part in a competition with other sculptors to create seven Amazons for the ornamentation of the Temple of Artemis at Ephesus. She placed third behind Polyclitus and Phidias.

Helena

5th c. B.C.; Greece
Helena was a painter during the Hellenistic period in Greece. Her paintings were presented to a temple dedicated to Venus.

Kora

7th c. B.C.; Greece
Kora is one of the earliest woman artists of whom there are reliable records. She is credited with having created the first bas-relief.

Lalla

4th c. B.C.; Greece
Lalla, an artist, was known as "The Painter" of her time. She mainly painted portraits of women and executed at least one self-portrait.

Timarete

fl. 800 B.C.; Greece
Timarete was an artist who produced an image of Artemis, one of the most ancient examples of painting. The work was on view at Ephesus.

The Greeks considered music divine and – for a long time – the province of women. Priestess-musicians and poet-musicians like Sappho were quite common.

Nanno

6th c. B.C.; Greece
Little is known of Nanno other than that she was a famous flute player. Many elegies were addressed to her, indicating that she was a prominent musician.

Megalostrata

fl. 600 B.C.; Greece
Megalostrata achieved prominence as a poet, composer, singer, and leader of girls' choirs in Sparta at a time when female choirs were especially active and important in Greek life. Unfortunately, none of her compositions have been preserved.

Penthelia

pre-6th c. B.C.; Egypt
Penthelia, like other Egyptian women, was part of the tradition of musician-priestesses who were trained for service in the temples. She described the events of The Trojan War in song and story; her technique was said to have inspired Homer and other Greek poets.

Praxilla

fl. 450 B.C.; Greece
Praxilla came from the city-state of Sicyon, which had retained the earlier customs in which women played a leading role in the religious and musical life of the times. Her songs were famous and were sung by choirs and soloists at banquets and festivals.

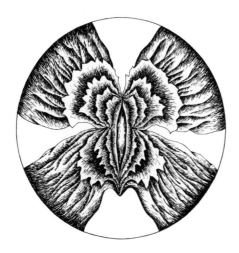

Aspasia
470–410 B.C.

Originally, all Greek women took part in the public councils with men and had a voice in decision-making. According to legend, however, when the women's vote defeated the men's over the question of a patron deity for the city of Athens, Poseidon – who had hoped to be elected – grew angry and submerged the city. In order to appease the god, the men deprived the women of the right to vote, transmit their names to their children, and be citizens. Women were relegated to total ignorance and obscurity except in religious and domestic matters.

This erosion of the position of Athenian women is clearly manifested by Aspasia's time, the presence of female goddesses notwithstanding. Male attitudes toward women were best summed up by Thucydides' famous remark: "That woman is best who is least spoken of among men, whether for good or evil." It is ironic that a society glorified for its democracy was probably harsher to its women than most other cultures of the time.

Aspasia exerted great influence in her day, and her accomplishments are even more remarkable when viewed in the context of women's exclusion from Athenian life. Her courage in speaking out encouraged others; there is evidence that because of her, Athenian women agitated for increased rights. Aspasia was not, of course, the only woman to make her voice heard. But those we know of have been described by history primarily as courtesans, rather than as the women of achievement they really were.

Arete of Cyrene
fl. 370–340 B.C.; Greece
Educated by her father, Aristippus, the head of a school of philosophy, Arete was unanimously elected to succeed him after his death. She was concerned with science and ethics and held a world-view that advocated equalized relationships among people. Forty works are attributed to Arete. She passed on the family tradition of scholarship to her son, whom she educated, just as her father had educated her.

Aristoclea
6th c. B.C.; Greece
Aristoclea, instructor of Pythagoras at the college at Delphi, was renowned for her wisdom and is said to have been responsible for improving Pythagoras' attitudes toward women. This resulted in many women becoming associated with the Pythagorean school of philosophy.

Damo
fl. 500 B.C.; Greece
Daughter of Pythagoras and one of his disciples, Damo was initiated into all the secrets of Pythagorean philosophy. She devoted much of her time to the education of other women.

Although poverty-stricken and tempted by many offers to sell her father's writings, she remained true to his wishes not to make them public.

Diotima
5th c. B.C.; Greece
According to the writings of Plato, it was Diotima who was responsible for instructing Socrates in social philosophy. She was a learned woman, a prophet, a priestess, and a Pythagorean philosopher whose theories on nature and life provided the basis for Socrates' dialogues.

Hipparchia
fl. 300 B.C.; Greece
A philosopher of the Cynic school of thought, Hipparchia was at one time the mistress of Alexander the Great and later became involved with another Cynic philosopher, Crates. She was resolved to live as he did, repudiating all comforts. Hipparchia wrote several tragedies, philosophical treatises, and other works, none of which are now extant.

Leontium

3rd c. B.C.; Greece
Leontium was among many young women who attended one of the "schools" for hetaerae in Athens. She became the companion of Epicurus – with whom she studied philosophy – but she owed her fame among her contemporaries primarily to her writings, none of which have survived. She was considered the most eloquent philosopher of her time.

Nicobule

fl. 300 B.C.; Greece
A celebrated author of the fourth century B.C., Nicobule wrote a history of Alexander the Great and composed many poems. Her works are no longer extant.

Perictyone

5th c. B.C.; Greece
Perictyone was a Pythagorean writer and philosopher who may have been the mother or sister of Plato. One of her works, *On Wisdom,* was praised by Aristotle, and another, called *Concerning the Harmony of Women,* dealt with the relationship between body and spirit, thought and action.

Phile

1st c. B.C.; Greece
Phile was elected to the highest municipal office in her city, that of magistrate, in which capacity she was responsible for the construction of reservoirs and aqueducts.

Salpe

1st c. B.C.; Greece
Salpe was both a physician and a poet, writing treatises on women's diseases and eye afflictions as well as poetry about athletics.

Theano

fl. 540–510 B.C.; Greece
A brilliant mathematician, Theano succeeded Pythagoras as head of his institute of philosophy and, when he was quite aged, married him. Theano, knowledgeable in medicine, hygiene, physics and early psychology, emphasized child-rearing and human relations in her writings. She first articulated the idea of the "golden mean," a major contribution of Greek thought to the evolution of social philosophy.

Theoclea

6th c. B.C.; Greece
Theoclea, a student at the Pythagorean school of philosophy at Delphi, later became a high priestess to Apollo there.

There were some women who, in an effort to be educated, disguised themselves as men.

Agnodice

fl. 506 B.C.; Greece
Agnodice studied medicine disguised as a man with the idea of becoming expert in gynecology and offering her services to women. After completing her studies, she revealed her true identity to women and they flocked to her, happy to have a gynecologist of their own sex. Male doctors were outraged that their female patients preferred Agnodice, though they did not realize she was a woman. They brought her to trial for malpractice and, when she publicly revealed her sex, tried to enforce the law prohibiting women from practicing medicine. Prominent women of the city protested and thus succeeded in having the law changed, at least until the twelfth century.

Aspasia of Athens

4th c. B.C.; Greece
Aspasia, who studied and practiced medicine in Athens a century after her famous namesake lived there, became renowned for surgery and was especially knowledgeable in the treatment of women's diseases. The titles of her medical writings were recorded by Aetius, a physician and writer of the fifth century A.D.

Some women, because they lived in parts of Greece where women retained some independence or because they refused to conform, lived as they wished.

Axiothea

4th c. B.C.; Greece
Axiothea was a student of philosophy who studied with Plato. As women were not admitted into his academy, she attended the lectures in male attire. Plato refused to commence without her, saying that he would not begin "before the arrival of the mind bright enough to grasp his ideas." It is not known whether he was aware of her sex.

Aglaonice

5th c. B.C.; Greece
Aglaonice was regarded as a sorceress because she was able to predict eclipses of the moon and sun by means of the lunar cycles discovered by Chaldean astronomers. Her observations were the result of her interest in astrology, rather than astronomy, and she insisted on referring to her scientific skills as "her will."

Cynisca

3rd c. B.C.; Greece
Cynisca, daughter of the King of Sparta, was celebrated for her skill in the Olympic Games. She won several victories in the chariot races and – as the first female to enter the Olympics – paved the way for others. She was also the first woman horse breeder in recorded history.

Elpinice

5th c. B.C.; Greece
In contrast to the women of Athens, Spartan women controlled two fifths of the land and property of Sparta through dowries, inheritances, and laws pertaining to property. Elpinice, an Athenian, took "The Spartan Woman" as her model and, rejecting the traditional domestic reclusiveness expected of Athenian women, participated fully in the intellectual life of the city.

Euryleon

3rd c. B.C.; Greece
In the tradition of the charioteer Cynisca, Euryleon won an Olympic victory in the two-horse chariot race. A statue of her was erected at Sparta in honor of her victory.

Hippo

5th c. B.C.; Greece

A martyr, Hippo killed herself rather than submit to the rape planned by a group of enemy sailors who were determined to violate her comitment to chastity. When her body was found and the reasons for her suicide understood, she was buried with veneration in a memorial built to celebrate her morality.

Lamia

4th c. B.C.; Greece

The most renowned flute player in antiquity, Lamia, a child prodigy, lived as an independent woman, traveling extensively and performing wherever she went. (She was considered a hetaera which – although it has come to mean a courtesan or prostitute – originally meant a woman who remained unmarried and free. Many hetaerae came from countries outside of Greece.) Altars were erected to Lamia, a festival was created in her honor and she was worshiped as a goddess.

Telesilla

fl. 50 B.C.; Greece

Telesilla, a lyric poet who wrote verses to Artemis and Apollo, saved her city during a battle with Sparta. She armed the women, repulsed the enemy, and was victorious. A statue in her honor was erected in the temple of Aphrodite at Argos.

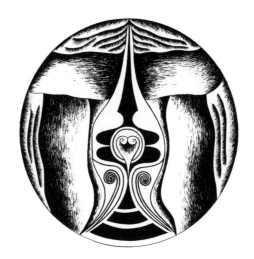

Boadaceia

1st c. A.D.

Tales of warrior women abound in myth, legend, and literature. Although there were probably not entire nations of warrior women, there is no question that our foremothers participated in battles, were involved in military strategy, and led armies in the countries they ruled. Celtic religion had powerful female deities who, much like Ishtar, conferred the right to rule on the king in a ritual mating designed to ensure the fertility of the land and the people. The worship of these goddess figures was reflected in the respect and independence Celtic women enjoyed. Boadaceia was not the only woman of the past to lead armies or to challenge the might of great powers. Invasion and occupation by the Romans, however, eventually led to the erosion of the original Celtic religions and, with it, the rights of women.

Basilea

n.d.; Celtic

Queen Basilea, the legendary daughter of Gaea and the first ruler of Atlantis, was a mythological figure who brought order, law, and justice to the world after the mythic war against the forces of evil and chaos.

Brynhild

n.d.; Germany

Brynhild was the most famous of the Valkyries, a band of German horsewomen and warrior goddesses and the counterparts of the Amazons. Depicted as virgins with swans' plumage who lived in forest lakes, they would become the slave of any man who stole their feathers. Brynhild's were stolen by King Agnar, whom she aided in a war against Hjalmgunnar. She defied the sky god, Odin, and he punished her by stripping her of her power and immortality and secluding her in a flame-encircled castle. She could only marry the man who would rescue her – and that was the German hero Sigurd, or Siegfried.

Medb of Connacht

n.d.; Ireland

A mythical warrior queen, Medb was the legendary ancestor of such historic warrior queens as Boadaceia and Cartismandua. Her predecessor was Macha, the fertility and warrior goddess who was worshiped in parts of pre-Celtic Ireland.

There were numerous women warriors, warrior-queens, and women who fought back when abused.

Artemisia I

5th c. B.C.; Halicarnassus
Because of the minority of her son, Artemisia assumed the throne upon the death of her husband. In 480 B.C. she became engaged in a military expedition against the Greeks, furnishing five ships and fighting in the great naval battle. She distinguished herself as a strategist comparable to any of the Persian generals. According to Herodotus, she was one of the most distinguished women of antiquity.

Artemisia II

4th c. B.C.; Halicarnassus
Artemisia II immortalized herself by erecting a tomb for her husband, Mausoleus. This *mausoleum* (from which all such subsequent monuments obtained their name) was considered one of the "Seven Wonders of the World." Though devastated by her husband's death, Artemisia ruled for the two years she outlived him. When the Rhodians attempted to dethrone her, she waged war against them and drove them back to the walls of their city, which she and her troops besieged in the year 351 B.C.

Cartismandua

1st c. A.D.; Britain
Cartismandua was one of the outstanding queens of Celtic antiquity. She ruled the Brigantes and led them to victory in several military campaigns, including one against her own husband. After triumphing against him, she challenged the Roman Empire, and – although she met defeat at the hands of the Roman general Agricola in 77 A.D. – she was celebrated as a heroine by her people.

Chiomara

fl. 180 B.C.; Gaul
When the Gauls were defeated by the Romans, Chiomara was one of the women taken captive. She resisted a centurion's attempts to seduce her, so he raped her. He then offered her her freedom in exchange for gold. She retaliated by cutting off his head, which she took to her husband as a symbol of her revenge.

Cleopatra

69–30 B.C.; Egypt
At the height of her power as the last great Queen of Egypt, Cleopatra fulfilled the prophecy that a woman would bring salvation to the strife-torn world. She was declared the New Isis, the embodiment of the goddess who exercised a passionate appeal for women and gave them equal power with men. Elevated to the position of ruler/deity after the death of her father, Cleopatra – who was well-educated, multi-lingual, and aware of her strength – was determined not to be used by nobles seeking power. Her foes, led by the guardian of her brother, young Ptolemy, drove the queen from the capital city. She then raised an army and, with Caesar's aid, conquered Ptolemy's forces and captured the throne.
In 47 B.C. Cleopatra had a son, whom she named Caesarion, and then joined Caesar in Rome until his assassination, after which she returned to Egypt. Two years later Cleopatra was proclaimed "Queen of Kings" by Mark Anthony. A new order was established by Cleopatra and Anthony which many thought would bring true partnership between Egypt and Rome.

The two leaders had a serious goal: the merging of the eastern and western parts of the empire. If they had accomplished their objective, the course of Western civilization would have been drastically altered.
Under Cleopatra's rule Egypt became an autonomous, allied, and protected kingdom. Her desire to extend the realm had been supported by both Caesar and Anthony at various times, but she was resented by the majority of Romans – both because she appeared on the battlefield with Anthony and because of her power. In 30 B.C. the army of Octavian defeated Anthony, who committed suicide, dying in Cleopatra's arms. She then killed herself by allowing a snake to bite her.

Cynane

4th c. B.C.; Macedonia
Cynane's father, Philip of Macedonia, arranged a marriage for her, but she was soon left a widow with a daughter, Eurydice. Cynane led her army to Asia to ensure that Eurydice would marry the heir to Alexander's lands. Certain leaders conspired against her and sent Macedonian warriors to kill her, but she persuaded them from their mission. Because the soldiers refused to murder her, one of the generals carried out the deed. Nonetheless, Eurydice then became Queen of Macedonia.

Eachtach

4th c.; Ireland
Eachtach was a warrior of such prowess that the men of Ireland saluted her with a distinguished burial, an unusual honor for a woman.

Macha

of the Red Tresses
fl. 330 B.C.; Ireland
Macha, a warrior queen, disguised herself as a leper in order to beguile her

enemies. She pursued them into the woods, captured them, and brought them – tied together – to Emhain. There a council ruled by women, instead of condemning the prisoners to death, made them slaves of the queen. The men then built Macha a fortress which became the capital of the province.

Muirgel

fl. 882 B.C.; Ireland
The warrior Muirgel slew the chieftan of the Northmen during an invasion of her country, thereby ridding Ireland of a longtime foe.

Tomyris

6th c. B.C.; Scythia
Tomyris was a Scythian warrior queen and founder of the city of Tamyris. Herodotus wrote admiringly of her, reporting that when Cyrus of Persia threatened invasion of her land, she placed her son at the head of an army to repel the invaders. After he was killed by the enemy, Tomyris led her forces in a fierce battle with Cyrus and was victorious. She then killed Cyrus, dipped his head in gore, and proclaimed that she was giving the bloodthirsty man his fill of blood for murdering her beloved son.

Veleda

1st c. A.D.; Celtic
A Celtic queen of the tribe of Batavi, Veleda was greatly respected by her people for her powers of prophecy. She was venerated as a goddess and lived alone in a tower. Approach to her was forbidden, and she directed affairs of state through one of her relatives.

Zenobia

ca. 240–300; Palmyra
Zenobia, the "Queen of the East," was a scholar, warrior, military strategist, and the administrator of a large empire. She accompanied her husband, the King of Palmyra, on all military ventures. After his death she took over the empire and waged war to conquer Egypt, Syria, and Asia Minor. She ruled for many years, and her court was the most splendid of that time. Because Zenobia's power was a threat to Rome, two emperors besieged her land. She repulsed the first attack, but was captured during the second while traveling to Persia to seek aid. She was taken to Rome as a valuable prisoner and lived to old age there as a highly respected noblewoman.

There were other Female rulers who were prominent in areas outside of Rome.

Alexandra of Jerusalem

d. 70 B.C.; Judea
The widow and successor of Alexander Jannaeus, Alexandra established peace in Judea after the bloody and turbulent reign of her husband. The later years of her rule were disturbed, however, by conflict surrounding her younger son's opposition to Alexandra's religious tolerance.

Aretaphila of Cyrene

fl. 120 B.C.; Cyrene
Widowed at the hands of a conquering tyrant and then forced to marry him, Aretaphila vowed to free herself and her country. Her desire was eventually fulfilled, and the people of Cyrene asked Aretaphila to reign, but she declined and retired for the remainder of her life.

Arsinoe II

3rd c. B.C.; Egypt
Arsinoe II ruled Egypt in conjunction with Ptolemy II, her brother and husband. Although the two were worshiped as divine and were both represented on Egyptian coinage, Arsinoe exercised the primary governing power, was responsible for the expansion of Egyptian sea power, and is credited with having founded a great city which bore her name.

Meave

n.d.; Ireland
A powerful ruler, Meave was married to King Ailill. She was the superior leader and strategist of the two and is credited with saving the city of Ulster from falling to the enemy. During peacetime, she provided stability in her kingdom through astute marriage alliances. Meave was also the original Queen Mab of fairy lore.

Olympias

fl. 350–320 B.C.; Macedonia
Olympias was the most prominent woman in Macedonia during the stormy period in history when her husband, Philip II, ruled that country. Devoted to her son, Alexander the Great, she worked to ensure his succession to the throne.

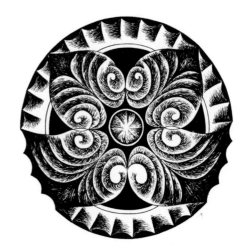

Hypatia

380–415
In the latter days of the Roman Empire, there were no legal or social barriers to stop an ambitious woman. Most women of Rome married and had children but were able to gain some control over the size of their families through contraception and abortion. Varied life-styles were tolerated by society, and, although women had cultural influence, they were totally shut off from the political sphere; however, most Roman women could exercise political influence through men. It is clear from their achievements that they had a great deal more mobility than their Athenian sisters.

Aemilia

4th c. Rome
Aemilia was a physician who wrote books on gynecology and obstetrics.

Clodia

1st c. B.C.; Rome
Clodia conducted a great salon which included many of the most gifted thinkers and the outstanding politicians of that era. She established a position of power through her salon and was considered a feminist in her day.

Cornelia Gracchi

fl. 169 B.C.; Rome
Cornelia's house was one of the social and intellectual centers of Rome. Fragments of her letters substantiate the fact that she corresponded with the most distinguished philosophers and scientists of her time. She was responsible for the education of her sons, known to history as the Gracchi, through whom Cornelia exercised a profound influence on Roman politics.

Cornelia Scipio

1st c. B.C.; Rome

Cornelia Scipio was well educated, a mathematician, a philosopher, and a musician. She was married to Pompey and traveled widely with him. Unfortunately, Scipio's later career is lost to history.

Hestiaea

2nd c.; Alexandria

Hestiaea, a Homeric scholar, was one of the first to attempt a scientific exploration of the actual locations of places named in the *Iliad*. She was also the first to throw doubt on the generally accepted view that new Ilium was the site of ancient Troy.

Hortensia

fl. 50 B.C.; Rome

Hortensia, an eloquent orator, represented fourteen hundred wealthy women who felt they were being unfairly taxed. An early advocate of "no taxation without representation," Hortensia argued that the tax money was being used for a military venture of which the women disapproved. She spoke before the Roman Forum and succeeded in having the taxes reduced.

Laya

fl. 100 B.C.; Greece-Rome

The first painter of miniatures, Laya was renowned for her paintings on ivory, particularly her portraits of women. Her work commanded large sums of money and is known to history through the writings of Pliny, who praised her highly.

Metrodora

2nd c. Rome

Metrodora was a physician who wrote a treatise on the diseases of women – the oldest extant medical writing by a woman. A twelfth-century copy, in the Laurentian Library in Florence, contains many valuable prescriptions for the treatment of diseases of the uterus, stomach, and kidneys.

Pamphile

fl. 20 A.D.; Greece

Pamphile was an essayist and historian who wrote a thrity-three-volume work as well as many shorter treatises. She was the daughter of a grammarian and the wife of a scholar.

Ima Shalom

fl. 70 A.D.; Hebrew

Despite the fact that Shalom's husband, a religious scholar, wrote, "Whoever teaches his daughter Torah, it is as though he taught her lechery." She was a highly educated and respected woman.

Sulpicia

1st c. A.D.; Rome

Sulpicia, the author of thousands of poems, was the first Roman woman to encourage other women to write poetry of as high a quality as that of the greatest Greek poets. Upset by the expulsion of Stoic philosophers from Rome, she wrote a satirical poem which chastised Roman men for not protesting this act. She also wrote a popular poem on conjugal affection.

Women were frequently brutalized, sometimes because of their sex and sometimes because of their religion. There were many female martyrs during the early days of Christianity.

Agatha

d. 251; Sicily

After Agatha – a noblewoman and Christian – refused the advances of the Sicilian governor, he used the pretext of her Christianity to avenge himself. He had her mutilated and rolled on burning coals, then left in prison to die.

Barbara

d. 235; Nicodemia

Barbara, a wealthy, well-educated woman, decided to convert to Christianity and remain a virgin. This so enraged her father that he delivered her over to a magistrate and exposed her as a Christian. She was cruelly tortured and then beheaded.

Blandina

d.177; France

Blandina was the slave of a Christian mistress and one of the forty-eight martyrs to die in Lyons during the persecutions of Marcus Aurelius, her body broken and mangled and then thrown to the beasts in the amphitheater. Somehow surviving all this torture, she was finally burned at the stake without once having recanted her faith. In her dying breath she cried out, "I am a Christian; no wickedness is carried on by us." Her courage impressed even her persecutors, who later regretted their actions.

Catherine

d. 307; Alexandria

Educated in the schools and libraries of Alexandria, Catherine was one of the most learned women of her time. When the Emperor ordered that all his subjects offer a sacrifice to the gods, Catherine – a Christian convert – tried to show him the falsity of his beliefs. He called together fifty famous university scholars to refute her, but instead she converted them all. Enraged, Maximinus had the men burned alive and Catherine brutally killed in a specially constructed machine, which had four wheels armed with points and saws that turned in opposite directions.

Epicharis

1st c. A.D.; Rome

A freed slave and revolutionary, Epicharis was involved in a conspiracy against Nero. The plot was uncovered and she was whipped, burned, and beaten, but she still refused to divulge any information or the names of others involved. The following day she was brought back to the tribunal in a chair because her body had been so badly broken that she could not stand or walk. She took off the girdle that bound her breast, tied it in a noose to the canopy of the chair, and hanged herself.

Philotis

fl. 380 B.C.; Rome

Philotis was a maidservant in Rome and led the female slaves in a plot against the invading Gauls, who demanded to be given the wives and daughters of the city. At the suggestion of Philotis, the slaves were dressed as Roman matrons and sent to the Gauls. When the troops fell asleep, Philotis lit a torch to signal the Roman soldiers, who then – together with the women – conquered the Gauls.

127

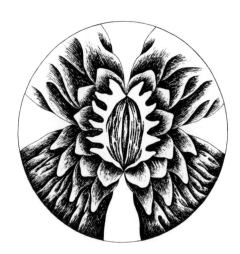

Marcella

325–410

Roman women were in a similar position legally to that of their Greek predecessors, but actually they were much freer. Although they were considered perpetual minors and were subject to the jurisdiction of their fathers and their husbands, public sentiment was at odds with the laws. These laws gradually improved, partly as a result of a protest organized by Roman women. Although their gains were later eroded, for a while women's opportunities were expanded; divorce was easily accomplished, and women could inherit property and exercise great control over their private lives. Generally, Roman women were able to participate in the cultural life of the times, and intellectual achievements enhanced a woman's reputation. Roman matrons could not, however, exercise political influence directly, which led to the political manipulations commonly practiced by upper-class Roman women.

Because the political powerlessness of these women has not been clearly understood by historians, many of their actions have been misperceived and their motives consequently maligned.

Agrippina I

13 B.C.–33 A.D.; Rome
Agrippina accompanied her husband, a Roman general, into battle and fought side by side with him. When her husband was poisoned, she attacked the man suspected of killing him, resulting in his death. She returned to Rome carrying her husband's ashes, and the city went out to meet her. She was exiled by the Roman ruler, who resented her popularity. When Agrippina challenged him, he had her blinded and her children persecuted. Finally driven to despair, she committed suicide by starvation.

Agrippina II

15–59 A.D.; Rome
Agrippina II ruled the Roman Empire in the name of her imbecile husband. Undeservedly vilified by history, in actuality her administration was brilliant and vigorous, and order was re-established during her ten-year reign. She was the first woman allowed to ride in the gilded imperial chariot reserved for priests, and on public occasions she sat next to her husband on an elevated throne. Agrippina was Nero's mother and was largely responsible for putting him on the throne. She soon realized, however, that he was going mad and would create chaos in the country. Nero eventually had her murdered to prevent her from threatening his power.

Caelia Macrina

2nd c.; Rome
Caelia Macrina, like other philanthropic noblewomen, invested in the future of her city by contributing to the welfare of its children. It is recorded that she personally provided for the support of over one hundred children.

Galla Placidia

ca. 390–450; Roman Empire
Although she suffered at the hands of powerful men who attempted to use her as a political pawn, Galla Placidia was the last significant empress in the crumbling Western Roman Empire. She ruled from Ravenna for twenty-five years as regent for her son and was responsible for many city improvements, including the construction of numerous public buildings.

Julia Domna

ca. 157–217; Rome
Well-educated in history, philosophy, geometry, and the sciences, Julia Domna communicated with the most distinguished and learned people of her time. She preserved literature and science, advised her husband in all governmental affairs, and became regent during the reign of her young sons. Banished by the ruler who succeeded her sons, she committed suicide by starvation.

administer property and in their husbands'

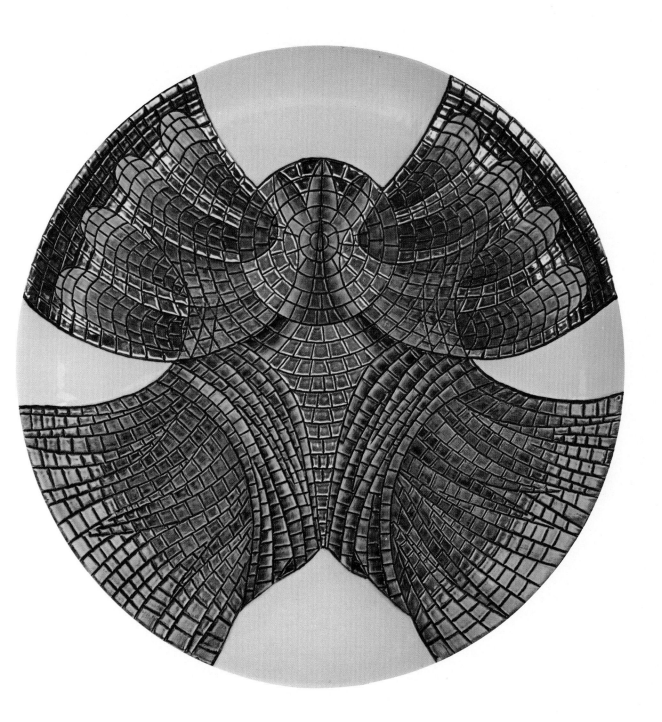

Theodora

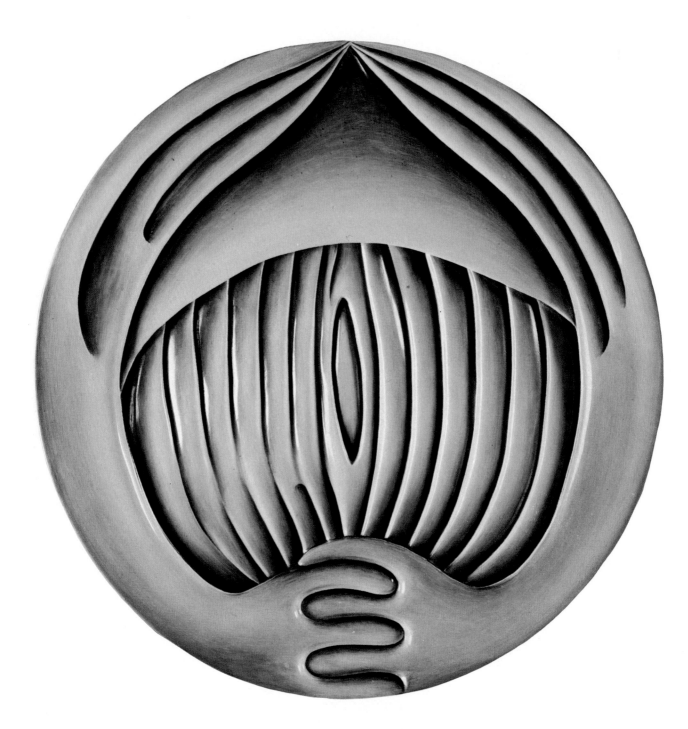

Hroswitha

the courts, signed treaties, made laws, and in

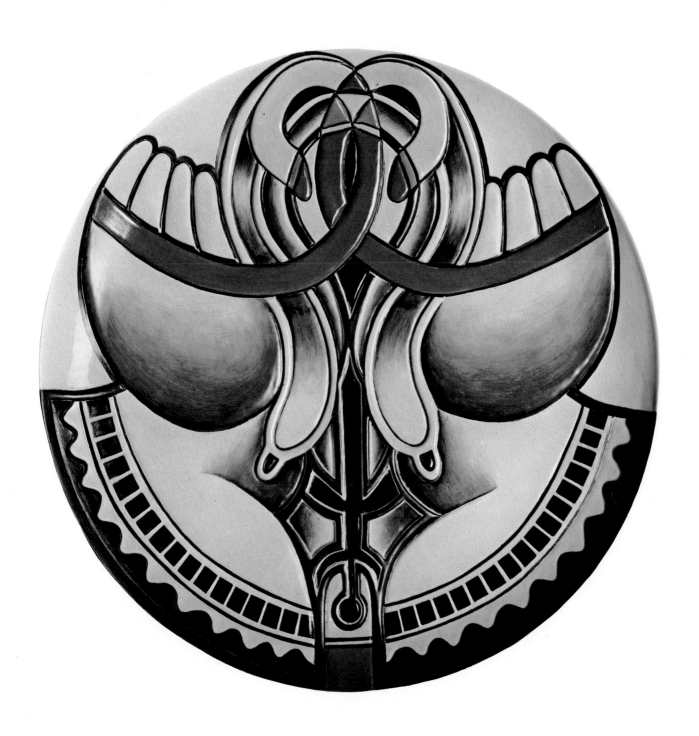

Trotula

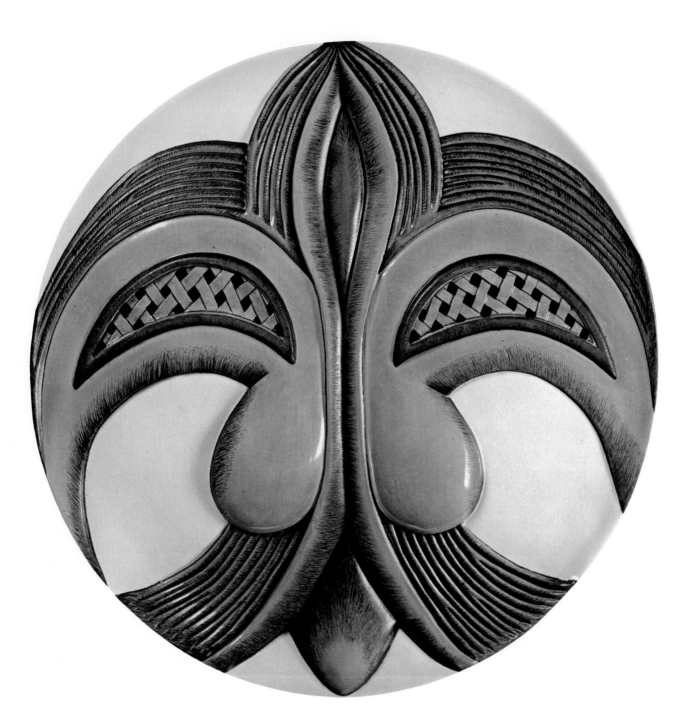

Eleanor of Aquitaine

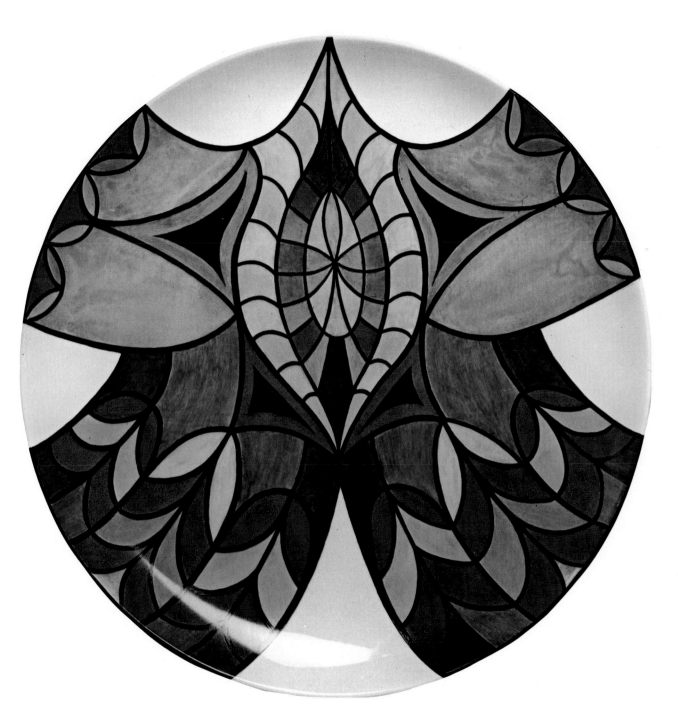

Hildegarde of Bingen

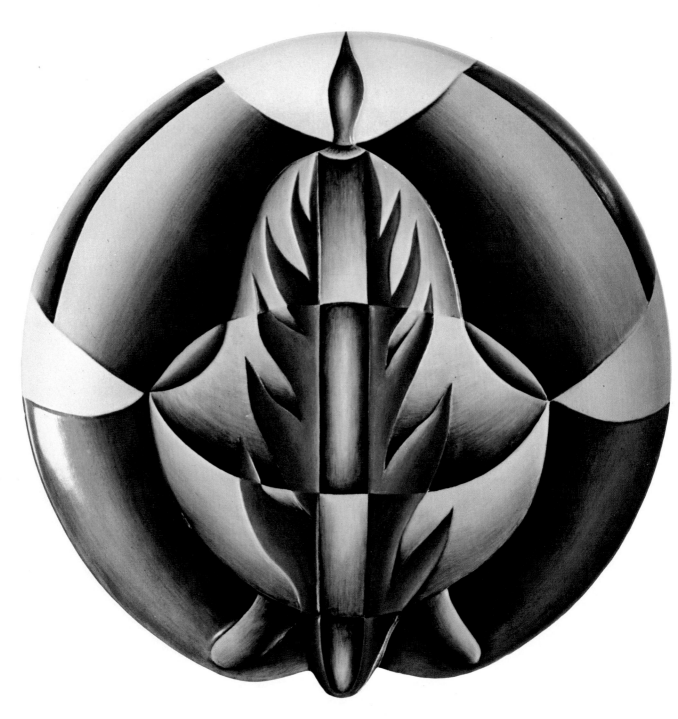

Petronilla de Meath

spread throughout Europe, it absorbed indigenous

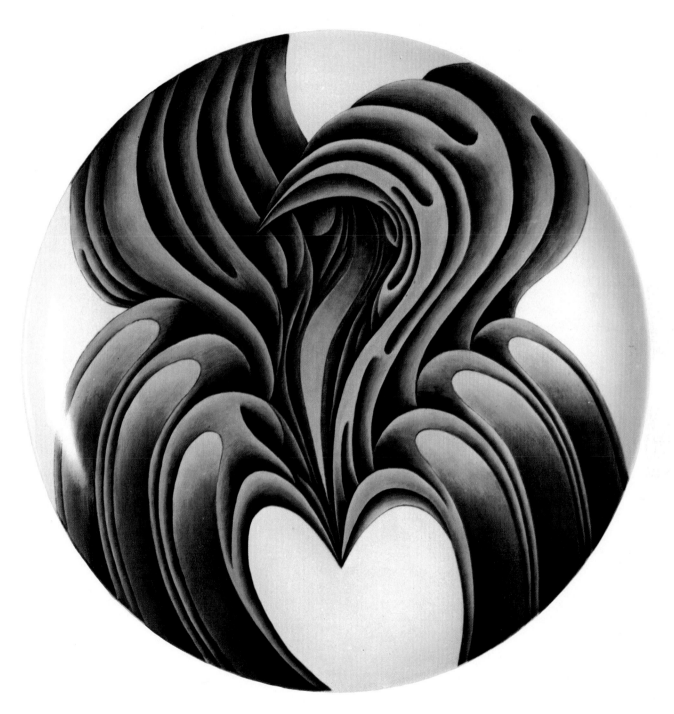

Christine de Pisan

religious practices, especially the continued

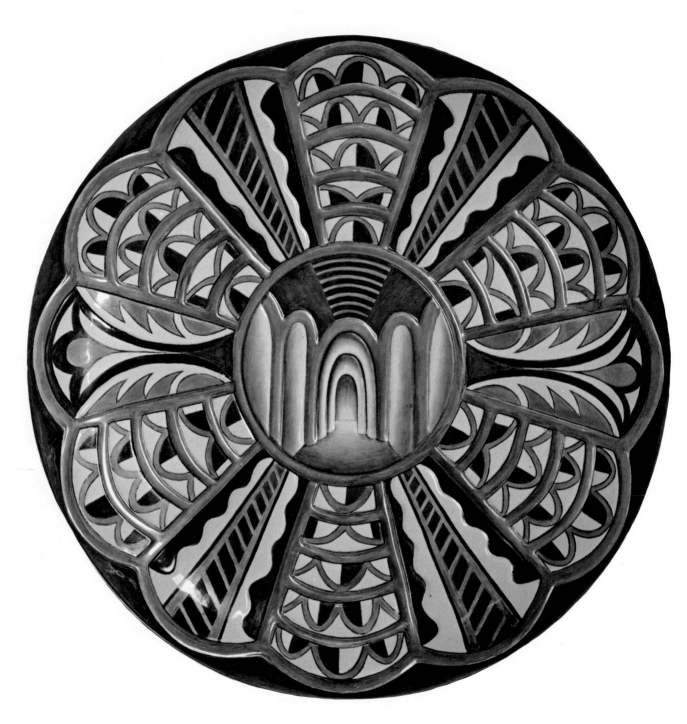

Isabella d'Este

Julia Maesa

fl. 217; Rome

Her knowledge of the workings of the Roman court led Julia Maesa to become skillful at manipulating political events. She was responsible for the respective ascents to the throne of her grandsons, Elagabalus and Alexander. Julia Maesa made a place for herself and her daughter Soemias in the Senate, and they participated fully in its governing activities. She became leader of the Senaculum, a body of women who decided issues pertaining to women, and she also acted as a military commander in the Roman army.

Julia Mamaea

d. 235; Rome

Trained in state affairs by her mother, Julia Mamaea led troops in a battle that established her reign in the name of her young son. Her reign was characterized by a level of peace, justice, and prosperity unprecedented in Roman history. She established a strong, democratic form of government, and the Senate, incensed at the incorruptibility of Julia Mamaea and her counselors, passed a law excluding women from its ranks. Although she spent money freely on public works and on such reforms as free public education for orphans, she failed to gain the loyalty of her soldiers, who felt that they were underpaid. The dissatisfied troops assassinated both the Empress and her son.

Livia Drusilla

56 B.C.–29 A.D.; Rome

As the first Roman empress, Livia Drusilla played a significant role in governing Rome for seventy years. Setting a precedent for future empresses, she was designated co-regent with her husband, Octavian, and was given the title "Julia Augusta." The couple's reign was marked by prosperity and tranquility, and Livia Drusilla was responsible for tempering her husband's harsh rule by modifying many of his decrees. She used her wealth to help the poor and persecuted and to establish a school for children. She worked to secure the crown for her son, who ultimately renounced her and thwarted the plans of Roman Senators to build an arch in her memory to honor her as the "Mother of Her Country."

Octavia

ca. 69–11 B.C.; Rome

As Roman Empress, Octavia was instrumental in preserving peace between two of the Empire's rulers – her husband, Mark Anthony, and her brother, Augustus. Although she had been recently widowed, Octavia's marriage to Antony was deemed so politically expedient that the Senate passed a special resolution allowing her to remarry before the end of the official mourning period. Marriage to Octavia strengthened Antony's political position in the governing triumvirate. However, when he sought to extend his power through alliance and marriage with Cleopatra, Antony secured the divorce against Octavia's wishes and sent his men to Rome to forcibly remove the Empress from her home. Despite this treatment, Octavia took responsibility for the welfare of all the children fathered by Antony, in addition to her own.

Plotina

d. 120; Rome

Plotina, Empress and wife of Trajan, was known for sound political judgment. She helped reduce governmental corruption, and she supported the Jews in a dispute between Jewish and Greek legations from Alexandria. She constructed harbors, highways, and buildings, fed orphans, improved the lot of slaves, and expanded the public education system. In recognition of her accomplishments, the Senate proclaimed her "Augusta." When Trajan died, Plotina, unable to rule in her own name, secured the throne for her favorite son, Hadrian. She continued to be active in government through Hadrian until her death.

Porcia

1st c. B.C.; Rome

When Porcia realized that Brutus, her husband, was planning a major coup and the assassination of Caesar, she inflicted wounds upon herself in order to discover how much pain she could bear without divulging her knowledge of the plot. When she learned that Brutus had committed suicide after Caesar's death, she followed his example, killing herself by swallowing burning coals.

During the earliest Christian centuries, there seems to have been little regulation of what was or was not "proper" Church work for a man or a woman. Women were involved in spreading the gospel, founding convents and hospitals, teaching, preaching, and administering religious houses.

Anastasia

d. 303; Rome

A noblewoman, Anastasia was raised as a Christian by her mother. Her father arranged her marriage to a wealthy Roman, who, upon discovering that she was a Christian, treated her harshly. After her husband died, Anastasia devoted herself to Scriptural studies and charitable works. She spent what was left of her fortune aiding the poor and Christians in prison. She was eventually imprisoned and burned for her refusal to practice non-Christian rituals.

Dorcas

1st c. A.D.; Jerusalem

An affluent woman whose name has become synonymous with charity, Dorcas made clothes for the needy. Out of her work grew the Dorcas Sewing Societies, now worldwide. Upon her death, Dorcas was said to have been resurrected by St. Peter.

Eustochium

d. 419; Rome

The daughter of St. Paula and a disciple of St. Jerome, Eustochium traveled with them to the Holy Land, where they founded the first women's convents in Bethlehem. Eustochium worked with her mother copying, translating, and revising the manuscripts of St. Jerome.

Fabiola

d. 399; Rome

Fabiola, a wealthy noblewoman, was converted to Christianity by Marcella. In divorcing her first husband she created a controversy, because divorce was by then regarded as a male prerogative. Upon the death of her second husband, Fabiola devoted herself to a ministry of mercy. In 390 she founded the first public hospital in Rome, where she was a nurse, physician, and surgeon, as well as a teacher of Christianity. She performed charitable works with Jerome, Paula, and Eustochium, and was important in the inception of a distinctly female order of Christian ministry. Thousands of people converged upon Rome to pay homage to her at her death.

Flavia Julia Helena

255–300; Rome

The first Roman Empress who was an avowed Christian, Helena was one of the most generous and influential supporters of the early Church. She and her son Constantine, the first Christian Emperor, were responsible for establishing Christianity as the official State religion. When her husband became Emperor in 292, he was forced to divorce Helena, who was a commoner, and marry a noblewoman. When he died, however, Helena saw to it that her son was proclaimed Emperor. Helena was then restored to power as Empress Mother.

Lydia

1st c. A.D.; Macedonia

A successful businesswoman in the city of Philippi, Lydia was engaged in the lucrative sale of purple dye and purple-dyed textiles – purple being the Imperial color of the Romans. She is mentioned in the New Testament as an early convert to Christianity, perhaps the first in Europe. Her entire household subsequently converted, and her home became a haven for Paul and his followers.

Macrina

327–379; Turkey

Macrina studied medicine in Athens and built a large hospital at Cappodocia in 370, including separate pavilions for different diseases and living spaces for nurses and physicians. Also a pioneer in monastic life, Macrina founded a women's community in Asia Minor. There she taught, preached, prophesied, and set an example of "no hatred, pride, luxuries, or honor." Her entire family was influential in the early Church, and she and her brothers, Bishops Gregory and Basil, were canonized.

Marcellina

4th c.; Rome

Marcellina received the Virgin's Veil in 353 at St. Peter's in the first known ceremonial recognition of a nun by the Church. She corresponded with her brother, St. Ambrose, who wrote his tract, *De Virginibus*, for her. This treatise clearly set forth the guidelines by which professed nuns were to live.

Martha of Bethany

1st c. A.D.; Jerusalem

Sister of Lazarus and Mary of Bethany, Martha was an early follower of Jesus. According to scripture, she prepared meals for Jesus, and was one of the women who opened their homes for the early practice of Christianity.

Mary of Bethany

1st c. A.D.; Jerusalem

Sister of Martha and Lazarus, Mary of Bethany was an early follower of Jesus. She anointed him before his crucifixion.

Mary Magdalene

1st c. A.D.; Jerusalem

Probably an influential and prominent woman from the town of Magdalen, Mary was one of the early female followers of Jesus. She was closely associated with him throughout his ministry, was present at his crucifixion and burial, and was the first to see and report the resurrection. The identity of Mary Magdalene has been obscured through various interpretations of the gospels; she has been confused with Mary of Bethany as well as with the unnamed "sinner" who anointed Jesus with oil and was forgiven by him for her sins. Around 600, Pope Gregory decreed that these three "Mary" identities be combined under the name Mary Magdalene, assigning her the character of the penitent prostitute. Thus Mary Magdalene and Mary, mother of Jesus, have come to symbolize the Church's polarized attitudes about woman – that she is either a virgin or a whore. Magdalene represents not only the Church's attitude that evil, associated with carnality, is embodied in woman, but that through Jesus she can find redemption.

Paula

347–404; Rome

A wealthy Roman noblewoman and scholar, Paula was converted by Marcella and became a philanthropist, ascetic, and founder of a circle of women who studied literature and practiced ascetic rituals honoring Jesus. She founded three convents, a monastery, and a hospital, and collaborated with St. Jerome on his translations of the Bible, many of which are dedicated to her.

Phoebe

1st c. A.D.; Rome

Phoebe was a deaconess of the early Church and was said to have carried Paul's *Epistle to the Romans* to Rome. After the persecution of Christians began, the deacons devoted themselves primarily to preaching, and the ministry of good works fell into the hands of women. An order of deaconesses arose who often wielded significant power in the early Church.

Priscilla

1st c. A.D.; Rome

An early Roman convert to Christianity, Priscilla, with her husband, Aguila, traveled with Paul to Ephesus. There they preached and held services in their home. Priscilla edited Paul's letters and was instrumental in having them copied and dispersed throughout the Empire. She was one of the most influential women in the early Church.

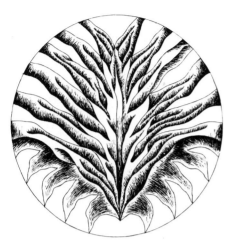

Saint Bridget

453–522

The Celts observed complete equality between the sexes. Women attended and often presided at the tribal councils; male chiefs were elected, but the monarchy was hereditary through the female line. Both sexes were educated equally and trained in sports. The existence of women poets, physicians, sages, lawyers, warriors, and judges is attested to by old records of Irish-Celtic society. When the Romans first encountered the Celts, they were outraged by a tradition so unlike their own – one that revered intuition and psychic knowledge. Invasions and the spread of the Roman Empire destroyed the Celtic culture and, in so doing, changed the shape of women's lives. The arrival of Christianity was at first beneficial to women, but later the Church became the source of great oppression, and that – especially in Ireland – has not changed.

Brigh Brigaid

70 A.D.; Ireland
Brigaid was a lawyer who rose to the position of judge, or brehan, and was responsible for many laws that were precedent-setting for centuries, particularly in the area of women's rights.

Cambra

n.d.; Britain
Cambra, a scholar and mathematician, was said to have invented the method of building and fortifying citadels. Because of her extensive knowledge and understanding, she was consulted by her father, a British king, on all important matters of state.

Martia Proba

4th c.; Britain
The English Common Law, upon which our legal system is based, was originated by Martia Proba, a Celtic queen. Perceiving the need for reform, she developed the Martian Statutes which introduced trial by jury – a concept unknown to Roman law – and incorporated ancient property laws that treated women and men equally.

Women throughout Europe were involved in the development and spread of Christianity. Some helped shape Christian dogma; others contributed to the organization of the Church. At first, women in the cloister were not required to take vows and were not enclosed. Unfortunately, as the Church became more formalized, women's freedom diminished.

Unknowingly, many women helped build a religious system that was ultimately destructive to them.

Basine

5th c.; France
Basine abandoned her husband, a king, to marry King Childeric of France, telling him that she had determined to marry him because of his great wealth and courage. Thought to be a prophet, Basine predicted that her son would possess the strength of a lion, but that later generations would be weak and would squabble like dogs. The predictions proved to be true. Her son, King Clovis, strengthened the Frankish kingdom and united it under Christianity, but later rulers, the Merovingians, weakened France through feudal wars.

Eugenia

d. 258; Egypt
Eugenia was a young, well-educated noblewoman, supposedly the daughter of the governor. She chose to convert to Christianity rather than submit to a political marriage. The bishop of Heliopolis allowed her to wear men's clothing and become a monk. She later converted her family and founded a convent in Africa. Upon her return to Rome, Eugenia was beheaded for her Christian beliefs.

Genevieve

b. 419; France
Patron saint of Paris, Genevieve was twice credited with saving the city. When Attila the Hun threatened to besiege Paris, Genevieve persuaded the women to pray for protection. They miraculously remained safe as Attila destroyed Orleans without touching Paris. A second time, she saved her people from famine by securing grain and distributing it among them. She is buried in a church whose construction she planned.

Lucy

d. ca. 303; Sicily
A noblewoman who converted to Christianity, Lucy refused a marriage proposal and was denounced as a Christian by the rejected suitor. Because she would not deny her faith, she was condemned to a house of ill repute, and when she would not move from the spot of the tribunal, she was tortured and murdered there.

Maximilla

3rd c.; Rome
Maximilla was one of the founders of Montanism, a movement that was a reaction to the increasing worldliness and ecclesiasticism of the Church. Montanism espoused fasts, trances, prophecy, and the religious equality of women and men. It defended the rights of women prophets, who were being attacked by conservative men in the Church.

Scholastica

480–547; Italy
Scholastica established the first religious order for women, and through her efforts, greater dignity was accorded to female monasticism. At her colony for religious women, the nuns devoted their time to worship, study, and manual labor. Through their spinning, weaving, and manufacturing of cloth, they developed a textile industry that was one of the triumphs of the Middle Ages. The women also copied religious and medical manuscripts.

Sylvia

fl. 398; France
St. Sylvia of Aquitaine was a noblewoman who left an extensive record – in the form of letters to nuns in a French convent – of a journey she made through the holy land.

Thecla

1st c. A.D.; Turkey
Thecla was one of the first women to preach and to baptize converts, and was responsible for converting many women to Christianity. She was closely associated with Paul, and the tract *Acts of Paul and Thecla*, accepted as authoritative for the first two centuries of the Christian era, calls her Paul's assistant. She may have been the unknown author of the books of *Luke* and *Acts* in the *Bible*.

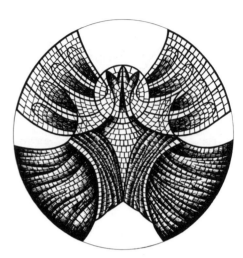

Theodora

508–548

Throughout the Middle Ages, there were a number of women rulers, many of them extremely forceful. The position of women in Byzantium, particularly as a result of Theodora's reforms, was higher than almost anywhere in the West. Moreover, Greek Church fathers continued to lay great stress on the basic equality of the sexes and the fundamental humanity of women. As they said: "Woman does not have one human nature and man another.... They both possess the same nature." Until the eleventh century, when an anti-feminist storm erupted, Byzantine women wielded considerable power.

Anna Dalassena Comnena

11th c.; Byzantium
Anna Dalassena, the mother of Anna Comnena, reestablished her family upon the Byzantine throne. Her son Alexius was declared Emperor, and Anna Dalassena Comnena was honored in recognition of the important role she played as mother and advisor to her son. For twenty years, she ruled the empire jointly with him.

Anna Comnena

1083–1148; Byzantium
Anna Comnena was a historian and one of the great medical writers of the twelfth century. Her fifteen-volume work, *The Alexiad*, the first extensive historical work written by a woman, was the history of the achievements of her father's reign and the events of the first crusade. She also was a physician, founded and supervised a hospital, and wrote medical treatises.

Her great ambition was to succeed her father to the throne, but her brother was the heir. Disappointed, she declared that nature had "made a pretty mess of things, clothing her masculine spirit with a woman's body." When her brother became Emperor, he put her in a convent. It was there that she completed her fifteen-volume history.

Damelis

9th c.; Byzantium
Damelis established factories where women wove magnificent silks, exquisite carpets, and fine linens. She owned much of the Peloponnesus and generously endowed the Emperor of Byzantium.

Eudocia

ca. 401–460; Byzantium
Eudocia was educated by her father, an Athenian philosopher, and eventually married the Emperor of Byzantium. A scholar, writer, and patron of education, Eudocia founded the University at Constantinople, where she encouraged the study of Greek literature. Later exiled to Jerusalem, she founded churches, medical schools, and a hospital where she personally tended the sick.

Eudoxia

d. 404; Byzantium
In the year 400, Eudoxia was crowned Augusta, Empress of Byzantium, and her portrait was sent throughout the Eastern Empire, a rare honor. She was a forceful and independent ruler, but her reign was cut short by an untimely and painful death through miscarriage.

Irene

752–803; Byzantium
In the five years during which Irene ruled the Eastern Roman Empire, she ended a war, restored a long-abandoned policy of religious toleration, lowered taxes and tariffs, reformed fiscal policies, founded charitable institutions, and proclaimed herself "Emperor," something no woman had done. Because there was a female head of state, the Pope severed all ties with Byzantium and named Charlemagne Emperor of the West. Irene sought reconciliation with the papacy, but she was ultimately dethroned and died in exile.

Leoparda

4th c.; Byzantium
Leoparda was a gynecologist of wide renown who practiced medicine at the Byzantine court.

Olympia

360–408; Byzantium
Olympia headed a community of women who cared for the sick and performed charitable works. She was a church deaconess and refused an offer of marriage from the Emperor to devote herself to her work.

Pulcheria

399–453; Byzantium
The daughter of Eudoxia, Pulcheria began to influence state affairs at the age of fourteen. When her father died, she formally took on the regency in the name of her brother, who was a minor. For forty years, she virtually ruled the Eastern Empire, even after her brother came of age. She counseled and directed him, and due to her wisdom, the Empire enjoyed an era of peace and prosperity.

Theodora II

d. ca. 867; Byzantium
Theodora II, like her predecessor Irene, possessed a natural talent for governing. Regent for her son, she preserved the tranquility of the Empire and enhanced its prestige. When her son reached his majority, however, he pressured his mother to retire to a monastery, and when she resisted, he had her removed from the throne.

Theodora III

980–1056; Byzantium

Zoë

980–1055; Byzantium
Theodora and her sister Zoë ruled the Byzantine Empire jointly after the death of their father, Constantine VIII, until Zoë forced Theodora into religious retirement. Because of the prevailing aversion to female sovereigns, Zoë adopted her nephew as a son. As soon as he attained the throne, he banished her to an island, forcing her to become a nun. But the people and the Senate revolted, insisting on the joint reign of the two sisters. Theodora, the more able of the two, gradually assumed control, and in order to prevent usurpation of her power, presided in person at the meetings of the Cabinet and the Senate and heard appeals as Supreme Court Judge in civil cases. Upon her sister's death, she took sole control of the throne, governing alone and refusing all offers to marry.

Pre-Christian German society was a loose association of clans, tribes, and groups of kin, which although already patriarchal, still retained strong evidence of an earlier, more matriarchal structure in their traditions, customs, and legends. Women's position in Germany was certainly not as good as in Byzantium, but nonetheless a few women were able to leave their marks.

Brunhilde

d. 613; Austrasia
Queen of the Franks, Brunhilde lived in Austrasia, a region peopled by the least cultivated of the Franks. She was originally from Spain and had brought with her many of the refinements of Roman civilization, which had been retained by the Visigoths there. Brunhilde tried to introduce a number of reforms; she oversaw the construction of highways, bridges, castles, churches, monasteries, and monuments, and she was an early patron of the arts. However, her efforts to improve the society met with great resistance. In 614, after a strenuous political life, she perished at the hands of Clothaire II, the son of an old political rival. He had the eighty-year-old woman paraded before the army on the back of a camel, then kicked to death by an unbroken horse.

Clotilda

475–545; France
Queen Clotilda was responsible for converting her husband, Clovis I, and three thousand of their subjects to Christianity, a turning point in the Christian history of Europe, and the act which resulted in Clotilda being honored by historians as the "Mother of France."

Engelberga

9th c.; Germany
Queen Engleberga, the wife of Ludovico II of Italy, was the first German woman of the Middle Ages to rule equally with her husband.

Maude

895–968; Germany
Queen Maude was convent-educated and continued to lead a pious, self-denying life, even after marrying Henry I of Germany. She favored her second son rather than the first as the successor to the crown. As a result, when the eldest, Otto, became king, he robbed his mother of her dowry, and forced her to take the veil. She took refuge in a convent while Queen Edith, Otto's wife, tried to accomplish a reconciliation between mother and son. Maude's wealth was finally restored. She used her dowry for philanthropic work – helping the poor and establishing hospitals, churches, and abbeys.

Radegund

518–587 Germany
Queen Radegund was a prominent figure in the medical annals of the early Middle Ages, and one of the first women to establish a convent in France. Kidnaped as a child, she was forced to marry her father's enemy, who became King of the Franks. She studied medicine with the most learned men of her court, converted her private palace into a hospital, and personally cared for all the patients. She eventually escaped from the court and took refuge in a convent, founding a religious house and hospital at Poitiers. Although she had abandoned court life, she still exerted influence on political affairs.

Theodelinda

580–628; Lombardy
Theodelinda, Regent of Lombardy, encouraged and improved agriculture, endowed charitable foundations, and built monasteries. She reduced taxes and attempted to allay the sufferings of the lower classes, something few male rulers of the time were able to achieve. Due to her influence, the Lombards converted to Christianity *en masse*.

Life in Europe during the early Middle Ages was extremely precarious. Invasions, warfare, and unstable governments left women vulnerable to rape, capture, and oppression. Unfortunately, the impact of this on the lives of women is only sketchily recorded. The information that does exist is, of course, about women of the ruling class.

Adelaide

931–999; Burgundy
Adelaide, a noblewoman and heiress, was married at the age of fifteen, widowed at eighteen, and then imprisoned and tortured for refusing to marry an invading conqueror. She escaped and was rescued by Otto I of Germany. Their son, Otto II, who succeeded his father, turned against her. Adelaide fled to Burgundy where she spread her wealth among the French abbeys and rebuilt the monastery of St. Martin of Tours. She returned to Germany and eventually re-established her influence.

Aethelburg

fl. 680–700; England
Aethelburg ruled jointly with her husband, Ine, King of Wessex. It was common for women to have influence and power within Anglo-Saxon governments.

Aethelflaed

d. 918; England
The daughter of Alfred the Great, Aethelflaed ruled jointly in England with her husband, the Earl of Mercia. She gained complete control of the country after his death and was given the title of King. She began establishing a network of fortresses which later developed into centers of government and commerce, and no other woman of the Saxon era conducted military operations on a comparable scale.

Balthilde

7th c.; France
Born in England, Bathilde was a princess who was captured, sold into slavery, taken to France, and married to Clovis II, the Frankish King. At his death in 657, she became ruler. During her administration she restored the rights of individuals, abolished the slave trade in France, and equalized taxation.

Bertha of England

d. 612; England
Through Bertha's influence, Christianity was introduced into England. In order to create a political alliance between England and France, Bertha, who was French, was married to the King of Kent. The marriage contract stipulated her right to practice Christianity. Bertha established the first Christian Church at Canterbury and was also primarily responsible for establishing the first body of written law in England.

Fredegund

d. 597; France
Queen Fredegund exerted influence directly upon the political and ecclesiastical affairs of her time. From a peasant background she rose to become the wife of Chilperic, the Frankish king. She is said to have planned and executed his assassination, a political act with precedents, for Chilperic had murdered his first wife in order to marry Fredegund. She became sovereign and the guardian of her infant son, holding this position for thirteen years.

Olga

892–971; Russia
Olga, Princess of Kiev, was married to Igor, second monarch of Russia. After his assassination, she ruled the country wisely and firmly, improving the system of government, regulating the amount of taxes to be paid by different provinces, and establishing courts of justice. Converted to Christianity in 959, she paved the way for the general conversion of the Russian people some thirty years later under her grandson Vladimir.

Wanda

8th c.; Poland
Legend attests that Queen Wanda's beauty attracted a German prince who fell in love with her and began a violent suit for her hand. When she refused him, he threatened to invade her domain and make her his wife by force. Rather than submit, she gathered a large army and defeated the Germans. She returned triumphantly to Cracow, but fearing that her beauty might cause more wars, threw herself into the river and drowned. Traditional poetry, art, and music have commemorated her self-sacrifice, but contemporary thought questions it.

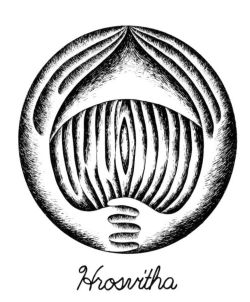

Hroswitha

935–1002

The early convent was the home of very spirited women, and there is no doubt that its immense popularity during the Middle Ages was largely due to women's need to escape, not from life, but from subordination. Many highborn women refused to relinquish their property to their husbands and established religious houses instead. There, they gathered other women and enjoyed opportunities not available at home. Convents became places of residence and training schools for women of the ruling classes. Girls came there to be educated and either considered the convents as their permanent homes or left to be married, frequently returning in later life. Those who wished to devote themselves to learning and the arts gathered there with or without taking religious vows. The convent fostered some of the best sides of intellectual, moral, and emotional life for some centuries. Religious women were held in great esteem and treated with respect. Many traveled widely and received visitors freely, thus allowing continual interchange with the religious, political, and intellectual leaders of the day.

"And how, I ask, does the wife stand it when she comes in, hears her child scream, sees the cat at the flitch and the hound at the hide? Her cake is burning on the stove, her calf is sucking up the milk, the earthen pot is overflowing into the fire, and the servant is scolding. Though it be an odious tale, it ought, maiden to deter Thee more strongly from marriage, for it does not seem easy to her who has tried it. Thou, happy maiden, to deter Thee more thy self out of the servitude as a free daughter of God?"
—Anonymous medieval nun

Agnes

fl. 1184–1203; Germany

Agnes, abbess at the monastery of Quedlinburg, supervised the manufacture of tapestries and collaborated with her nuns on ecclesiastical embroidery as well as manuscript illumination.

Athanasia

d. 860; Greece

Because vows of celibacy were forbidden due to the small population, Athanasia's parents arranged a marriage despite her desire for a religious life. Her husband later chose to become a monk, and she inherited all his possessions. Athanasia opened her house to other women and founded a great convent.

Begga

d. 698; Belgium

Begga was the daughter of Blessed Ata and the sister of St. Gertrude. Begga established a convent at Ardenne and was believed to be the founder of the Order of the Beguines.

Berthildis

d. 680; France

One of the most famous ruling abbesses of the seventh century, Berthildis restored the Abbey of Chelles, near Paris. She abolished slavery and oppressive taxation within the region. Her reforms aroused strong opposition, and she was forced to retire to another monastery and devote her life to medical work.

Bertille

652–702; France

Daughter of a propertied family near Soissons, Bertille became a nun. At the request of Queen Bathilde, with whom she worked, she became abbess of the convent at Chelles, remaining in that position for forty-six years.

Eanswith

fl. 630; England

With land given to her by her father, Eadbald of Kent, Eanswith founded the first religious settlement for women in Anglo-Saxon England.

Ebba

10th c.; Ireland

In the ninth and tenth centuries, a new wave of non-Christian invaders assaulted Europe. Although the convents protected women, they were vulnerable because of their property holdings. Nuns were commonly raped and tortured by invading armies. When the Danish soldiers drew near, Abbess Ebba persuaded the nuns of her monastery to disfigure their faces. The whole community cut off their noses and upper lips, and when the Danes saw them, they were so enraged that they set fire to the convent and all the nuns were killed.

Ethelberga

d. ca. 616; England

Ethelberga established the first Benedictine nunnery in England, where she taught medicine to women and healed and tended the sick. She prepared the way for the mission of St. Augustine to England in 597 when thousands of people were baptized.

Gertrude of Nivelles

626–659; Belgium

After the death of her father, Gertrude and her mother, St. Ata, retired to a convent and Gertrude became the abbess at Nivelles. She brought monks from Ireland to educate her nuns. Devotion to her was widespread in Belgium, Germany, and Poland.

Gisela

d. 807; Germany

Gisela founded a Benedictine abbey where she became a nun and later an abbess. She directed the first major convent scriptorium which created thirteen manuscripts, among them a three-volume commentary on the Psalms, signed by nine female scribes who were probably under Gisela's direction. She was also a member of the scholarly circle in the court of her brother, Charlemagne.

Hilda of Whitby

614–680; England

Hilda, Abbess of Whitby for thirty years, was the most distinguished churchwoman of Anglo-Saxon times. The abbey that she established was a celebrated religious and educational center. The monastery housed both men and women and was a training ground for bishops, abbesses, and priests. Hilda was also the patron of Caedmon, the first religious poet to write in English. Hilda's power extended far beyond her convent and she greatly influenced the political and religious affairs of her time.

Lioba

d. 779; Germany

A pioneer in the Christianization of Germany, Lioba left England around 740 and traveled to Germany at the request of St. Boniface, a distant relative. He placed her in charge of all nunneries under Benedictine rule. She was thoroughly acquainted with religious writings, theology, and ecclesiastical law and became so learned that she was consulted in church matters and was considered the most important churchwoman in Germany.

Mathilda

10th c.; Germany

Mathilda was the abbess of the monastery at Quedlinburg and Hrosvitha's cousin. Because of her extensive knowledge of both medicine and history, she was able to supply Hrosvitha with information for her writings. She, together with Adelheid, regent for Otto III, practically ruled the Empire during Otto's minority. Later, the king entrusted her with the control of affairs during his prolonged absences, a common practice in the Middle Ages when abbesses were members of the ruling families. In 983, Mathilda raised an army and defeated the invading Wends.

One of the great attractions of the religious life was that it allowed women career options that were not available in secular life. In the convents, women wove and embroidered the great medieval vestments, copied and illuminated manuscripts, and wrote, studied, and engaged in musical activities.

Frau Ava

d. 1127; Germany

Frau Ava was a sacred singer and the first woman known to compose biblical and evangelical stories in the German language. As most religious writings were in Latin, Ava's work made Christian ideas available to the common people.

Claricia

fl. 1200; Germany

Claricia was a painter and illustrator and knowledgeable in manuscript illumination and bookmaking. There is a signed self-portrait of her in the Walters Art Gallery in Baltimore, Maryland. It was quite unusual at the time for a work to be signed.

Diemud

12th c.; Germany

A nun who worked as a calligrapher and manuscript illustrator, Diemud reproduced forty-five volumes that were greatly prized. One, a *Bible*, was so valued that it was exchanged for an estate. Her work, distinguished by its ornate letters and small elegant writing, was said to be of exquisite beauty.

Gisela of Kerzenbroeck

d. 1300; Germany

Gisela was a manuscript illuminator who worked independently in the town of Rulle in Westphalia until her death.

Guda

12th c.; Germany

Guda wrote and decorated a discourse on morality which is now in Frankfort. She signed it with a self-portrait, which is possibly the first surviving self-portrait of a woman in the West.

Harlind Reinhild

fl. 850–880; Germany

Harlind and her sister Reinhild were trained in religious practices and the arts at a convent in France. Returning home, the sisters found no secular use for their talents and decided to return to religious life. Their parents helped them establish a settlement in Germany devoted to weaving and embroidery. The women there, under the sisters' direction, created vestments and altarcloths and transcribed gospels and psalms.

Joanna

fl. 1200; Germany

With the help of several nuns, Joanna, the Prioress of Lothen in Germany, wove a series of tapestries telling the tumultuous history of their convent.

Medieval nunneries recruited largely from among the upper classes, primarily because of the narrowness of options available to noblewomen. In the lower classes, a woman could work in the fields with her brothers or spin and weave at home with her mother and earn a supplementary, if not a living, wage. Lower-class women actually had other choices than marriage

– if they didn't find a husband or didn't want to marry, they could be apprenticed to a trade or go into domestic service. But for upper-class women, the only alternative to marriage was the convent.

Baudonivia
6th c.; France

Baudonivia was educated in the monastery of St. Croix at Poitiers, which was founded by Radegund. After Radegund's death in 587, Baudonivia wrote a study of her life which was included in the first volume of *The Acts of the Saints of St. Benoit.*

Dhuoda
9th c.; France

Dhuoda, a devout and aristocratic woman, wrote the *Manual*, which chronicles the time when the Empire of Charlemagne was breaking up.

Ethylwyn
11th c.; England

Ethylwyn embroidered ecclesiastical vestments and was a friend of Queen Edith, who was a patron of needlework. Ethylwyn's needlework was renowned throughout England. The designing of this work was often a collaborative effort among the women needleworkers, the archbishop, and the queen.

Gormlaith
10th c.; Ireland

Gormlaith was influential in planning the Battle of Clantarf, which drove the invading Danes from Ireland. She was also Ireland's first female historian, writing verse and history to preserve Irish traditions.

Hygeburg
8th c.; England

Hygeburg recorded the recollections of Willibald, Bishop of Eichstat, the first Englishman known to have traveled in the Near East. Her book is the earliest extant travel documentation and the first book written by an Englishwoman. She was an English nun who accompanied Boniface and helped him convert Germany.

Liadain
9th c.; Ireland

A renowned poet of Ireland, Liadain benefited from the monastic system of the Middle Ages in which women could obtain education.

Mabel
13th c.; England

Mabel was a professional embroiderer who was commissioned by Henry III of England to execute a gold and ruby banner for Westminster Abbey.

Elizabeth Stagel
ca. 1300–1360; German Empire

Stagel was a Dominican nun, as well as a historian, writer, and religious reformer. She wrote biographies of forty of the sisters who lived in her convent in what is now Switzerland. She was also associated with an informal religious group known as the Friends of God and was largely responsible for recording much of their history.

Lady Uallach
d. 932; Ireland

A learned woman in the tradition of St. Bridget of the sixth century, Uallach was one of the great poets of Ireland.

Outside of the cloister, women usually wielded power in conjunction with men. They were mothers, daughters, sisters, or wives of rulers and came by their positions through marriage or heredity. Because the following women were all connected to Charlemagne, we know quite a lot about them, although some of the information is contradictory.

Bertha
d. 783; Frankish Empire

Queen of the Franks, Bertha was a very strong-willed and able ruler. During the reign of her husband, Pippin III, she performed administrative duties and ran the royal household. She also held a court of women which made laws concerning women. Bertha was responsible for her son Charlemagne's education, and many of his later religious policies can be directly attributed to her influence.

Bertha of France
8th c.; Frankish Empire

Bertha was one of the daughters of Charlemagne, all of whom were forbidden to marry because their father "loved" them so much he couldn't bear to part with them. She was a scholar and musician, singing famous poems of the day and accompanying herself on a stringed instrument.

Carcas
8th c.; France

Carcas courageously sustained the city of Carcasonne during a siege in which her husband, the king, was killed. Charlemagne, King of the Frankish Empire, was so impressed with her bravery that he named her governor of the city. Later, the Saracens attacked her, jesting at the idea of a female warrior who should be "spinning rather than fighting." Carcas was so angered by this insult that she armed herself with a lance to which she attached a bundle of hemp, leaving only the point exposed. She set fire to it and rushed into the midst of the enemy, who were so terrorized that they fled.

Eadburga
fl. 730; England

Eadburga, Queen of Wessex, is an unclear figure. Some historians say that she achieved a reputation for her supposedly radical methods of gaining power. Accused of poisoning her enemies deliberately and inadvertently poisoning the king, she is then supposed to have fled with a huge treasure and been welcomed by Charlemagne. He is said to have proposed marriage, which she declined, stating that she favored his son. Outraged, Charlemagne said she could have neither and made her an abbess, perhaps thinking that celibacy was a fitting punishment for a woman who preferred his son to him.

But conflicting evidence suggests that Eadburga was an artist and manuscript illuminator and lived a relatively quiet life. Whether this contradictory information means that there were two different women with the same name, or one woman whose actions have been maligned, is unclear.

In Spain, during the Moorish occupation, there was emphasis on language and the intellect. Throughout this period, the high point of Muslim civilization, women had a great deal of educational freedom. This resulted in a flowering of female creativity, particularly around Andalusia, where there were a number of women poets, writers, and scholars.

Aisha

12th c.; Spain

A distinguished poet, Aisha left a large body of work, a well-selected library, and a reputation for having frequently presented her verses and orations at the Royal Academy of Cordova.

Maria Alphaizuli

10th c.; Spain

A poet, Alphaizuli was referred to as the "Arabian Sappho." Repeatedly in history, women are linked to a few earlier women as if there were certain "unchangeable" types of female achievers. Thus, Alphaizuli has not been compared to male poets of her period, but to Sappho, who lived over fifteen centuries before her, and whose work bears no resemblance to

that of this Spanish writer. Extant examples of Alphaizuli's compositions are preserved in the library of the Escorial.

Ende

10th c.; Spain

Ende, an artist and illuminator, executed the first extensive cycle of miniatures known to be by a woman. She also helped to produce the *Gerona Apocalypse.*

Leela of Granada

13th c.; Spain

Leela of Granada was a Moorish Spaniard who was celebrated for her learning.

Libana

d. 995; Spain

A Moorish Spaniard of noble parentage, Libana was an established poet as well as a philosopher and musician.

Maryann

9th c.; Spain

Maryann founded a school for girls in Moorish Spain which provided instruction in science, mathematics, and history.

Thoma

d. 1127; Spain

A distinguished scholar, Thoma wrote highly celebrated books on grammar and jurisprudence. She was also known as Habeba of Valencia.

Valada

d. 1091; Spain

Daughter of the King of Cordova, Valada was well educated, celebrated for her scholarship, and known for her skill in debate.

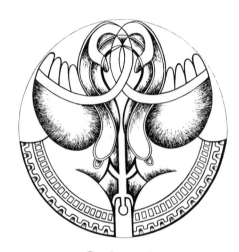

Trotula

d. 1097

From the beginning of time, women were considered the natural doctors, the bone-setters, the gatherers of medicinal herbs, and the only obstetricians. The study and treatment of women's diseases had traditionally been in women's hands, and there had been women surgeons in Sumeria, Greece, and Egypt. In the Middle Ages, because the men were so often away at war, much of the responsibility for medical care fell upon women. At home, they nursed their families; they rendered first aid for bruises and wounds and attended to the medical needs of servants and guests. Women were the pioneer medical missionaries as they went out from the convents to help the infirm, heal the wounded, and treat the lepers. Noblewomen provided nursing services on the battlefields, and, in addition to providing relief for the suffering, performed innumerable medical tasks, including the setting of broken limbs.

Abella of Salerno

14th c.; Italy

An instructor and lecturer in Salerno, Abella wrote highly esteemed medical treatises and lectured on the nature of women.

Adelberger

8th c.; Italy

Adelberga, also known as Bertha, was a member of the guild of lay physicians in Northern Italy.

Etheldreda

ca. 630–679; England
Etheldreda founded the church and convent at Ely in 673, where she later became the abbess. She practiced medicine, taught the nuns how to treat disease and to care for the poor.

Francesca of Salerno

fl. 1321; Italy
Francesca, in the tradition of earlier Italian women doctors, studied medicine at the School of Salerno, but was only able to receive her degree in surgery after she had proven herself to a panel of male judges. She was able to practice medicine, however, only after obtaining permission from the Duke who governed the area.

Stephanie de Montaneis

13th c.; France
History reveals only that De Montaneis was taught the art of healing by her father, a physician in Lyons, and that she was a practicing physician.

Odilla

8th c.; Germany
In 720, Odilla built and ruled a monastery and a hospital which became famous for its cures of eye diseases.

Sarah of St. Gilles

fl. 1326; France
A Jewish physician in St. Gilles, Sarah practiced and taught medicine. She conducted a large medical school, and there is a document, dated August 28, 1326, sanctioning her to teach medicine to her husband.

Urraca

13th c.; Portugal
Queen of Portugal and sister of Blanche of Castile, Urraca was famous for her hospital work and support of advanced medical practices.

Walpurgis

710–778; England
Walpurgis was an English princess who studied medicine in order to practice among the poor. She went to Germany as a missionary and became an abbess at a monastery she founded in Heidenheim, near Munich.

Medieval records are full of independent women who, despite prevailing ideas of either women's inferiority or superiority, enjoyed a kind of equality.

Aloara

d. 992; Italy
From 982 until her death, Aloara ruled the principality of Capua with her son Landenulph. She was recorded as having been a wise and courageous ruler, and the two had equal authority.

Angelberga

fl. 875; Italy
A woman of great strength and ability, Empress Angelberga was responsible for the building of one of the most famous monasteries in Italy. Her own daughter, wishing to utilize Angelberga's political knowledge, had her kidnaped and brought to Germany for the purpose of aiding in the overthrow of the French king. Her eventual release was due to the Pope's intervention.

Ageltrude Benevento

9th c.; Italy
Determined to maintain her estates and her rights, Empress Ageltrude defended her property against invasions and intrigues by both political and religious leaders. Her domains and hereditary rights were respected – unusual for a woman at that time, when women were often married by force for their property.

Bertha of Sulzbach

d. 1162; Germany
Bertha's marriage to Manuel, brother of Anna Comnena, was arranged as a political alliance between Germany and Byzantium. Manuel inherited the throne at Constantinople, and thus Bertha, the German countess, became Empress of the Byzantine Empire in 1127. She did all she could to support the continuing alliance between Germany and Byzantium.

Constantia

ca. 1147–1200; Italy
Empress Constantia, a Princess of Sicily and Naples, inherited those lands and set out with her husband, Henry VI, Emperor of Germany, to claim them. Later, he returned with armies he had raised for the Crusades, stopping in Sicily to put down a rebellion against his government. Outraged by her husband's brutal torture of the rebel leaders, she renounced her loyalty to him, and encouraged her people to recover their freedom. She raised an army, and at age fifty personally led them to victory over Henry VI.

Rachel

ca. 1070–1100; Hebrew
Rachel, the daughter of a famous Biblical and Talmudic scholar, received a sound education in the Jewish tradition. She was also taught law by her father and wrote and made many legal decisions for him.

Theodora the Senatrix

901–964; Italy
Theodora's influence was so great during the tenth century that popes were chosen and disposed of at her bidding. Never before or since has a woman gained such an ascendency over papal affairs. She and her daughter Marozia con-trolled the election of the pontiffs between the years 901 and 964, and for over sixty years their sons and grandsons were selected.

There were a few medieval women who felt they could do what they wanted to only if they presented themselves as men.

Bettisia Gozzadini

d. 1249; Italy
Born of a noble family in Bologna, Gozzadini so desired a university education that she attended classes disguised as a man. She had the highest standing in the college when she took her degree. At age twenty-seven, she became a doctor of civil and canon law and later obtained a professor's chair, devoting her life to teaching and writing about law.

Pope Joan

d. 855; Italy
A brilliant scholar, Joan disguised herself as a man to study in Athens, obtaining a degree in philosophy. Still in the attire of a monk, she went to Rome where Pope Leo IV made her a cardinal. Upon Leo's death in 853, she was elected pope by her fellow cardinals. After two years, four months, and eight days as pope, she was discovered to be a woman when she gave birth, whereupon she and the child were stoned to death. She remained recognized as a pope until 1601 when Pope Clement VIII officially declared her mythical and all record of her was utterly demolished.

made them brutal, and they brought these habits back to civilized society. Feudal ladies often had jurisdiction over these unruly knights, and it was against this general background that the Courts of Love emerged. A more cultured world slowly developed in the feudal castles, encouraged primarily by women who were generally the literate members of society. The improved status of women did not last very long, but for a while feminine values reigned.

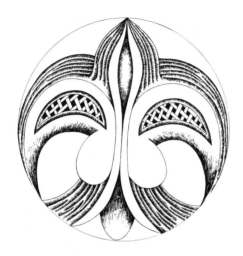

Eleanor of Aquitaine

1122–1204

Out of the convulsions of the early Middle Ages, the family emerged as the most stable force. Women, as part of the family, played a central role and thereby achieved a new measure of personal freedom. They could own and administer property and during their husband's absence, usually managed the estates, presided over the courts, took charge of the vassal service, administered justice, signed treaties, made laws, and – in some cases – commanded troops. But marriage was not always a pleasant proposition. For noblewomen, it was almost always based on economic or political gain. A landed man could improve his status by marrying a woman with property of her own.

If there were sons, property passed only to the eldest. Because families were usually large, this resulted in large numbers of landless men who roamed the countryside. They were encouraged to go on the Crusades and enlarge Christian lands; the long years of warfare

The whole body of doctrine associated with chivalry was profoundly influenced by the intensive veneration of the Virgin Mary, which definitely affected attitudes toward women. As far back as the fifth century, the popular worship of Mary showed signs of going beyond the bounds the Church had established. During Eleanor's lifetime, worship of Mary became increasingly manifest. The troubadours in particular venerated the Virgin and sang of her in hymn and prayer.

Virgin Mary

In choosing the characters for the *Dinner Party* table, I contemplated including Mary, primarily because her image has had such a profound effect on women's lives. I saw her as the Christian incarnation of the Mother Goddess, transformed into a major but circumscribed figure of patriarchal religion. The ancient reverence for a humane and nurturing female deity found its expression in the veneration of the "Mother of God." The image of the Virgin with her son at her knee derived from the traditional representation of the Goddess with her son/lover (e.g., Isis and Horus or the nameless goddesses with their male progeny). Often, Mary was easier for the populace to accept than the wrathful God of the Christians or even his less forbidding son. The Church allowed Mary-worship to flourish in an effort to draw new converts to the fold, but by the Middle Ages, Mariolatry had reached such heights that one bishop complained, "In the thirteenth century, God changed sex."

Because the deification of Mary reached such heights at the time Eleanor of Aquitaine reigned, I grouped her with the queen. Moreover, the adulation of a female deity reflected the enhanced status of women in the High Middle Ages. Women in the Church and the cloister blossomed under the beneficent gaze of their Lady, but soon all that remained of her was the concept of Our Lady of Sorrow, whose diminished identity both reflected and reinforced the end of female power.

The Courts of Love idealized women and enforced an elaborate code of manners. Women held court and laid down codes of behavior concerning the relation between the sexes, judged men's worth as lovers, and were the arbiters of personal disputes. The service of love was patterned on the feudal system of vassalage with woman as lord. But women were not only the patrons and commanders of the minstrels, but troubadours as well. Of the one hundred known minstrels between 1150 and 1250, twenty were female. The age of the troubadours was finished, however, in a merciless inquisition in the thirteenth century. The degradation of the clergy was a popular theme among the satirists of the troubadour poets, and this eventually led to the destruction of those whose castles had been open to the minstrels.

Almucs de Castenau

fl. 1140; France

A troubadour from a town near Provence, De Castenau wrote at the height of the classical period of troubadour poetry.

Beatrice de Die

12th c.; France

Die was a noblewoman who wrote poems and songs derived from personal experience, such as her work, "Of Deceived Love." Only five short poems still exist.

Fibors

12th c.; France

Fibors is the earliest female troubadour thus far recovered from history. Little is known of her other than that her brother was also a famous troubadour.

Marie de France

12th c.; France

Marie de France was the first professional woman writer in France. It is not known exactly who she was, but she probably lived in England for a time and was most likely connected to the court of Eleanor of Aquitaine. She composed poems and stories and collected folk tales, legends, and songs from the oral tradition of Europe. Her writing, recognized as the finest example of storytelling in any European vernacular up to that time, presented a woman's perspective on the activities of people of her age, and stood in sharp stylistic contrast to the masculine genre of the *chanson de geste*, or heroic epic.

Maria de Ventadorn

b. ca. 1165; France

DeVentadorn, a noblewoman, was an important patron of the troubadours, as well as an innovative troubadour herself.

Barbe de Verrue

13th c.; France

A "troubadouresse" who earned a considerable fortune traveling and performing her own compositions, De Verrue lived to an advanced age and was much admired by her contemporaries.

As a result of feudalism, noblewomen throughout Europe enjoyed greater freedom. Among the serfs, women and men had a rough equality throughout the Middle Ages, primarily because they worked together. As serfdom gave way to the growth of mercantile and artisan activities, guilds developed to which both women and men belonged.

Adela of Blois

1062–1137; France

Adela, a noblewoman, scholar, and an extremely gifted needleworker, participated in the creation of the Bayeaux Tapestry. This embroidery, which is two hundred feet long and depicts the Norman Conquest of England, was designed by Queen Matilda of Flanders and executed by her and the women of her court. William the Conqueror, set aside her needlework to help her husband seek support for his crusade. She became regent when he was killed, successfully carrying on the affairs of state until her son Theobald came of age.

Adelaide of Susa

1091–1150; Italy

Adelaide, a witness to constant war and slaughter, led an army in defense of the territory she would inherit from her father. She married Otto of Savoy, with whom she shared authority over the state, governing it more freely after his death. Adelaide was also a patron of the arts, supporting and protecting poets and troubadours.

Agnes of Poitou

11th c.; France

As Empress of the Holy Roman Empire, Agnes of Poitou became regent for her son Henry III in 1056. She governed during a turbulent period and continued to exert great influence after her son assumed the throne. This was a period when the ambitious designs of her son and the growing independence of the papacy were in conflict. Agnes acted as an intermediary between Pope Gregory VII and Henry in their struggle for power. Although historians have attempted to hold her responsible for the weakening of the realm, she actually tried to hold off its inevitable disintegration.

Lady Beatrix

11th c.; England

Lady Beatrix was a skillful and daring swordswoman whose prowess in combat earned her the name "LaBelle Cavalière." Discovered practicing sword drills in private, she was encouraged to engage in public displays of her ability.

Berenguela

12th c.; Spain

Berenguela was a princess and the granddaughter of Eleanor of Aquitaine. She astonished all of Europe by challenging the authority of a king and a pope. A defiant and independent woman, she refused to submit to a marriage arranged by her father, the King of Castile. When she chose her own husband, the Pope annulled the marriage, but Berenguela continued to live with Alfonso IX of Leon for seven years. When her parents died, she returned to Castile, becoming regent for her younger brother. He died unexpectedly and the crown passed to her. Described as the "fittest ruler in all Spain," she successfully arranged for her son to become King of both Castile and Leon, thereby increasing their domains and reuniting the two provinces under a single ruler.

Blanche of Castile

1188–1252; France
Another granddaughter of Eleanor of Aquitaine, Blanche's marriage at the age of twelve was one of the conditions of a cease-fire agreement between England and France, who were at war. A political pawn like many royal women, Blanche was married to the French king. After the death of her husband, Blanche became regent. French nobility and the King of England organized against her, but she was able to repress the insurrection and conclude a peace treaty with England. She remained in power for ten years – until her son was old enough to assume the throne.

Dervorguilla

1213–1290; Scotland
Dervorguilla – one of Scotland's wealthiest women – married John de Balliol, who founded Balliol College at Oxford University. When he died in 1269, she continued to be involved with the college, purchasing more land for it and generally placing it in a secure financial position. She influenced the tenor of the institution by drawing up a strict code of conduct for scholars. In addition to supporting the college, she brought about the construction of bridges, convents, monasteries, and abbeys.

Edith

fl. 1043–1066; England
Noted for her skill with the needle, Queen Edith was also extremely literate. She was adept at the subtleties of argument and often took part in debates at court, which was unusual for a woman of her time.

Failge

13th c.; Ireland
An intellectual and a noblewoman, Failge opened her home to all those who wished to discuss ideas and worship according to the old traditions. She thus helped to preserve and transmit culture in Ireland.

Isabella de Forz

fl. 1249–1260; England
Through skillful manipulation of the laws of inheritance and dowry, a woman in thirteenth-century England could still control a vast complex of estates, which is what De Forz was able to do. Married at twelve and widowed at twenty-three, she maintained her property throughout her life. She acquired so much land that the king, who regarded her property holdings as being too great for any subject – particularly a woman – tried to buy it from her. But he did not succeed until she was on her deathbed, and even then she sold only a portion of her holdings.

Lady Godiva

fl. 1040–1080; England
The story of Lady Godiva portrays her as a rebel against the oppressive tax her husband levied against the people of Coventry. He agreed to rescind the tax if she would ride through the town on horseback, unclothed, in daylight. Convinced of the unfairness of the tax, she did. The people honored her noble purpose by staying inside and drawing their blinds. Recent research, however, reveals an early Celtic religious ceremony as the root of the Godiva myth.

Hawisa

12th c.; England
One of the great ladies of twelfth-century Anglo-Norman society, Hawisa's marriage to the Earl of Essex in 1180 was the social event of the year. He died leaving no heir, and she was forced by King Richard I to marry a man of lower status. Her land and stock were then seized on behalf of the crown.

Jeanne of Navarre

1271–1309; France
Jeanne, the heiress of Navarre and Champagne, kept title to both of her kingdoms despite her marriage to Phillip IV of France, who could have taken them from her by law. When Champagne was attacked, she placed herself at the head of the army and personally defended her lands. She is best known for having founded the famous college of Navarre, a school for the French nobility, and for her patronage and support of intellectual and literary activities.

Margaret of Lincoln

13th c.; England
After the death of her husband, Margaret took over the management of a large estate, running a farm, a dairy, and a household.

Margaret

1045–1093; Scotland
Margaret was an Anglo-Saxon princess raised in Hungary and married to the King of Scotland. An educated woman, she brought culture to a rude country, teaching her husband to read and the ladies of her court to embroider. She was an able diplomat and played an important role in the political affairs of Scotland. A philanthropist, she built churches and monasteries and housed the destitute in her own palace.

Marie of Champagne

fl. 1170; France
Marie of Champagne was the daughter of Eleanor of Aquitaine and an important patron of literature. She worked with her mother to develop the elaborate code of chivalric manners in the Courts of Love and was influential in cultivating the art of the troubadours. One of the most famous, Chrétien de Troies, author of *Lancelot or Le Comte de la Carette,* was directly inspired and influenced by Marie.

Matilda of Flanders

d. 1083; England
Queen Matilda is credited with having designed and supervised the execution of the Bayeux Tapestry. This monumental work, which took years to produce, depicts events related to the Norman Conquest of

England in which her husband, William the Conqueror, figured prominently. Although called a tapestry, the piece is actually an elaborate embroidery in worsted wool on linen. Over two hundred feet long and containing seventy-two scenes filled with people, horses, castles, ships, and churches, it is probably the world's most famous embroidery. It is believed to have been completed in England by Matilda and the women of her court and then brought to France where it was displayed in the Bayeux Cathedral.

Mathilde of Tuscany

1046–1115; Italy

As the daughter of the most powerful nobleman of the time, Mathilde became the sole inheritor of his vast estate, which she ruled with her mother as advisor. She established churches, convents, monuments, public baths, and a hospital. She also took an interest in the guilds of Florence, promoting and protecting them. A devout Catholic and niece of the Pope, Mathilde became involved in the power struggle between the German Emperors and the papacy. She led her troops to victory on the side of the Pope and further attempted to solidify the power of the papacy by willing all her land to the Holy See. Although Italy was united under Mathilde, it did not remain so after her death.

Matilda

fl. 1100–1135; England

Queen Matilda founded two free hospitals at which she personally nursed the sick. She also enacted a welfare program to provide for underprivileged pregnant women. She influenced her husband, Henry I, to grant the important legal charter

that was the model and precedent for the Magna Carta. She protected the civil rights of the Saxons, paving the way for peace between them and their Norman conquerors. She endowed religious institutions and built, repaired, and improved bridges.

Melisande

d. 1161; Jerusalem

In 1143, Melisande became the sole ruler of Jerusalem. When her son came of age, she refused to relinquish her power, and a struggle between them ensued. She was forced to surrender and in her last years worked on behalf of the church.

Sobeya

10th c.; Spain

Sobeya became regent for her son, Heschem II. Her lover helped her to secure her position but then began to usurp her power. She attempted to overthrow him and was nearly successful. At one time considered the most powerful of the Moslem Sultanas, she was forced to withdraw into seclusion for the rest of her life.

Violante

14th c.; Spain

Famed for its elegance, good manners, and courtly grace, Queen Violante's court recreated the brilliant atmosphere of the French Courts of Love and attracted poets and knights from all over her realm. Many women, encouraged by the contact with the literary figures Violante brought to her court, began writing verse. Eventually, the funds necessary to maintain a cultured court life were cut off, and Violante's activities were restricted.

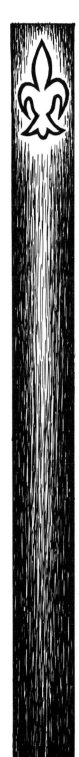

An Imaginary Correspondence Between Eleanor of Aquitaine and Hildegarde of Bingen

To Hildegarde, Tabernacle of the Divine Spirit, from Eleanor, Duchess of Aquitaine and Queen:

I salute you, gracious lady,
noble abbess
Mighty woman with the status
of a feudal lord
Though I have never seen you,
yet I think you
A Sister who worships Mary's
power
I am told you dress in
snow-white linen
And in your hand the crozier
of your rank
A prophet, a healer, a mystic,
a saint
So filled with the passion of
your vows
Yet wishing no bounds
But rather to soar like a bird
Two queens, you and I
Of cloister and of court
Two gentle hearts, twin flowers
of our age.

To Eleanor, Most Royal Majesty and Queen of the Heart:

Oh, how much I wish I could be with you, for my soul longs for its twin. Through our efforts in court and cloister, new virtues are taking hold. The cult of Our Lady is spreading, and through her power women could be redeemed. Though Eve has been blamed for our downfall, the worship of Mary exalts us all. Reverence for our Mother is rising though I fear it will not last. But the people need the figure of a woman to soften the harshness of the world. The priests grumble that God has changed sex, but there is little that they can do. No father, not even in heaven, can provide all that the human heart craves.

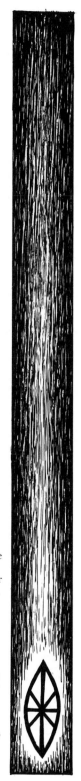

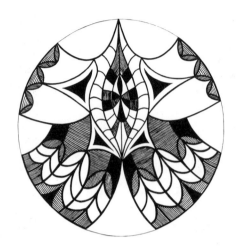

Hildegarde of Bingen

1098–1179

The twelfth century was not only the high point for women in the courts but also in the cloister. The ruling abbess of an important monastic center had the rights and privileges of a feudal baron. Many times, she was a member of the royal family and acted as the representative of the king in his absence. She usually owned and administered vast lands; managed convents, abbeys, and double monasteries of both men and women; provided her own men-at-arms in war; had the right of coinage; entertained the royal family when they traveled; exercised great political power, and was consulted in religious affairs.

But the rights of abbesses were gradually curtailed. New religious houses were set up as priories and the prioress became subject to the abbot's control. Women increasingly turned toward spirituality and mysticism as an avenue of personal expression. This gave birth to a female mystic movement cen-

tered in Germany in the thirteenth century. Other religious women became involved in reform of the church, perhaps in the hope that re-establishing the purity of Christianity would accomplish a renewal of their power. From the twelfth century forward, women were very prominent in heretical movements which began to threaten the church. They also took part in and led peasant uprisings against feudal oppression, all of which suggests that women did not passively accept their steadily diminishing roles but instead attempted to resist their loss of status.

Gertrude of Hackeborn

13th c.; Germany

Gertrude, a mystic and writer, was an important abbess at Helfia for forty years. She encouraged intellectual activity, and her convent became a center of the mystic movement.

Agnes d'Harcourt

13th c.; France

Abbess at Longchamp, D'Harcourt wrote a biography of Isabel of France. The manuscript, originally written on vellum, was published in 1668 and is still of great interest to medieval scholars.

Héloïse

1101–1164; France

The story of Héloïse and Abelard has been told many times, but the identity of Héloïse has remained unclear. While still quite young, she became known for her extraordinary intelligence. Abelard, a philosopher and theologian, was impressed by her reputa-

tion and became her tutor when she was seventeen. They fell in love and had an affair; Abelard proposed marriage, but Héloïse at first refused. He was persistent and they were married secretly, then Abelard arranged for her to be sent to a convent. Héloïse's uncle, discovering that she was pregnant, was outraged, and thought Abelard had deserted her. He and his friends took revenge and castrated Abelard, who then sought refuge in a monastery.

Héloïse became prioress and then abbess of the convent in which she had been placed by Abelard. She elevated the intellectual level of her order and established a college of theology. She was probably the most learned woman doctor in France in the twelfth century. Her letters to Abelard established her as one of the first great female writers in France.

Herrad of Lansberg

d. 1195; Germany

Herrad, Abbess of Hohenberg, created the encyclopedic work, *Hortus Delicarum* (Garden of Delights), for the purpose of educating the nuns in her convent.

Destroyed by fire in 1870 when Strasbourg was bombarded by the Germans, what knowledge remains of it derives from tracings made in the nineteenth century.

Las Huelgas

12th c.; Spain

Las Huelgas was an abbess who practiced medicine as well as preached, a common practice, particularly in the heretical sects of the time.

The contraction of woman's authority did not progress evenly everywhere. In areas removed from the centers of church and state powers, women continued to exercise their rights. Women also played a major role in the medieval mystic movement, which emphasized breaking down the barriers between the church and the people. Mystics urged reform within the church and state, and inveighed against wealth, luxury, and the oppression of the populace.

Birgitta

1303–1373; Sweden

Birgitta, or Bridget, was the dominant figure of Swedish politics, religion, and literature during the fourteenth century. After the death of her husband in 1344, she began to experience revelations that inspired her to form a new religious order, the Bridgettines – a religious order that encouraged humility, simplicity, and the contemplative life. She became involved in church reform and traveled extensively throughout Sweden, becoming a favorite of the people and an advisor of kings and princes. Respected as a visionary and a prophet, her revelations were published, widely read, and translated into several languages. They exerted a profound influence on the literary history of Sweden.

Catherine of Siena

1347–1380; Italy

Catherine, one of the greatest mystics of the Western world, was born at a time of great conflict and extensive church corruption. She reconciled enemy factions, traveled, preached, wrote to and advised all the rulers in Europe, and exercised considerable influence on the political affairs of the church. She had numerous disciples. No woman in history understood church matters better than Catherine. She tried to restore the church to its original purity through the establishment of a spiritual community, which, she hoped, would include all humankind. Catherine claimed that Christ had appeared to her when she was a young girl, saying, "You must know that in these days pride has grown monstrously among men and chiefly among those who are learned and think they understand everything.... I have chosen unschooled women...so that they may put vanity and pride to shame. If men will humbly receive the teaching I send them through the weaker [*sic*] sex, I will show them great mercy; but if they despise these women, they shall fall into even worse confusion and even greater agony."

Clare of Assisi

1194–1253; Italy

From a noble family, Clare, as a co-worker with Francis of Assisi, organized the Poor Clares, a religious order for women that spread throughout Europe. The order stressed preaching and ministry to the body and soul, and Clare founded branches of the order throughout Italy, France, and Germany. She was also a visionary and was said to possess the ability to see and hear things happening miles away.

Cunegund

1224–1292; Poland

Daughter of the King of Hungary, Cunegund was well-educated. Although married at sixteen to a king, she insisted on retaining her chastity and vowed to live a religious life. The queen lived austerely, spending her time caring for the poor and the sick. When the king died, she refused the wish of the nobles that she assume the throne, preferring to become a Poor Clare at the convent she had founded. She built churches and hospitals and saved the nuns in her convent when Poland was invaded.

Alpis de Cudot

12th c.; France

De Cudot was a visionary who argued that the earth was a round globe and a solid mass and that the sun was larger than the earth. She was totally ignored.

Elizabeth of Schönau

d. 1164; Germany

Elizabeth of Schönau was a contemporary of Hildegarde of Bingen, and like Hildegarde was regarded as a divinely inspired messenger of God. Elizabeth entered the convent at Schönau in 1141 and became its superior in 1157. Her ideas appeared in three books, which related her visions and mystical experiences from 1152 to 1160. Her writings were extremely popular and her prophecies, messages, and sermons were taken to be the word of God.

Gertrude the Great

1256–1301; Germany

A great mystic and healer, Gertrude was one of the eminent religious figures of the Middle Ages. Brought to the convent at age five, she studied Latin, philosophy and the liberal arts. In 1281, she had a vision that caused her to pursue only religious studies. Thereafter, she spent her time studying and writing, recording her revelations and her personal experiences in books that are still used today.

Isabel of France

ca. 1225–1270; France

Influenced by her mother, Blanche of Castile, Isabel chose a disciplined life dedicated to prayer and education. She studied the scriptures, natural history, medicine, logic, Eastern languages, and Latin. She refused many offers of marriage – including one that would have made her Holy Roman Empress – preferring to be "last in the ranks of the Lord's virgins to being the greatest empress in the world." She founded the Abbey of Longchamp.

Juliana of Norwich

ca. 1342–1413; England

Juliana of Norwich wrote the *Revelations of Divine Love*, which was one of the first spiritual works written by an Englishwoman. Her inspired and artistic book is regarded as a rare reflection of the spirit of the Middle Ages and enjoyed a popular revival when it was reprinted in 1902.

145

Jutta

12th c.; Germany

Jutta was the first ruling abbess of the Benedictine Abbey, where Hildegarde of Bingen was educated. Jutta personally supervised Hildegarde's studies and when Jutta died, Hildegarde succeeded her as abbess.

Loretta

fl. 1207; England

After her family died, Loretta lived a simple life as an anchoress, attended by a few servants in a modest house. She disposed of the property she had inherited and was fed by people of position in the neighborhood.

Margaret

1242–1271; Hungary

Margaret was educated by the Dominican Sisters of Hare Island (now Margaret Island), where she became the spiritual advisor of the order. She lectured publicly and was renowned throughout Europe. Her advice and diplomatic skills were often sought by the royal family.

Mechthild of Hackeborn

13th c.; Germany

A nun at the convent of Helfde, Mechtild wrote, with the help of other nuns in the convent, the widely read *Book of Special Grace* which described her visions. Her book inspired other women to take their visions and revelations seriously and record them. Famous for her musical abilities, she often sang during her visions.

Mechthild of Magdeburg

1210–1297; Germany

One of the greatest religious figures of the Middle Ages, Mechthild was a mystic and a member of the Beguines. An educated woman, she wrote *The Flowing Light of God,* a beautiful collection of visions, parables, reflections, letters, and dialogues in both prose and verse. At the center of the literary and mystic movement in Germany, she attempted to reform the decadence of the Church and was persecuted for her efforts, charged with being "unlearned, lay, and worst of all, a woman." She was helped and protected by Gertrude the Great, who admired her writing, courage, and visionary powers.

Finola O'Donnell

d. 1528; Ireland

A nun for twenty-two years and co-founder of a Franciscan Monastery in 1474, O'Donnell is primarily important because references to Irish nuns during this period are so rare.

Rosalia of Palermo

fl. 1130–1160; Italy

A well-known saint of the medieval period, Rosalia is said to have delivered the town of Palermo from the plague in 1150. It was for this action that she was canonized.

Thérèsa of Avila

1515–1582; Spain

"The very thought that I am a woman is enough to make my wings droop," wrote Thérèsa of Avila, a monastic reformer, a visionary, and one of the greatest mystic writers of all time. A valiant and capable woman, Thérèsa challenged the apostolic precept which forbade women to teach. She reformed the Carmelite order and established sixteen nunneries for women and fourteen religious houses for men. Her objective was to restore the former purity of the order and to thereby bring about the regeneration of the church. Thérèsa wrote a number of mystic works, one of which was *The Way of Perfection,* which can be seen as a feminist book. Admonishing her nuns to be disciplined and strong, she urged that their lives have purpose. She continually stressed that although convent life was difficult it was better than being a wife.

Medieval noblewomen continued to be involved in medicine, often using their wealth to found hospitals, which they then administered. Upperclass medical women became the targets of the university-trained physicians, who set out to eliminate them because they competed for their clientele.

Agnes

1218–1282; Bohemia

Agnes's father, a king, tried to force her to marry against her will, but his death allowed her to remain single and devote her life to religious work. She founded a nunnery and a hospital in Prague, helped women who were sick or in trouble, and washed and mended garments of the lepers she tended.

Anna

fl. 1253; Bohemia

Princess Anna, sister of Agnes, was trained in medicine and specialized in the treatment of children. In 1253, she founded a nunnery and hospital at Kreutzberg and another at Neumarkt which is still in existence.

Phillipe Auguste

1164–1225; France

Phillipe Auguste was a prominent member of the Augustinian Sisters, the oldest nursing order in existence. She worked at a hospital in Paris that originated in 650 A.D.

Berengaria

d. ca. 1230; Spain

Queen of Castile, sister of Blanche of Castile, and mother of Ferdinand of Spain, Berengaria was known for her knowledge of medicine and sanitation. She personally attended to the sick and suffering among her people.

Douceline

13th c.; Germany

Douceline was the founding member of the Beguines of Marseilles, an order of lay nuns devoted to charitable works. Part of a reform movement, these women lived communally, supporting themselves by nursing, weaving, lacemaking, and embroidering. The Beguines appealed particularly to single, independent women. The order survived despite persistent attempts of the authorities to discredit them as heretics.

Elizabeth

1207–1230; Hungary

Elizabeth was one of the most noted medical women of the century and the daughter of a king. Betrothed at four and married at fourteen, she was widowed with several children while still quite young. Elizabeth was treated brutally by her brothers-in-law, deprived of the regency, and driven from court with her children. While queen she had used her royal revenue to relieve suffering among her people, building a hospital and home for lepers, nursing the sick, and feeding the poor. During the terrible famine of 1226, she provided bread and soup for thousands, causing the king's treasurers to accuse her of squandering money. Because of this, she was deprived of even her dowry when she was forced from court.

Hedwig

1174–1243; Poland

Famous for her medical skill, Hedwig's main work was in founding hospitals. Educated at a convent ruled by her sister, Hedwig was taken from the convent and forced to marry at the age of twelve. As soon as her husband died, she resumed the religious life, founding a nunnery and educating the nuns. At her convent, Hedwig and her nuns cared for the sick, particularly the lepers. In an effort to simplify their lives and work, she urged the women in her order to adopt plain dress.

Hersend

fl. 1249; France

As physician to Louis IX, Hersend accompanied him to the Holy Land in 1249. There she provided care for the queen as well as for the other women who followed the armies. The king rewarded her service with a lifelong pension.

Marguerite of Bourgogne

fl. 1293; France

Daughter of Blanche of Castile, Marguerite built a hospital that was a vast improvement over most hospitals of the period. Its wards were 270 feet long and well-ventilated; it afforded privacy, as each bed was screened as well as comfortable; the ceilings were high, and stained glass windows depicted scenes from the Bible.

Yvette

1158–1228; Hungary

Yvette was married against her will at a young age and was left a widow with two sons at the age of eighteen. Rather than remarry, she spent the next ten years nursing lepers and thirty more as an anchoress in a walled cell.

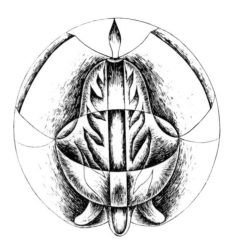

Petronilla de Meath

d. 1324

There were only a handful of licensed physicians but thousands of lay healers at the end of the Middle Ages. Hildegarde's compendium of natural healing methods gives some indication of the methods employed by these healers, most of whom were women. But the rising medical profession was determined to limit its ranks to men, and when the witch hunts began, doctors joined forces with the church to suppress the female healers of the lower classes. Bringing these women to trial, the male physicians made judgments about whether they were witches, and the church reinforced the judgments of the physicians by pronouncing nonprofessional healing as heresy, saying, "If a woman dare to cure without having studied, she is a witch and must die." Of course, women were not allowed to study in the universities where the only authorized medical training took place. The charges leveled by the witch hunters included inspiring lust through copulation with the devil; rendering men impotent or causing their penises to disappear; having an insatiable sexual appetite; and miscarrying, even when the miscarriage was the result of a husband's brutality. Some of the accusations, however, were more obvious in their intent: If a woman engaged in lesbian activity or in a sexual relationship outside of marriage, if she bore an illegitimate child, used contraception, or aided in an abortion, she was accused of witchcraft and – with or without evidence – usually killed.

Angèle de la Barthe

d. 1275; France
De La Barthe was found guilty and executed in the first witchcraft trial in France in 1275. She was accused of copulating with the devil. The basis for this accusation may have been a misinterpretation of certain fertility rituals which were related to the ancient practice of the sacred marriage. These rituals intrigued the Christian judges, who totally misunderstood them but examined them with a perverse fascination.

Madeleine de Demandolx

1593–1670; France
At the age of fourteen, Demandolx became a novice in a convent in Marseilles, where she confessed to having had intercourse with her family's priest. She later experienced fits, severe cramps, and hallucinations. The priest was summoned to exorcise her, and her hysteria became even more uncontrollable. She was put in jail "to protect her from the devil"; the priest, who denied the relationship, was tried by the Inquisition and executed for witchcraft. After his death, De Demandolx became subdued but

was charged with witchcraft several years later. She served a lengthy prison sentence and was finally released.

Catherine Deshayes

d. 1679; France
Deshayes, a fortune teller, was charged with witchcraft, tortured, and executed for her alleged involvement in a scandal involving the nobility. Supposedly, members of the ruling classes went to sorcerers for the purpose of obtaining poison and spells to kill their spouses. The practice was exposed but only Deshayes was arrested. She was accused of killing two thousand infants with her potions. The fact that she was of the peasant class was a factor in her accusation.

Geillis Duncan

d. 1590; Scotland
Duncan was one of the first witches tried in the famous North Berwick trials that launched a purge that was officially sanctioned by James I of England. A lay healer, Duncan worked as a servant in the home of a town official. Believing that

her ability to heal the sick was a power given by the devil, her employer tortured her and forced her to say that she had made a pact with the devil. He then had her arrested, whereupon she was further tortured to name accomplices. Confessions obtained in this manner were consistently used in these trials.

Jacobe Felicie

b. 1292; France
Felicie was a physician who was brought to trial by the University of Paris Medical Faculty in 1322. Her competency was not the issue (six cured patients testified on her behalf), but rather that she was practicing without a degree. She defended herself and argued for the need for women doctors, especially for treating female patients. Despite the validity of her argument and the absurdity of the charges, she was forced to pay a heavy fine and forbidden to practice medicine.

Goody Glover

d. 1698; Massachusetts Bay Colony
Glover was executed at the Salem witchcraft trials. She purportedly bewitched the children of the family for whom her daughter worked, and they supposedly contracted strange illnesses after Glover scolded them. A doctor accused her of witchcraft and brought her to trial. The evidence used against her included her inability to recite the Lord's Prayer in English and the existence of dolls found in her home. Glover may or may not have been a witch, but she was clearly irreligious, and that combined with her sex made her a victim of persecution.

Guillemine

13th c.; Bohemia
Guillemine was the founder of a religious sect for women and a reformer who questioned prevailing Church doctrine on the nature of woman. She argued for the right of women to prophesize, interpret the Scriptures, and commune directly with God. Her sect was denounced by the Inquisition because of her direct challenge to the clergy's authority.

Joan of Arc

1412–1431; France
When Joan was thirteen, she began to hear voices that convinced her that she would save France and obtain the crown for the exiled Dauphin, Charles VII.

At age seventeen, she obtained an audience with the king and convinced him that she was destined to be his savior. She led a small army to Orleans, where she won battle after battle against the English, and Charles was crowned the King of France. Considered by many historians to be a military genius, Joan employed martial strategies that were not commonly used until later centuries. Convinced that her mission had been fulfilled, she attempted to return home, but Charles insisted that she lead more campaigns. She was defeated, captured, and sold to the English, who charged her with heresy and witchcraft. She was also accused of wearing male attire, cutting off her hair, and listening to inner voices rather than to the authority of the Church.

Charles, for whom she had won the throne, made no attempt to gain her release. There is some possibility that he feared the power she had acquired, for many people believed that Joan was God incarnate. Another theory suggests that she was actually a heretic and a member of a Dianic cult that practiced witchery.

At any rate, she refused to reassert her faith in the Church during her trial. Confined and tortured for three months, she was finally forced to sign a submission to the Church, and although there was no legal proof against her, she was burned at the stake. Twenty-four years after her death, she was acquitted of all charges against her.

Margaret Jones

d. 1650; Massachusetts Bay Colony

Jones was a medical practitioner who so aroused the jealousy and distrust of the male physicians that she was accused of witchcraft, brought to trial, and convicted. She became the first woman executed as a witch in America.

Margery Jourdemain

d. 1441; England

Jourdemain allegedly used her powers of magic to help the Duchess of Gloucester achieve her political ambitions. The Duchess was said to have asked Jourdemain to make a waxen image of the king in order to destroy him and secure the crown for her husband. The king arrested all three, but only Jourdemain was executed.

Ursley Kempe

d. 1582; England

One of two women hanged in a famous witchcraft trial, Kempe was a typical target of witch hunts. She was a midwife and wetnurse, and because she lived as she pleased and bore several children out of wedlock, her neighbors considered her to be a loose woman. Kempe's

children testified against her, a common occurrence in witchcraft trials. She was pressured into a confession by a magistrate who believed that convicting a notorious witch would enhance his prestige. In exchange for a promise of clemency, Kempe implicated others. (The instinct for self-preservation led many like Kempe to denounce their friends and family members.) Despite the promise, Kempe was executed.

Alice Kyteler

fl. 1324; Ireland

In 1324, Kyteler and the members of her coven were tried for worshiping a diety other than the Christian God. In Ireland, Mother Goddess worship remained the chief religion of the majority of the people, and there was a direct connection between the ancient practices of Mother Goddess religion and witchcraft. Kyteler was able to escape safely to England, but her personal maid, Petronilla de Meath, was not so fortunate.

Margaret of Porète

d. 1310; Germany

Margaret of Porète, a mystic and a member of the Beguines, wrote a religious tract espousing a form of mystical pantheism that so outraged the Church that she was brought to trial. She refused to recant and was publicly burned as a heretic.

Pierrone

d. 1430; France

Pierrone, a follower of Joan of Arc, was accused of witchcraft and burned at the stake. She insisted that her god had appeared to her in human form and had spoken to her personally. There are repeated instances of people tried as witches who refused to deny their belief in non-Christian deities.

Anne Redfearne

d. 1612; England

Redfearne was initiated into the craft in 1596 by her mother, with whom she was accused by the local magistrate of "witchcraft by common complaint." She was later charged with causing the death of Robert Nutter, a man who had once tried to rape her. When the court found the evidence against her inconclusive, the crowd and the judges, outraged by the verdict, demanded that she not be allowed to go free. To appease the mob, a second trial was held in which she was accused and found guilty of murdering Nutter's father, who had died twenty years before. Redfearne was then executed.

Maria Salvatori

d. 1646; Italy

An old woman, Salvatori was brought to trial as a witch on the grounds that she used the communion wafer for casting spells. Her inquisitors were so zealous in their torture of her that she died in prison before she could be executed. Old women were especially vulnerable as targets of witchcraft charges because they were poor and alone and many were nonconformist or eccentric.

Agnes Sampson

d. 1592; Scotland

Sampson, a lay healer, was one of the chief witnesses in the North Berwick witch trials. Under torture, she confessed that her coven was involved in a plot against the life of the King and Queen of Scotland, and she was strangled and burned.

Alice Samuel

d. 1593; England

Samuel was a victim of the Warboys witchcraft trial in 1593, the first trial in which the accusers were children. The three young children who sent this eighty-year-old woman to the gallows first tormented her for four years. They scratched Samuel's face until it was raw, in the belief that if bewitched persons could scratch and draw blood from the bewitcher, they would immediately recover. The children's parents forced Samuel, who worked for them, to stay with the children despite her mistreatment of her. By the time of her trial, she was completely deranged, and in an effort to gain sympathy from her accusers she pleaded that she was pregnant. Despite the pathetic state to which she'd been driven, she was hanged two days after the trial.

Anna Maria Schwägel

d. 1775; Germany

Schwägel was the last woman to be tried and executed for witchcraft in Germany – the scene of the most extensive and brutal of the witch hunts. She fell in love with another servant who worked for the same family, then discovered that he was married. Shocked by his betrayal, she ran away and was later found half-demented and begging for alms. She confessed that she was a lapsed Catholic and that her lover was a Satanist who had convinced her to renounce Christianity. The authorities found *her* guilty of witchcraft.

149

Elizabeth Southern

d. 1613; England
Southern was one of the main defendants in England's first mass witchcraft trial. She reportedly became a witch in 1591 and was involved in a feud between her family and another. They attempted to use witchcraft against each other for several years. Their activities became common knowledge, and they were charged with "witchcraft by common complaint." Southern gratuitously provided the magistrate with details of her career as a witch, as she was extremely proud of her craft. She was placed in prison, where she died awaiting trial.

Gertrude Svensen

d. 1669; Sweden
Svensen was the first victim of the worst mass witch hunt in Sweden. She was arrested and accused of kidnaping children in order to hand them over to the devil. She implicated others; seventy people were charged with witchcraft (fifteen were children). A spectacular trial followed which attracted three thousand people. Despite an absence of evidence, all seventy were found guilty and burned.

Tituba

fl. 1697; Massachusetts Bay Colony
On the word of three little girls in whose household she was a slave, Tituba was arrested as a witch. Because she practiced herbal medicine, she was accused by the children of knowing spells and magic. She confessed, telling an imaginative story of orgies, witches' Sabbaths, and other strange activities, which threw Salem into a panic. Eventually she was released for lack of evidence and became the property of whomever paid her prison fees.

Agnes Waterhouse

d. 1566; England
Waterhouse was brought to trial at the age of sixty-four, accused of employing her cat in acts of murder and violence. Her daughter testified against her in an effort to save her own life (she had been accused as well). Despite a lack of any real evidence against her, Waterhouse was hanged. This set a precedent for the acceptance of uncorroborated evidence in witchcraft trials and served as a pretext to eliminate old women.

Jane Weir

d. 1670; Scotland
Weir was charged with practicing witchcraft; committing incest with her brother, who was said to be a god of the witches; consulting other witches; and keeping a "familiar" (a supernatural being often embodied in an animal). She and her brother confessed their witchcraft freely, and both refused to recant. This would appear to be a genuine case of witchcraft, revealing that the adherents of witchery persisted despite widespread persecution, and that real witches were tried along with those who were falsely accused.

María de Zozoya

d. 1610; Basque
De Zozoya, an elderly Basque woman, was brought to trial as a principal member of a large group of witches who were tried for heresy and burned alive.

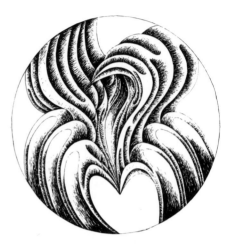

Christine de Pisan

1363–1431
The decline of feudalism, the consequent contraction of women's position, the gradual loss of educational rights, and the advent of witch hunts combined to create a situation in which most women were intimidated into submission.

Some women realized what was happening, and it is no accident that women began to produce feminist literature at this time. As soon as women were systematically relegated to an inferior position, they began arguing for the equality of the sexes. This argument would continue for several centuries, waxing and waning as women's position improved, then worsened, during the historical changes that occurred between the Renaissance and the Industrial Revolution. Women's situation from the fourteenth to the nineteenth centuries also has to be understood in the context of their difficulty in gaining education.

Anastasia

14th c.; France
An artist, Anastasia may have executed the illuminations in the works of Christine de Pisan. She is described in *La Cité des Dames,* in which De Pisan tells stories about a number of famous women to support her thesis of the essential nobility of the feminine character.

Jane Anger

fl. 1589; England
Anger wrote *Protection for Women,* an early example of feminist literature, protesting a misogynist tract written by a man whose unfortunate experiences in love led him to denounce and slander all women. Anger chastized women for spending too much time catering to men, with the result that "Our good toward them is the destruction of ourselves; we being well-formed, are by them foully deformed."

Maddalena Buonsignori

14th c.; Italy
Buonsignori gave instruction in law and wrote a Latin treatise which was a detailed study of the legal status of women.

Teresa de Cartagena

15th c.; Spain
A mystic and writer, De Cartagena's major work, *Arboleda de los Enfermos,* caused a great deal of discussion. In it, she defended women and argued on behalf of their capacities.

Angela Merici

1474–1540; Italy
A strong advocate for education for women, Merici founded the first women's teaching order of the Catholic Church in 1494. She then went on to organize the Ursuline Order, whose aim was educating girls through individualized attention. Merici was noted for opposing the common use of physical punishment in the schools.

Isotta Nogarola

1418–1466; Italy
By the time she reached the age of eighteen, Nogarola's knowledge and eloquence had been recognized by prominent humanists. But because she was a woman, her attempts to pursue an intellectual career by corresponding with leading scholars, a common practice at the time, were ignored. After several years of trying and failing to gain acceptance as a serious scholar, she renounced secular studies and retreated to her home in Verona, where she spent the rest of her life as a virtual recluse devoted to religious studies. Her choice of religious scholarship, combined with her vow of chastity, was apparently more acceptable and won her the praise and encouragement of the same men who had previously rejected her. They exchanged letters with her and carried on theological debates. She never accepted her ascetic life happily, however, and was chronically ill for the rest of her life.

A number of her scholarly works and hundreds of her letters have been preserved, including a famous dialogue with a male humanist on the question of whether Adam or Eve was the greater sinner in eating the forbidden fruit. Though she defended Eve, Nogarola rationalized that, because Eve was created as an "inferior being," she was not responsible for her actions.

Aliénor de Poitiers

fl. 1430–1480; France
De Poitiers was the daughter of a lady-in-waiting to Isabelle, wife of King Philip. She wrote *Les Honneurs de la Cour* (The Honors of the Court), a detailed biographical record of famous women in the French court from 1380 to 1480, which provides an invaluable account of court etiquette, tradition, and style. The book placed particular emphasis on women who broke with tradition to assert themselves.

Modesta Pozzo

b. 1555; Italy
Pozzo was a feminist writer whose book entitled *The Merit of Women* maintained that women are equal to men in understanding and integrity. She also wrote poetry, including a work on the passion and resurrection of Christ.

Throughout Europe, there continued to be women who were able to make a mark, but the great age of female achievement was at an end. Occasionally, because of her social position, her family's attitudes toward women, her extraordinary abilities, or particular social or political circumstances, a woman was able to transcend the restrictions on women's lives.

Agnes of Dunbar

1312/13–1369; Scotland
The Countess of Dunbar, or Black Agnes, as she was called, embodied Scottish independence and resistance to English domination. While her husband was at war with the English, she successfully defended their castle against the most memorable siege in Scottish history. She plotted the defense, walked the battlements, and nearly killed the enemy leader herself. After five months of her heroic resistance, a cessation of arms was concluded, and the Scots had triumphantly repulsed the English attack.

Martha Baretskaya

fl. 1471; Russia
Baretskaya, one of the few Russian women of the Middle Ages to make a mark on history, was the mayor of Novgorod, an ancient northern republic. She was also leader of a movement to resist the subjugation of Novgorod by Moscow. In 1471, a majority group under her direction appealed to the King of Poland, offering their allegiance if he would respect their rights. This was a threat to Ivan III of Moscow, who sent in an army to sever the new alliance. Baretskaya was captured and sent to a convent.

Margaret Beaufort

1441/3–1509; England
The mother of Henry VII, Beaufort was one of the first female writers in England. She wrote books dealing with theological issues, and she lectured on divinity at Oxford and Cambridge. Interested in education, she founded several free grammar schools, built and endowed Christ College, and founded St. John's College. In addition, she studied medicine in order to aid the poor and sick, founded hospitals at which she personally attended patients, and provided refuge for the indigent in her own home.

Juliana Berners

b. ca. 1388; England
A well-educated noble-woman, Berners was trained in hunting, hawking, and fishing. Her technical knowledge was so vast that she wrote a book, *Julyan Barnes, Her Gentleman's Academy of Hawking, Hunting, Fishing and Armorie,* published in 1481. This work may be the first book by an English-woman to appear in print and is even more note-worthy for its subject matter because Berners' expertise was in areas that were definitely regarded as male provinces.

Bourgot

14th c.; France
A famous manuscript il-luminator of the 14th cen-tury, Bourgot learned the art from her father. The decoration of books was particularly accepted as an occupation for women, but individual contributions were usually anonymous.

Rose de Burford

14th c.; England
De Burford was from a wealthy London family. She and her husband were wool merchants and worked to-gether, as was common in the Middle Ages. After her husband's death she carried on the business and was quite successful as a trades-woman.

Beatrix Galindo

1473–1535; Spain
Educated in Italy, Galindo became a professor of phi-losophy, rhetoric, and medi-cine at the University of Salamanca. Her knowledge of Latin was so extensive that she was appointed Queen Isabella's instructor, and was known as "La Latina."

Clara Hätzerlin

1430–1476; Germany
A scholar who worked as a professional scribe, Hätzer-lin made a collection of German folk songs and poems which documented major trends in German literature. This collection, which contains 219 exam-ples, many of an erotic nature, represented the tran-sition from the medieval to the modern style.

Ingrida

15th c.; Sweden
Ingrida was a nun at the convent of St. Birgitta and a distinguished literary stylist. An epistle that she wrote to her lover is consid-ered to be a classically elegant example of the use of the Swedish language.

Margareta Karthauserin

15th c.; Germany
A nun from a Dominican convent in Nurnberg, Karthauserin was an artist and a scribe. A number of handsomely written and illustrated manuscripts from 1452 to 1470 are signed by her.

Margery Kempe

1373–1438; England
Kempe was the author of the first known autobiog-raphy in English – the first work other than religious writings by a woman. Un-educated and illiterate, but driven by inner voices, she was determined to record her life's struggles. She dic-tated her story to scribes, but the book was lost to his-tory for five hundred years. It was discovered in a li-brary in England in 1934.

Francisca de Lebrija

15th c.; Spain
De Lebrija was educated by her father, a humanist scholar. She taught history at the University of Alcala.

Cobhlair Mor

fl. 1395; Ireland
Mor was a preserver of Gaelic customs at a time when they were under-mined by Edward III and his government. A fore-runner of the salonists, she gathered people in her home to practice Gaelic cul-tural traditions, which had been declared illegal by the Statute of Kilkenny in 1367.

Margaret O'Connor

15th c.; Ireland
O'Connor was a wealthy woman who devoted herself to social, artistic, and reli-gious causes. An important patron of medieval litera-ture, she supervised the construction and adorn-ment of many churches and was a benefactor of numer-ous causes. Her home was known as a center of cul-ture and charity.

Margaret Paston

1423–1484; England
Paston, a member of the ris-ing English gentry class, conducted extensive corre-spondence with her family. The letters provide impor-tant information on English social history and the role of women in it. As mistress of the manor, she not only ran the household and managed the land, but was also her husband's agent and transacted all business while he was away. She had an intimate knowledge of the law, and during the tur-bulent period of Civil War in England she preserved her family's property.

Margaret Roper

1505–1544; England
Roper was considered the greatest pre-Elizabethan Tudor woman of learning. The favorite child of Sir Thomas More – who be-lieved that women should be given the same education as men – she was educated in Greek, Latin, philosophy, astronomy, physics, mathe-matics, logic, and music. A friend of Erasmus, she translated his *Treatise on the Lord's Prayer.* It was printed with an introduction by a man who used her accom-plishments as an argu-ment for university educa-tion for women. When her father was beheaded and his head put on London Bridge, Margaret defied the king by rescuing it, for which she was arrested and imprisoned. However, her eloquence before the judges won first their respect and admiration, and then her release.

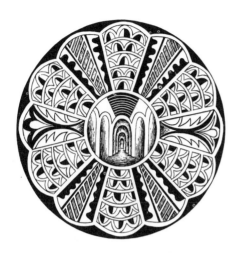

Isabella d'Este

1474–1539

Isabella d'Este's situation mirrors that of many Renaissance noblewomen. They had little independent power, for the kind of economic and political base that supported their medieval predecessors had disappeared. It was the male – not the female – ruler who served as the arbiter of culture, and women were completely unable to shape cultural values in their own interests. Even in their courts, they were expected to facilitate, not participate in, the evening discussions among the predominantly male guests they had assembled. And although Italian women were educated, sometimes held chairs in philosophy and law, discoursed in Latin before bishops and cardinals, and wrote and performed music – ultimately, the new concept of individualism born in the Renaissance was applied only to men.

Catherine Adorni

1447–1510; Italy
Adorni worked in the hospital of Genoa, where she was a nurse and supervisor of a group of disciples. When the Plague broke out, she organized open-air wards. She wrote mystical and theological works such as *Purgatory* and *A Dialogue Between the Soul and the Body.*

Laura Ammanati

1513–1589; Italy
Considered one of the finest poets of the sixteenth century, Ammanati was a scholar in philosophy and literature, and a member of the Academy at Siena. Her best works include the *Glory of Paradise* and a translation of *Penentential Psalms.*

Novella d'Andrea

14th c.; Italy
D'Andrea was a scholar in law and literature. Instructed by her father, she became his assistant when he was professor of canonical law at the University of Bologna.

Isabella Andreini

1562–1604; Italy
Andreini was famous as an actress, a poet, and a musician. Many of her sonnets, madrigals, and songs, as well as her letters, were printed in Venice in 1610.

Lucrezia Borgia

1480–1519; Italy
Behind the myth of Lucrezia Borgia – the image of feminine evil – was an innocent woman who became a political pawn of her father, Pope Alexander VI. He manipulated her physical charm and political acumen to further his own ambitions. Her third husband was the Duke of Ferrara, to whom she became devoted.

As Duchess of Ferrara, she made her court a lively center of intellectual activity. She founded hospitals and convents, proclaimed a special edict to protect Jews from persecution, and once pawned her jewels to aid famine victims.

Dorotea Bucca

fl. 1436; Italy
The daughter of a physician and philosopher, Bucca received a doctorate from the University at Bologna and succeeded her father there as Professor of Medicine and Moral Philosophy. She taught for forty years.

Caterina Cornaro

1454–1510; Italy
A member of the Venetian nobility, Cornaro was used by the Doge to further his political ambitions by arranging a marriage for her with the King of Cyprus. She had been in Cyprus a year when her husband was killed, and she was declared regent for her unborn child. Ultimately, the Venetian government relieved her of her responsibility, having achieved control of Cyprus through her. Sent back to Venice with honor and given an estate in the Alps, she established a salon which became an international retreat. She also founded hospitals and institutions for the poor.

Laura Cereta

1469–1498; Italy
An eminent scholar and professor, Cereta devoted most of her life to work in philosophy and the languages, both ancient and modern. Little of her work is extant.

Vittoria Colonna

1490/92–1547; Italy
Colonna was the most influential woman of the Italian Renaissance and was considered Italy's greatest woman writer. Her works dealt with nature, religion, patriotism, and the human condition. She was concerned with religious reform, as were other great thinkers of the day, such as her friend Margaret of Navarre. The greats of the Italian Renaissance gathered at the Colonna castle at Ischia. Colonna was a friend and inspiration to Michelangelo, who wrote of her, "Without wings, I fly with your wings; by your genius I am raised to the skies; in your soul my thought is born."

Her written work was voluminous and hundreds of her sonnets have been preserved. Unfortunately, history has obscured her own achievements and focused primarily on her relationship with Michelangelo.

Isabella Cortesi

d. 1561; Italy
Cortesi wrote books on the subjects of chemistry, alchemy, and medicine. One extant title is *Secreti Medicinal: Artificiosi de Alchemici*, published 1561 – 1565.

Tullia d'Aragona

1505–1556; Italy
One of the most illustrious women of her time, D'Aragona's poems include a treatise on embittered love, *Dell Infinita d'Amor*, and an epic poem, *Il Meschino* (the unfortunate). She established an academy in her home, where Platonic thought and Latin and Greek were studied, as well as music, singing, and poetry.

Cassandra Fidelis

fl. 1484; Italy
Fidelis was renowned for her knowledge of medicine and was also a poet and accomplished musician. She gave public lectures in Padua and corresponded with the leading figures of the Italian Renaissance. Her letters and orations were published in 1636.

Veronica Gambara

1485–1550; Italy
Gambara was a poet and musician. Widowed early in life, she devoted her time to study, correspondence, literature, and the education of her two sons, with the result that one became a general and the other a cardinal. In 1528, she moved to Bologna and established a salon where the most eminent literati gathered.

Alessandra Giliani

1307–1326; Italy
A pioneer of anatomical injection, Giliani devised a means of drawing blood from the veins and arteries of cadavers and then filling them with different colored liquids to render them more visible. She was an assistant to the surgeon Mondino, the father of modern anatomy, and was pictured in his anatomy text. (Women were still included in the professions in Renaissance Italy.)

Elizabetta Gonzaga

15th c.; Italy
The court of Duchess Gonzaga was the heart of the intellectual and cultural life of the city of Urbino. Gonzaga, a sister-in-law of Isabella d'Este, received at her court Piero della Francesca, Jan Van Eyck, Raphael, and Baldassare Castiglione, whose *The Courtier* was based on conversations in her drawing room.

Baptista Malatesta

d. 1460; Italy
A scholar and philosopher, Malatesta lectured and wrote on philosophy and theology. She administered her estates alone after the death of her husband and eventually retired to a convent.

Olympia Morata

1526–1555; Italy
Educated by her father, Morata became a distinguished classical scholar and professor of philosophy and was respected by the greatest thinkers of her day. Her Greek and Latin dialogues and poems, as well as her letters and translations, were published in 1555. Sympathetic to the Reformation, she was forced to move to Heidelberg because her religious views were unpopular. The University offered her the professorship of Greek, but the plague cut short her brilliant career.

Caterina Sforzia

1463–1509; Italy
Sforzia was an illegitimate daughter of the heir of the Duchy of Milan. He was assassinated, and she was married off to strengthen an alliance between her family and another which controlled the papacy. Caterina's husband was made a count, and when the pope died and her husband was later assassinated, she decided to take command of the territory as regent for her son. Her title as regent was not the source of her power, but rather her military strength and political skill. Though she was finally overthrown by Cesare Borgia, she was one of the few Renaissance women to seize power so directly.

Lucrezia Tournabuoni

ca. 1430–1482; Italy
A Florentine woman, powerful in all spheres of public life, Tournabuoni was a politician, businesswoman, and banker, as well as a writer, an art patron, and a philanthropist. Her counsel was sought and respected, for – as the wife of Piero de Medici and mother of Lorenzo the Magnificent – she wielded much influence over political appointments and financial transactions. A cultivated woman, she supervised the education of her grandson, who became Pope Clement VII. She also patronized the arts and wrote several religious works.

In the late fifteenth century, with the breakdown of the Church – which had considered the female voice lewd and lascivious – professional female musicians began to appear, inspired in part by the tradition of the courts of love where women both wrote and played music. These women musicians enjoyed great popularity in the Renaissance courts, where there was intense competition for those skilled in playing and composing music.

Francesca Caccini

b. 1581; Italy

A versatile musician to the Court of the Medicis, Caccini sang and played the harp, guitar, and harpsichord. She composed many songs which were published as *Il Primo Libro,* one of the largest collections of solo songs to appear in print. In the 1620's, she received a commission to compose a work that is believed to be the first opera written by a woman.

Tarquinia Molza

1542–1617; Italy

A musician at the later D'Este Court, Molza was a singer, composer, and the conductor of an orchestra of women musicians. Her career was cut short when she was dismissed from court over her involvement in a love affair. Unfortunately, her music may have been banished as well, for none remains. A true Renaissance woman, Molza was also a poet, translator, and scholar.

Gaspara Stampa

15th c.; Italy

Stampa was a famous Venetian poet, musician, and composer. Though abandoned by her lover, the Count of Collato, she gathered her love lyrics into a volume and dedicated it to him. Her verses enjoyed wide publication and great acclaim after her death.

Barbara Strozzi

16th c.; Italy

Strozzi was a singer who performed her own compositions. She was one of the earliest female musicians to receive recognition as both performer and composer.

As members of ruling families in Europe, women, of course, continued to be regents and queens. But there was an outbreak of resentment toward female monarchs, perhaps as a result of their continued power. A new development saw the king's mistress gain a major role, exerting influence on him indirectly, which became an increasingly common way for women to affect politics.

Anne of Beaujeu

ca. 1462–1522; France

One of the most important political figures of her day, Anne was so distinguished for her knowledge of government that her father, Louis XI, declared her regent during her brother Charles' minority. The appointment was disputed by the Duke of Orleans, who provoked a civil war. He was not only defeated but became Anne's captive for several years. An astute stateswoman, she weathered many diplomatic storms and challenges to her authority.

Anne of Brittany

1476/77–1514; France

Anne of Brittany took over the administration of France when her husband Charles VIII fought in the Italian Wars. She later married Louis XII. She was a patron of the arts, and she won privileges for the office of queen, such as her own guard. Although she lived in rude times, Anne was considered learned, refined, and pious, and was the first queen to give women an important place at court.

Annabella Drummond

d. 1401; Scotland

Drummond was an intelligent and successful ruler of Scotland. She and her husband ascended to the throne in 1390, and, because he was often ill, the responsibility of governing was largely assumed by Annabella. She died during the Plague in 1401, but Scotland enjoyed a period of relative tranquility during her ten-year reign.

Isabella of Lorraine

fl. 1429; France

A wise ruler, Isabella of Lorraine assembled an army of nobles to rescue her husband when he was taken prisoner in 1429. While a prisoner, he inherited another kingdom which Isabella went to claim, reigning there quite successfully. She was the patron of Agnes Sorel and one of the most illustrious women of the fifteenth century.

Mahaut of Artois

d. 1329; France

A noblewoman and lady of the manor, Countess Mahaut inherited first her father's estate of Artois, then her husband's estate of Burgundy. She ruled the two domains for many years, surviving intrigue, scandal, and insurrection. She proved to be an able administrator, a skillful diplomat, a dedicated art patron, and a conscientious philanthropist. Not only did she study medicine – leaving many illustrated manuscripts on the treatment of disease – but also built eighty hospitals and thirty lazarettos.

Mathilda of Germany

fl. 1470; Germany

Mathilda was largely responsible for the advent of humanism in Bavaria and Swabia. Interested in literary reform, she collected old court poetry, encouraged the oral tradition of Germanic folk songs, promoted poetry writing based on ancient Germanic tradition, and had valuable works translated into German. She inspired the humanist Nicholas von Wyle to compose a eulogy for her which praised the many blessings women had brought into the world. This tribute was intended to counteract many of the coarse, offensive, and obscene images of women that were being promulgated in contemporary literature.

Marie de Medici

1573–1642; France

De Medici married Henry IV of France in 1600, and during their ten-year marriage she became an important patron of the arts. In order to ensure the political legitimacy of her offspring, she had herself formally crowned queen in 1610, and when Henry was assassinated she became regent for her son Louis XIII. In 1617, her son exerted his authority and exiled her. She was allowed to return to Paris two years later, where, as Queen Mother, she remained an influential art patron, building and decorating the Luxembourg Palace and Gardens and commissioning Rubens to paint a series of works depicting events from her life. She also commissioned eight statues of famous women to surround the entrance to her residence.

Jeanne de Montfort

fl. 1341; France

De Montfort played a key role in the Hundred Years' War, a major war of succession. She supported her

155

husband in his claims to the Duchy of Brittany. Together, they took certain towns and fortresses and garrisoned them. When De Montfort was captured, his wife, a good military strategist and fearless leader, obtained the aid of the English and thereby won.

Agnes Sorel

1409–1450; France
Sorel was a politically astute woman and won a powerful position as advisor to King Charles VII. Together with Yolanda of Aragon and Joan of Arc she helped to consolidate and strengthen the French kingdom.

Yolanda of Aragon

15th c.; France
Yolanda was an important political figure in French history. After marrying into the French nobility, she sought to strengthen the interests of France against the English, who had conquered much of France. She supported Joan of Arc's army financially and exerted pressure on Charles VII to favor Joan's plans. Yolanda proclaimed her belief in Joan's divine mission, and when Joan went to trial, Yolanda testified in her behalf. Realizing the political ineptitude of Charles VII, Yolanda introduced Agnes Sorel to him, with the idea that Sorel would become, as his mistress, a political force. Together Sorel and Yolanda exercised a positive influence on the King; then, Yolanda made an alliance with Navarre and Brittany, uniting those provinces and thereby strengthening the French crown.

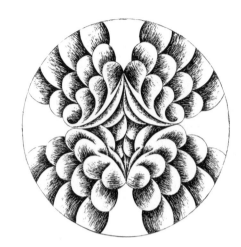

Elizabeth R

1533 – 1603

The position of women improved during Elizabeth's reign. This was partly a result of her enlightened rule, her reforms, and her example as a powerful role model on the throne. She virtually eliminated England's witchcraft trials by insisting that a woman could not be executed without evidence. Another factor in the improving status of women was that some of the early reformers were descendants of the humanists and believed in educating women. For a little while, women's educational opportunities were expanded, aiding the erudition and learning of many female rulers of the time. These queens then supported humanist studies in their royal schools, which produced many female scholars, a flowering of female achievement, and a startling number of exceptional female rulers. However, later the Reformation stressed that women's education should be limited to basics and also brought with it the dissolution of the convents. Thus, the primary source of women's education disappeared.

Anne Bacon

1528–1610; England
Scholar, translator, and tutor and governess to Edward VI, Bacon's reputation among the literati extended beyond her own country. In 1550 she published a translation of twenty-five sermons by Bernardine Ochine, a celebrated Italian religious figure. She also translated Bishop Jewel's *An Apology for the Church of England* from Latin to English. The book was an important and controversial document, and her translation made it accessible to the common people. She was also the mother of Sir Francis Bacon and an obvious influence on his thought and life.

Georgiana Cavendish

1757–1806; England
Influential as the most important female member of the Whig party in England, Cavendish took an active part in politics. As the Duchess of Devonshire, she was extremely liberal and progressive and supported middle-class commercial interests as well as favoring a representative government.

Elizabeth Danviers

16th c.; England
Danviers was one of the learned women during the reign of Elizabeth I. She was a noted authority on Chaucer.

Elizabeth Hoby

fl. 1558; England
By the age of twenty-five, Hoby was managing an estate comprising two hundred houses and four mills. She was a midwife, surgeon, and general medical practitioner.

Jane of Southerland

1545–1629; Scotland
A pragmatic yet visionary businesswoman, Jane was responsible for turning the town of Brora into an industrial center. She oversaw the working of a new coal mine and established a saltworks. As a Catholic, she was often out of favor politically, but she remained true to her faith.

Sarah Jennings

1660–1744; England
A major force and influence in Queen Anne's court, Jennings ultimately disagreed with royal policies and became leader of the opposition Whig Party. Jennings, the Duchess of Marlboro, also known as "Queen Sarah," was a shrewd businesswoman and became one of the richest peeresses in England. When she became too old to leave her rooms, she transacted her own business from her bed, six hours a day, until her death. Jennings left a record of her life and time in her memoirs, which she published herself.

Lilliard

d. 1547; Scotland
In a war between England and Scotland, Lilliard, a Scottish soldier, fought in retaliation for a raid in which her parents and lover were killed. Wearing a suit of armor, she joined the battle at Ancrum, where she killed the English leader. Although she died in battle, the Scots won, and their success is attributed to her heroism.

Elizabeth Lucar

1510–1537; England
An exquisitely skilled needleworker, Lucar was also an excellent calligrapher. She was proficient in mathematics, knew Latin, Italian, and Spanish, and was an accomplished musician.

Margaret of Desmond

fl. 14th c.; Ireland
A Gaelic warrior and stateswoman, Countess Margaret governed her estates jointly with her husband and maintained and led her own private band of warriors. As a patron of the arts and education, she invited weavers from Flanders to teach and establish tapestry-making and she also founded a school.

Grace O'Malley

fl. 1580's; Ireland
A sea captain and pirate, the "Lady Chieftain of the O'Malleys" commanded a fleet of three galleys and two hundred of the most lawless men in the British Isles. She ruled the sea for years, a terror to all merchant ships on the Atlantic. She was so powerful that Elizabeth I, in order to curtail O'Malley's activities, invited her to court and offered to make her a countess. O'Malley refused, saying that she would serve no one but herself. This meeting did, however, cement an alliance between their two countries.

Mary Sidney

1555/61–1621; England
Sidney established a salon in her home where she exchanged ideas with the most illustrious people of the period – Raleigh, Shakespeare, Jonson, and Donne. With her brother, she translated a book of psalms into English verse, called the *Sidnean Psalms*.

Elizabeth Talbot

1518–1608; England
Talbot was a successful architect and businesswoman who designed and built houses on property that came to her through inheritances from two husbands. She was also a moneylender, farmer, and a merchant of lead, coal, and timber. Multititled, Elizabeth, known as Countess of Shrewsbury and Bess of Hardwicke, represents the power of the aristocratic woman of Tudor England.

Jane Weston

fl. 1560; England
Well-traveled and highly educated, Weston was internationally known for her prose and verse and was considered one of the leading Latin poets of the sixteenth century.

There were exceptional women elsewhere in Europe in the sixteenth century, but we know less about them than about those Englishwomen who benefited directly from Elizabeth's rule.

Maria de Coste Blanche

fl. 1566; France
An instructor of mathematics and physics in Paris, De Coste Blanche published *The Nature of the Sun and the Earth* in 1566.

Catharine Fisher

d. 1579; Germany
One of the most precise linguists of the sixteenth century, Fisher was responsible for the education of her son James, the celebrated philosopher.

Penette de Guillet

16th c.; France
De Guillet was an accomplished musician and poet. Fluent in Spanish and Italian, she composed verse in Latin as well, and many of her works have survived to present times.

Kenau Hasselaer

1526–1589; Holland
Hasselaer was a successful businesswoman from a brewer's family. She married a shipbuilder, and was widowed, with four children, in 1561; she registered as an independent shipwright and carried on the business. She traveled extensively, competing successfully for business in the Netherlands and Scandinavia. She achieved fame for her participation in the defense of Haarlem during the Wars of Liberation in 1573.

Helene Kottauer

1410–1471; Austria
Kottauer was a middle-class servant to Queen Elizabeth of Hungary. She wrote her memoirs, recounting her experiences in the court and describing the struggles of Elizabeth to maintain her power.

Isabella de Joya Roseres

16th c.; Spain
A theologian and preacher, De Joya Roseres was one of the few women to address the congregation in a Catholic church. She preached in the cathedral at Barcelona, and later went to Rome where she was a member of the papal court of Paul III. There, she discoursed on theological problems before the College of Cardinals.

Maria-Christine de Lalaing

1545–1582; Belgium
De Lalaing organized the military defense of her city when it was besieged by the Spanish in 1581. Continuing to fight even while wounded, she was a valiant model for her soldiers. The city was forced to surrender when the food and ammunition were gone, but even the conquerors celebrated her heroism.

Isabella Losa

1473–1546; Spain
A brilliant scholar, Losa was illustrious for her knowledge of Greek, Latin, and Hebrew. After she was widowed, she entered the Order of St. Clair and went to Italy, where she founded a hospital.

Gracia Mendesa

Beatrice de Luna
1510–1569; Portugal
Mendesa was a philanthropist who spent much of her large fortune relieving the suffering of persecuted Jews. She founded synagogues, gave support to Jewish scholars, and worked to prevent the Inquisition from entering Portugal. Denounced as a Jew, she was put in prison in Venice, and her property was confiscated. Liberated in 1550, she and her daughter settled in Constantinople.

Olivia Sabuco

16th c.; Spain
Sabuco produced a body of work that investigated the relationship between mental and physical health and the effects of culture and environment on human development. She also wrote on political and social reforms. Her theories were quite advanced, and her writings were attacked by the Inquisition, which destroyed all but two volumes.

The fact that women were able to continue to exert power as rulers is not surprising, for upper-class women always retained some privileges. But it is of interest to note how many enlightened, progressive, and independent female rulers there were throughout Europe during the course of a few centuries.

Jeanne d'Albret

1528–1572; France
Daughter of Margaret of Navarre, D'Albret was a scholar, a poet, a religious reformer, and the Queen of Navarre. She ardently opposed Catholicism and withstood the Inquisition, which was invoked against her in 1563. She established Protestantism throughout the country, seizing the property of the established Church and using it to support ministries and schools. New religious ideas were studied at her palace, and she designed and worked a series of tapestries with religious liberty as the theme. She influenced her son, Henry IV, to establish religious toleration in France.

Anna Sophia

1531–1585; Denmark
Known as the Mother of Her Country, Anna Sophia improved education, built schools and churches, and established botanical gardens. Interested in agriculture, she raised her own medicinal herbs and founded an apothecary that remained in existence for three hundred years. She was the daughter of the King of Denmark and wife of August I of Savoy.

Catherine of Aragon

1483/5–1536; England
Catherine's classical education was supervised by her mother, Isabella of Castile, who brought such scholars as Beatrix Galindo and Francisca de Lebrija to her court. When Catherine married Henry VIII of England, she continued her intellectual pursuits, patronizing writers and advocating education for women. Many treatises on the education of women were written under her auspices, and her ideas affected women's education for the next hundred years. Because she did not produce a male heir, she was forced from her royal position.

Catherine II

Catherine the Great
1729–1796; Russia
Catherine's ability to reform, refine, and organize affected nearly every phase of life. In agriculture, she introduced improved animal breeding techniques, crop rotation, and silk worm cultivation. In industry, Catherine encouraged immigrants to settle in labor-short regions, broke up monopolies, and extended manufacturing and mining. She advanced the education available to girls and built many schools. Her support of the advancement of medicine was underscored by her willingness to be the first in Russia to receive a smallpox inoculation. She intended to free the serfs but the nobility resisted.

Christina of Sweden

1626–1689; Sweden
As sole heir to the throne of Sweden, Christina, age eighteen, was the first woman to be crowned king. During her ten-year reign she tried to raise the standards of Swedish culture and attracted many of the leading intellectuals of the day to her court, including Descartes and Scarlatti. Christina's refusal to marry, coupled with her desire to travel and live her life free from courtly criticism, led to her abdication. She settled in Rome, converted to Catholicism, founded academies, compiled a comprehensive library, and collected paintings and antiques.

Isabella of Castile

1451–1504; Spain
Isabella of Castile is known as the supporter of Columbus' expeditions to the New World. This act was in keeping with her breadth of vision, which led to the founding of new universities and the subsidy of scholars in the sciences and the arts. New opportunities for women were made possible by Isabella as she assigned women to University posts and supported several female scholars in her court. She insisted upon a formidable education for her daughters, and one of these, Catherine of Aragon, passed on this tradition to her step-daughter, Elizabeth I. Industry flourished during her reign as did conservation. Her reign was severely blemished, however, by her support of the Inquisition and the persecution of the Moors and the Jews.

Jadwiga

1370–1399; Poland
In default of a male heir, Jadwiga ascended to the throne in 1384, the first legitimate queen to rule Poland. Her reign ushered in the heroic age of Poland, which lasted for two hundred years. She tried to bring religion and learning within the reach of all her people, re-established the University of Krakow, supported and improved Church music, and did all she could to raise the cultural level of her country.

Margaret of Austria

1480 – 1530; Austria
As Regent of the Netherlands from 1507 until her retirement, Margaret brought about financial stability and negotiated important trade agreements in Western Europe. The Treaty of Cambrai (1529) between Margaret and Louise of Savoy was called "The Ladies' Peace." After using her political influence to secure the crown for Charles V, she retired and devoted herself to study, encouraging the "new learning" of the Renaissance.

Margaret of Navarre

1492–1549; France
Margaret of Navarre contributed more to the development of learning in France than any other individual of the period. A patron of the arts and literature, her salon became the stronghold for those who advocated and initiated the Reformation. Margaret wrote a volume of religious poems, *The Mirror of the Sinful Soul*, and the *Heptameron*, a collection of medieval tales.

Margaret of Scandinavia

1353–1412; Denmark
Margaret, daughter of the King of Denmark and wife of the King of Norway, became regent of both thrones – in the name of her son – when the kings died. After her son also died, Margaret was unanimously elected Queen of Denmark, despite the fact that there was no precedent there for a ruling queen. She took control of Norway, and was such a popular ruler that the people of Sweden, oppressed by their king, offered her the throne. She accepted, defeated the Swedish king in battle, and tried to unite the three countries and end the constant warring among them. She established a fair legal system and laid the foundation for future commerce.

Maria Thérèsa

1717–1780; Austria
Maria Thérèsa ascended the throne in 1740 and ruled for forty years. Leaders of several nations began to plot her downfall, but she engaged the support of Hungary in the Seven Years War against Prussia and established an alliance with Holland, Denmark, and Russia. Through collaboration with Mme. de Pompadour, Maria Thérèsa gained the support of France, which resulted in Prussia's defeat. With peace restored, she began many needed reforms in the army, the courts of law, and the educational system. She suppressed the Inquisition, lowered taxes, and founded orphanages and hospitals. As the economy improved, the arts flourished under her rule. During her reign, Vienna became the musical capital of Europe, fostering the talents of Mozart, Haydn, and Gluck. Maria Thérèsa was the mother of Marie Antoinette and eighteen other children, all of whom were born in her first nineteen years of marriage.

Mary of Hungary

d. 1558; Spain
The daughter of Philip of Spain, Mary married Louis, King of Hungary, in 1521. Upon his death she became the ruler of the Netherlands, and she reigned there until 1555, when she returned to Spain. She was remembered as a patron of the arts and friend to the Protestants.

Catherine Pavlovna

1788–1819; Russia
A Grand Princess of Russia, Pavlovna formed associations for women, promoted education for all her people, established agricultural societies, and provided food for her subjects during a famine.

Elizabeth Petrovna

1709–1762; Russia
As Empress of Russia, Petrovna ruled the nation singlehandedly from 1741 to 1761. She refused all offers of marriage, preferring love affairs and absolute sovereignty. Influenced by the West – she founded the University of Moscow and later the Academy of Arts at St. Petersburg to encourage popular education and native literature. She eradicated long-standing corruption in Russian government, established alliances with France and Austria, introduced a better system of taxation, encouraged pioneer settlements in Eastern Russia, opened mines, and established banks.

Philippa of Hainault

1314–1369; England
Queen Philippa triumphantly led an army of twelve thousand against the Scots, captured the King of Scotland, and became a heroine to the English people. Recognized throughout Europe for her remarkable innovations in social welfare and her concern for the poor, especially women, she also established the wool industry at Norwich and the coal industry at Tynedale – enterprises which became the backbone of the English economy.

Sophia of Mechlenberg

16th c.; Germany
Due to the influence of Sophia of Mechlenberg, Scandinavian midwives have led the world in the prevention of maternal and infant mortality. Sophia tried to change the custom of "a baby a year," which led to the deaths of so many mothers. She taught birth control, encouraged mothers to nurse their babies, and stressed that midwives must study their art carefully. She instituted sanitation reforms such as isolating the sick, enforcing stricter burial laws, and encouraging frequent bathing and she put a stop to the killing of illegitimate babies. After her husband's death, she ruled Norway and Denmark until her son Christian IV reached his majority.

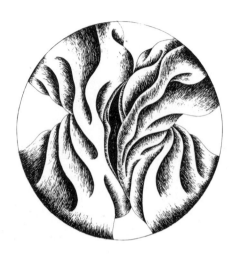

Artemisia Gentileschi

1590–1642

Although women artists generally encountered enormous obstacles in obtaining training, commissions, and recognition, women's position varied in different parts of Europe and as a result, women artists appeared in various countries at different times, depending upon the social and political circumstances. An improvement in women's status usually brought with it the appearance of more women in the arts. Thus, between the fifteenth and seventeenth centuries, Italy produced a large number of female artists, partly as a result of the continued convent tradition there and also because humanism encouraged female achievement. But when a woman artist appeared, she was always claimed as an example of the creative genius of a Renaissance city, rather than being seen as a representative of the talent of her sex. In France, the eighteenth century brought a period of greater freedom for women, but, as Vigée-Lebrun commented about the early eighteenth century, "The

women reigned then; the Revolution dethroned them." And, of course, successful women artists disappeared. Despite the evidence of history, however, as to the difficulties women artists faced, the question "Why are there no great women artists?" continues to be asked. Studying the lives of women artists of the past makes it abundantly clear that even when women were able to establish themselves, their work was later underestimated, obscured, or attributed to men.

Sophonisba Anguisciola

1527–1624; Italy

Renowned for her portraits, Anguisciola became the court painter to Philip II in 1560. As a member of the nobility, she received a well-rounded education, which led to the discovery of her artistic talent. Not only was she the first woman to emerge as an eminent, professional painter, she was also a member of the aristocracy.

Rosalba Carriera

1675–1757; Italy

Carriera was the greatest painter of pastels and miniatures of her day. By 1720, when she visited Paris and did portraits of Watteau and the young Louis XV, her work had become extremely popular and she was elected to the French Academy. However, she began to go blind, and treatments could not prevent it. The loss of her sight so depressed her that she is said to have ended her life in a state of complete mental collapse.

Lavinia Fontana

1552–1614; Italy

Fontana was trained by her father and was the most prolific woman artist before the eighteenth century. Her subject matter was not confined to portraiture and still lives, as was many women's (primarily because they were not permitted to study anatomy), but included figurative works, some portraying female and male nudes. She painted large-scale works and executed many public and private commissions. Usually signed and dated, her work also included portraits, small religious pieces, and altar pieces for churches in Bologna, Cento, and Rome.

Fede Galizia

1578–1630; Italy

Famous for her still lifes and portraits, Galizia's artistic talent was mentioned in print when she was twelve years old; by her late teens, she was an established portrait painter. She produced still lifes and religious works, received public commissions, and was responsible for the high altar piece of Santa Monica Maddalena in Milan in 1616. Some of her work in Milanese churches survives today, and her painting *Judith and Her Handmaiden* is in Sarasota, Florida.

exterminated, but contemporary feminist scholars

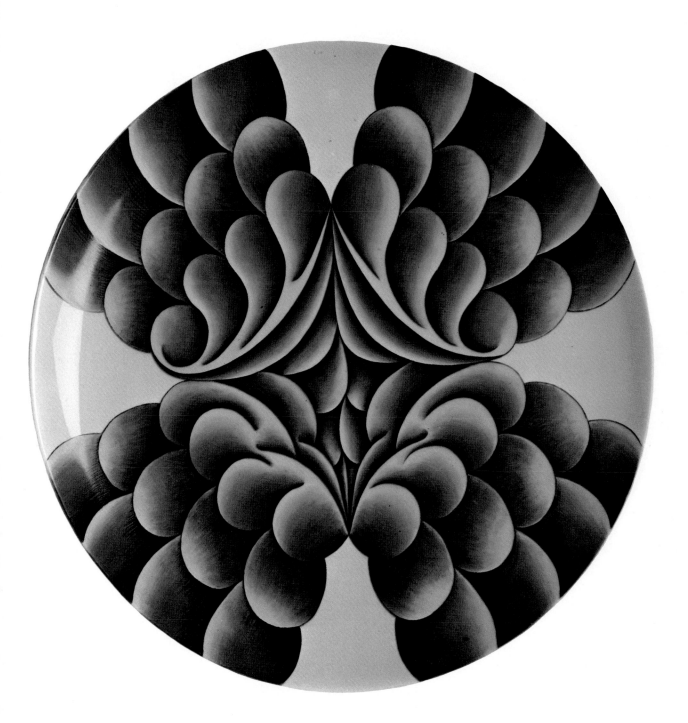

Elizabeth R

are beginning to suspect that there were probably

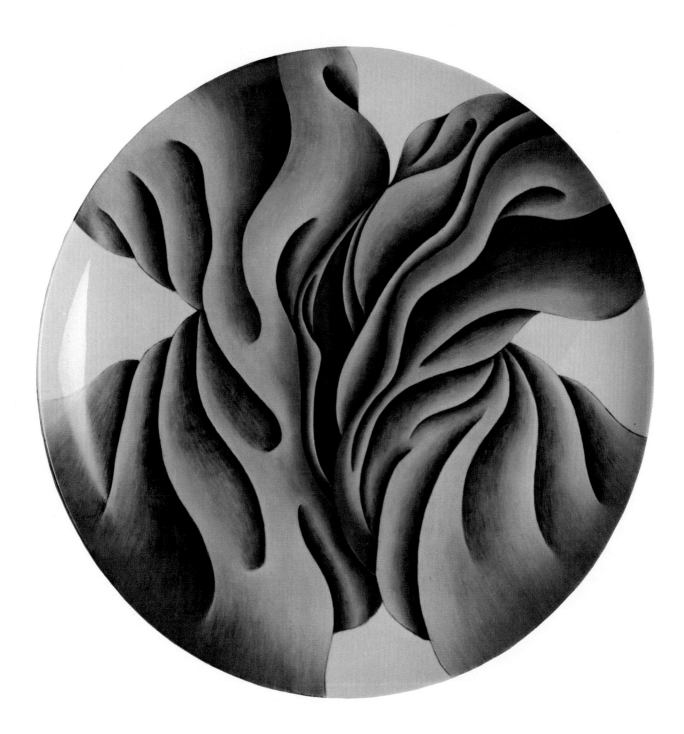

Artemisia Gentileschi

between six and nine million killed. Eighty-five

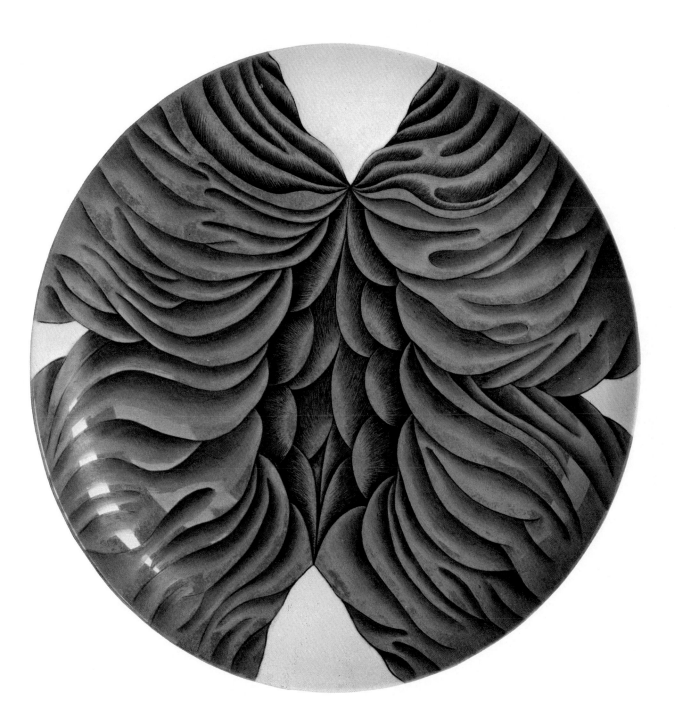

Anna van Schurman

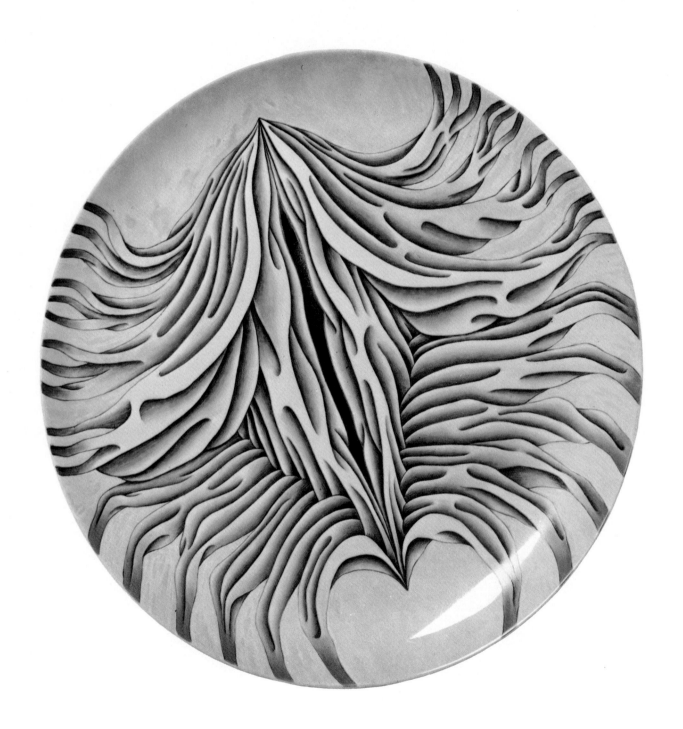

Anne Hutchinson

Renaissance women had little independent power,

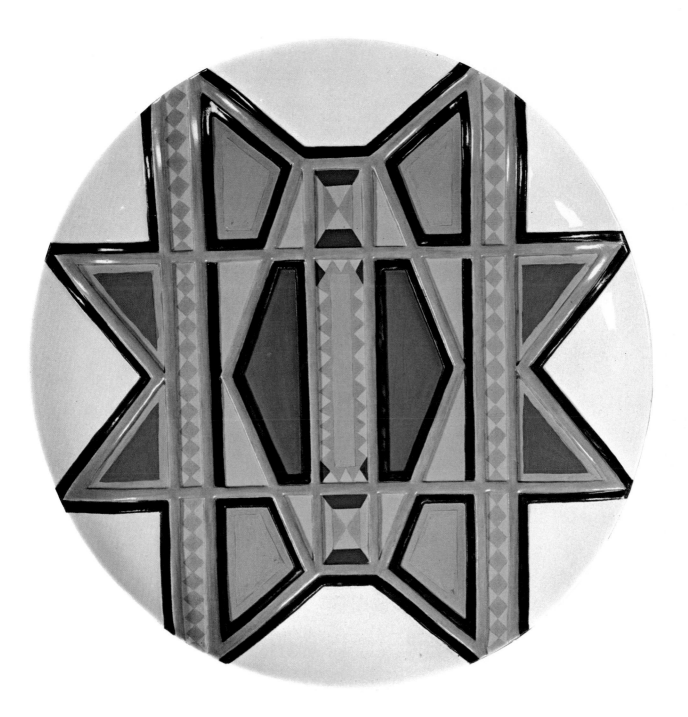

Sacajawea

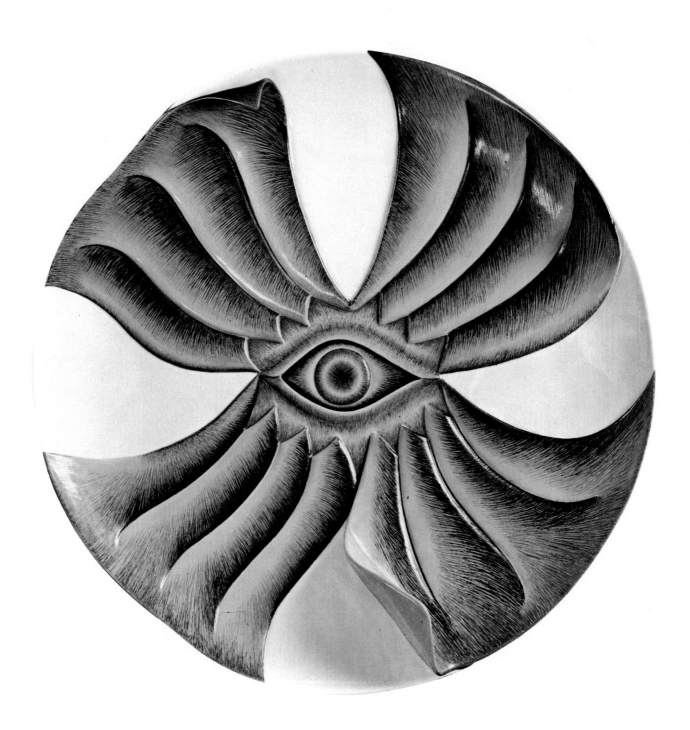

for the economic and political base that

Caroline Herschel

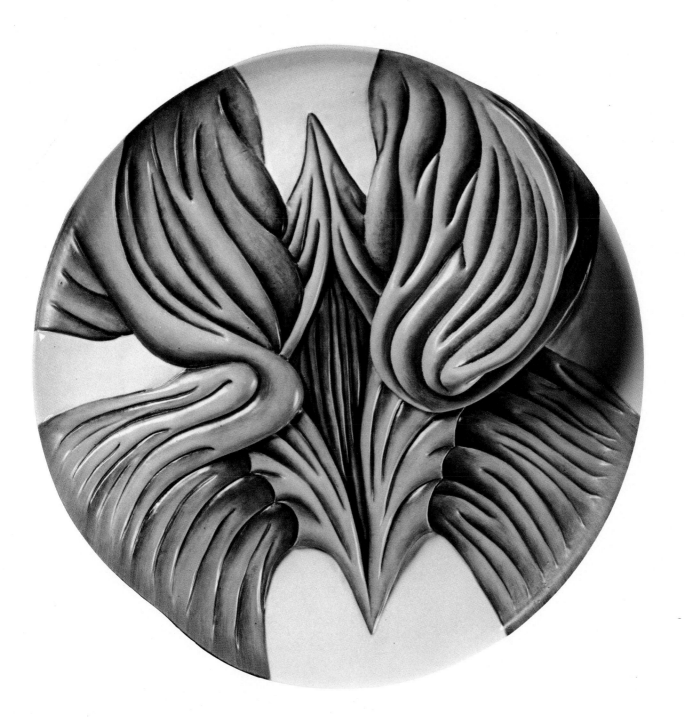

Mary Wollstonecraft

had disappeared. The decline of feudalism,

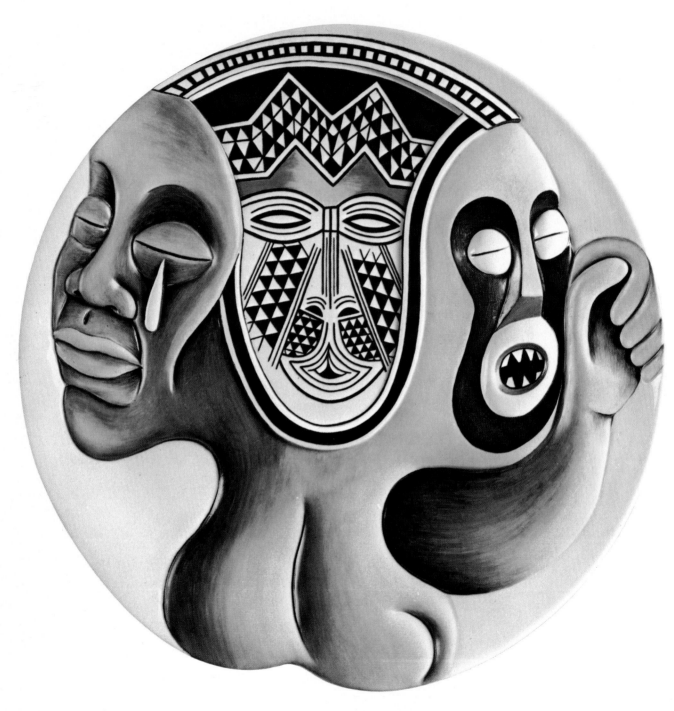

Sojourner Truth

Honorata Rodiana

d. 1472; Italy

Rodiana was the only woman fresco painter in fifteenth-century Italy. Unfortunately, none of her works are extant, probably due to improper attribution. It is said that she worked for the ruler of Cremona until one of his courtiers attempted to – or possibly actually did – rape her. Rodiana fatally stabbed him, fled, and, disguised as a man, joined a band of professional soldiers. Thereafter she divided her time between painting and fighting. She died defending her birthplace of Castelleone.

Properzia de Rossi

1490–1530; Italy

De Rossi was a sculptor who worked in several media, the most unique of which was peach stones. A series of these miniature carvings, which depict the Saints and Apostles, is in the Grassi Museum at Bologna. She also sculpted two angels for the Church of St. Petronius as well as bas-reliefs of Potiphar's wife and Joseph.

Elisabetta Sirani

1638–1665; Italy

Sirani was a professional artist and the instructor of an entire generation of women artists. She was extremely prolific during her short lifetime. She produced at least 150 paintings on subject matter ranging from portraits to religious, allegorical, and mythological scenes.

Marie Antoinette was the patron of a number of women artists who vied with each other for fame and fortune. Paintings by Labille-Guiard and Vigée-Lebrun fill a room at the Palace of Versailles, but not all the French women artists of this period enjoyed as much status as they had.

Elizabeth Cheron

1648–1711 France

Cheron's historical paintings and portraits won her the admiration of the Royal Academy, although membership in the Academy by women was not allowed. Her work was so respected that she was given an annual pension by Louis XIV.

Marguerite Gérard

1761–1837; France

Gérard's sister was married to Fragonard and summoned Gérard to Paris, where she became a part of the artistic community surrounding her sister's husband. By 1789, Gérard's reputation equaled that of Vigée-Lebrun and Labille-Guiard. She was the first woman to succeed as a genre painter, an area that was particularly male-dominated. She was also a portraitist and miniaturist.

Adélaïde Labille-Guiard

1749–1803; France

From a low social class background and with no artistic tradition in her family, Labille-Guiard became one of the most active and influential artists of the eighteenth century. She worked as a portrait painter and was admitted to the Royal Academy in 1783 on the same day as Vigée-Lebrun. Labille-Guiard was a vocal member of the academy, arguing for such things as the appointment of women art professors.

As a supporter of the Revolution, she was able to remain in Paris and build up a clientele among the leaders of the new regime. She embarked on a monumental work that not only challenged her ability but would have elevated her to the status of historical painter in the Academy. Unfortunately, the work glorified the royalty and was unacceptable to the new government, who had it destroyed. Her productivity declined steadily until her death a few years later.

Elizabeth Vigée-Lebrun

1755–1842; France

Vigée-Lebrun was one of the most prolific and popular artists of her day. While still in her teens, she began receiving commissions from the aristocracy and eventually became the favorite at Versailles and court painter to Marie Antoinette, who became a close friend.

A Royalist, Vigée-Lebrun fled with her daughter to Italy on the eve of the Revolution. She spent twelve years in exile, living and working in the courts of Europe and becoming a member of the Academies of Rome, Florence, Bologna, St. Petersburg, and Berlin.

She returned to Paris and spent the remaining twenty-two years of her life in France under the Napoleonic Regime. She painted over eight hundred portraits and landscapes and maintained a journal which provides a fascinating account of the life and times of a successful professional woman.

Angelica Kauffman

1741–1807; Switzerland

Kauffman was one of the major artists and intellectuals of the eighteenth century. She was equally gifted in music and painting, but recognized that to become a professional she must devote herself to one or the other. She chose painting and years later depicted the difficulty of that decision in an allegorical work entitled *Angelica Hesitating Between the Arts of Music and Painting*. In Italy she became involved in the emerging style of Neoclassicism and was elected to the prestigious Academia di San Luca. Kauffman received vast numbers of commissions from the royalty and nobility of Europe and painted portraits of the leading artists, writers, and intellectuals of her day. She was equally renowned for her historical and allegorical paintings.

Kauffman was one of the original founding members of the British Royal Academy, and only one other woman – Mary Moser – was allowed membership until 1922. In the official portrait of the Academy, Kauffman and Moser are represented by small portraits on the wall and their male colleagues are pictured painting from a nude female model.

In Northern Europe, women's status was higher than in other areas and thus they emerged into prominence earlier. However, a number of women artists throughout Europe also had significant and important careers.

Maria de Abarca

d. 1656; Spain

A celebrated portrait painter, De Abarca was a contemporary of both Rubens and Velasquez and held in high esteem by them.

Joanna Koerton

1650–1715; Holland

Koerton was an artist who excelled in drawing, painting, embroidery, and cut-paper portraits and landscapes. Her work was admired by Peter the Great and commissioned by the Emperor of Germany.

Judith Leyster

1609–1660; Holland
Leyster was a major Dutch artist of the seventeenth century. Her career was unusual because there was no artistic tradition in her family. By 1635, she was a member of the Painters' Guild in Haarlem and had three male pupils. Her paintings are characterized by her interest in the psychology of the sitter and by her dramatic use of light and shadow. Leyster's domestic scenes display a special sensitivity toward the everyday life of women.

Maria Sibylla Merian

1647–1717; Switzerland
Naturalist and artist, Merian produced definitive works on the insect life of Switzerland and the Dutch colony of Surinam in South America. She revolutionized the sciences of zoology and botany, laying the foundation for the classification of plant and animal species in the eighteenth century. Merian wrote and illustrated a three-part catalog of flower engravings called *The New Flower.*

Luisa Roldán

1656–1704; Spain
Roldán executed life-sized carved wooden terracotta sculptures for the churches of Spain, work that so impressed Charles II that he appointed her his court sculptor. Trained by her father, she soon surpassed him in technique and sensitivity.

Rachel Ruysch

1664–1750; Netherlands
Ruysch was one of the first women to achieve an international reputation as a major artist. Her artistic talent was evident early, and at age fifteen she was apprenticed to one of Holland's finest painters. In 1701, she was received into the Painters' Guild at the Hague and later became the court painter to the Elector in Dusseldorrf. She had ten children, but despite her domestic responsibilities produced a total of eighty-five works and remained an active painter until three years before her death.

Levina Teerling

ca. 1520–1576; Flanders
Teerling was a court painter to Henry VIII, Edward VI, Mary I, and Elizabeth I. Trained in the tradition of her father and grandfather, she was a painter of miniatures. Her fame spread throughout England and the Netherlands, but unfortunately no works can be securely attributed to her.

Caterina van Hemessen

ca. 1528–1587; Flanders
Van Hemessen, one of the earliest recorded female artists in Northern Europe, was probably trained as a painter by her father and collaborated with him on some of his works. She received commissions not only from the upper class families of Flanders, but also from Queen Mary of Hungary, whom she accompanied to the court of Philip II of Spain. Best known for her small, elegant portraits, mostly of women, she also executed at least two elaborate religious paintings, signed and dated as are most of her works. Unfortunately, the end of her productivity seems to have coincided with her marriage in 1554.

Sabina von Steinbach

fl. 1318; Germany
Von Steinbach has been credited with sculpting the stone figures on the south portal of Strasbourg Cathedral in the fourteenth century. The master builder died, and she received the contract to complete the work. Although there is some dispute as to the validity of this attribution, there is an inscription on one of the sculptures that bears her name.

Women did not appear on the European stage until the 1600's, when they performed in the Commedia Dell'Arte and the Comédie-Française. Prior to this, all female parts had been played by men and young boys. Charles II of England saw actresses perform while he was in exile in Europe, and upon his restoration to the throne he not only reopened the theatres (which the Puritans had shut down), but passed a special decree allowing women to enter the profession.

Leonora Baroni

17th c.; Italy
Famous for her fine voice and musical talents, Baroni possessed a profound knowledge of music. A poet as well, her work was widely published.

Marie Champmeslé

1642–1698; France
An actress who was instrumental in the formation of the Comédie-Française,

Champmeslé achieved fame for her portrayals of Iphigenia and Phaedre in the dramas by Racine.

Elizabeth Farren

1759–1829; Ireland
Farren was a leading English actress who attempted to play male parts, but her efforts were not well received. She also performed in the plays of Elizabeth Inchbald, one of the first woman dramatists in Ireland.

Nell Gwyn

1650–1687; England
One of England's greatest actresses, Gwyn was born to a lower class family and made her theater debut in 1665. A favorite on the London stage for nearly twenty years, she was a singer, dancer, and comedienne as well. A mistress to Charles II and well known for her generosity, she influenced Charles to build Chelsea Hospital and willed most of her fortune to the poor.

Sarah Siddons

1755–1831; England
Siddons, the greatest tragic actress of her day, ruled the London stage for thirty years. Her farewell performance as Lady MacBeth was so moving that the play was stopped after her sleepwalking scene.

Luiza Todi

1753–1833; Portugal
An internationally famous soprano, Todi performed throughout Europe during the latter part of the eighteenth century.

Marie Venier

1590–1619; France
Venier was the first French actress recorded by name and was famous for her portrayal of tragic heroines.

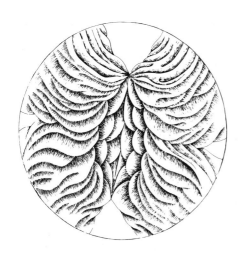

Anna van Schurman

1607–1678

As a result of the Reformation, marriage became the only acceptable option for Protestant women, although within the family women enjoyed new respect. Their lives were busy and productive, as work was centered in the home, and the activities of all the family members were crucial to its economic survival. Both father and mother were involved in child-rearing, but the mother was responsible for the religious education of the children. If a woman was content to function primarily within the family, her life could be relatively satisfying, particularly if her marriage was good. But if she had other ambitions, life was very difficult. A number of women spoke out against such restrictions, many arguing for women's right to education. Some suffered greatly for their ideas; others were respected but ultimately unheard.

Maria Agnesi

1718–1799; Italy
Agnesi, a child prodigy, spoke fluent French by the time she was five, Greek by the age of eleven, and at nine, spoke publicly for an hour in Latin on the rights of women to study science. She was so gifted in mathematics that by age twenty she had embarked on a monumental work – a treatise in two volumes on calculus – to which she devoted ten years of uninterrupted labor. When the work was completed, it caused a huge sensation in the intellectual community as it demonstrated that women could attain to the highest eminence in science. The French Academy of Science sent Agnesi a letter congratulating her on her work. They then apologized for not being able to offer her membership in the Academy, as this would be against their rules. After this, Agnesi retired from the world, devoting the rest of her life to charity. She made her views on life as a woman clear when she wrote, "…nature has endowed the female mind with a capacity for all knowledge and…in depriving women of an opportunity for acquiring knowledge, men work against the best interests of the public welfare."

Mary Astell

1666/68–1731; England
Astell's precursory treatise, *A Serious Proposal to the Ladies for the Advancement of Their True and Greatest Interest…*, was published in 1694 and dealt with the defects of the educational system for women. As a result of her work, a wealthy woman pledged the money needed to build a college for women, although she was later dissuaded by the local bishop. Though disappointed, Astell continued her work, writing *An Essay in Defense of the Female Sex.* Her goal was to raise "the general character of women and rescue them from ignorance and frivolity."

Anne Baynard

1672–1697; England
Baynard received a classical education from her father; her studies included Latin, Greek, astronomy, natural science, mathematics, and religion. She was respected for her intellect and scholarship.

Aphra Behn

1640–1689; England
A novelist and playwright and the first Englishwoman to earn her living as a writer, Behn was the author of a number of plays and eighteen novels. Determined to make her living by writing, she defied convention by competing with male playwrights. Her courage in expression, coupled with her honest criticisms of her contemporaries, brought her a great deal of hostility, particularly because she defended her own work and the rights of women writers.

Helena Cornaro

1646–1684; Italy
Cornaro challenged the practice of excluding women from academia when, in 1672, she made formal application to enter the prestigious University of Padua to qualify for the Doctor of Philosophy degree. Despite opposition, she achieved a unique place in the history of education for women. On June 25, 1678, before an immense audience of male scholars,

ecclesiastics, and foreign dignitaries, Cornaro stood to defend her thesis. Her scholarly dissertation ended to a unanimous shout of approval, and she was formally invested with the academic symbols which designated her "Prima Donna Laureate del Mondo" – the first woman in the world to receive the degree of Doctor of Philosophy.

María le Jars de Gournay

1565–1645; France
A writer and early feminist, and one of the staunchest defenders of women in sixteenth-century France, De Gournay wrote *L'Egalité des Hommes et des Femmes,* which argued for equality between the sexes. Attacks upon women – or praises of their merit – had been commonplace in French literature, but her originality lay in her insistence that the sexes were equal. She felt that the existing gulf between men and women was due largely to the limited educational opportunities available to women.

Bathsua Makin

fl. 1670's; England
Involved in the beginnings of English feminism, Makin was a teacher and educational theorist. *An Essay To Revive the Ancient Education of Gentlewomen in Religion, Manners, Arts and Tongues* was published in 1673, as was her treatise on education. Her friendship with Anna van Schurman was influential in her philosophy and work. Makin supported herself through writing and teaching.

Lucretia Marinelli

1571–1653; Italy
Marinelli was best known for her eight-volume work of 1601, *The Excellence of Women and the Defects of Men.* Her literary output also included poetry, *The Life of St. Francis,* and *The Life of the Virgin Mary.*

Marie de Miramion

1629–1696; France
De Miramion founded a school for young women, trained teachers and nurses, established a dispensary, and instructed women in the preparation of salves and plaster for which she had become famous. She also opened a home for former prostitutes where they could develop other means of support.

Hortensia von Moos

1659–1715; Switzerland
Von Moos was a scholar, a supporter of the emancipation of women, and a writer. Her published works dealt with such subjects as medicine, geology, physiology, and childrearing. From a wealthy family, she led an active and independent life, managing her estates both before and after her husband's death.

Hannah Woolley

b. 1623; England
Woolley, a professional educator, was one of many women active in the early stages of English feminism. She published many writings, the most widely read being the *Gentlewoman's Companion,* 1675. She believed that if women could obtain the same education as men, their "brains would be as fruitful as their bodies." She supported her views by providing information on role models such as Anna Comnena and Anna van Schurman.

Many women were punished, obscured, or saw their work destroyed as a result of the biases of the societies in which they lived.

Maria de Agreda

1602–1665; Spain
De Agreda was a nun, an abbess, and an essayist who had recurrent visions in which she felt God was commanding her to write the life of the Virgin Mary. The work filled nine volumes and became very controversial when it was published, primarily because De Agreda portrayed Mary as a powerful queen. Under the advice of a priest, she destroyed the wor¹, but began it again after continued visions. It took her thirty years to complete the rewriting. Although the Inquisition at Madrid permitted publication of her work, the Inquisition at Rome was not so tolerant, particularly of women's writings. Her entire body of work was condemned and destroyed.

Anne Askew

1521–1546; England
Askew, a Catholic, became convinced of the necessity of the Reformation after intensive study of the Bible. She became a Protestant, which so enraged her husband that he drove her from the house. She escaped to London, but at her husband's request she was taken into custody and examined as a heretic. Tortured on the rack, all her bones were dislocated, yet she continued to reason calmly with her tormentors. She refused an offer to recant and was burned at the stake. The published account of her martyrdom helped to strengthen the Protestant cause.

Jeanne Marie Guyon

1648–1717; France
Guyon established hospitals and aided the poor but is most remembered as a mystic and religious educator. She traveled throughout France and Spain and wrote over forty books in her campaign to educate others in the philosophy of Quietism, a system of mysticism which emphasized the inner religious experience as the true way to attain spiritual perfection. Persecuted for heresy, the books she had written were burned publicly, and she was imprisoned for seven years, only obtaining her release because of ill health. Guyon lived another fifteen years, virtually a prisoner in her own home, but continued writing about her religious beliefs.

Charitas Pirckheimer

fl. 1524; Germany
An abbess who presided over the convent of Santa Clara at Nuremberg during the period of extreme Lutheran agitation, Pirckheimer strongly opposed the Reformation and wrote a memoir expressing her beliefs.

Luise Gottsched

18th c.; Germany
In the eighteenth century, French had almost replaced German as the polite language of Germany. Gottsched was partly responsible for re-establishing the use of German, although her husband has received total credit for this work. She gave up her own literary efforts in order to help her husband write a Dictionary of the German language and a model grammar.

Despite the attitude that "a woman in this age is considered learned enough if she can distinguish her husband's bed from that of another," there were cultivated and educated women in Europe.

Marianna Alcoforado

1640–1723; Portugal

Alcoforado wrote *Letters of a Portugese Nun,* which is a major piece of self-analytical writing, as well as an important record of the life of seventeenth-century Portuguese religious women.

Anna Amalia

1739–1807; Germany/ Prussia

Although best remembered as a music collector, Anna Amalia, the sister of Frederick the Great and regent for her son, was also a highly skilled performer and composer. She composed music to accompany the words of her close friend, Goethe, and took an active part in the musical life of Weimar. Distinguished artists and women and men of letters were drawn to her court, either as visitors or as permanent residents under her patronage. In 1775, she retired from court and devoted her life to the study of music and the arts.

Laura Bassi

1711–1778; Italy

Bassi received a liberal education in the sciences and languages. She earned a doctorate in philosophy in 1732, carried on experimental philosophy at the University of Bologna, and became a famous and popular teacher, drawing students from all over Europe.

She maintained a steady correspondence with the most well-known intellectuals of Europe – among them Voltaire, whom she aided in gaining admittance to the Bolognese Academy of Science.

Luisa de Carvajal

1568–1614; Spain

One of the most illustrious writers of the sixteenth century, De Carvajal wrote lyric poetry that was unsurpassed in Castile. She was determined not to marry and took a vow of chastity. De Carvajal was an outspoken Christian, publicly destroying paintings and writings that offended her faith. She also opposed the monarchy of Spain and went to England, where she founded a free community for pious women.

Bernarda de la Cerda

17th c.; Portugal

De la Cerda was a scholar and writer whose poems and prose were known throughout Spain and Portugal. She received recognition in the academies of both countries. Fluent in several languages, De la Cerda also knew rhetoric, philosophy, and mathematics. Among her extant works are *Political Selection* and *Volume of Comedies.*

Isabela Czartoryska

1746–1835; Poland

A princess and a writer, Czartoryska attempted to spread a universal culture and national consciousness among the Polish people. She founded an educational institute for young people, a school for girls, and a

school for peasant children. She made her estate the center of the literary and political life of Poland, always emphasizing in her writing and dialogues the need to spread knowledge and culture to all aspects of community life.

Anne Dacier

1651–1720; France

Dacier was one of the most famous women in seventeenth-century France and a scholar unequaled in her knowledge of classical literature. Her translations into French and Latin include the works of Anacreon, the sixth-century B.C. lyric poet; the existing poems of Sappho; and Homer's *Iliad* and *Odyssey.* Dacier was educated by her father – but only after he discovered that she was supplying her brother with the answers for his lessons. Dacier knew and corresponded with other important scholars of her time and was invited by Queen Christina to join the Swedish court. She declined the invitation and went to the French court, which was then the center of intellectual activity in Europe.

Susanna Lorantffy

1600–1660; Hungary

As the economical and financial head of her family, Lorantffy managed the estates and was influential in securing her husband's appointment as Prince of Transylvania in 1636. Her great legacy was the systematic development of Hungarian cultural life. She founded the Reformed College of Sarospatak, established boarding schools, and created scholarships and endowment funds. During the war in 1644–1645, she organized the army and ran military operations.

Bridget Tott

17th c.; Denmark

Tott translated the works of the most celebrated authors of antiquity into Danish.

Barbara Uttman

1514–1575; Germany

Uttman was the founder of the lace industry in Annaburg, Saxony. She had learned the then little-known art in Nuremberg and opened a school in her home, which was the beginning of a vast and profitable industry for the impoverished town of Annaburg. Through her efforts, schools were opened throughout Germany, and by 1561 lacemaking was an active trade employing thirty thousand people.

Glueckel von Hameln

1646–1724; Germany

Although she was not recognized as a historian in her lifetime, Von Hameln's work on her family's history is now viewed as a classic. The seven-volume set – published in 1896 – presents a cross-section of Jewish-German history in the seventeenth century and provides information about the customs and lifestyle of the time.

Maria Antonia Walpurgis

1724–1780; Germany

Walpurgis, the Electress of Saxony, was a composer, poet, painter, singer, and patron. She was a member of the Arcadian Academy in Rome under a pseudonym and used the initials E.T.P.A. to sign her works. Her most important compositions were two operas, *Il Trionfo della Fedelta,* produced in Dresden in 1754, and *Talestri, Regina della Amazoni,* first performed in Munich in 1760.

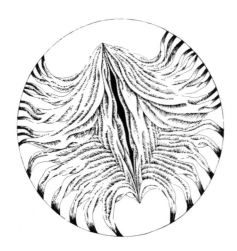

Anne Hutchinson
1591–1643

Theories about the spiritual equality of the sexes continued to appear and disappear in European and then American religious ideas. Women were unusually active in the formation of new religions and persisted in trying to reform traditional religious practices. In the early stages of a religion, women were generally allowed a certain amount of freedom. But ultimately, the pattern was always the same; liberal ideas gave way to the formation of an increasingly patriarchal structure unless control remained in the hands of women, as it did in the case of those who actually founded and organized religions. Then, equality between the sexes continued in theory and usually – but not always – in practice. Those women who looked to America for both religious tolerance and political freedom discovered that in the early days of the colonies – as in all communities that had not yet solidified – women enjoyed a great deal more liberty than in Europe, as long as they functioned within the accepted roles for women. Although colonial society lacked the consciousness about delineated sex roles that marked later American culture, Puritans emphasized the dignity of the female *within* the family structure and with the condition that women accept ultimate male authority. If a woman challenged that, as Anne Hutchinson did, the limits of female freedom became all too clear.

Women continued to be active in religion, either working for reform, fighting persecution, trying to reaffirm Christian ideals, or actually building new religions.

Helena Blavatsky
1831–1891; Russia

Born in Russia, Blavatsky left when she was seventeen and traveled extensively, visiting India, Tibet, Mexico, the United States, and Canada. Influenced by ancient religions, Hinduism, the Kabbala, occultism, and spiritualism, she established the Theosophical Society of New York in 1875. Its goals included familiarizing people with ancient thought and investigating the laws of nature to develop the divine powers Blavatsky believed were inherent in the human race. By the time of her death in 1891, the Theosophical movement had spread to England, France, and India and included more than a hundred thousand members.

Mary Bonaventure
fl. 1630's; Ireland

Bonaventure was one of the founders of the historic community of the Poor Clares in Galway, the oldest existing order in Ireland, and recorded the struggles of the Poor Clares under the persecution of the Catholics by Oliver Cromwell. Ultimately, Bonaventure and others were forced into exile in Spain.

Mary Dyer
d. 1660; United States

Despite the threat of punishment for associating with an ostracized person, Dyer publicly supported Anne Hutchinson during her trial. At a time when Massachusetts law condemned avowed Quakers to death, and in defiance of prohibitions against women preaching, Dyer preached and openly visited imprisoned Quakers. Upon her own arrest, she agitated for repeal of the laws against Quakers by writing tracts from her jail cell. Arrested twice, sentenced to hang twice, given reprieves and banished twice, and repeatedly forbidden to preach, Dyer returned to Massachusetts and continued preaching and speaking out against religious persecution. Because of her popularity and influence, the governor had resisted executing her, but finally had her hanged in 1660. Only one other Quaker was executed after Dyer was, and the law against Quakers was finally changed.

Mary Baker Eddy
1821–1910; United States

Eddy, was the founder of Christian Science, a

metaphysical and scientific system of healing. She was the first woman to establish a major religion. She explained her philosophy in *Science and Health* and after founding Christian Science in 1866 developed a worldwide organization. She established her own publishing house, which printed periodicals that included *The Christian Science Monitor,* a daily newspaper devoted to world events. It is now circulated in 120 countries and is consistently honored for its excellent reportage.

Margaret Fell Fox

1614–1702; England
Fox, a founder of the Quaker religion, wrote a tract in 1666 entitled, *Women's Speaking Justified, Proved and Allowed by the Scriptures,* which supported the ministry of women. She also established women's meetings that provided training in midwifery and aid to the poor. Her lobbying resulted in the King James III Declaration of Indulgence of 1687 and the Toleration Act in 1689, signaling the end of persecution of the Quakers in England.

Selina Hastings

1707–1791; England
Hastings' home was the center of early Methodist activity. She built over sixty chapels, founded a religious school, and helped establish missions throughout the British Isles. She originally hoped to reform the Church of England but eventually, disillusioned, became a strong dissenter.

Ann Lee

1736–1784; United States
Known as "Mother Wisdom," Lee was the founder of the American Shaker Society. The Shakers established a number of communities based on their belief in the absolute equality of sexes. The Shakers became the largest and most significant American religious utopian community.

Marie de l'Incarnation

1599–1672; Canada
De l'Incarnation, a Frenchwoman, established an Ursuline mission in Quebec at a time when that city was merely a trading post. Hoping to build a bridge between cultures through language and religion, De l'Incarnation took Algonquin girls into her care and tutelage. She studied and mastered several native dialects and wrote a French-Algonquin Dictionary. She spent thirty-two years working among the indigenous people of the Quebec region.

Susanna Wesley

1669–1742; England
Wesley had nineteen children in twenty years and educated all of them at home. She conducted a "household school" for six hours a day for twenty years, giving the same education to boys and girls. Neighbors began to send their children to her, and she soon had two hundred in attendance. Because she also wrote religious textbooks and conducted services for the children, she met some opposition from the local curate, as women were forbidden to preach. Her son John Wesley founded Methodism, and it was said that Methodism began in her home.

Until the end of the Revolutionary period in America, the distinction between men's and women's work was flexible in the colonies. Women moved freely into most occupations and received equal pay.

Though women had no formal political rights, they were active in public affairs and thoroughly involved in the Revolutionary struggle. But when the war was over and the new government formed, women found themselves left out again, as they had been so many times in the past.

Abigail Adams

1744–1818; United States
A patriot, revolutionary, abolitionist, writer, and feminist, Adams was self-educated. She managed all the business and farm affairs for her family, advised her husband, John, and was one of the great letter writers of her time. She spoke out against slavery eighty-five years before the abolition movement, writing, "I wish most sincerely that there was not a slave in the province. It always appeared a most iniquitous scheme to me to fight ourselves for what we are daily robbing from those who have as good a right to freedom as we have." Advising her husband of the need to include a women's rights clause in the Declaration of Independence, Abigail said, "…remember the ladies and be more generous and favorable to them than your ancestors. Remember all men would be tyrants if they could… give up the harsh title 'master' for that of 'friend' …If particular care and attention is not paid to the ladies, we are determined to foment a rebellion and will not hold ourselves bound by any laws in which we have not voice or representation."

Hannah Adams

1755–1831; United States
With the publication of her *History of the Jews* in 1812, Adams became the first female historian in the United States and the first American woman to support herself by writing.

Mary Alexander

1694–1760; United States
Alexander invested her inheritance in trading ventures and developed a prosperous business. It was said that hardly a ship docked in New York harbor without a consignment for her. She sold these goods, together with colony products, in her own store.

Penelope Barker

18th c.; United States
A Revolutionary War heroine, Barker singlehandedly drove off British soldiers when she discovered them leading horses from her stables. She also was the leader of a women's group that drew up a document opposing taxes levied by the British Parliament on the colonies.

Anne Bradstreet

1612–1672; United States
Bradstreet was America's first published poet. Her work appeared in 1650 and was the first volume of original verse to be written in New England.

Margaret Brent

1601–1671; United States
In 1647, Brent, a businesswoman, was one of Maryland's largest landowners and the executor of the Governor's estate. The first woman in America to demand suffrage, she applied to the Maryland Assembly for the right to vote. Her request was denied.

Hannah Crocker

1765–1847; United States
An advocate of women's education, Crocker wrote *Observations on the Real Rights of Women* in 1818. She said "The wise author of nature has endowed the female mind with equal powers and faculties and given them the same right of judging and acting for themselves as he gave to the male sex." Crocker believed that Christian doctrine insisted that the sexes share equally in divine grace, and she argued that marriage should be a state of mutual affection and trust, with all responsibilities shared by both partners, including earning the family income.

Mary Goddard

1736–1816; United States
In 1775, Goddard became the publisher and manager of Baltimore's first newspaper. Her press printed the Declaration of Independence. Appointed by Benjamin Franklin as Postmistress of the country, she was later replaced by a man. Goddard complained to the government, but her complaint was ignored and the job declared "too strenuous" for a woman.

Catherine Greene

1731–ca. 1794; United States
Greene invented a method for separating cotton from its seed. She entrusted the fabrication of the machine she designed to her boarder, Eli Whitney, who nearly abandoned the project several times, but Greene continued to support and encourage him. By law, women were not able to apply for patents, so Whitney received credit for the invention of the cotton gin.

Henrietta Johnston

1620–1728; United States
Johnston, one of the earliest artists to work in pastels, was possibly the first woman artist in America. She supported herself by painting portraits of public officials, prominent families, and the clergy.

Judith Murray

1751–1820; United States
In 1779, Murray wrote an essay declaring that the sexes have equal minds and demanding education for girls. Her first published piece concerning women's education was *Desultory Thoughts upon a Degree of Self Complacency Especially in Female Bosoms* (1784). In it she agreed with Mary Wollstonecraft's ideas about education for women and argued that all women should be equipped to make their own livings. Her play *The Medium* was the first American play to be produced at the Federal Street Theatre in Boston. *The Gleaner*, a three-volume book of her essays, is considered an American classic.

Margaret Philipse

d. ca. 1690; United States
Philipse was a merchant and shipowner before her marriage to a merchant trader, and after she was married, she carried on her business in her maiden name. When her husband died in 1661, she took over his trading interests and made frequent business trips overseas.

Sarah Peale

1800–1885; United States
Peale and her sister Anna are considered the first professional women painters in America. Sarah studied with her father, a miniaturist, and her uncle, the portraitist Charles Willson Peale, who inspired her to become a portrait painter. She was commissioned to paint over one hundred portraits by Baltimore's leading families. During this time, she also made several trips to Washington, where she did portraits of cabinet members, senators, and foreign dignitaries.

Eliza Lucas Pinckney

1723–1793; United States
Pinckney experimented with diversified crops in the South Carolina soil and helped develop indigo as a major resource. Indigo sales sustained the Carolina economy for three decades, until the Revolution cut off trade with England. As a young woman, she tutored her sister and taught reading to two black girls whom she intended to train as school teachers for the rest of the Negro children. Pinckney's correspondence is one of the largest surviving collections of letters of a colonial woman.

Molly Pitcher

1750/54–1832; United States
Pitcher was one of the women who followed the Revolutionary Army to care for the wounded. When her husband was shot, she took his place as gunner and is said to have won the battle. It is also recorded that she fired the last shot against the British at the Battle of Fort Clinton and that she carried a wounded soldier two miles to safety and nursed him back to health. She was honored by General Washington and was buried with military honors.

Deborah Sampson

1760–1827; United States
In 1782, dressed in men's clothing, Sampson enlisted in the Continental Army. She fought in a number of battles, and it was not until a year and a half after she was discharged from the Army that her true identity was discovered. She later began to travel and lecture, telling her life story in towns throughout New England. When she became ill as a result of old army wounds, Congress granted her a pension.

Mercy Otis Warren

1728–1814; United States
Warren was one of the most significant Revolutionary women. Self-educated, she was a poet, satirist, and historian, publishing a major document, *The Rise, Progress and Termination of the American Revolution,* in 1805. She maintained a large correspondence with the important figures of the Revolution, who consulted her on political issues. She believed that women should have equal education, rights, and opportunities.

Phillis Wheatley

1753–1784; United States
Bought directly off a slave ship in Boston, Wheatley was only eight years old when she became the personal maid to Mrs. John Wheatley. Educated by her mistress, she began to write verse, becoming the first black poet in America. Although her poems were not well-received, her achievement was remarkable and helped prove the abolitionist arguments that educating blacks was both possible and desirable. She died at the age of thirty-one after an unhappy marriage and what must have been a terribly difficult life. In one of her poems, she wrote about the feelings of a captured African slave:
"I, young in life, by seeming cruel fate
Was snatch'd from Afric's fancy'd happy seat;
What pangs excruciating must molest,
What sorrows labour in my parent's breats?"

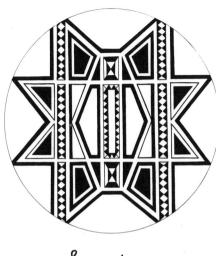

Sacajawea

1787–1812

Grouped around Sacajawea are other Native American, Mexican-American, Mexican, Hawaiian, and Latin-American women. I put them together because they shared – either during their lifetimes or in their past – the experience of colonization by Europeans. Some of these women represent the intact traditions of their heritage; others reflect a later amalgamation of cultures; still others demonstrate women's efforts to resist or come to terms with the domination and destruction of their societies.

One thing shared by all the early women was incredible brutalization by white men. Upon their arrival in the Americas, early European conquerors raped thousands of women, with army officers handing out three or four hundred women at a time to their men. Previously, rape was unheard of, and women were highly regarded in both North American tribes and pre-Columbian societies, many of which were matriarchal. Socially and politically advanced tribes accorded women leading positions in religious and civil affairs, and most Indian myths relate that men and women were created simultaneously,

with each dependent on the other for existence. This concept of interdependency pervaded Indian cultures generally and resulted in deep reverence for the balance of life.

The confrontation with European civilization – with its emphasis on controlling and exploiting nature, expanding frontiers, and subordinating women and Native American culture – pitted two totally different world views against each other. Unfortunately, the more humane philosophy was not only overpowered but nearly obliterated in a genocidal campaign.

In the Americas, the particular forms of exploitation and genocide varied, but invariably the women suffered – not only at the hands of conquerors but often because their own men, frustrated by their powerlessness, took out their anger on them. The women of the Americas have had to struggle to maintain their dignity as women while also fighting to retain their cultural identities.

Europeans developed many misconceptions about North American Indian societies, particularly about the position of women. Some of these occurred because Europeans perceived Indian social structure through the prism of their own patriarchal, hierarchical, and authoritarian societies. They made the assumption, for example, that because Native American women worked hard, they were oppressed, and because men walked in front of women, women were subordinate. On the contrary, women's work was respected; they generally had property rights and possessed their own tools and household articles. In some societies, they held the ultimate political authority. Men preceding women in public was an act of deference and was intended as a way of protecting women from harm. Women had lower

slowly eroded over centuries, were totally eliminated.

status in some Indian societies that usually depended upon hunting, not agriculture, for survival.

Anaconda

fl. 1562; North America
Anaconda was a warrior who attempted to stop the invasion, exploitation, and colonization of her land by the European conquerors. She led a war party to destroy a Spanish settlement. However, the Spanish retaliated by sending more troops to re-establish the settlement. They captured Anaconda and executed her.

Awashonks

fl. 1671; North America
Awashonks was the leader of the people who inhabited the lands that now comprise the State of Rhode Island. In an effort to protect her home and people, she led many battles against the encroaching English settlers. In 1671, Awashonks signed a peace treaty at Plymouth Colony, but four years later, with the support of the French forces, she again fought the English, who had violated the terms of the treaty.

Rosana Chouteau

fl. 1875; North America
Chouteau was elected chief of the Osage Beaver Band in 1875 after the death of her uncle. Her election was unusual because the Osage were a patrilineal tribe. About this, Chouteau said: "I am the first one (female chief) and expect to be the last one. I think my band obeys me better than they would a man."

Ehyophsta

fl. 1869; North America
Ehyophsta, "Yellow-Haired Woman," was a Cheyenne woman who belonged to a small select group of female warriors. During an invasion by the Shoshonis, she saved a fellow warrior by stabbing his opponent.

Marie Iowa

19th c.; North America
Iowa was a guide whose knowledge of the terrain and expertise in survival techniques in the wilderness aided in the opening up of the Pacific Northwest. Like Sacajawea, her ability to endure hardship and to maintain a supply of food from the wilds proved invaluable to the exploration parties.

Kaahumanu

1772–1832; Hawaii
In Hawaii by the eighteenth century, women's freedom was severely restricted by the "kapus," or taboos, of the religion. Women were segregated from men and certain foods forbidden them. When Kaahumanu, the first female ruler and lawmaker, took power, she abolished these practices. After her husband – King Kamehameha I – died, she dressed in warrior's clothing and announced to her son, who was heir to the throne, that his father wished that they rule together. After learning to read and write, she helped establish schools and educational rights for women and then passed laws to rid the islands of the abuses of the traders, who had brought drunkenness, venereal disease, vandalism, social disruption, and sexual exploitation of the women. A major figure in Hawaiian history, Kaahumanu is an outstanding example of a woman who used her position to secure rights for women.

Maria Montoya Martinez

b. ca. 1880; United States
Martinez, an acclaimed craftswoman, perfected an exquisite pottery-making technique that had been lost for almost seven hundred years. A Tewa Indian from the pueblo of San Ildefonso in New Mexico, Martinez became acquainted with the ancient pottery-making techniques of her village and, with her husband, redeveloped the lost art of black work pottery. They began teaching their technique in the 1920's, building a pottery industry that benefited their entire pueblo. Her entire family learned the art of blackware, and through their efforts, the industry continues to flourish.

Mary Musgrove

18th c.; North America
The Creek Indians were one of the societies that accorded women respect and power. Musgrove, a Creek Indian warrior chief, was an important political leader in the history of her tribe and of Georgia. By deciding which alliances were advantageous for her people and which wars her people should fight, she influenced the politics and trade of Georgia during the early days of its settlement.

Pocahontas

1595–1617; North America
Pocahontas was instrumental in the survival of the early colonists in America, giving them advice on their agricultural problems and saving the Jamestown colony more than once from starvation. She is most remembered for having saved the life of John Smith after he was taken prisoner, but it would be more appropriate to honor her for her work in bringing about peaceful relations between the colonists and the Indians.

Nancy Ward

1738–1822; North America
Ward, a member of the matriarchal Cherokee tribe, was head of the Women's Council and a member of the council of chiefs. She was called Aqi-qa-u-e, or "Beloved Woman," by her tribe. She was in the forefront of the peace negotiations between her tribe and the settlers. She attempted to pacify both sides and thereby bring about friendly relations. While she warned the settlers of Cherokee invasions and saved one white woman from the stake, she also supported the Cherokee Council's decision not to part with any more land.

Wetamoo

d. 1676; North America
Wetamoo was responsible for aiding King Phillip in his war against the English during 1675 and 1676, and she attempted to prevent expanding British colonization by uniting the East Coast Indian tribes. She led attacks on fifty-two of the ninety existing English towns, twelve of which were completely destroyed. By 1676, however, her forces had all been captured; Wetamoo escaped, but drowned.

Sara Winnemuca

fl. 1870–1880; North America
Translator, arbitrator, and Indian scout, Winnemuca became the translator for her tribe, the Southern Paiutes, who were agricultural and wanted to live peacefully, working and living side by side with the whites. Other tribes were not so tolerant of the Europeans, and one of these, the Bannock, kidnapped the Chief (Winnemuca's father) her brother, and others from her village.

Marriage became the only acceptable option

They planned to force the Paiutes to fight the settlers and the military. Winnemuca traveled 223 miles on horseback for three days and two nights in order to rescue them. After a six-year struggle, Winnemuca, who was revered by her tribe, obtained government farmland, where the Paiutes were able to continue their self-sufficient existence.

The Spanish conquest of Mexico brought with it a traumatic change in the culture. Thousands of women had their faces deformed with branding irons as they were marked and then sold as slaves. Sexual relations with the conquerors, both forced and voluntary, produced an interracial, intercultural society that created race and class distinctions that divided women. Additionally, the repressiveness of the Catholic church, compounded by severe poverty, made the situation of Mexican women extraordinarily difficult. The emergence of Mexican Independence movements in the nineteenth and twentieth centuries stimulated the growth of a Mexican feminist consciousness. The development of a large Mexican-American community, however, brought with it cultural and economic problems that Chicanas have struggled with for several decades.

Maria Bartola

16th c.; Mexico

Bartola, whose Aztec name is not known, was the first female historian from Mexico. She wrote an account of the Spanish conquest of Mexico from the point of view of an Aztec experiencing the destruction of her world.

Juana de la Cruz

1651–1695; Mexico

Born in a farmhouse, De la Cruz taught herself to read and began writing verse at a very early age. She begged her mother to let her dress as a boy so that she could attend the university, but instead she was sent to live in her grandfather's house in the city, where she read all the books in his library. She became famous for her erudition and poetry and as a result was invited to live in the home of a noblewoman as one of her attendant ladies. When De la Cruz was seventeen, she was paraded before forty university professors and made to "defend herself" in an examination of her intellectual merits. Realizing that her accomplishments as a woman made her vulnerable to attack, De la Cruz entered a cloister in order to pursue her studies. But even in the convent, she was harassed and rebuked for her scholarly interests. The pressure to give up "unwomanly" pursuits finally forced her to sell her four thousand books and her scientific and musical instruments and to devote the remainder of her life to helping the poor. She died at forty-three, after nursing the nuns in her convent who were stricken by the Plague.

Josefa de Dominguez

1773–1829; Mexico

De Dominguez was a heroine of the Mexican Independence movement in the 1820's. As wife of the mayor of the city of Queretaro, she had access to information on the movements and plans of the Spanish troops. Dominguez passed this information to the revolutionaries, and when her activities became known to the Spaniards she was imprisoned for three years. When offered compensation for her service in the Revolution, she refused, stating that she needed no reward for doing what was right. On her deathbed, she said: "My struggle has been as a *Méxicana* against the Spaniards who have come to steal the land, enslave Mexicans, exploit their labors, degrade their families, humiliate their dignity, and torment their flesh more cruelly than if they were beasts."

Maria del Refugio Garcia

fl. 1931; Mexico

Garcia, the Secretary of the United Front for Women's Rights, was an active promoter of political justice and equality for women. As a delegate to the Women's National Congress in 1931, she accused the provisional president of Mexico of reneging on his promised support of women's suffrage. She was arrested and imprisoned for this, but a huge women's demonstration forced the president to release Garcia. She was elected to federal office, then denied her seat because the constitution did not allow women to hold office. She appealed to the Supreme Court and won. Garcia improved working conditions and worked for the legal protection of women, and the development of work training centers for unemployed women.

Jovita Idar

fl. 1911; Mexico/United States

Idar wrote for *La Cronica,* a Spanish newspaper published in Texas in the early 1900's. In 1911, she organized the first Mexican Congress, which was held in Laredo, Texas, and she later became the president of the Mexican Feminist League.

La Malinche

16th c.; Mexico

To understand La Malinche's life, it is important to understand that after the advent of the Conquistadores the position of Mexican women was reduced to near slavery, and one of the few ways possible for a woman to improve her situation was through association with a Spanish male. La Malinche was sold by her parents as a slave to Cortez so that her half-brother could inherit her property. Fluent in Spanish, Mexican, and Aztec, she became Cortez's interpreter and translator and eventually his lover. She gave birth to a child and was later rejected by Cortez when he brought his wife from Spain. Because of her role in the colonization of her people, La Malinche has been represented as a traitor and as symbolically responsible for their oppression. Contemporary Chicanas, however, reject this idea, arguing that when La Malinche was deposed of her rightful position by her family, she made the best choice she could given her circumstances.

Luisa Moreno

fl. 1940's–50's; United States

Moreno was a major figure in labor organizing and worked for the Agricultural and Packing Workers of America. She organized the Congress of Spanish Speaking Peoples, which brought together Mexicans, Puerto Ricans, and Cubans to talk about labor conditions and police brutality. As a result of her activities, Moreno was deported to Mexico in the 1950's, even though her birthplace was Guatemala and she was married to a United States citizen. Moreno's deportation demonstrates the way Hispanic-American leaders were separated from the mainstream struggle of the labor movement in the United States.

Laura Torres

fl. 1900's; Mexico

Torres, a labor organizer, was employed at a cigar factory where the women were forced to work seventeen hours a day for extremely low wages. The company did not allow them to be educated, and their social activities were strictly regulated. One of the women tried to get food for her sick child from the company store and was refused because she had no money. The child died. The women were outraged and went out on strike. The local police were called in to control them, but when Torres confronted them with the question, "Men of Mexico, will you shoot your sisters?" they retreated. The army came in, slaughtered the police, and arrested the six hundred women as well as the three thousand men who had also gone out on strike. They were sent to labor camps where most of them died. This "Rio Bravo Massacre" was part of a series of labor struggles that eventually led to the 1914 Revolution.

Andrea Villarreal

fl. 1910; Mexico

Teresa Villarreal

fl. 1910; Mexico

The Villarreal sisters were feminists, anarchists, and revolutionaries who worked for both the cause of women and the independence of Mexico. They founded a feminist club for political action and published *La Mujer Modern* (the modern woman). They were members of the Mexican Liberal Party and were active throughout the Mexican Revolution.

Xochitl

fl. 900; Meso-America

Xochitl was a queen of the Toltecs and wife of Tecpancaltzin. During her reign, women were soldiers in battalions that she led. Legend has it that she was killed in battle and that the blood that flowed from her wounds foretold the destruction of the Toltec Nation.

Until the wars of independence in the early nineteenth century, Latin American countries were "kingdoms" of Spain or Portugal. The same laws and attitudes toward women that prevailed there were applied to the women of South America. The idea that women should be submissive, frugal, industrious, and sequestered was reinforced by the Catholic Church. Many women fought in the independence struggles, and in some countries women's rights became one of the goals.

Ana Betancourt

fl. 1850's; Cuba

Betancourt, a feminist, was actively involved in Cuba's struggle for independence from Spain. At the constitutional assembly of the new Republic, Betancourt stood and demanded equal rights for women.

Capillana

16th c.; Peru

Capillana, a friend of Pisarro, illuminated manuscripts. There is one that contains paintings of ancient Peruvian monuments and a short historical text that is in the Dominican library in Peru.

Isabel de Guevara

fl. 1535; Spain

In 1535, Guevara set sail for the New World with a large Spanish expedition, eventually settling with her husband among the Guarani Indians in what is now Argentina. After their colony was established, she wrote to the Spanish ruler, describing the hard physical labor performed by the women who had planted, raised, and harvested the first crops. Although they had defended the colony and cared for the ill and dying, De Guevara complained that they had been forgotten in "the glory of the men."

Candelaria Figueredo

1852–1913; Cuba

Figueredo, a revolutionary soldier, was the first woman to fight in the Cuban ranks in her country's attempts to achieve liberation from Spain. She joined the army at age sixteen and participated in the defense of Cuba until 1871, when she was taken prisoner.

Carlota Matienzo

1881–1926; Puerto Rico

Educated at the University of Puerto Rico and Columbia University in New York, Matienzo was offered work in Venezuela, Nicaragua, Mexico, and the United States, but chose to return to her native Puerto Rico. She was instrumental in the revitalization and expansion of the public school system in Puerto Rico during the first quarter of the twentieth century. A strong feminist, Matienzo was posthumously honored when a hall was named after her by female students at the University of Puerto Rico. The Carlota Matienzo Prize is awarded every year to the graduate who shows the greatest aptitude for teaching.

Isabel Pinochet

fl. 1870's; Chile

It was due to Pinochet's efforts that the women of Chile gained the right to higher education and the chance to receive professional degrees. She founded a school for women in 1875, and two of her graduates later became the first women physicians in South America.

Magda Portal

fl. 1930's; Peru

Portal was a leading socialist, a political activist, and a founder of a revolutionary political party that was unfortunately against women's suffrage. They believed that women would be influenced by the Church and their husbands to vote conservatively. Portal, like many Latin American and European women, felt that the socialist revolution must come first and that once society was free women would be ready to become full political participants.

Maria Luisa Sanchez

20th c.; Bolivia

Sanchez, a writer and translator, was the founder and organizer of the Women's Atheaem, a group that worked for the consolidation and continuation of the culture and education of women. Elected the group's first president, she continued as head of the organization for twenty-eight years. After women gained the right to vote in Bolivia, Sanchez organized the first all women's political conference. In 1929 in La Paz, Sanchez tried to bridge the gap between liberal and radical women and stressed the importance of women working together to achieve equality with men.

Ofelia Uribe de Acosta

20th c.; Columbia

Uribe De Acosta was an active feminist who worked to improve the position of women in Columbia. Concerned with raising women's consciousness, she argued that in order to begin to put an end to their exploitation, women must be educated to free themselves from prevailing myths and to build confidence in their own self-worth. Because she understood that women's oppression cut across all class barriers, she agitated on behalf of both working and middle-class women, urging joint action. She wrote many articles calling for working women to join unions and for housewives to organize. Arguing for the improvement of women's condition generally, she also dealt with such issues as the abusive treatment of female workers and the low status of the female office worker.

Saaredra Villanueva

fl. 1916; Bolivia

Poet, teacher, intellectual, and feminist, Villanueva founded a Women's Legion for Popular Education which investigated women's issues and commissioned articles advocating civil and political rights for women and civil rights for children. An active official in the Ministry of Defense, she founded a Women's Auxiliary Service and the Intra-American Organization for Women, which expanded educational opportunities for women. She developed career opportunities for women and helped open the professions. She also edited an anthology of women poets, and her own writing concerned itself with women's experience.

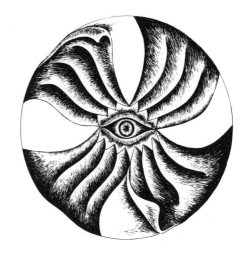

Caroline Herschel

1750–1848

The seventeenth century invention of the telescope and the microscope brought with it an interest in science and the possibility of pursuing scientific studies at home. Countless women were drawn to work with the telescope by night and the microscope by day. The more gifted of them wrote books that made scientific thought available to still more women.

However, for most women the pursuit of science remained an informal pastime. In order for a woman to become a professional scientist, she had to overcome prejudice, discrimination, and the deeply entrenched ideas about her intellectual inferiority, for – less than three hundred years ago – debate raged as to whether women could be considered human, much less capable of the achievements of men.

One way that a woman could participate in scientific and other professions was through a brother or a husband, but this usually meant oblivion for the sister or wife, no matter what her contribution was to his success. Some women were still able to practice medicine, but this tradition was almost entirely taken over by men. Only midwifery and nursing were available to the female sex, and even midwifery would soon fall into male hands.

In *A Room of One's Own,* Virginia Woolf asks the question: "What if Shakespeare had a sister? What would her life have been like?" The answer can be clearly seen in the life of Caroline Herschel. But she was not the only woman – there were many like her – who benefited from association with a famous man and also suffered because of it. Women were able to share their brothers' or husbands' work and to also express their own intellectual drives. Yet their achievements were obscured by the men's fame, although without the women, no accomplishments might have occurred.

Frau Cramer

1655–1746; Holland
Because she was married to a physician, Cramer was able to study medicine with the leading doctors of her day. She established a successful practice in obstetrics, and for fifty-two years kept a journal of case histories of all of the deliveries she made. Her writings were given to the Medical Association of Holland and were published in 1926.

Maria Kirch

1670–1720; Germany
Kirch was taught by her husband, a Berlin astronomer, and went on to become his assistant. In 1702 she discovered a comet, and in 1710 she published *A Discourse on the Approaching Conjunction of Jupiter, Saturn, Etc.* Her daughters became astronomers also, working for the Berlin Academy of Sciences.

Mary Lamb

1764–1841; England
Educated as a child with her brothers Charles and John, Lamb was forced to give up her schooling and work as a needlewoman to help support her brothers while they completed their educations. Her ambitions thwarted, she went mad when she was thirty, killed her mother, and was sent to an asylum. When she was released her brother Charles took care of her, but he also subsumed her. The *Tales of Shakespeare,* a classic in English literature, was primarily authored by Mary but was published under Charles' name. Mary also wrote a fascinating but little-known essay on needlework in which she argued that women should be paid for the work they do in the home. Charles' stature in the literary world brought Mary in contact with the leading writers of the day and allowed her work to become visible, albeit under her brother's name.

Marie Lavoisier

1758–1836; France
Lavoisier assisted and enriched her husband's scientific work, devoting herself entirely to his career. She learned Latin and English in order to translate books that might be useful to him; she wrote descriptions of the result of his experiments and executed the engravings for his textbook, the first on modern chemistry; she promoted her husband's ideas and after his death edited his memoirs and distributed them among prominent scientific figures, with whom she maintained intellectual relationships throughout her life.

Dorothy Wordsworth

1771–1855; England
Known primarily as the devoted muse of her poet-brother William, Dorothy Wordsworth claims an independent place in English literature as one of the earliest writers on the beauties of nature. She wrote poetry and journals, and frequently read passages from them to William to revive his memory of their experiences in nature. Her journals recorded descriptions of their travels and their walks in the Lake District in England where they lived for fifty years, even after William's marriage. She also wrote of her endless household chores as William's housekeeper – the washing, cleaning, baking – noting that, "William, of course, never does anything."

From Greek times until the latter half of the nineteenth century, women interested in science were discriminated against by law, custom, and public opinion. They were excluded from the universities and from intellectual societies, and in most countries they rarely had the opportunity to develop their innate capacities. Women had to overcome the opposition of family and friends, and even when they attained excellence in their field they were usually deprived of the rewards ordinarily received by men for equivalent accomplishments.

Baroness de Beausaleil

17th c.; France
The first female mining engineer in France, De Beausaleil prophetically wrote of the relationship between a country's power and independence and its use of natural resources. In her report, *La Restitution de Reuton,* she recorded the location of mines and ore deposits in France and encouraged the French to be aware of the proper use of the resources in augmenting the economy. She also detailed the qualifications for becoming a mining engineer, stressing knowledge of chemistry, mineralogy, geometry, mechanics, and hydraulics.

Katherine Bethlen

1700–1759; Hungary
Bethlen wrote about current scientific developments, publishing *A Strong and Protecting Shield* in 1751, and *Monuments to Immigration* in 1753. She supported a wide variety of scientific activities through her donations and her work.

Annie Jump Cannon

1863–1941; United States
Cannon, a noted astronomer, discovered three hundred variable stars and five novae and produced the enormous and invaluable *Henry Draper Catalogue* (1918–24) through her classification of the spectra of all stars from the North to South Poles. She studied astronomy and physics at Wellesley, then worked at Harvard Observatory for forty-five years, where she built their astronomical research collection into the largest in the world. Cannon received many honorary degrees, was appointed to numerous learned societies – including the Royal Astronomical Society in 1914 – and won many prizes. As an ardent supporter of women scientists, Cannon established a prize to be given to women astronomers. She was a strong believer in women's suffrage, joining the National Women's Party. Unlike Herschel, Cannon achieved scientific fame in her own right because of the substantial gains of the women's movement.

Margaret Cavendish

1624–1674; England
The emergence of the "scientific lady" began with Cavendish, the first woman to write extensively about science. Before 1653, when she published her first book, there had been no attempt to direct science to women, and Cavendish was interested in making scientific ideas more accessible. She experimented with microscopes and telescopes and published her findings under her own name, thereby shocking English society, which not only doubted women's capacity for abstract thought but also believed it inappropriate for a woman to write and publish her work. Cavendish forced an invitation to present her work to the Royal Scientific Society, thereby symbolically opening the doors of science to women.

Émilie du Châtelet

1706–1749; France
Primarily a mathematician, Du Châtelet was also an astronomer, a philosopher, and a scientific writer. Her most noted achievement was the first translation into French of Newton's *Principia,* which was published after her death. Her philosophic and scientific views opposed those of Descartes and Newton, but were in accord with scientific thought of the twentieth century. Sleeping only three hours a night, Du Châtelet used her time to work, study, and correspond with the other major philosophers of the eighteenth century and give women-only dinner parties at her chateau. Despite her accomplishments, she is remembered as the companion of Voltaire, with whom she lived for fifteen years.

Maria Cunitz

1610–1664; Germany
Cunitz is the earliest known European woman to have been active in astronomy. Her simplification of the Rudolphine Tables was acclaimed throughout Europe. Fluent in seven languages, including Latin, Greek, and Hebrew, she also excelled in the arts.

Jeanne Dumée

fl. 1680; France
A celebrated Parisien astronomer, Dumée wrote *Entretiens sur l'Opinion de Capernic Touchant la Mobilité de la Terre,* in which she defended and corroborated the findings of Copernicus. She championed the right of women to study science, challenging the prevailing notion that a woman's brain was smaller in size – and therefore inferior – to a man's.

Sophie Germain

1776–1831; France
Germain was a French mathematician and a founder of mathematical physics. She won the Grand Prix of the French Academy of Sciences for her theoretical work on the vibration of elastic surfaces. In 1816, she became the first woman invited to attend sessions of the Institute de France. She wrote a work on the philosophy and history of science, but the general prejudice against women in the sciences obscured her achievements after her death.

Josephine Kablick

b. 1787; Czechoslovakia
A paleontologist and naturalist, Kablick began her career by collecting specimens for her own herbarium as well as for schools and colleges in Czechoslovakia and other parts of Europe. Many fossil animals and plants are named in her honor.

Hortense Lepaute

1723–1788; France
An important astronomer, Lepaute investigated the oscillation of pendulums, studied Haley's comet, calculated and charted the path of eclipses, prepared and published a table of parallactic angles, edited the astronomical annual of the Academy of Sciences, and was the author of a number of scientific works.

Renier Michiel

1755–1832; Italy
Michiel, a renowned scholar, was educated in literature, music, and the sciences. She wrote and published treatises on botany.

Maria Mitchell

1818–1889; United States
Mitchell was the first distinguished American woman astronomer, receiving international acclaim when she discovered a comet in 1847. When Vassar opened in 1865, she was offered the chair of astronomy, which she held for twenty-three years. She was an effective and innovative educator, inspiring her students and refusing to give grades, arguing that the work, not the reward, was important. She felt strongly about the need for women to make advancements in science and became the first woman to be admitted to the American Academy of Arts and Sciences in 1887. Through her achievements, her tutelage, and her pioneering efforts, Mitchell was responsible for opening an exclusively male field to American women.

Mary Somerville

1780–1872; Scotland
Somerville was considered the leading scientific writer and thinker of her day. In 1827, she translated *The Mechanism of the Heavens* into English, adding her own comments. Most honored for her work in astronomy, Somerville also contributed to the field of physics with two important treatises, *Connection of the Physical Sciences* and *Physical Geography.*

Despite the prohibitions against them, women continued to practice medicine, primarily as midwives. The male physicians, arrogant about their university training, looked down on midwifery, but the women felt their duties were preordained and resisted the encroachment of male doctors into this field.

Louyse Bourgeois

1563–1638; France

Bourgeois was instrumental in the advancement of midwifery as a science. She learned her profession from the midwife who had delivered her children, from books, and from a physician who favored medical education for midwives. Her book *Observations* (1609), covered the various stages of pregnancy, abnormalities occurring in labor, the anatomy of the female pelvis, and the care of mother and child. In 1635 a group of midwives petitioned the king to allow Bourgeois to give a public course in obstetrics, but this was not permitted.

Mrs. Cellier

fl. 1662; England

An intelligent and progressive midwife, Cellier tried to elevate the status of her profession and improve the practice of midwifery. She claimed that high mother-and-infant mortality rates could be improved through the education and organization of professional midwives. She attempted to organize a clean, well-staffed royal hospital to provide education for nurses, and she tried to establish a program that would find homes for unwanted babies. All her plans failed because of lack of support, however, and she was actually put in the stocks several times for her efforts.

Marie Colinet

16th c.; Switzerland

Colinet, a physician and a highly skilled surgeon and bonesetter, was taught by her husband, himself a famous surgeon. He recorded a spectacular case in which Marie Colinet cured a man whose ribs were so severely injured that she had to wire them in place. She also devised a method of using hot bags to stimulate and dilate the uterus during childbirth, and she was the first to employ a magnet for extracting steel from the eye – a method historians wrongly attributed to her husband.

Angélique du Coudray

1712–1789; France

A noted obstetrician, Du Coudray was the head of the maternity section of a French hospital. Her delivery methods had a major impact on the education of midwives.

Geneviève d'Arconville

1720–1805; France

A great anatomist, D'Arconville wrote on chemistry, medicine, natural history, and philosophy. She also did work in osteology, translating a major text on the subject and supervising illustrations drawn directly from the cadaver. In addition to being an important scientist, D'Arconville wrote several biographies, including a three-volume work on Marie de Medici.

Justina Dietrich

fl. 1689; Germany

Dietrich was one of the most important obstetricians in seventeenth-century Europe. She published and illustrated a textbook on midwifery, which demonstrated the most advanced techniques of the time. She educated peasant women to be skilled midwives.

Anne Halkett

1622–1699; England

Born into the court of Charles I, Halkett received a thorough scientific and religious education. She became skilled in surgery and also wrote theological works, leaving thirty-six books in manuscript form at her death.

Mother Hutton

18th c.; England

Hutton was a biologist and pharmacist and the discoverer of digitalis as a treatment for heart conditions. In 1785, Dr. William Wilhering bought her prescription, analyzed its content, and arranged for the inclusion of digitalis in the new *London Pharmacopoeia*. The product and its discovery have been associated with his name rather than hers ever since.

Louise Le Gras

1591–1671; France

Le Gras was one of the first leaders of the society of visiting nurses established by St. Vincent de Paul. Born into nobility and well-educated, she learned medicine and surgery from her husband. After his death, she devoted her life to the sick and destitute. Le Gras prepared the medicines and instructed her helpers – the first Sisters of Charity.

Dorothea Leporin-Erxleben

1715–1762; Germany

Leporin-Erxleben was trained by her father, a physician. Her talent was so exceptional that, despite the prohibitions against women, Frederick the Great permitted her to attend the University in 1741. Her studies were interrupted because of illness, then by marriage in which she bore four children. Her husband died and she resumed her studies, becoming the first woman to graduate from a medical school in Germany. She practiced medicine for a number of years. The medical schools, however, did not allow any other women to attend for over 150 years.

Jeanne Mance

1606–1673; Canada

In 1641, Mance crossed the Atlantic to open the second hospital in North America. Mance was its physician, nurse, administrator, and fundraiser. When she returned to France for funds and nurses, she succeeded in convincing the women of the court of Louis XIII to provide for the needs of her hospital in Quebec. In 1902 the Jeanne Mance School of Nursing was founded in her honor in Montreal.

Anna Manzolini

1716–ca. 1774; Italy

Manzolini was a professor of anatomy at the University of Bologna for many years and was noted for the discoveries she made as a result of her dissections of cadavers. The anatomical models that she made in wax were known throughout Europe. They became the prototype for subsequent models, and upon her death they came to be considered as among the most prized possessions of the university.

Martha Mears

fl. 1797; England

In 1797, Mears wrote *Candid Advice to the Fair Sex on the Subject of Pregnancy*, a practical book on gynecology and obstetrics in which she stressed the hygiene of pregnancy and the naturalness of childbirth. In part, this was an attempt to dispel certain beliefs concerning pregnancy, one of them being that it was a pathological state.

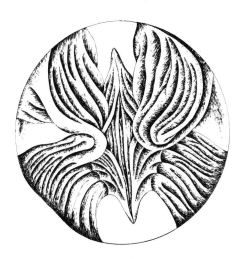

Mary Wollstonecraft

1759–1797

Grouped around Wollstonecraft are the women of the French Revolution, feminist and nonfeminist writers, women who influenced their cultures in various ways, and explorers who found world travel infinitely more stimulating than traditional roles. The lives of these women indicate that opportunities for women had expanded, partly as a result of new ideas about human rights and democratic concepts. The salons were one impetus for the expression of feminist ideas. There women not only presided over intellectual dialogue but participated in it as well. This resulted in social criticism of these "daring" women, who began to defend both their ability and their right to think. In the process, they gave birth not only to a great deal of feminist theory but also to the French Revolution. Women joined and sometimes led the protests against the excesses of the aristocracy; they wrote pamphlets, posted notices, organized radical societies, and agitated for women's rights. The Revolution was fought in the name of Liberty, Equality, and Fraternity, but unfortunately, the last word was taken too literally. Despite the fact that women played a significant role, it was the men who accrued most of the benefits. Women did win laws protecting their rights in marriage, property, and education, but the few advantages they gained were swept away when Napoleon came to power and enforced a code of laws that was more restrictive than before the Revolution.

Charlotte Corday

1769–1793; France
Horrified by the violence of the Revolution, which she had believed would bring a new order, Corday assassinated Marat, whom she held responsible for the execution of hundreds of thousands of people. She was arrested, tried, and guillotined, saying before she died, "I have killed one man to save the innocent – a famous monster – to procure peace for my country." Unfortunately, her act was used as a pretext for antifemale sentiment and a reaction against women in politics.

Olympe de Gouges

1745–1793; France
In response to the 1789 "Declaration of the Rights of Man," the preamble to France's new constitution, De Gouges wrote the *Declaration of the Rights of Woman*. She demanded equal rights for women before the law and in all aspects of public and private life. Realizing that the revolutionaries were enemies of the emancipation of women, she covered the walls of Paris with bulletins – signed with her name – expounding her ideas and exposing the injustices of the new government. She attacked Marat, Robespierre, and the Jacobins openly, and when she was put on trial she cried out to the women in the crowd, "What are the advantages you have derived from the Revolution? Slights and contempt more plainly displayed." Then De Gouges, who had established clubs for women all over France in the name of the Revolution, was sentenced to death by Robespierre and guillotined.

Théroigne de Méricourt

fl. 1789; France
On July 14, 1789, the French celebrated the storming of the Bastille, which signaled the outbreak of the Revolution. Although it is a documented fact that Méricourt led this assault, her name is usually left out of history.

Marie Tussaud

1760–1850; Switzerland
Tussaud began her career in her uncle's studio, where she modeled parts of the human body in wax. During the French Revolution, she cast Marat's head and those of Marie Antoinette and Louis XVI after they were guillotined. Later, she gained the favor of Napoleon and became a state portraitist. Eventually, she went to London and set up her collection as the still famous "Madame Tussaud's Wax Museum."

Jeanne Manon Roland

1754–1793; France
Roland, a stateswoman and political leader, became aware of the inequities of society as a child and brooded over class distinctions. She married the politically active M. Roland, and her house soon became the center for his political group, the Girondists. The discussions in her salons centered on transforming France from a monarchy to a republic, and Roland became increasingly outspoken in her support of revolutionary ideas and acts. Arrested and taken to prison, she wrote a letter protesting her incarceration, then began work on her life story. Given a mockery of a trial, Roland was taken to the guillotine, pronouncing the now immortal words, "O Liberty, what crimes are committed in thy name!" Unfortunately, Roland's concept of liberty did not extend to women, for she was a supporter of Rousseau, who believed that women existed only to please men.

Neither the Reformation nor the Enlightenment brought positive benefits to women directly. But the breakdown of the authority of the Church, the questioning of the "divine rights of kings," and the debates about the "rights of man" stimulated discussion of the "rights of woman." As a result, women and some men began to articulate feminist viewpoints.

Josefa Amar

b. 1753; Spain
Deeply concerned with the position of women, Amar, a linguist and writer, presented a dissertation defending women and their aptitude for government service, as well as for other positions then held only by men. In her works, she addressed the need for women's education and condemned men's attempts to judge, define, or constrict women in any way.

Jeanne Campan

1753–1822; France
Campan, who founded the first secular school in France to give girls a liberal education, opened the school to students from modest and upper-class families, an unusual precedent in class-conscious France. She also published a number of important books on education.

Elizabeth Carter

1717–1806; England
Carter belonged to the Bluestocking Society, a salon known for its support of women's rights and the first of its kind in England. Carter was a linguist, a translator, a poet, and an excellent conversationalist and noted wit.

Elizabeth Hamilton

1758–1816; Scotland
Hamilton was a successful novelist and historian and an astute observer of Scottish rural life. In her book, *The Letters of Education,* she promoted education for women of the lower classes.

Mary Hays

1760–1843; England
After she read Wollstonecraft's *Vindication,* Hays immediately became her friend, supporter, and follower. She and her sister Elizabeth praised Woll-stonecraft in their *Letters and Essays Moral and Miscellaneous* (1793) and urged women to insist upon their rights. In her *Appeal to the Men of Great Britain in Behalf of the Women,* Hays argued for the need for more equitable property and ownership laws, inveighed against marriage, and strongly supported women's sexual freedom. In *The Memoirs of Emma Courtney* (1769), the heroine is an active and educated woman who not only pursues a career but initiates a relationship with the man who becomes her husband. In *A Victim of Prejudice* (1799), Hays describes the persecution of an illegitimate daughter whose mother has died. She also wrote a six-volume *Female Biography,* published in 1803.

Mary Monckton

1747–1840; Ireland
A member of the Bluestocking Society, Monckton was a social leader and influential figure in London society. She encouraged women to frequent her salon and was a noted participant in the literary community in England.

Elizabeth Montagu

1720–1800; England
Montagu, a writer and critic, assembled the first literary society in London, The Bluestockings. The people who were invited to her salon were asked because of their merit more than their rank and included many accomplished women. Montagu gained fame for her intellectual and conversational talents and produced many critical works, including an *Essay on Shakespeare*.

Mary Radcliffe

fl. 1799; England
An early feminist, Radcliffe wrote *The Female Advocate, or An Attempt to Recover the Rights of Women from Male Usurpation,* published in 1799.

Rachel Varnhagen

1771–1838; Germany
Varnhagen was a Jewish leader of the intellectual life of Berlin who believed that the evils of Europe were the slave trade, war, and marriage. She challenged the existing view of women as the incarnation of sin and proclaimed their honor and moral purity. She advocated equality of the sexes and education for women, and argued that women, as citizens, had a right to work. In a statement that reflected how she thought women should regard themselves, she stated: "I am at one with myself and consider myself a good, beautiful gift."

Although the Enlightenment did not improve the position of women, it apparently produced some men progressive enough to publish women's work. Because the Reformation had encouraged women to learn how to read (although only for the purpose of teaching the Bible to their children), a growing female audience for literature developed, which benefited these women writers.

Marie de Lafayette

1634–1693; France
Madame Lafayette's major works, *La Princesse de Cleves* and *Zaide,* marked an important development in the history of literature and were precursors of the psychological novel. Lafayette shared serious intellectual companionships with many women, including a forty-year friendship and correspondence with Madame de Sévigné. She became an insider to the intrigues of the court, which provided her with material for her memoirs and novels; she held a salon which was the most aristocratic and learned in Paris; and she was renowned as a businesswoman and legal expert.

Mary Manley

1663–1724; England
An early British journalist, Manley published political tracts challenging the ideas of the Whig party. After the publication of her *Secret Memories* in 1709, she was arrested and charged with libel but later released. In 1711, Manley became a newspaper editor.

Hannah More

1745–1833; England
More and her sisters were educated by their father, the village schoolmaster. Hannah's father encouraged her to write, and her first work, *The Search for Happiness,* was published in 1762. An immediate success, it established More's reputation, and from 1775 on she spent her time in the heart of London life. A member of the Bluestocking Society, she wrote *Bas Bleu,* which described this circle. More became involved in the anti-slavery movement and wrote political commentaries and a series of religious and moral reflections that were among the most widely read books of the day.

Karoline Pichler

1769–1843; Austria
Pichler was a leading salonière of Vienna and an extraordinarily prolific writer. Her salon became the center of literary life in Vienna. She wrote a number of works on the French Revolution, Napoleon, and the Congress of Vienna. Further, she wrote sixty romances and plays whose production she supervised. Like many women writers, her work has not been made widely available through translation, and she is therefore known primarily in Germany.

Mary Shelley

1797–1851; England
Shelley, the author of *Frankenstein,* was a pioneer in the development of the Gothic novel and the creator of the genre of science fiction. The daughter of Mary Wollstonecraft, Shelley was never able to forget that her mother died of complications resulting from her birth, and she grieved at never having known her. When she was seventeen, she ran away with the then unknown poet, Percy Shelley (whom she later married), thereby provoking her father, William Godwin, to disown her. By the time she was twenty-two, she had borne four children, three of whom died, and shortly thereafter her husband drowned. By then, she had already published *Frankenstein,* a tremendously popular success and a best-seller for thirty years in England. To support herself and her remaining child, Shelley wrote novels, short stories, newspaper and scholarly articles, and edited and published the major editions of her husband's poetry. She devoted the last thirty years of her life to his work, which served to ensure his place in English literature.

Germaine de Staël

1766–1817; Switzerland
A novelist, philosopher, and political writer, De Staël was an important figure in post-revolutionary France. In 1794, she published a book that advocated the immediate end of revolutionary wars and the re-establishment of the absolute monarchy, which of course brought her the friendship of Napoleon. But she quickly came to oppose Napoleon's ambitions, and her drawing room became the meeting place for his enemies and the center of a powerful opposition. *Dulphine,* published in 1802, stated her views on the limited intellectual climate in France under Napoleon and became so popular that Napoleon exiled her. She began work on a three-volume book, not published until 1814, which challenged the prevailing literary ideas in France and set the stage for the later French Romantic movement. In 1807, her novel *Corrine* was published, in which she described the passions, struggles, and difficulties of a woman of genius. After Napoleon's downfall, De Staël returned to France and although in bad health, continued to write.

Deprived of the option of exercising power directly, many women found ways to shape the values of their societies through patronage and cultural activities – acting as hostesses and facilitating dialogue in the salons, influencing male creators, or becoming the mistresses of kings.

Leonor d'Almeida

1750–1839; Portugal
D'Almeida conducted a salon which became an intellectual center and brought European literary ideas to Portugal. She introduced English, French, and German pre-Romantic and Romantic works into the culture and in this way exerted an influence on the development of Portuguese literature.

Bridget Bevan

1698–1779; Wales
A noted patron of Welsh schools, Bevan established and directed two schools herself, then became director of the school system. She supported many of the liberal philosophical, religious, and educational movements of her time.

Yekaterina Dashkova

1744–1810; Russia
Dashkova, a scholar and author, was appointed by Catherine II to head the Russian Academy of Arts and Sciences, which had been founded at her suggestion. She established public lectures, increased the number of student fellowships, and organized a translator's department which made the best foreign literature available to the Russian public. She was instrumental in the writing of a dictionary of the Russian language, published and wrote for several periodicals, translated foreign works, wrote poetry and plays, and generally tried to popularize fine literature.

Françoise de Maintenon

1635–1719; France
Born in a prison cell where her parents were incarcerated for being Huguenot agitators, De Maintenon eventually became tutor to the children of Louis XIV, then his mistress, and later, secretly, his wife. For forty years, De Maintenon's insights affected French government and education. She was responsible for the passage of laws that improved the quality of life of the French people, and she established homes and educational institutions for poor young women. She also founded the convent of St. Cyr, where she retired after the death of Louis.

Suzanne Necker

1739–1794; Switzerland
Necker received a classical education, which enabled her to support herself as a teacher in her native Switzerland. After the death of her parents, she went to Paris and married a wealthy banker who became a prominent political figure. She opened a literary salon that marks the transistion between two distinct phases in the salons: the first more literary and the second more political. As the Revolution approached, the opinions of her daughter, Germaine de Staël, gave her salon a political and semi-revolutionary character. From 1776 on, Necker devoted herself to prison and hospital reform, establishing a model hospital in 1778.

Jeanne de Pompadour

1720/21–1764; France
As the mistress of Louis XV, De Pompadour influenced the choice of ministers and the making of government policy. Her extensive patronage of the arts included the construction of a theatre at Versailles and the funding of the Gobelin Tapestry Factory and the Sevres Porcelain Factory. By 1754, De Pompadour was considered a "world force" and the indispensable agent of the French government.

Alison Rutherford

18th c.; Scotland
In 1731, Rutherford arrived in Edinburgh and established a literary salon patterned on those in Paris, where she entertained the leading artists, writers, and political figures. She wrote character studies of her contemporaries, satirical poems about government officials, and serious poetry. Throughout her lifetime she corresponded with, supported, and encouraged women and their work.

Caroline Schlegel

1763–1809; Germany
Schlegel grew up in the university atmosphere of Göttingen, where her father was a professor. She joined a group of "Republicans" who were ardently sympathetic to the French Revolution; she was arrested in 1793 and imprisoned. After her release, she became important in the German Romantic Movement. Schlegel's writings included transcribing manuscripts, critical essays, and letters, which she exchanged with many leading Romantic figures. She was married to both Schlegel and Schelling, inspiring and influencing the formation and direction of their philosophies.

Elizabeth Vesey

1715–1791; England
An aristocratic salonist, Vesey, like her contemporary, Elizabeth Montagu, gathered people of influence around her and exerted immense influence on English life through her salon.

During the eighteenth and nineteenth centuries, a number of female explorers emerged. Perhaps it was a natural result of the widening understanding of the geography of the world, and perhaps it was because travel allowed women freedoms they could never have at home.

Isabella Bishop

1831/32–1904; England
One of the first women world explorers, Bishop traveled extensively throughout Asia and wrote travelogues which are considered masterpieces. She was the first woman elected to the Royal Geographical Society.

Celia Fiennes

1662–1741; England
Between 1687 and 1702, Fiennes took a series of journeys through England, Scotland, and Wales, riding about in a "spirit of pure curiosity." She made a record of her travels which encouraged women in the "study of those things which tend to improve the mind."

Mary Wortley Montagu

1689–1762; England
Writer, explorer, and social leader, Montagu is best known for having introduced smallpox innoculation into England, a practice she had observed in Turkey during her travels. The record of her journey, entitled *Letters from The East,* is the first account of that region by a woman.

Ida Pfieffer

1797–1858; Austria
Pfieffer, an explorer, anthropologist, and naturalist, traveled nearly two hundred thousand miles, recording her observations and collecting artifacts. After raising her family, she embarked on her first journey at the age of forty-five, then wrote *Woman's Voyage Round the World,* in which she described her experiences. In many countries, she was the first European visitor. Her collection of artifacts was distributed among British and European museums.

Hester Stanhope

1776–1839; England
The niece of the English Prime Minister William Pitt, Stanhope was his advisor and confidante and acted as his secretary and hostess until his death in 1806. With her lifelong female companion, she later settled in Palestine, adopted Arab manners, customs, and dress, and soon gained such powerful influence over the wandering Arab tribes that she came to be regarded as a queen of the desert. She established a refuge for the persecuted and distressed at an unused convent in Lebanon, saying: "Show me where the poor and needy are and let the rich shift for themselves." Stanhope wrote six volumes of her travels and memoirs, leaving a marvelous record of a near-legendary woman.

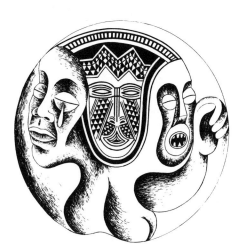

Sojourner Truth
1797–1883

The first English settlers landed in America in 1607, and just twelve years later the first slaves were brought over and sold to the early colonists. By 1720 the slave trade was widespread. Slave ships were loaded with as many Blacks as could be forced into the dark, airless holds. They were chained into wooden decks, deprived of their dignity, and systematically degraded.

From the beginning of slavery, there were whites who protested the contradiction between democratic principles and the horrible reality of slavery. In the decades before the Civil War, anti-slavery societies sprang up everywhere. Many of these were female organizations, and it did not take the women long to realize that – even though their work provided an enormous amount of support for the abolitionists – they were expected to remain in the background. As a result of their experiences in the anti-slavery movement, women began to agitate for their own rights. Their arguments, however, often had no meaning to black women who didn't even own themselves. They belonged to their white masters, and it was difficult for them not to scoff at white women who enjoyed so many privileges, yet complained about their lot. But southern women, in particular, had direct knowledge of the intimate connection between the slavery of both women and Blacks. They knew that the concept of white womanhood that imprisoned them was based on the sexual exploitation of the Blacks.

For black women, the contrast between the rights most of them had enjoyed in their homelands and the degradation they experienced in America must have been particularly cruel. In the North and the South, black women were used for sexual pleasure and to breed more slaves. Rape, a common occurrence, was an *institutional* crime, part of the deliberate dehumanization of both men and women. The humiliation of the women devastated them and also caused black men to feel emasculated by their inability to protect their women from brutality. This has had severe consequences for the relationships between black men and women and has made black women's struggle extremely complex. Still, in the face of oppression, lack of education and opportunity, and often extreme poverty, a number of black women have emerged to challenge racism, and sometimes sexism as well. They have tried to bring education and help to their people and to achieve places in the professions, even more difficult for them to break into than for white women.

Marian Anderson
b. 1902; United States

Anderson's talent was recognized by her family at an early age, and through donations from church and community members, she began her musical training. She joined the all-black Philadelphia Choral Society and was granted a Rosenwald Scholarship in 1930. She traveled to Europe, where she studied and began her professional career. As with many other black American performers, her initial fame was achieved in Europe. On Easter Sunday, 1939, Anderson was scheduled to sing at Constitution Hall in Washington, D.C., but the Daughters of the American

Revolution owned the hall and refused to allow her to perform. This prompted her friend Eleanor Roosevelt to resign her membership and arrange for the concert to take place instead at the Lincoln Memorial. The first Black to perform with the Metropolitan Opera, Anderson also performed at the White House and at Eisenhower's Inauguration. She is the recipient of twenty-three honorary doctorates and was a delegate to the United Nations.

Josephine Baker

ca. 1908–1975;
United States
Baker began her fifty-year career as an entertainer in Harlem night clubs, then appeared with the Révue Nègre in Paris and became the sensation of Europe. The star of the Folies Bergère, Baker epitomized the Jazz Age with her flamboyant and exuberant singing and dancing. She performed in films, operettas, and extravagant revues. During World War II, she was active in the French Resistance, receiving the Croix de Guerre, the Legion of Honor, and the Rosette of the Resistance. In later years, she campaigned for civil rights in the United States.

Mary McLeod Bethune

1875–1955; United States
Born of slave parents, Bethune graduated from the Moody Bible Institute in Chicago in 1895 and began her lifelong involvement in expanding opportunities for Blacks. In 1904, she opened the Institute for Girls in Daytona Beach, raising all the money herself to start it and maintain it. When her school merged with a men's school in 1923, Bethune became president of Bethune-Cookman

College. She served on federal commissions and worked in the administrations of four presidents.

Mary Ann Shadd Cary

1829–1893; United States
Cary was the first black woman to practice law in the United States and the first to edit a newspaper. She taught in Canada during the 1850's, and while there she edited the abolitionist newspaper, *The Provincial Freeman*. With the outbreak of the Civil War, Cary returned to the United States and became active in the recruitment of Blacks into the militia. After the war, she attended Howard University and earned a degree in law.

Milla Granson

19th c.; United States
Granson, a slave in Kentucky, learned to read from the children of her owner. Although it was illegal to teach slaves, she organized a clandestine school and, from midnight until 2 a.m., taught reading and writing. Hundreds of slaves were educated this way, and many wrote their own freedom passes to escape to the North. She carried on her project for seven years in Kentucky and then in Louisiana. The school was discovered by authorities in Kentucky and became a subject of debate in the state legislature. After much deliberation, a bill was passed stating that it was not illegal for a slave to teach a slave, and Granson resumed her work.

Frances Harper

1825–1911; United States
Harper's novel about the Reconstructed South, *Iola Leroy, or Shadows Uplifted* (1892), was the first book published by a black American. Born of free parents,

she was self-educated. She worked as a nursemaid, seamstress, needlework teacher, and writer, producing ten volumes of poetry, her novel, and many articles. Harper toured as a lecturer, advocating abolition and women's rights at the 1866 Women's Rights Convention and at the 1869 meeting of the Equal Rights Association. When the schism developed between white abolitionists and feminists, Harper sided with Frederick Douglass, who felt that the issue of race had priority over that of sex. Nonetheless, Harper continually worked for black women and founded the National Association of Colored Women, serving as its vice-president until she died.

Zora Neale Hurston

1901–1960; United States
Dedicated to the preservation of black culture and tradition, Hurston traveled throughout the South collecting folklore and mythology. During the thirties, she received WPA grants and a Guggenheim Fellowship to pursue her work. She published several collections, such as *Mules and Men* (1935), as well as novels and an autobiography, *Dust Tracks on a Road*. By the 1950's, no longer able to find support for her writing, she worked as a maid, a librarian, and a teacher. She suffered a stroke in 1959, and died in 1960, a patient in a county welfare home. Thirteen years later, the writer, Alice Walker, and Hurston scholar, Charlotte Hunt, placed a tombstone on the previously unmarked grave. It read, "Zora Neale Hurston, A Genius of the South, Novelist, Folklorist, Anthropologist, 1901–1960."

Edmonia Lewis

1845–1890; United States
Lewis was America's first black woman sculptor. Born to a Chippewa mother and

a free black father, Lewis was orphaned at age twelve and adopted by abolitionist parents. She received a scholarship to study at Oberlin College in Ohio and developed into an accomplished neoclassical sculptor. She went to Rome where she worked and exhibited with Harriet Hosmer's group of women sculptors. Her finest works depict important Native American figures, manifest her concern with her black heritage, and generally incorporate images of heroic women.

Bessie Smith

1894–1937; United States
Born in Chattanooga, Tennessee, Smith made her stage debut at the age of nine. As a teenager, she appeared with Gertrude ("Ma") Rainey's minstrel show on the black vaudeville circuit. Influenced by Rainey, she developed her own unique art form – a blend of classical blues, country blues, and jazz. She sang to packed houses wherever she performed and worked with every great jazz musician of her day. Her music reflected the oppression she experienced as a woman, as a Black, and as a victim of alcohol and hard times. At one time, she was Columbia Records' most valuable artist, but her career experienced a decline in the early Depression years. She was beginning to make a comeback when she died in an automobile accident.

Maria Stewart

1803–1879; United States
In the early 1830's, Stewart gave a series of lectures in which she asked her people to work for the abolition of slavery and to take pride in their race and heritage. This marked the first time an American-born woman spoke in public. Because of the criticism she received as a woman, however, she gave up lecturing and devoted

the remainder of her career to work in education and in the church. She started schools in Baltimore and Washington, founded and taught Sunday Schools, and worked as a matron in the Freedman's Hospital in Washington.

Harriet Tubman

1826–1913; United States
Tubman was born into slavery, escaped to the North in 1849, and established her "underground railroad," from which she "never lost a single passenger." Tubman led over three hundred men, women, and children from slavery into freedom during the 1850's, risking her freedom nineteen times on her trips into the slave states. Called "Moses," she became a legendary figure, and a reward of forty thousand dollars was offered for her capture. During the Civil War, she worked as a spy, a scout, a nurse, and a commander of both black and white troops for the Union Army. Like Sojourner, Tubman spread her beliefs in freedom and liberty by speaking, organizing, and inspiring others. In her later years, she attended women's suffrage conventions and helped organize the National Federation of Afro-American Women (1895).

Ida B. Wells

1862–1931; United States
The child of slave parents, Wells began her struggle for equality when she sat in the "white" railroad coach and was forcibly removed. She sued and won, but a higher court struck down the decision. She then became part owner of the *Memphis Free Speech,* for which she wrote articles condemning the lynchings of Blacks. After the destruction of her office by mobs in 1892, she began a one-woman campaign against lynching. Wells lectured in New York and Boston,

founded anti-lynching societies and black women's clubs, and in 1895 published *A Red Record,* an account of three years of lynchings. An uncompromising militant, she never gave the conservative National Association for the Advancement of Colored People her full support, although she had participated in its founding.

Margaret Murray Washington

1865–1925; United States
Washington founded the National Association of Colored Women in 1896, which united the two major national black women's associations with hundreds of local organizations. She graduated from Fisk University in 1889 and became a principal at Tuskegee Institute. She married its founder, Booker T. Washington, and worked with him in the expansion of the school. She became the Institute's first director of girls' industries, and later, Dean of Women.

In addition to the black women grouped around Sojourner, there are a number of white women who either played a part in the Civil War or worked to help their black sisters.

Anna Ella Carroll

1815–1893; United States
Carroll who was responsible for the Union victory in the Civil War, wrote books, pamphlets, and articles on the state of American politics and was involved in espionage for the Union in the Civil War. These activities attracted the attention of Lincoln, who sent her on a mission to the West to investigate and evaluate the Union's war policy. During

that trip Carroll became aware of the inadequacy of the Union's military strategy, and she masterminded the Tennessee plan which finally won the war. She was never given recognition for her monumental achievement, as Lincoln and the War Department felt it necessary to "protect" the public from the knowledge that it was Carroll – not their generals – who had ended the strife that divided the nation.

Prudence Crandall

1803–1889/90; United States
Crandall, a pioneer educator of black girls in the "free North," became a victim of persecution for her courageous stance on the right of Blacks to an education. In the 1820's she started a girls' school in Connecticut and was respected by the community until she admitted a black girl. When parents withdrew their daughters, Crandall, undaunted, began another school for black girls. She was jailed in 1832, and her trial attracted the attention of abolitionists who came to her support. Eventually mob violence forced the closing of the school.

Angelina Grimké

1805–1879; United States

Sarah Grimké

1792–1873; United States
The Grimké sisters were the first women to speak publicly for the abolition of slavery in the United States. Cultured and well-educated, the Grimkés had come north from South Carolina with first-hand knowledge of the condition of the slaves. In 1836, Angelina wrote a lengthy address urging women to assume their responsibility to work actively to free the Blacks. The sisters' lectures elicited violent criticism, as it was considered improper for women to speak out on political issues.

The Grimkés became acutely aware of their own oppression as women and began to address that issue as well. A severe split developed in the anti-slavery movement, with some abolitionists arguing that it was the "Negro's hour and women would have to wait." The Grimkés refused to accept this and insisted on arguing for the equality of all. Sarah became a major theoretician of the women's rights movement. She challenged all the conventional beliefs about women's place and, addressing men, said: "All I ask of our brethren is, that they will take their feet from off our necks…"

Mary Livermore

1820–1905; United States
During the Civil War, Livermore worked in hospitals and was a correspondent for numerous journals. She wrote books, edited her husband's newspaper, and was the only woman reporter at Lincoln's nomination. After the Civil War, she was active in the temperance and suffrage movements.

Harriet Beecher Stowe

1811–1896; United States
Stowe's novel, *Uncle Tom's Cabin,* is a landmark in American history and is often cited as a cause of the Civil War. Deeply moved by accounts of the injustice and cruelty of the slave system, Stowe traveled to the South to witness it herself. The material she gathered became the source for *Uncle Tom's Cabin; or Life Among the Lowly,* published in 1851 in serial form in an abolitionist newspaper. The work became an immediate sensation and gained worldwide popularity. Stowe was also an ardent supporter of women's rights and collaborated with her sister Catherine Beecher on nineteen domestic science books.

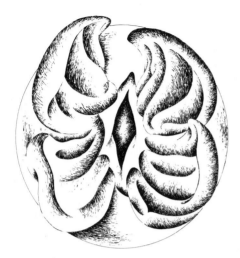

Susan B. Anthony

1820–1906

Anthony's plate rests on a runner embroidered with a series of memory bands, each commemorating a major figure in the international women's movement that Anthony inspired. The women's names surrounding the place setting comprise the largest grouping on the floor. We traced the history of the women's movement and tried to represent the most significant leaders in various parts of the world. Each woman also symbolizes the thousands who worked to change women's condition and bequeath a better world to us.

In America, the women's rights movement was part of the great social reform movements of the nineteenth century, including abolition and temperance. As a result of sexism experienced in the anti-slavery societies, women realized that it was time to organize in their own behalf. Women's clubs and reform activities provided members with the organizational skills that they brought to the formation of the National Woman Suffrage Association. The radical views of Association leaders Anthony and Stanton, however, frightened some of the Association's more conservative members, who broke away and formed another organization under the leadership of Lucy Stone. The two groups worked separately until 1890, when the schism that divided them was healed and a unified group was formed.

Alice Stone Blackwell

1857–1950; United States
Blackwell was the daughter of Lucy Stone and the niece of Elizabeth Blackwell. She was instrumental in reuniting the two major factions of the suffrage movement in the United States with the formation of the National American Woman Suffrage Association (NAWSA) in 1890. As a reporter for the *Woman's Journal* at the 1891 national convention of the Women's Christian Temperance Union (WCTU), Blackwell wrote, "multitudes of women who began by seeing only the drunkard are learning through the WCTU to look beyond him to the principle..." Women temperance workers were becoming aware of their powerlessness without the vote, and, as a result, strong ties between temperance and suffrage emerged. As a second-generation suffragist, Blackwell voted in the first national election following the passage of the Nineteenth Amendment.

Carrie Chapman Catt

1859–1947; United States
Catt assumed leadership of NAWSA after the deaths of Stanton in 1902 and Anthony in 1906, and it was due partly to her twenty years of dedicated work that the Nineteenth Amendment was ratified in 1920. Catt founded the International Woman Suffrage Alliance in 1904 and traveled around the world to forge an international feminist movement. She founded the League of Women Voters in 1920 and brought together eleven national women's organizations to create the National Committee on the Cause and Cure of War. After World War II, she used her influence to see that qualified women were placed on crucial United Nations committees. Despite her achievements, she has remained relatively unknown.

Charlotte Perkins Gilman

1860–1935; United States
Gilman's feminist perspective made her the voice and conscience of a generation of women taking their first steps outside the domestic sphere. Her widely acclaimed book *Women and Economics* was a declaration of women's economic independence from men. "The labor of women in the house, certainly, enables men to produce more wealth than they otherwise could; and in this way women are economic factors in society. But so are horses." She also proposed a model for modern day care centers and suggested cooperative kitchens to free women for nondomestic activities.

Lucretia Mott

1793–1880; United States
Mott was a major figure in the early organization of the women's suffrage movement in the United States and a leading abolitionist. As a Quaker minister and a member of the liberal Quaker community, she taught school, opened her home as a station on the underground railroad, and, in 1833, founded the first integrated anti-slavery society in the United States.

Mott and Stanton, unable to gain power in the world anti-slavery convention in London because they were women, decided to organize a convention and form a society to advance women's rights. In 1848, the historic Seneca Falls Convention convened. Mott addressed the convention concerning the social, civil, and religious restrictions placed on women. It was resolved there "that it is the sacred duty of the women of this country to secure for themselves their sacred right to the elective franchise," a right that would be withheld for another seventy-two years.

Carrie Nation

1846–1911; United States
Nation was one of the radical activist leaders of the WCTU, which was formed in 1874 to combat the growing alcoholism problem that was disrupting a vast number of American families. Because women had few social and political rights, they had no protection from alcoholic fathers and husbands. Nation experienced this situation and struck out in whatever way she could. She and her female followers entered saloons and smashed their stocks of liquor. The liquor interests massed against the women, opposing temperance and, later, women's rights. Though arrested over thirty times for her

militant reform tactics, Nation continued her temperance campaign. Maligned by history and represented as eccentric, Nation's place in women's struggles needs to be re-examined in the context of a wider understanding of nineteenth-century women's lives.

Alice Paul

ca. 1885–1976; United States
A militant suffragist in the early women's movement, Paul drafted the Equal Rights Amendment in 1923, kept the issue before Congress for nearly twenty years, but died without seeing it passed. From a Quaker family, Paul was an extraordinary organizer, fundraiser, and politician.

Convinced by her work with the Pankhursts in England that the only way to gain suffrage in America was through militant pursuit of a federal amendment, she returned to America a dedicated, militant suffragist. Paul and her colleagues were arrested and jailed for their political activities, and were force-fed during prison hunger strikes.

Annie Smith Peck

1850–1933; United States
A feminist, scholar, lecturer, and mountaineer, Peck traveled around the world. In 1912, at age sixty-one, she climbed Mt. Coropu in Peru and planted a "Votes for Women" sign at the summit. She was also the first to scale Peru's Mt. Huascaran, which at the time was believed to be the highest peak in the Western Hemisphere.

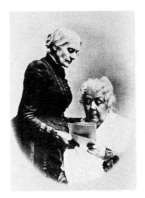
Susan B. Anthony and Elizabeth Cady Stanton, about 1892.

Elizabeth Cady Stanton

1815–1902; United States
The lifelong friend and colleague of Susan B. Anthony, and one of the giants of the women's movement, Stanton devoted her life to the struggle for equal rights. Her initial involvement in social and political reform was, like many feminists, as an abolitionist. After realizing that even in the anti-slavery movement women were discriminated against, she turned her attention entirely to gaining women's educational opportunities, suffrage, and property and divorce law reforms. She gradually expanded her vision and developed theories advocating a total transformation of relations between the sexes: "…we have every reason to believe that our turn will come again…not for women's supremacy, but for the as yet untried experiment of complete equality, when the united thought of man and woman will inaugurate a just government…a civilization at last in which ignorance, poverty, and crime will exist no more…" Neither she nor Anthony, who joined with her in 1851, ever imagined that obtaining the vote would be so difficult or require the efforts of so many women. Rather, they saw it as one small step in the struggle for complete equality.

Lucy Stone

1818–1892; United States
Stone was one of the first women to attend liberal Oberlin Collage when it opened its doors to women and Blacks. She graduated valedictorian in 1841, but, because she was a woman, had to sit in the audience while a male student read her speech. She become an avowed feminist and expressed her discontent with the plight of women and with the plight of the slave, speaking for women during the week and for slaves on the weekend. When the Anti-Slavery Society objected, she offered to resign, saying, "I was a woman before I was an abolitionist; I must speak for women." When the suffrage movement split into liberal and conservative factions in 1869, Stone headed the American Woman Suffrage Association, which worked for suffrage at state and local levels first. In 1855, Stone married Henry Blackwell, who actively supported the women's rights movement and Stone's involvement in it. Their marriage contract was unconventional in specifying that their relationship would be totally equalized.

Mary Church Terrell

1863–1954; United States
Terrell, a leading black educator, lecturer, writer, and activist, was an influential leader in the suffrage and civil rights movements. She graduated from Oberlin College at the head of her class in 1884, taught school, and served for eleven years on the Board of Education in Washington, D.C., the first black woman ever appointed. She was the first president of the National Association of Colored Women (1896–1901).

Frances Willard

1839–1898; United States

In order to pursue women's social and political equality, Willard gave up a promising career as an educator. She boosted the membership of the WCTU to two hundred thousand and expanded its focus to include such wider social concerns as woman's suffrage. Arguing that women needed the vote to protect their homes and children against alcoholic husbands, Willard skillfully led otherwise conservative women into the active suffrage campaign. In 1879 she became president of WCTU – a position she held until her death.

Victoria Woodhull

1838–1927; United States

Woodhull's career was as varied as it was criticized. A stockbroker, Woodhull joined the women's movement as a speaker. In 1872, she ran for President of the United States, demonstrating the absurdity of laws that allowed a woman to run for public office while denying her the vote.

Because of her Marxist leanings and open advocacy of free love, Woodhull frightened many women and became a target through which critics attacked the entire women's movement. Woodhull was forced to flee the United States after she candidly exposed an affair between an important minister and a female member of his congregation in an attempt to point out the hypocrisy of leading moral figures. Disillusioned by the rigidity of the system, she advocated that women declare their independence from the United States and set up a government of their own.

Frances Wright

1795–1852; United States

In 1828, Wright spoke publicly in support of women's rights and education, an event signaling the beginning of women's rights agitation in the United States. A Scotswoman, she became interested in the slavery issue. Unsuccessful at integrating Blacks into American society, she accompanied freed slaves to Haiti and gave them money for a new life there.

In England, both the suffragists' tactics and the government's response were far more violent than in the United States. Repeatedly arrested and imprisoned, the women initiated hunger strikes and were cruelly force-fed, then released only to go through the same thing all over again. The English movement was more militant but ultimately less effective in challenging the basic structure of both a classist and a sexist society.

Annie Wood Besant

1847–1933; England

Besant was a feminist, a birth control advocate, and an early convert to Fabian socialism. She also worked as a strike leader, union organizer, and social and educational reformer. She was elected president of the Indian National Congress in 1918.

Barbara Bodichon

1827 – 1891; England

A leading feminist in the early stages of the English women's movement, Bodichon was instrumental in securing passage of the Married Women's Property Act, worked to extend university education to women, and helped establish a women's college in Cambridge. In 1857, she formed the first women's employment bureau in Britain and participated in publishing the *Englishwomen's Journal,* which became the voice of the suffrage movement.

Millicent Fawcett

1847–1929; England

Fawcett was a founder, in 1866, of the first Woman's Suffrage Committee, which by 1867 had gathered enough momentum to present Parliament with the first women's suffrage petition. The Committee began holding public meetings to agitate for the vote, and although suffrage measures were continually defeated, improvements were made in women's rights to work.

An advocate of education for women, Fawcett helped her sister, Elizabeth Garrett Anderson, open the medical profession to women. In 1897 she helped create the National Union of Women's Suffrage Societies, becoming its first president.

Annie Kenney

1879–1953; England

An early English suffrage leader, Kenney began working at a mill at age ten. The deplorable conditions at the mill led to her involvement in the textile unions, and after meeting the Pankhursts in 1905, she joined the Women's Social and Political Union (WSPU). She and Christabel Pankhurst were the first women arrested in connection with suffrage activities. In 1912, with the WSPU leadership in prison, Kenney became director of the movement, receiving guidance from Pankhurst. She continued to be arrested and to participate in hunger strikes until the outbreak of World War I.

Constance Lytton

1869–1923; England

A member of the aristocracy, Lytton passionately believed in women's rights and in the eradication of class distinctions. She joined the WSPU, took part in demonstrations, and was arrested many times. On trial, she testified, "I have been more proud to stand by my friends in their trouble than I have ever been of anything in my life."

Because of Lytton's class and the prison officials' knowledge that she had heart trouble, she received preferential treatment. To protest such privileges, she carved a "V" for "votes" on her chest with a hairpin. Upon her release she attempted to disguise her identity, was arrested again, and was released after her identity was discovered. Shortly thereafter she suffered a heart attack and partial paralysis. She began recording her prison experiences, painfully learning to write with her left hand. She died an invalid.

Caroline Norton

1808–1877; England

A prominent writer of books, Norton used her talent to work for social reform. Her widely read poem "A Voice From the Factories" was an exposé of child labor conditions. Norton first became involved in women's rights when she was sued for divorce by her husband and stood to lose her possessions and custody of her children. Through lobbying and pamphlet-writing, Norton contributed to the passage of the Infants' Custody Bill of 1838 and the Marriage and Divorce Act of 1857.

Christabel Pankhurst

1880–1958; England

In 1903, with her mother, Emmeline, Pankhurst organized the WSPU. She became an able administrator, inspiring leader, brilliant theoretician, and militant crusader. When the government attempted to subvert the movement by imprisoning WSPU leaders, Pankhurst escaped to Paris and directed its activities through Annie Kennedy. At this time she launched the radical newspaper, *The Suffragette*. After women's suffrage was achieved in 1918, she became a lawyer and continued the struggle for women's rights.

Emmeline Pankhurst

1858–1928; England

Through Pankhurst's bold leadership, suffrage was won for Englishwomen. Working as Registrar of Births and Deaths, she came into contact with the plight of working-class women. Convinced that men regarded women as the servant class, she determined to change society's inequities. When she and her daughter Christabel created the WSPU, their goal and motto was "Votes for Women." WSPU membership cut across class barriers, and mill workers and aristocrats worked together.

When it became clear that the government was completely unsympathetic to feminists, Pankhurst, with daughters Christabel and Sylvia, inaugurated violent tactics that shocked the world. Crying, "Deeds, not words!" the women engaged in window-breaking demonstrations, chained themselves to the gates outside the prime minister's house, and even committed arson. This led to arrests and imprisonments. While many women suffered incredible hardships in prison, they continued to subject themselves to arrest and brutality in an effort to force a moral confrontation with the government.

At the outbreak of World War I, Pankhurst directed her energy toward the war effort, encouraging women to join her. Indeed, partly because of women's wartime contributions, the vote was granted to women over thirty in 1918. In 1928, the bill was amended to grant the vote to women over twenty-one.

Sylvia Pankhurst

1882–1960; England

An artist who put aside her work to engage in the suffrage cause, Sylvia Pankhurst worked closely with her mother and sister in the early WSPU by organizing, speaking, and officiating as treasurer. She worked with women in London's East End slums, and her experience there strengthened her socialist tendencies and beliefs in the need for social reform for women and men.

Expelled from the WSPU by her mother and sister because of their sole commitment to suffrage, Sylvia had a large working-class following and soon formed the East London Federation for Women's Suffrage. She continued her East End work, organizing clinics, day nurseries, and communal restaurants, and working to improve factory conditions. Because Sylvia was a pacifist, she broke with her family on the war issue, but although she differed with her mother and sister as to methodology, ideologically all three were committed to the same goal – the re-ordering of a society rife with injustice.

Emmeline Pethick-Lawrence

fl. 1900's; England

Pethick-Lawrence was an upper-class woman active in feminist and socialist causes. She and her husband did philanthropic and labor movement work and through Emmeline Pankhurst became involved in the WSPU, raising more than one hundred thousand pounds for the cause. They also published *Votes for Women*, a suffrage journal, and were imprisoned many times for participating in demonstrations.

The nineteenth-century feminist movement in America created a convulsion in the fabric of society. The women's rights issue was debated everywhere for several decades. Moreover, as a result of Anthony's organization, in 1888, of the International Council of Women, in the early twentieth century, feminism became an enormous international movement that changed the status of women in most European countries, in some parts of eastern Europe, and in South America. It forced open the professions and created a climate that permitted artists and writers to begin to find an authentic female voice. A great deal of research on women's history was done during this period, and a number of theoretical works were written that established the basis for an overall understanding of our past.

Baroness of Adlersparre

fl. 1880's; Sweden

In 1859, the Baroness began advocating feminist ideas in her magazine *For the Home*, and later she founded the Fredrika Bremer League, named for the early Scandinavian women's rights advocate and mainstay of the German feminist movement.

Gunda Beeg

20th c.; Germany

Beeg was a founder of Germany's dress reform movement. She designed a loose-fitting dress to replace the restrictive Victorian style of women's clothing.

Frederika Bremer

1801–1865; Sweden

Bremer's writings launched the Swedish women's rights movement. Her 1856 book, *Herha*, became the textbook for the Swedish women's movement. Bremer tried to organize a universal women's league to promote peace through social legislation.

Minna Canth

1844–1897; Finland

Canth was a realist – novelist and playwright who dealt with women's issues and working-class problems. In 1885, having become an ardent feminist, she wrote a novel, *The Worker's Wife*, criticizing the Church's attitude toward women.

Minna Cauer

1841–1922; Germany

Cauer played a major role in the German suffrage and political rights movement. Influenced by Anthony, she started a magazine, *The Women's Movement*, and began lecturing on women's rights. With Anita Augsburg and Lili Braun she challenged the reactionary Prussian law prohibiting women from holding or attending political meetings.

Frances Power Cobbe

1822–1904; Ireland

A feminist educator, author, and philanthropist, Cobbe was deeply concerned with higher education for women. She wrote the introduction to *The Woman*

187

Question in Europe, an 1884 publication chronicling the progress of the suffrage movement. Her writings, including *The Duties of Women,* addressed women's issues.

Augusta Fickert

1855–1910; Austria

An educator and feminist, Fickert worked to improve Austrian women's social and economic position. Her activities included organizing the General Women's Club of Austria, which sought to improve women's wages; opposing state sanction and regulation of prostitution; initiating free legal aid for women; editing a women's magazine; working for higher education and employment opportunities for women; and setting up community kitchens to serve families with working mothers.

Margarete Forchhammer

20th c.; Denmark

Forchhammer was a peace and women's movement activist who won international acclaim for her work, which included the founding in 1899 of the Danish National Council of Women, a group that fought for suffrage and women's rights. Sixteen years later, leading a procession of twenty thousand women to celebrate women's suffrage in Denmark, Forchhammer became the first woman to address the Danish Parliament.

During World War I many Danish women lost their jobs, and Forchhammer organized ways of helping them. In 1920, a conference held by the International Council of Women decided that female delegates should be chosen to represent their governments at the League of Nations. Only Norway, Sweden, and Denmark appointed women delegates – Forchhammer among them.

Vida Goldstein

1869–1949; Australia

Goldstein was the major leader of the Australian women's suffrage movement. She devoted herself full-time to the suffrage cause, speaking, lobbying at Parliament, and publishing the *Australian Women's Sphere,* a feminist journal. Women received the right to vote in federal elections in 1902, and the following year Goldstein became the first woman in the British Empire nominated for Parliament. She ran for that office five times and, although never elected, used her campaigns as opportunities to educate the public on women's issues.

Hasta Hansteen

b. 1824; Norway

Hansteen, an early feminist writer, was the founder of the women's rights movement in Norway.

Amelia Holst

fl. 1802; Germany

Holst was the first German woman to write a book advocating women's educational opportunities. She provided an early impetus for the women's movement through her writings, which later feminists used as a theoretical foundation for their political and social activities.

Aletta Jacobs

1849–1929; Holland

The first woman physician in the Netherlands, Jacobs she joined Catt in a world tour to build support for an international women's suffrage and political rights movement.

Eliska Krasnohorska

b. 1847; Czechoslovakia

A poet, educator, and patriot, Krasnohorska was also a leader in the women's education movement. She founded the *Women's Journal,* which advocated unrestricted education for women in 1875; became the leader of the Women's Industry Society, which opened educational opportunities in technical work and the arts; and founded the Minerva Society, whose goal was to secure higher education for women. By 1890, the society opened a school for girls which was so successful that it became state-supported. Krasnohorska was an important poet, and she also became known for her translations of English, Polish, Russian, and German works.

Mary Lee

fl. 1895; Australia

Lee was the founder and leader of the suffrage movement in the state of South Australia where women won the right to vote in state elections in 1895, seven years before Parliament granted them voting rights in federal elections.

Bertha Lutz

20th c.; Brazil

The daughter of an intellectual family, Lutz was educated at the Sorbonne and became a linguist, naturalist, and secretary of the National Museum. Out of her concern with improving the educational, civil, and political status of women, she organized the Brazilian Association for the Advancement of Women to work for child welfare and women's suffrage and educational opportunities.

In 1923 Lutz was a delegate to the Pan-American Association for the Advancement of Women, which tried to stimulate the development of feminist and suffrage orgainzations in South and Central America and Mexico. One of her major ambitions was realized when Brazilian women won the vote in 1932. Significantly, four years later Lutz was elected to Parliament and continued her activism in the government as an official of the Federation for the Advancement of Women.

Mary Müller

1820–1902; New Zealand

Müller was an early theorist in New Zealand's women's suffrage movement and advocated women's suffrage in a series of newspaper articles. In 1869, under the pseudonym "Femina," She published the pamhlet *An Appeal to the Man of New Zealand,* which argued for women's rights and influenced passage of the Married Woman's Property Act of 1884. In 1893 New Zealand became the first country to grant women the vote.

Luise Otto-Peter

1819–1895; Germany

Otto-Peter, founder and leader of the German women's movement, used her writing and administrative skills in the struggle for equality. She began work in the 1840's, advocating women's emancipation in the Revolution of 1848 and founding a newspaper suppressed by the government for supporting women's equality. The Association for Women's Education was formed in 1865, with Otto-Peter as president, and became the basis for the National Association of German Women (NAGW), which supported the goals of civil equality and women's right to work.

Kallirhoe Parren

fl. 1896; Greece

A feminist and writer, Parren organized the Federation of Greek Women in 1896. This organization worked for women's political and social freedom and belonged to the International Council of Women, which developed communication channels and strategies for women's organizations around the world. In addition to writing several women's rights dramas, Parren was editor of a women's magazine in Athens for eighteen years.

Adelheid Popp

1869–1939; Austria

The founder of the Socialist Women's Movement in Austria, Popp was considered the "awakener" of European feminist socialists. Her dedication to women's issues and socialism was reflected in her fifty years as a party organizer, administrator, writer, speaker, and elected official to the Austrian government.

Käthe Schirmacher

fl. 1911; Germany

Schirmacher was a suffrage leader who wrote two books on the women's movement. In *The Riddle Woman,* she argued that women not only needed equal rights and opportunities, but had to forge their own vision and plans for their future as women. In *The Modern Woman's Rights Movement,* a history of the movement, she examined the status of feminism internationally.

Augusta Schmidt

19th c.; Germany

Working with Otto-Peter, Schmidt helped found the German women's movement. As a member of the executive committee of the NAGW and associate editor of its official paper, *New Paths,* she helped develop the NAGW's activities and goals, supporting women's right to education, choice of work, and participation in public life.

Katherine Sheppard

1848–1934; New Zealand

Sheppard succeeded Müller as head of New Zealand's suffrage movement. Active in the WCTU, she became a leader of that organization after it decided to spearhead the movement for women's suffrage. In 1888 Sheppard drew up and submitted a petition to the House of Representatives, but it was defeated. She continued the drive, submitting petitions in 1891, 1892, and 1893. The petition of 1893 was signed by one third of New Zealand's adult females and finally led to passage of the bill granting women suffrage that year.

Alexandra van Grippenberg

1856–1911; Finland

An author and leader of the Finnish feminist movement, Van Grippenberg published a collection of tales advocating temperance and women's rights. She attended the 1888 Women's Congress in Washington, D.C., organized by Anthony, after which she became an activist in the international struggle for women's rights, establishing a branch of the International Council of Women in Finland. For twenty years she was president of the oldest Finnish society for the promotion of women's rights. Feeling that women's efforts to secure liberation should be permanently recorded, Van Grippenberg wrote an extensive history of the feminist movement.

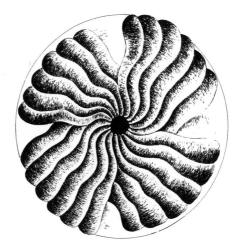

Elizabeth Blackwell

1821–1910

By the late nineteenth century, it seemed that women would not have to continue to face the enormous difficulties of earlier pioneers in medicine and the other professions. But even though there was a remarkable increase in the number of women doctors by the early twentieth century, there were fewer in 1950 than there had been in 1890; the institutional barriers were really not radically altered. Women's initial thrust into the professions were powered by the enormous strength and visibility of the feminist movement. This caused a male backlash that organized around the slogan, "God never intended women to be doctors," and similar phrases aimed at pushing women back into traditional female roles and out of competition with men. Women's professional training schools – formed by the first wave of successful female professionals to provide education for the next generations – merged with established colleges and universities, and within just a few decades, there were no longer women in positions of authority. Additionally, the passage of the Nineteenth Amendment brought with it the illusion that the vote marked the end of the quest for equal rights. Feminism declined, and its decline brought the rapid erosion of the progress made in the nineteenth century. The professions had all been forced open, but by the mid-twentieth century, they had almost closed again.

"A blank wall of social and professional antagonism faces the woman physician and forms a situation of singular and painful loneliness, leaving her without support, respect or professional council," wrote Elizabeth Blackwell. Her struggle epitomizes that of many women in medicine. Ironically, the areas in which women met the most resistance were obstetrics and gynecology – despite the fact that only a century before, female midwives prevailed. After the medical profession absorbed midwifery, women were told they were too delicate for obstetrical work. With male domination of childbirth and delivery, pregnancy became an illness. Childbed fever was introduced along with the use of forceps, and women's bodies became the passive fields upon which men plied their various skills.

Elizabeth Anderson

1836–1917; England
Anderson was the first and only female member of the British Medical Association for nineteen years. When Elizabeth Blackwell returned to England, the intense campaign to open the medical profession to women was already underway, and Anderson was deeply involved. She became the general director and chief surgeon of the new hospital for women (renamed the Elizabeth Garrett Anderson Hospital after her death in 1917) and was instrumental in establishing the London School of Medicine for Women, of which she became president.

Clara Barton

1821–1912; United States
Barton, the founder of the American Red Cross, began her professional career as a schoolteacher. With the outbreak of the Civil War she went to the front to nurse the soldiers without pay. She spent four years there and all of her own money. In 1870, she went to Europe to work with the International Red Cross, establishing military hospitals during the Franco-Prussian War. Barton returned to the United States determined to organize a branch of the Red Cross, which she did in 1881. She served as its president until 1904, extending Red Cross services to deal with disasters other than war.

Emily Blackwell

1826–1910; United States
Emily, the sister of Elizabeth Blackwell, was a physician who devoted her life to training women medical students and to treating women patients. She was admitted to medical school in Chicago in 1852, only to be turned away the next year because of her sex. She was finally accepted to medical school in Cleveland and, after graduating in 1854, traveled to Britain for postgraduate work in obstetrics. In 1856, Blackwell, her sister, and Dr. Marie Zakrzewska opened the New York Infirmary for Women and Children. By 1868, they had established a first-rate medical school for women for which Emily Blackwell assumed full responsibility after Elizabeth moved to England. For the next thirty years, she served as dean and professor of obstetrics and diseases of women.

Marie Bovin

18th c.; France
Considered the first great woman doctor of modern times, Bovin was awarded the honorary degree of Doctor of Medicine for her important work and research in gynecology. Denied admission to medical school, she was self-taught, as were most women doctors until the nineteenth century.

Edith Cavell

1865–1915; England
Before the outbreak of World War I, Cavell was head of nursing at the Birkendall Medical Institute in Brussels. When the Germans invaded Brussels, the school became a Red Cross hospital. Cavell treated all wounded soldiers regardless of their nationalities and also allowed the hospital to be used as an underground stop for French

and British soldiers going to Holland. Discovered by the Germans, Cavell was arrested and court-martialed. She admitted to having helped Allied soldiers cross the border, and her confession led to her conviction and death in 1915.

Marie Dugés

1730–1797; France
Dugés married an officer of health, studied medicine with him, then reorganized the maternity department of the hospital in which she worked, generally improving the medical care. She wrote several books on midwifery.

Marie Durocher

1809–1895; Brazil
Durocher was one of the first woman doctors in Latin America. Born in France and raised in Brazil, she studied obstetrics and in 1834 became the first recipient of a degree at the new medical school in Rio de Janeiro. She then carried on a successful practice for sixty years.

Salomée Halpir

18th c.; Poland
Halpir initially received training from her husband, an oculist. She went on to become a renowned specialist in cataract surgery.

Marie Heim-Vögtlin

1846–1914; Switzerland
One of the first professional woman physicians in modern Europe, Heim-Vögtlin received her degree in 1873 from the Zurich Medical School. She then established her own practice, specializing in gynecology and obstetrics. She and another doctor, Anna Heer, raised funds for a hospital and nurse-training school, which they opened in 1901. This excellent hospital treated only women and children and was run by an all-woman staff.

Kate Campbell Hurd-Mead

1867–1941; United States

Hurd-Mead, a physician and pioneer medical historian, wrote the first comprehensive chronicle of women in medicine. She established the Baltimore Dispensary for Working Women and Girls and became a specialist in the diseases of women and children. Hurd-Mead also helped establish a nurses organization and the Medical Women's International Association. But the absorbing interest of her life was the history of women in medicine. She spent years collecting information in the United States, Europe, Africa, and Asia, especially after 1925 when she retired from her practice. She published two books, *Medical Women of America* (1933) and *A History of Women in Medicine From the Earliest Times to the Beginning of the Nineteenth Century* (1938).

Marie La Chapelle

1769–1821; France

Trained in obstetrics by her mother, Marie Dugés, La Chapelle took over as head of maternity and midwifery at the hospital after her mother's death. She organized the maternity and children's hospital at Port Royal, trained midwives, and wrote a three-volume work on obstetrics that was the major text on midwifery for many years.

Rebecca Lee

fl. 1860's; United States

Lee was the first black woman doctor in the United States, receiving her degree in 1864 from the New England Female Medical College. She returned to the South after the Civil War and established a successful practice in Richmond, Virginia.

Florence Nightingale

1820–1910; England

At a time when nursing was considered menial labor which needed neither study nor intelligence, Nightingale elevated the practice to a professional level. In 1853 she became Superintendent of the Hospital for Women in London. When the Crimean War broke out, Nightingale and thirty-eight other nurses, whom she trained, went to the Crimea. There she was put in charge of all hospitals in the war zone and within a few months had reduced the death rate from 42 percent to 2 percent. When she returned to England, she established the Nightingale School and Home for Nurses with money she had received in recognition of her war work. Her achievement was formidable. She not only elevated nursing in her time; she established standards and educational programs and laid the foundation for the entire system of modern nursing.

Susan La Flesche Piccotte

fl. 1900; North America

Piccotte was the first Native American woman to study western medicine. A daughter of the chief of the Omaha tribe, she graduated from the Women's Medical College of Pennsylvania in 1889 and returned to practice medicine among her people.

Anna Schabanoff

19th c.; Russia

Schabanoff was the first woman to graduate from the Academy of Medicine in St. Petersburg. She received her M.D. in 1877 and became an excellent pediatrician in addition to establishing a child welfare association.

Miranda Stuart

1795–1865; England

"Thee must go to Paris and don masculine attire to gain the necessary knowledge," a Quaker gentleman advised Elizabeth Blackwell when she was struggling to be accepted into medical school. Stuart did just that and thereby became the first English-speaking woman in the world with a medical degree from an established school.

Amelia Villa

d. 1942; Bolivia

Bolivia's first woman doctor, Villa received her degree in 1926. The Bolivian government decorated her for her work in pediatrics and honored her by founding a children's ward that bears her name at the hospital in Oruro.

Mary Walker

1832–1919; United States

Walker served with the Ohio regiment as an Army surgeon and for her heroic work on the battlefield she was awarded the Congressional Medal of Honor. After the war, she continued her medical practice and also became a feminist activist. She was particularly involved in dress reform, considering trousers as the calling the corset "a coffin of iron bands." A review board revoked her medal in 1917, saying that fifty years earlier she had been awarded it by mistake. She refused to give it up and continued to wear it until she died. Her great-grandniece campaigned successfully to have it officially restored in 1977.

Nathalie Zand

fl. 1930's–40's; Poland

Zand was involved both nationally and internationally as a physician and feminist between World Wars I and II. She specialized in the pathology of the central nervous system, and her papers were published in Poland, England, and France. She disappeared during World War II.

As a result of feminist agitation and a half-century of arguments about women's rights, a new breed of women appeared. College-educated and independent, they set about opening the professions one by one. The pattern was usually the same; a few women won entry into a field and then established women's professional schools to counteract the continued resistance of male-dominated institutions.

Marianne Beth

b. 1890; Austria

The first Austrian woman to receive a doctorate of law, Beth specialized in international law, gained a reputation for her politically liberal views, and wrote influential papers on women's rights issues. Academically qualified to study law, she was at first allowed only to study the history of Church law, earning a Ph.D. Later, after it became possible for women to earn law degrees, she went back to school, graduated, and succeeded as a lawyer.

Sophie Blanchard

d. 1819; France

Blanchard was the first woman in the world to earn her living as a professional balloonist. In 1810, she became the Chief of Air Services to Napoleon and performed at royal functions.

Marie Curie

1867–1934; Poland/France

Educated by her father in chemistry, Curie became his laboratory assistant, then went to Paris and entered the Sorbonne, and finally found a job as a poorly paid assistant in a laboratory. As a result of her extraordinary talents, she was promoted to work on original research. She met and married Pierre Curie, and began a long series of experiments on the compounds of uranium and theorium. The Curies worked together intensively, resulting in the discovery of radium, an event that caused many long-held theories to be challenged and a new view of the nature of energy and the constitution of matter. They received many joint awards for their discoveries, among them the Nobel Prize for Physics and the French Legion of Honor. But because the Legion of Honor was awarded only to men, Pierre Curie declined it. The Curies sprang into worldwide fame, but their shared joy was cut short by Pierre's premature death in 1906. Marie was appointed Pierre's successor as special lecturer at the Sorbonne, the first time a woman obtained a full professorship. She continued her scientific research, sharing another Nobel Prize in 1903 for her discovery of radioactivity and radioactive elements. In 1911, she won the Nobel Prize in Chemistry.

Amelia Earhart

1898–1937; United States

Earhart's pioneering efforts in aviation were intended to improve the industry as well as to create opportunities for women in this new field. In 1936, she embarked on an around-the-world flight, Throughout the journey, she documented the effects of prolonged air travel on the human body, conducted mechanical tests on the aircraft, and recorded her observations on the lives of women in the countries where she stopped. It is believed that her plane went down in the Pacific Ocean, and no trace of her has ever been found. Before she left she wrote: "Women must try to do the things men have tried. When they fail, their failure must be but a challenge to others."

Emily Faithfull

1835–1895; England

In 1863, Faithfull founded *The Victoria Magazine,* which explored the problems of the working woman and demanded "equal pay for equal work." The periodical was printed by Faithfull's Victoria Press, established in 1860, and employing only women compositors. Although initially criticized, her publishing house soon acquired a reputation for excellent work.

Charlotte Guest

1812–1895; Wales

Guest was the first British woman to manage an ironworks, the Dowlais Iron Company. She inherited the business after her husband's death and was able to assume control immediately because she had been operating the company with him, overseeing the finances and familiarizing herself with the technical aspects of the manufacture of iron. She successfully averted a threatened strike by dealing reasonably with the workers' demands. She was also a writer and patron and was known for her excellent china collection, which she donated to the Victoria and Albert Museum.

Jane Harrison

1850–1928; England

Harrison became the Assistant Director of the British School of Archaeology in Rome and by 1925 had been awarded more honorary university degrees than any other woman in the world. Her interpretation of Greek culture, myths, and religion revolutionized the study of the classics.

Irène Joliot-Curie

1897–1956; France

Joliot-Curie, no doubt strongly influenced by her mother Marie Curie, was a leading scientist in the field of radioactivity. She and her husband discovered the neutron, a fundamental subatomic particle, for which they received the Nobel Prize for Chemistry. An ardent feminist and anti-facist, Joliot-Curie served in the Popular Front Government in 1936 and appeared twice before the Academie des Sciences to argue the right of women to become members. After 1937, she and her husband worked on nuclear fission and after World War II helped develop nuclear reactors and establish the French Atomic Energy Commission. In 1946, Joliot-Curie became Director of the Radium Institute but was removed without explanation by the government in 1950.

Betsy Kjelsberg

20th c.; Norway

Kjelsberg was the first woman elected to the Norwegian Legislature. She founded a businesswomen's union, and worked for legislation to protect factory workers, and inspected factories to ensure safety health standards for workers.

Sofia Kovalevskaya

1850–1891; Russia

Unable to obtain higher education in her native Russia, Kovalevskaya went to Germany to earn her doctorate in math. She finally was able to get a job in math at the New University of Stockholm, becoming the first woman outside of Italy to gain a university chair.

Belva Lockwood

1830–1917; United States

Lockwood was the first woman to plead a case before the Supreme Court. Originally a teacher, she founded a girl's school in Washington, D.C., and began to study international law. She applied to Columbia Law School, was turned down, and had to fight first for admission and then to actually receive her diploma. When she was admitted to the bar in 1873, a justice remarked, "I have no qualms about admitting you because I don't believe you'll succeed." Despite his doubts, Lockwood's practice flourished, and one of her cases went to the Supreme Court. But she was not allowed to plead the case, and she struggled during the next five years for passage of the bill allowing women lawyers to appear before the Supreme Court.

Margaret Murray

1863–1963; England

Murray was an archaeologist and the first woman to conduct her own digs. She was also a professor, folklorist, and author who did extensive research and writing in Egyptology. She wrote an original study of matrilinear descent of property in early Egypt and later did work on witchcraft, which resulted in two major works, *The Witch Cult in Western Europe* and *The God of the Witches.* She was the first to promulgate the theory that the witches of Western Europe were adherents of an earlier religion that was displaced by Christianity.

there is little wonder that a women's revolution began.

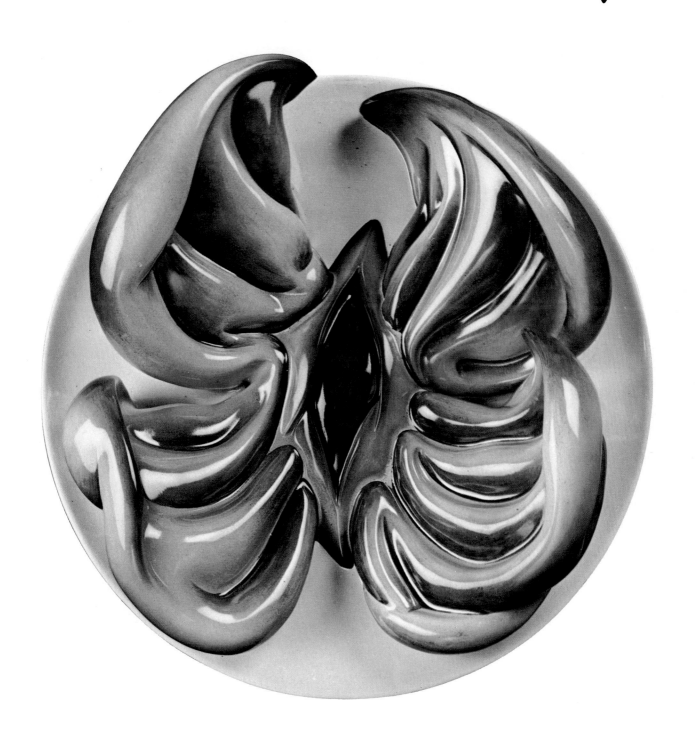

Susan B. Anthony

In 1792 Mary Wollstonecraft published a book

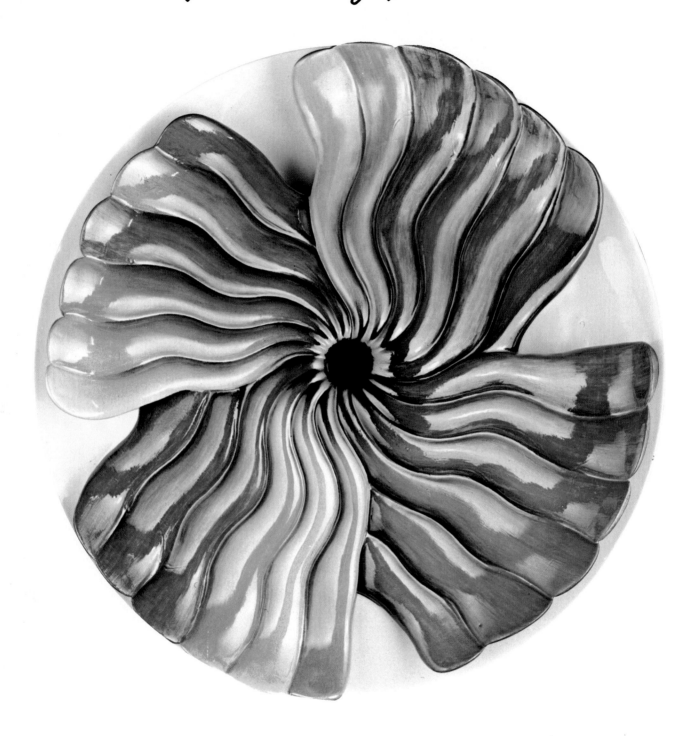

Elizabeth Blackwell

which provided the foundation for feminist theory and

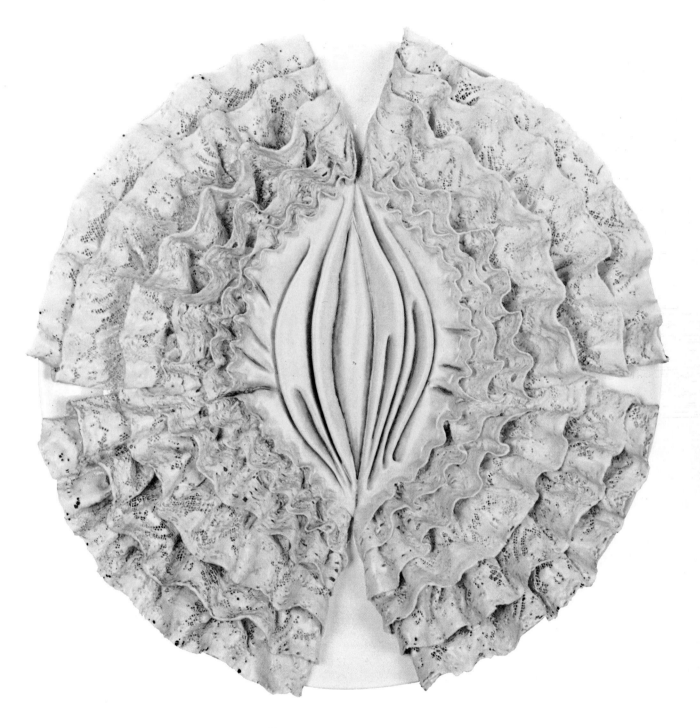

Emily Dickinson

the subsequent revolution. She argued that if women

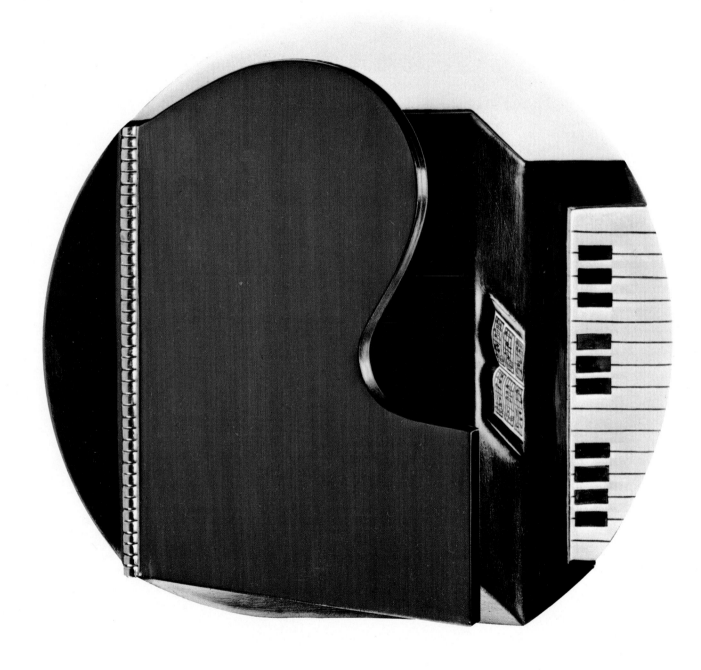

Ethel Smyth

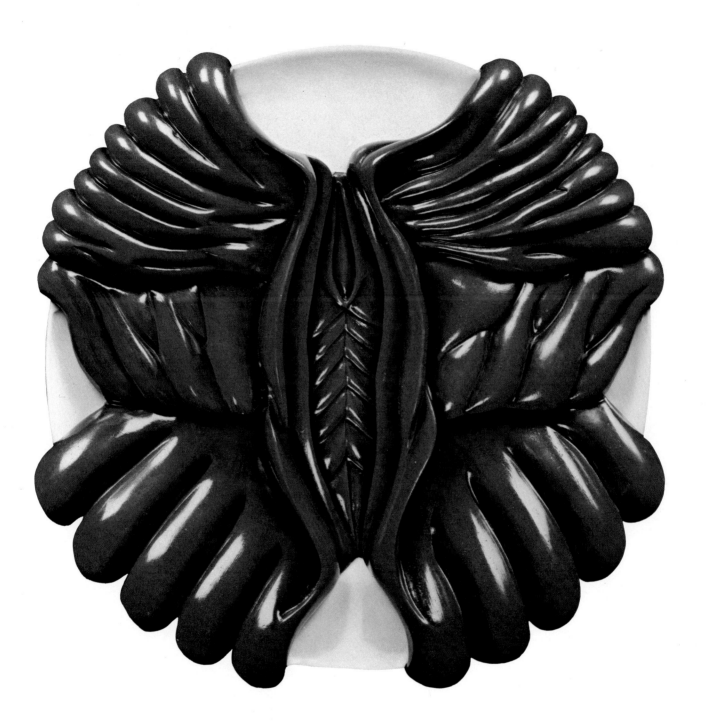

Margaret Sanger

human knowledge and virtue would be halted, and,

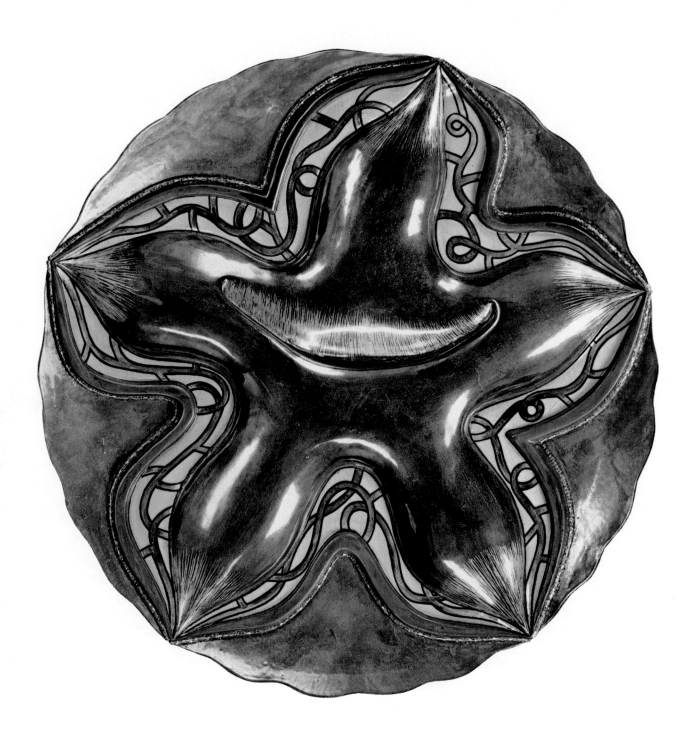

Natalie Barney

moreover, that the tyranny of men had to be broken

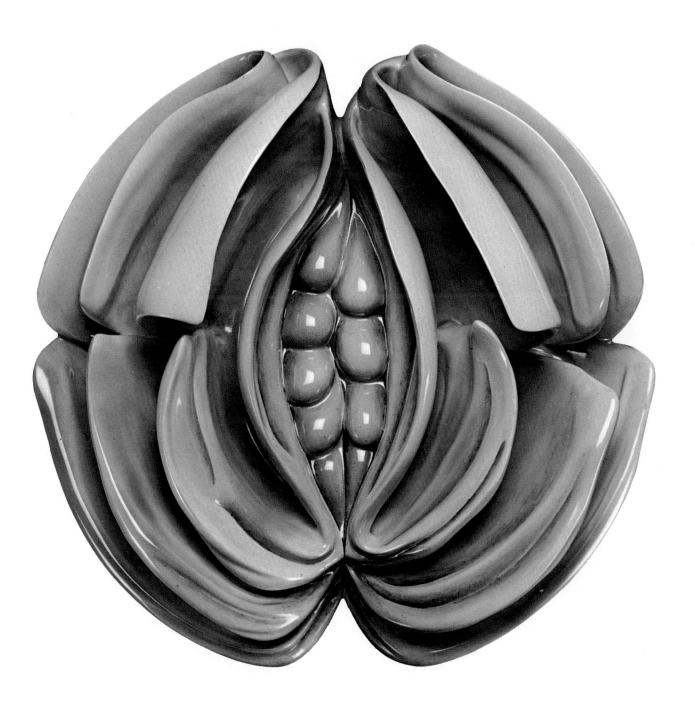

Virginia Woolf

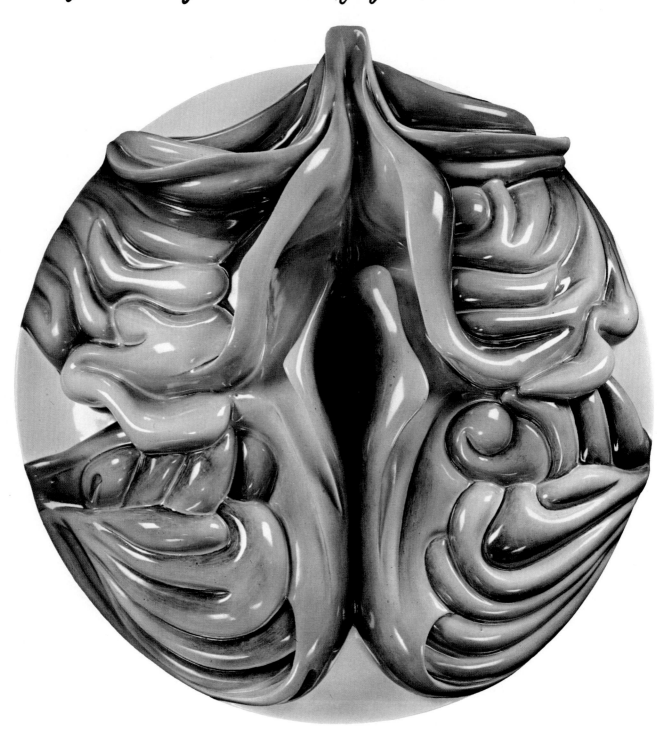

Georgia O'Keeffe

free. **In 1848 a group of American women met in**

Emmy Noether

1882–1935; Germany

A mathematical genius, Noether made extensive contributions to the development of modern algebra and in addition was an innovative and effective teacher. With the rise to power of the Nazi regime, Noether was dismissed from the University and forbidded to participate in any academic activities. As an intellectual woman, a Jew, a liberal, and a pacifist, she was an obvious target for persecution. She escaped from Germany and migrated to the United States to work as a professor at Bryn Mawr and a lecturer at the Institute for Advanced Studies.

Marie Popelin

1846–1913; Belgium

Popelin was the first woman to earn a degree as professor of law in Belgium, but she was then denied admission to the bar in 1888 because she was a woman. Angered by this injustice, she became the driving force behind the first Belgian feminist organization, established in 1892. As President of the Belgium League of Women's Rights, Popelin organized an International Feminist Congress at Brussels five years later.

Clemence Royer

1830–1902; France

An expert in the fields of anthropology and prehistoric archaeology, Royer received acclaim for her French translation of Darwin's *Origin of the Species* in 1862. She wrote an introduction to the edition, which informed her readers of the implications of this controversial work. She later published her own treatise on evolution entitled *Origine de l'Homme et des Societes.*

Emilie Snethlage

1868–1929; Brazil

Snethlage, a zoologist, ornithologist, and ethnologist, traveled on foot, by canoe, and on horseback to collect zoological specimens. Born in Germany, her life work was done in Brazil, where she specialized in the study of birds. She wrote about her findings and was the director of the Zoological Museum and Gardens at Porto Belho, Brazil.

Dorothea von Rodde

1770–1825; Germany

Von Rodde was taught by her father only because he wanted to prove that women were capable, intelligent, and could be highly educated. By the time she was eleven, she knew numerous languages, then studied mathematics, the sciences, and history. At seventeen, she was paraded before a group of professors and tested, then awarded a doctorate. But this was done in a private home, as women were not allowed to take part in academic ceremonies.

Nineteenth-century Victorian ideas of womanhood confined women in clothing that not only restricted their movements but often caused real physical harm. Tight corseting resulted in broken ribs and prolapsed uteri. This, combined with idleness and sexual repression, created weak bodies and frequent cases of hysteria and psychosomatic illness. The freeing and strengthening of women's bodies through dress reform and physical activity was a revolutionary step.

Babe Didrikson

1914–1956; United States

Considered the world's greatest woman athlete, Didrikson set world records in the 1932 Olympics and won gold medals in the javelin throw and the 80-meter hurdles. She was a member of the Amateur Athletic Union's All-American women's basketball team and once scored 106 points in a single game. In the later thirties and forties, she concentrated on golf and won seventeen consecutive professional tournaments and every important title for women golfers. In addition, she swam, boxed, and played tennis, billiards, football, and baseball. She was said to have once struck out Joe DiMaggio. After recovering from a major operation for cancer, she won the National Women's Open Golf Tournament in 1954, but died two years later at the age of forty-two.

Althea Gibson

b. 1927; United States

Gibson, whose ambition was to be "the best woman tennis player who ever lived," was the first black tennis player to win the United States National Tennis Championship. Brought up in Harlem, Gibson began to play tennis seriously at age thirteen, quitting school and working as a chicken cleaner and factory worker in order to support herself. Finally, a prominent Southern black family became her "foster" family, and Gibson was able to improve her game, finish high school, go to college, and get a degree in physical education. In 1950 she was the first Black invited to play in the U.S. Lawn Tennis Association championships, and in 1957 she was the first Black to win at Wimbledon; she then went on to win the U.S. Championship at Forest Hills.

Sophia Heath

1890–1934; England

An advocate for women's sports, Heath founded the Women's Amateur Athletic Association in 1922, then challenged the Olympic policies which banned women. She was the only woman to speak before the Olympic Committee in Prague in 1925, where the debate on participation by women was taking place. It was largely as a result of her work that women competed in the Olympics for the first time in 1928.

Sonja Henie

b. 1913; Norway

Henie, a championship figure skater, was the first woman to win the Olympic Gold Medal for figure skating. She won the award again in 1936 and was the World Champion ten years in a row. Henie earned more money than any athlete before her. She later starred in motion pictures.

Elin Kallio

1859–1927; Finland

Kallio, who helped popularize gymnastics in Finland, began teaching the sport at age seventeen, training other teachers and publishing books on the subject. To bring women athletes together, she founded an athletic association for women, the first of its kind in Northern Europe.

Madame A. Milliat

fl. 1921; France

An advocate for women's athletics, Milliat founded the Federation Sportive Feminine International. Because women were denied the right to take part in the Olympic Games of 1922, Milliat organized an Olympic Games for women, held in Paris that same year.

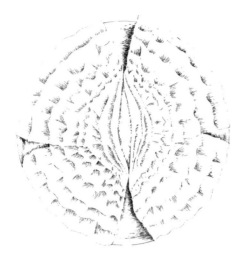

Emily Dickinson

1830–1886

The Industrial Revolution took the means of earning a livelihood out of the home. Thus most women were left, for the first time, with the entire burden of domestic duties and child-rearing. In earlier times, when most work was done at home, men participated in some aspects of the home life, just as women took part in the economic life of the family. Suddenly, women had to make a choice between household activity and work, although in reality there was hardly a choice. The pervasive Victorian ideal was of a submissive and dependent wife; there was a decrease in work available to middle-class women, and women were poorly educated in general. Working-class women, of course, *had* to earn money, but were always paid less than men.

The conflicts resulting from this situation were expressed by a number of women writers, who began to articulate women's experiences from a woman's point of view.

Jane Austen

1775–1817; England

The first major female novelist, Austen created a body of work known for its luminous language and considered some of the most well-crafted literature ever written. Austen, who was the educated, unmarried daughter of a clergyman, began writing at an early age, ostensibly to entertain her family. She did expect to publish her work, but, aware of the attitudes of the time, she was always sure to preserve a genteel demeanor, keeping a piece of needlework close by to cover her literary efforts if anyone came to call. However, her demure façade covered a penetrating intelligence which enabled her to realistically describe the lives and limited options of her female characters. Marriage was the focus of her women's lives; marriage measured a woman's success and established her status; and a bad marriage was considered better than no marriage at all, as gaining a husband was the only aspiration a woman was expected to have.

Joanna Baillie

1762–1851; Scotland

Baillie published poems and several plays anonymously. Since these were well received, they were attributed to a man. In 1799 a woman decided to produce the plays, claiming that their author must be female because the heroines were clever, captivating, and rationally superior. When Baillie revealed her identity, her works continued to be well received by the public, but the critics withdrew their previous support.

Elizabeth Bekker

1738–1804; Holland

Bekker wrote a number of works considered classics in Dutch literature, the most important written with her friend Agatha Deken.

Charlotte Brontë

1816–1855; England

When asked for her opinion on the condition of women, Brontë replied that there were "evils, deep-rooted in the foundation of the social system, which no efforts of ours can touch; of which we cannot complain; of which it is advisable not too often to think." Nevertheless, Brontë continually expressed her dissatisfaction with women's lot. *Jane Eyre*, published in 1847 under the pseudonym Currer Bell, was the first modern English novel in which a woman explored her feelings without reservation. Brontë's second novel, *Shirley*, was more openly feminist than any of her other works. The heroine longed to have a trade instead of the vacant, weary, lonely life of a woman of her class, even if it made her, according to society's standards, "coarse and masculine." *Villette*, Brontë's next novel, took two years to write and was interrupted by her illness and the deaths of her sisters and brothers. She eventually married her father's curate and died as a result of illness caused by her pregnancy.

Emily Brontë

1818–1848; England

Emily, like her sister Charlotte, was brought up in the isolated environment of their father's parish house. Her mother died, leaving three young daughters and one son. The children spent their time making up stories and creating little books. From these activities grew the novels written by Charlotte, Emily, and Anne, all published under male pseudonyms. Emily's *Wuthering Heights* is considered the greatest piece of romantic fiction ever written. She died young and left only one other work, a book of poems.

Frances Brooke

1724–1789; Canada
The first Canadian novelist, Brooke wrote *The History of Emily Montague* in 1769.

Fanny Burney

1752–1840; England
Burney's diaries span seventy-two years and are her most widely known works today. She began writing as a child, but destroyed her early work because of her stepmother's disapproval. Her novel *Evelina* was written secretly, although, Burney became famous after its publication in 1778. Her popularity as a writer later declined, and following her marriage she stopped writing novels.

Elizabeth Barrett Browning

1806–1861; England
The daughter of a tyrannical father and a meek mother, Barrett was the eldest of twelve children. After becoming an invalid at fifteen, she began studying languages and literature. A series of family tragedies drove her more deeply into illness and invalidism until, in 1845, Robert Browning read a volume of her poems and wrote to her, thus initiating their relationship. With Browning's encouragement, Barrett slowly threw off the cloak of illness that had protected her from the world and allowed her time to read and write. She ran away with Browning, married him, and bore a child. Theirs was a relationship of peers – a union that lasted until Elizabeth's death in 1861, which devastated Browning. Her *Sonnets for the Portuguese* were considered the greatest sonnets since Shakespeare, and in *Aurora Leigh* she published one of the earliest autobiographical discussions of female role conflict.

Elizabeth Druzbacka

1695–1765; Poland
Druzbacka, one of the best Polish writers of the eighteenth century, was a poet whose subject matter ranged from religious hypocrisy to the need to broaden women's experience.

Maria Edgeworth

1767–1849; Ireland
Edgeworth's nearly fifty books earned her an important place in Irish literature. Her novels and stories, which depict Irish customs and heritage, inspired her friend Sir Walter Scott to write similar romances of Scotland. Like Austen, she produced her work amidst the goings-on of the family sitting room.

George Eliot

1819–1880; England
Born Mary Ann Evans, Eliot wrote under a man's name and established a reputation as a major novelist. She understood the pain of women who tried to realize their talents in the repressive atmosphere of Victorian ideals, and in *Daniel Deronda* she wrote, "You may try – but you can never imagine what it is to have a man's force of genius in you, and yet to suffer the slavery of being a girl."

A contradictory woman, Eliot lived openly with her lover, yet took a rather conservative political stance. Her heroines reflected the self-sacrificing masochism of the Victorian woman, and although they chafed under the restrictions imposed upon them because of their sex, none openly rebelled.

Margaret Fuller

1810–1850; United States
Fuller was a forerunner of the women's rights movement in the United States. Educated by her father, who was inspired by Mary Wollstonecraft's ideas, she shared her knowledge with other women by inaugurating "parlor lectures." These gatherings provided a forum (for women who were still excluded from the academic and intellectual life of New England) to discuss politics, art, philosophy, literature, and science.

As an editor, writer, and critic for the *New York Tribune* and the transcendentalist journal *The Dial*, Fuller was one of America's first women journalists and its first female foreign correspondent. She is best known for her feminist manifesto *Woman in the Nineteenth Century* (1845), which prepared the way for the Seneca Falls Convention of 1848.

Anna Karsh

d. 1791; Germany
Karsch, a peasant woman, was educated by an uncle and started to write poetry at an early age. She was "discovered" by a count who brought her to Berlin, where she was celebrated for a short time. Soon forgotten, however, she died in poverty and obscurity.

Harriet Martineau

1802–1876; England
After a lengthy struggle to get her work published, Martineau became quite well known. She wrote on political economy, history, philosophy, and travel. She toured Europe, the Middle East and the United States, where she became an ardent abolitionist. Her economic theories helped shape British fiscal policy, and she was also extremely influential as a social reformer.

Hedwig Nordenflycht

1718–1763; Sweden
The first Swedish woman poet of national importance, Nordenflycht published her poems in the form of "yearbooks" called *Womanly Thoughts of a Shepherdess of the North*. In 1753, she formed an important literary society known as the "Thought Builders."

Christina Rossetti

1830–1894; England
One of the greatest English poets of the nineteenth century, Rossetti traditionally has been characterized as the reclusive, otherworldly, sexually repressed sister of Dante Gabriel Rossetti. Critics have categorized her as a religious poet, yet there is a range in her work that transcends the limitations of this description. Her first major poem, "Goblin Market" (1861), is an uninhibited, bizarre tale of childhood erotica, laden with sexual imagery in which she contrasts bestial male sexuality with women's passionate, but spiritual, love. Educated by her mother, Rossetti began writing as a child and chose, like Dickinson, to live her adult life at home, devoted to literature.

Susanna Rowson

1762–1824; United States
Rowson's novel *Charlotte Temple* was the first bestseller in America. In it, she exposed the double standard by which women were ostracized for their love affairs, while men were not. Her writing protested women's dependent status, and she opened one of the first girls' schools to offer education above the elementary level.

to vote, to be educated, to enter any occupation,

George Sand

1804–1876; France

Sand – the most prolific woman writer in the history of literature, author of 120 books, several of which are masterpieces – has been remembered, until recently, only as Chopin's lover. Born Aurore Dupin, she not only published under a male pseudonym but also adopted male attire, which gave her greater mobility in Paris, allowing her to frequent cafés with her male literary friends, sit in the cheapest theater seats (where no women were allowed), and in general participate fully in a cultural life that was closed to women.

Her feminist views were expressed in her first novel, *Indiana* (1831), which protested the restrictions imposed on married women in a society that regarded them as the property of men. The book was an immediate sensation and established Sand's literary reputation. In her later work, her writing style at its best exemplifies the Romantic movement.

Bettina von Arnim

1785–1859; Germany

A writer of the German Romantic movement, Von Arnim sympathetically depicted the lives of poor women, illustrating the conditions of slum living and the environment which forced many women into lives of prostitution. She advocated women's emancipation, questioned the sanctity of the institution of marriage, and belonged to a group of writers who actively worked toward the social reforms that led to the German Revolution of 1848.

Bertha von Suttner

1843–1914; Austria

Von Suttner's first book, *Down with Weapons*, raised the European consciousness about the reality of war, much as Harriet Beecher Stowe's *Uncle Tom's Cabin* had exposed slavery to Americans. Von Suttner wrote and lectured on pacifism, and many of her works were published posthumously as her views became pertinent again with the outbreak of World War II.

For centuries women fought for the right to learn. Young women were allowed only rudimentary education and continued to be barred from universities. In some countries, the daughters of the economically privileged went to private academies, but these generally were inferior institutions. The demand for adequate education accompanied all feminist agitation. Finally, in the nineteenth century, a few established colleges began to admit women, and then some women's institutions were founded, but the latter usually had male faculties.

Anne Clough

1820–1892; England

Clough founded Newnham College, the first university for women in England. She was secretary and later president of the North of England Council for Promoting the Higher Education of Women and campaigned to allow women into all universities. By 1880 Newnham had been built, and Clough was its first president – a position she held until her death. It was at Newnham College that Virginia Woolf delivered her famous lecture on women and fiction, published as *A Room of One's Own*.

Mary Lyon

1797–1849; United States

A pioneer in women's education in the United States, Lyon opened Mt. Holyoke in 1836. She spent four years raising funds, speaking publicly, and soliciting from door to door. This behavior was criticized as appalling for a "proper" woman, and when her friends pleaded with her to stop, she replied, "I am doing a great work, I cannot come down."

Baba Petkova

1826–1894; Bulgaria

Petkova established a system of education for young women in eastern Europe. She began teaching in 1859 and hundreds of girls attended her classes. Though they and their parents supported Petkova's efforts to bring education to women, government officials attempted to stop her. She was arrested and her home searched for seditious books. Forced to stand trial, she was released for lack of evidence and continued her campaign to educate women.

Albertine Necker de Saussure

1766–1841; France

De Saussure, daughter of Germaine de Staël, wrote *Progressive Education*, which supported higher learning for women. Like Wollstonecraft, De Saussure also advocated physical education for girls, which would lead to strength and health for women instead of the continual ill health that resulted from their enforced idleness.

Hermine Veres

1815–1895; Hungary

Veres was responsible for making higher education available to Hungarian women. Her own educational background was limited, but she felt strongly that her daughter should be educated. In 1867, she made a public appeal for more adequate schools for women and helped found the Society for the Education of Women. Within two years a women's school was opened – the first step toward a more equitable system of learning.

Emma Willard

1787–1870; United States

Willard was the first American woman to take a public stand on the need for women's education. In 1821 she opened the Troy Female Seminary, later known as the Emma Willard School. In addition to teaching subjects considered "suitable" for girls, she introduced more serious subject matter and proved that girls were capable of comprehending all subjects, including mathematics, science, philosophy, and history. She also became the first to provide scholarships for women; one of the first women to write geography, history, and astronomy textbooks; and the first female lobbyist in the United States.

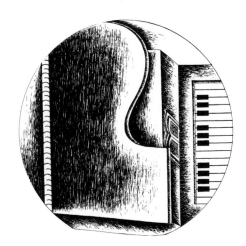

Ethel Smyth

1858–1944

Literature was one of the first creative fields women were able to penetrate. If a woman was sufficiently motivated and personally strong enough to withstand isolation, lack of support, and social censure, she could – with sufficient time and privacy – find the means to write. Only the publisher then stood between her and the public, and if that publisher was sympathetic, a woman's voice might be heard. But in music it was different. Although women have a rich musical heritage dating back to ancient times, and much of women's music centered on the female voice, the Church viewed that voice as lewd and lascivious and insisted it be suppressed. Even after the reappearance of female singers, the continued use of *castrati* limited women's chances for professional work. For centuries women were unable to obtain a serious musical education. Until, finally, women's colleges were established and women had a chance to be trained as performers, teachers, and musicologists.

Despite the fact that a number of women have proven themselves capable of composing and conducting, most have encountered a solid wall of resistance based on the continued prejudice holding that major music is the property of men. Unlike a writer or even a painter, a composer or conductor can't bring her work to visibility without the participation of many other people; a woman can't conduct in her bedroom or play all the instrumental parts of her symphony herself. Composing and conducting require patronage, support, and the real commitment of the musical world – none of which women have ever received.

Elfrida Andrée

1844–1929; Sweden

Andrée studied at the Stockholm Conservatory from 1858 to 1861, during which time she was a cathedral organist and gave over eight hundred peoples' concerts. Elected to the Swedish Academy of Music in 1879, she composed works including a piano quintet and trio, two organ symphonies, an orchestral symphony, a Swedish mass, organ sonatas, and solo pieces.

Amy Beach

1867–1944; United States

A pianist and composer, Beach began piano lessons at age six and later taught herself theory and composition. She began a concert career in 1883, often performing her own compositions. She was the first American woman to write a symphony; her oeuvre further included piano concertos, cantatas, string quartets, an opera, religious and patriotic pieces, and over a hundred choral works. She made a successful European concert tour and was commissioned to write the composition played at the opening of the Women's Building in Chicago in 1893.

Antonia Bembo

ca. 1700; Italy

Bembo, court musician to Louis XIV, was one of only three women composers to attain this position. She was required to produce a steady stream of music – a demand not often made upon women (and one reason why women usually created smaller oeuvres than men). One of her most successful compositions was a trio for women's voices, written to celebrate the birth of her child.

Faustina Bordoni

1700–1783/93; Italy

Bordoni was one of the great opera singers of the eighteenth century. She enjoyed an international reputation, performing in Venice, Vienna, London, and ultimately Dresden, the the major European music centers of the 1730's and 1740's.

Lili Boulanger

1893–1918; France

A member of a famous musical family, Boulanger showed enormous musical aptitude by age three, and by sixteen she was an accomplished pianist, cellist, violinist, and harpist. In 1913, for her cantata, "Faust et Hélène," she became the first woman to win the Grand Prix de Rome. This award allowed her to pursue her career in Italy, but after a short time her failing health forced her home to Paris. She died at age twenty-five, but during her brief career composed more than fifty works and was considered a genius.

Nadia Boulanger

b. 1887; France
Boulanger is considered a major force in shaping modern music, particularly American music. Although she is a composer and conductor, it is as a teacher of composition that her primary impact has been felt. Her role as a teacher has, of course, obscured her own creative accomplishments, which have remained relatively unknown. She has written orchestral pieces, chamber music, and choral works, conducted symphonies, and performed in concert.

Antonia Brico

b. 1902; United States
One of America's few women conductors, Brico has enjoyed an international reputation since her debut with the Berlin Philharmonic in 1902. Always painfully aware of the obstacles barring women from the profession of music, she was determined to succeed despite the prejudice she encountered. She graduated with honors from the University of California and studied orchestration and conducting in Berlin. Her conducting debut there made headlines throughout Europe and

the United States, partly because a female conductor was considered newsworthy. She toured the continent as guest conductor of many major orchestras and made a triumphal New York debut in 1933. To prove the excellence of women musicians – and also to create jobs for the many unemployed women musicians – she founded the Women's Symphony Orchestra in New York. This later developed into the "mixed" Brico Symphony Orchestra, which she formed because she wanted women and men to work together. Because this orchestra was not considered a novelty, however, it was disbanded, and her career suffered a decline.

Marguerite-Antoinette Couperin

1676–1728; France
Couperin was a member of the famous family that dominated French music from the seventeenth through nineteenth centuries. She was the principal soprano in the Musique du Roi and played the clavichord at the French court.

Marguerite-Louise Couperin

1705–1778; France
Following in the musical tradition established by her mother, Couperin became musician to the king. She also was the first woman to be appointed to the Ordinaire de la Musique (in 1723).

Margarethe Dessoff

1874–1944; Germany
Dessoff conducted the first public appearance of a women's chorus in 1912. From 1925 to 1935, she directed the fifty-woman Adesor Choir in New York

City – a chorus performing only music that had been composed specifically for female voices. Due in part to Dessoff's efforts, women's choruses began to flourish.

Sophie Drinker

fl. 1948; United States
Drinker spent twenty years researching and writing *Music and Women*, published in 1948. She traced women's role in music from early matriarchal societies to the modern period, showing that a long tradition of authentic women's music existed, that for centuries music was considered the province of women – part of their magic and creative powers – and that there were special rituals and songs written and performed by women for all the important occasions in people's lives. Drinker argued that women's music was directly connected to women's social and political authority, and when this authority ended, their music ceased to exist. She documented this process in a thorough, but disheartening, examination of our musical heritage.

Jeanne Louise Farrenc

1804–1875; France
Farrenc entered the prestigious Paris Conservatory of Music at age fifteen. During her career, she gave concerts throughout France and composed a remarkably ambitious series of piano pieces. One of only two women on the faculty of the French National Conservatory in the entire nineteenth century, she composed chamber music, overtures, and symphonies. She was also a musicologist, publishing a twenty-three volume work which revived interest in such composers as Scarlatti and Couperin.

Carlotta Ferrari

1837–1907; Italy
Ferrari endured more than just the usual hostility and criticism confronting women in music, for after her first opera was performed she was arrested and forced to stand trial for the crime of being a female composer.

Elisabeth de la Guerre

1664–1729; France
De la Guerre, a child prodigy, began composing at an early age. She wrote an opera, a trio sonata, six cantatas, and fourteen harpsichord pieces; composed and performed for the Theatre de la Faire; and gave harpsichord recitals that were acclaimed throughout France and England.

Wanda Landowska

1877–1959; Poland
Landowska, a musician and musicologist, was responsible for reviving interest in the harpsichord as a concert instrument. While teaching in Paris she began researching old music, which led her to bring the harpsichord out of the museum, first playing it publicly in 1903. She founded a school for the study of old music, supervised the manufacture of authentic replicas of ancient instruments, and gave concerts which reintroduced them to audiences in Europe and the United States. Her theories and techniques became the basis for contemporary harpsichord playing and have influenced modern keyboard composers.

Jenny Lind

1820–1887; Sweden
Known as the "Swedish Nightingale," Lind was one of the most celebrated sopranos of all time. She was trained at the Royal Theater of Stockholm, sang her first leading role at age

eighteen, and by age twenty had attained the distinction of court singer to Sweden's royalty. She created a sensation throughout Europe and the United States on her highly successful concert tours, donating most of her vast earnings to charity.

Fanny Mendelssohn

1805–1847; Germany
A superior musician and composer, Mendelssohn was overshadowed by her brother Felix. He was encouraged in his musical pursuits, while she was forbidden by her father to perform in public. As Felix and his contemporaries agreed, however, she developed into an incredibly accomplished musician, and Felix published some of her compositions in his name. In 1829 she married a man who also encouraged her work, and after her father died she performed in public for the first time. Felix suddenly reversed his position and became opposed to her entry into public life, insisting that she would neglect her family obligations. She retreated once more. Finally, in 1846, a small number of her best works were published. The following year she performed her last work, and she died shortly thereafter.

Rose Mooney

18th c.; Ireland
There were a number of celebrated female harpists in Ireland in the eighteenth century. Mooney was exceptional, however, in that she was blind. She was an extremely proficient musician and repeatedly won prizes at competitions in which all the best harpists performed.

Clara Schumann

1819–1896; Germany
The greatest woman pianist of the nineteenth century, Schumann began to study piano with her father at the age of five. A concert tour of Germany and France

when she was twelve years old firmly established her fame, and her first published works, four pieces for piano appeared at that time. She married Robert Schumann in 1840 and continued to perform during their sixteen years of marriage. She brought public attention to her husband's compositions as well as those by Chopin and Brahms. After her husband's death, she supported her seven children through her concerts.

Maria Theresia von Paradis

1759–1824; Austria
Although Von Paradis became blind during her childhood, she was an active musician, composer, and teacher throughout her lifetime. She was supported by Maria Theresa of Austria, who was her godmother, and she performed extensively throughout Europe. As a composer, she used an innovative notation system involving the use of pegs and a pegboard. In her later years she founded a music school for young women and devoted herself to teaching.

Mary Lou Williams

b. 1910; United States
Williams is considered by many to be jazz's finest pianist and one of its most brilliant composers. Largely self-taught, by the age of twenty she was the pianist for a big band and began arranging and composing. She influenced a generation of musicians through her radio show, "The Mary Lou Williams Workshop," and encouraged the exchange of ideas in her home – once a gathering place for jazz musicians in New York. She established the Bel Canto Foundation to aid down-and-out musicians, taught music at Duke University, and composed numerous works, including religious hymns.

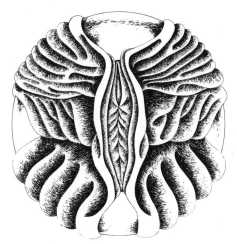

Margaret Sanger

1879–1966

The resistance encountered by the early advocates of contraception was immense, as any effort on women's part to confront their own sexuality and take control of it was viewed by the culture as enormously threatening. Sanger rightly perceived that without understanding of and authority over their own bodies, women's pursuit of other rights was meaningless. The present-day abortion controversy and the prevalence of pornography, which makes the female body the property of every man who can buy a magazine, makes it clear that this issue is a long way from being resolved.

Many of the women grouped around Sanger worked for women's rights. Only a few of her contemporaries, however, grasped the philosophical relationship between the position of women and the larger issues of human freedom on the planet. Rather, most put their faith in national revolutions or specific reforms as a means of obtaining equal rights. Sanger was in the tradition of Anthony and Stanton in her understanding that women's freedom could not be obtained unless society's structures were changed worldwide.

Sanger was not the only woman active in the birth control movement. Throughout the Western world, women were struggling for control of their bodies and the right to regulate reproduction.

Katti Møeler

20th c.; Norway
Møeler wrote and spoke on behalf of liberalized abortion laws; fought for legal protection of unwed mothers and their children; was involved in the organization of Oslo's first family-planning center (1924); and advocated contraception and improved hygiene practices in maternity and infant wards.

Marie Stopes

1880–1958; England
Stopes founded England's first family-planning center. She received excellent training in the sciences, won a scholarship for her research on ovules and eggs, and became Manchester University's first female lecturer in science. In an effort to combat the general ignorance about sexuality, Stopes wrote *Married Love*. She proclaimed the need for more intelligent attitudes about sexuality, sympathized with women who feared pregnancy and unwanted children, and eventually developed and perfected one of the most effective means of contraception – the diaphragm. After attending a conference on birth control in New York, she wrote to Woodrow Wilson in defense of Margaret Sanger, launched the Society for Constructive Birth Control, and withstood a trial defending her clinics.

The Victorians thought women were inherently more moral than men and saw them as "ministering angels" who spread comfort wherever they went. As an extension of this idea and an acceptable outlet for their frustrated energies, many women became actively involved in social reform. Moreover, when women entered colleges, many gravitated (or were encouraged) toward activities that seemed consistent with women's traditional nurturing role, and, as a result, a number of women emerged in education and humanitarian work.

Jane Addams

1860–1935; United States
Addams opened Hull House, the first "social service" center in America, on September 18, 1889. It provided education, job training, recreation and entertainment to the many immigrants who had settled in Chicago at the turn of the century. Addams fought for legal protection of immigrants, for the regulation of child labor, and for women's suffrage. She helped immigrant women regenerate the fine crafts they had brought from the old country and encouraged other women to learn new and useful skills. Addams was also the central figure in the international women's peace movement during World War I, and in 1931 she became the first woman to win the Nobel Peace Prize.

Sylvia Ashton-Warner

b. 1908; New Zealand
A teacher and author, Ashton-Warner devised new teaching methods while working with Maori children in New Zealand. She felt that children's natural impulses should be encouraged, and rather than using textbooks, she taught from primers that the children had written themselves. Her "Creative Teaching Scheme" was initially criticized, but Ashton-Warner was eventually recognized internationally as a brilliantly progressive educator. Her memoirs, *Teacher*, were published in 1963.

Catherine Beecher

1800–1878; United States
The sister of Harriet Beecher Stowe, Beecher's dream was to restore value to women's traditional activities. In 1843 she published her *Treatise on Domestic Economy*, in which she explained every aspect of domestic life from the building of a house (including designs for plumbing) to the setting of a table. Beecher's book was the beginning of household automation and the servantless household, and its success probably lay in its ability to combine a convincing domestic ideology with practical advice. Beecher's ideas directly opposed those of the Grimkés, who argued that women needed to escape domesticity and enter the world. These two approaches to women's situations – i.e., the elevation of women's role to a position of respect and authority versus the total breakdown of traditional roles – remained the fundamentally different arguments of nineteenth-century feminism.

Ruth Benedict

1887–1948; United States
Benedict, one of the world's leading anthropologists, did her early research on Native American cultures. She taught at Barnard in 1922, and it was there that she inspired Margaret Mead to pursue anthropology. Benedict's landmark book, *Patterns of Culture,* is a study of the relationship between human culture and the human personality. During World War II she wrote a work that was intended to combat racism and was distributed in an abbreviated version by the Army and after the war she produced an important study of Japanese culture.

Rachel Carson

1907–1964; United States
A marine biologist, naturalist, and writer, Carson used her book *Silent Spring* to focus national attention on the danger of pesticides. In this work, inspired by her concern for the survival of the human race, she said, "Along with the possiblity of the extinction of mankind by nuclear war, the central problem of our age has become the contamination of man's total environment with substances of incredible potential for harm." She was attacked by business interests, but defended her theories at Senate hearings which led to stricter regulation of the use of toxic chemicals such as DDT and heightened public awareness of the problem of pollution.

Dorothea Dix

1802–1887; United States
Dix, a philanthropist, teacher, writer, social reformer, and nurse, developed an interest in prison reform and visited prisons, county jails, and poorhouses in eighteen states and several European countries. She founded over a hundred asylums dedicated to the humane treatment of mental patients. When the Civil War broke out, Dix volunteered and was made Chief of Nurses for the Union Army. She developed the Army Nursing Corps, mobilizing thousands of women and turning public buildings into hospitals.

Elizabeth Fry

1780–1845; England

Fry was a Quaker minister, a philanthropist, the chief promoter of prison reform in England, and the first to suggest that prisons should be a place of rehabilitation. Called to appear before the House of Commons, she influenced the passage of a prison reform bill in 1821 and also instigated prison changes in Scotland, Australia, France, Germany, and Holland.

Rachel Katznelson

b. 1888; Israel

Russian-born Katznelson emigrated to Israel and was active in the formation of the new state's policies concerning the status of women. She was a co-founder of the Women Workers Council and established and edited the weekly newspaper, *Savor Hapocht.*

Helen Keller

1880–1968; United States

Keller was deprived of sight and hearing by an attack of scarlet fever when she was nineteen months old. At age seven, she was put under the care of Anne Sullivan of The Perkin Institute for the Blind in Boston. Slowly and painstakingly, Sullivan taught the Keller child how to read and write and finally, after enormous effort, how to speak. In 1907, Keller graduated from Radcliffe with honors. She published a series of books, mastered several languages, and was active in radical politics, joining the American Socialist Party and writing and speaking in its behalf. During World War I, she traveled around the country inveighing against the military and advocating peace.

Margaret Mead

1901–1978; United States

The author of numerous books on primitive societies, Mead – a distinguished anthropologist and social critic – also wrote on issues central to American life. Her first major book, *Coming of Age in Samoa,* became a bestseller. Her later studies of six different South Sea societies focused on women's role, childrearing, and other topics that illuminated both the cultures she was investigating and, by implication, our own society. She examined personality differences between men and women, suggesting that so-called masculine/feminine characteristics are not based on fundamental sex differences, but reflect the cultural conditioning of their societies. Arguing against the specialized role conditioning of women and the polarization of the sexes, she concluded in *Sex and Temperament*: "If we are to achieve a richer culture, rich in contrasting values, we must recognize the whole gamut of human potentialities, and so weave a less arbitrary social fabric, one in which each diverse human gift will find a fitting place."

Golda Meir

1898–1978; Israel

Raised in the United States after her Russian parents fled the Czar's pogroms, Meir worked as a teacher here until her increasing involvement in Socialist and Zionist causes led her to emigrate to Palestine in 1921. Her political activities there contributed to the formation of the State of Israel, and she was one of the original signers of its Proclamation of Independence. The first woman member of the legislature, Meir, a formidable stateswoman, became Israel's fourth premier in 1969.

Maria Montessori

1870–1952; Italy

Montessori, a pioneer educational theorist, was the first woman to graduate from the University of Rome. In 1907 she attracted nationwide attention for her innovative work in the slums with children previously considered educationally hopeless. By 1912 her first book, *The Montessori Method,* was translated into English and she became world-renowned. Montessori believed that "The fundamental problem in education is not an educational problem at all; it is a social one. It consists in the establishment of a new and better relationship between the two great sections of society – children and adults."

Frances Perkins

1882–1965; United States

The first woman to hold a Cabinet position in the United States Government, Perkins was appointed Secretary of Labor in 1933. As a pioneer in factory reform, she was instrumental in the formulation of New Deal policies and laws which helped to better the workers' condition.

Jeannette Rankin

1880–1976; United States

Rankin, the first woman elected to the United States Congress, began her political career as a suffragist. An ardent pacifist, she voted against U.S. entry into World War I and cast the only dissenting vote when the country declared war on Japan – a vote which virtually ended her congressional career. Nonetheless, Rankin worked incessantly as a peacemaker and pacifist and in 1967 led the Jeannette Rankin Brigade of five thousand women in a march on Washington to protest U.S. involvement in Vietnam.

Eleanor Roosevelt

1884–1962; United States

Eleanor Roosevelt, America's most distinguished First Lady, used her position to create a bridge between the Presidency and the people. She made speaking tours throughout the country, wrote a newspaper column, and delivered radio broadcasts. During the war she traveled internationally, conferring with world leaders on behalf of the United States. After FDR's death, Roosevelt continued to be a world figure. From 1945 to 1952 she was a delegate to the U.N. Assembly, Chairperson of UNESCO's Commission on Human Rights, and America's roving ambassador of good will. At home she lent public support to such causes as the civil rights movement, continued to be influential in the Democratic Party, and recorded her experiences in a series of memoirs.

Ellen Richards

1842–1911; United States

Over a hundred years ago, Richards, through her examination of the effects of chemicals on air, water, and food, and her insistence on the need for a balance between human beings and the environment, launched the science of ecology. She was the first woman admitted to MIT, its first to receive a degree in chemistry, its first woman faculty member, and the first woman science consultant to industry. Yet in 1873, when she graduated from

MIT, she was refused a doctorate because she was a woman. She did stay on, however, as an unpaid assistant professor in charge of the Women's Laboratory, which was dedicated to training women scientists. Her work in the field of sanitary chemistry, which involved analyzing air and especially water for pollutants, laid the foundation for the public health movement in the United States. She wrote *Food Materials and Their Adulterations,* which influenced the passage of the Pure Food and Drug Acts.

Henrietta Szold

1860–1945; United States
Szold was the first woman to attend the Jewish Theological Society, but was only admitted when she promised she would not attempt to become a rabbi. She was active in many Jewish and Zionist organizations, where she met with discrimination constantly because of her sex. She worked toward creating health and social welfare agencies in Palestine, and although her contribution to the world Zionist movement was considerable, her insistence on equal rights for women kept her from being elected to leadership positions until she was sixty-seven years old.

Women continued to be active in revolutionary movements, where they were always welcome, at least in the early stages of political activity. In Russia many women looked to the Revolution to bring them equal rights. As had happened so many times before, however,

the rhetoric of "women's issues" dissolved as the men took over the new government that women had worked so hard to create.

Inesse Armand

1874–1920; Russia
Armand was an ardent feminist and an important figure in international socialism and the Bolshevik Revolution. A political associate of Lenin, her correspondence with him helped shape his ideas on women's position in communist society.

Angelica Balabanoff

1878–1965; Russia
A social reformer and revolutionary, Balabanoff joined the Socialist Party in 1900 and worked closely with Lenin until after the Revolution, when, unable to support the authoritarian dogma of the Bolshevik regime, she left the party. After meeting Emma Goldman, Balabanoff became an anarchist.

Yekaterina Breshovskaya

1844–1934; Russia
Breshkovskaya, called the "Grandmother of the Russian Revolution," became politically prominent as a young woman. Although she was a noblewoman, she agitated for the rights of the serfs, setting up village schools, libraries, and hospitals for them. Breshkovskaya was periodically jailed for her political activities and eventually exiled herself to Prague.

Vera Figner

1852–1943; Russia
Figner, from an upper-class, land-owning family, involved herself with leftist student organizations and became progressively a socialist, a revolutionary, and a terrorist. She worked as a

paramedic and for ten years was a leader, organizer, and propagandist of the People's Will, an underground revolutionary group. She participated in the terrorist activities which finally led to the Czar's death in 1881. She was arrested, tried, and served over twenty years in solitary confinement. After the revolution, she wrote of her activities and remained in the USSR until her death.

Elizabeth Gurley Flynn

1890–1964; United States
Socialist, union organizer, and activist, Flynn began her political life at age fifteen when she delivered a speech on "What Socialism Will Do for Women." She was an organizer for the IWW and the Workers Defense League as well as for the Lawrence Textile Workers Strike of 1912. She was repeatedly arrested for her activities, but she continued organizing strikes. She also agitated for prison reform and free speech, and founded the American Civil Liberties Union. She joined the Communist Party in 1957 and as a result spent most of the fifties in prison. Released in 1959, she became the first woman president of the American Communist Party, a position she held until her death at age 76.

Emma Goldman

1869–1940; USSR/ United States
Goldman, the "Mother of Anarchy" in America, was a feminist, a revolutionary, a social reformer, and a political organizer and theorist. She published the anarchist periodical "Mother Earth"; wrote essays, books, and over two hundred thousand letters; and was an early advocate of birth control, urging women "to keep their minds open and their wombs closed." She was arrested many times and, in

1919, was deported back to her homeland. Disillusioned by the oppression she saw there, she left, settling in Europe. On the issue of women's suffrage she once said, "True emancipation begins neither at the polls nor in courts. It begins in women's soul."

Dolores Ibarruri

b. 1895; Spain
One of the leading figures in the Spanish Civil War, Ibarruri was dedicated to the ideals of the socialist movement. In 1930 she was elected to the Central Committee of the Spanish Communist Party. She was sent the following year to Madrid, where she edited the party's newspaper and took charge of women's activities. A leading propagandist for the Republic, Ibarruri went to live in the Soviet Union after the Republic's collapse in 1939. She was awarded the Lenin Peace Prize in 1964.

Mary Jones

1830–1930; United States
Born to an immigrant working-class family, Mother Jones devoted her life to fighting for the dignity of the worker. After the devastating loss of her husband and four children in a yellow-fever epidemic, Jones started a dressmaking business and began her work in the labor movement. She was a skillful organizer, an effective speaker, and a powerful leader, staging dramatic demonstrations which drew attention to the labor cause. Agitating against child-labor abuse and for improved conditions in coal mines and factories, Jones was often arrested but never deterred.

Aleksandra Kollontay

1872–1952; Russia
Kollantay, a feminist and leader of the Russian revo-

lutionary movement, was especially notable for her work on behalf of Soviet women. The daughter of a Czarist general, she became a successful organizer, writer, and propagandist for the Bolsheviks. In 1917 she was appointed to the post of People's Commissar of Social Welfare and later founded the Central Office for the Care of Mother and Child.

Nadezhda Krupskaya

1869–1939; Russia
Krupskaya, wife of Lenin, devoted her life to women's rights, educational reform, and the Russian Revolution. From a well-educated and politically oriented family, she became a teacher and joined a Marxist group in 1891. She met Lenin three years later when both were exiled to Siberia for their involvement in radical political agitation. She and Lenin worked toward the Revolution, with Krupskaya struggling to ensure that women's rights would be an essential part of Communist doctrine. After Lenin's death in 1924, she worked in vain to oppose the repressions of the Stalinist regime.

Rosa Luxemburg

1870–1919;
Poland/Germany
A major political theorist, Luxemburg had to flee her native Poland at the age of nineteen because of her political activities. For the next twenty years, she shaped socialist theory through writing and speaking. She moved to Germany, joined the Socialist Party, and was instrumental in the founding of what later became the German Communist Party. Luxemburg wrote over seven hundred books, articles, and pamphlets; because many of these challenged the party line, she and her companion,

Leo Jogiches, were captured, bludgeoned with rifle butts, and shot to death.

Louise Michel

1830–1905; France
Michel, an Anarchist, fought in the barricades to establish the Paris Commune, which envisioned itself as a permanent world republic but lasted just two months. While it existed, however, it initiated sweeping reforms. The Commune was sacked by government troops, who massacred twenty-five thousand men, women, and children. Michel was arrested and spent nine years in prison. Upon her release, she immediately resumed her political activities.

Federica Montseny

b. 1905; Spain
Montseny, brought up by anarchist parents, became an important speaker and anarchism's leading theoretician. Appointed Minister of Health and Public Assistance by the government, she was the first woman in Spain to hold such a position. She was also active in the Spanish Civil War and the struggle for women's rights.

Emma Paterson

1848–1886; England
A labor leader, Paterson organized three London unions; fought for protective legislation for women workers; became the first woman inspector of working conditions for women's trades; and founded the Women's Trade Union League. In 1875, Paterson was the first woman delegate to the Trade Union Congress at Glasgow and did much to overcome the prevailing prejudices of the male delegates against female agitators.

Sofia Perovskaya

1853–1881; Russia
Perovskaya was arrested for advocating social change among the villagers with whom she worked as a health worker and teacher. She was sent to Siberia, escaped in 1881, and became involved with the revolutionary organization called the People's Will. Perovskaya took part in the assassination of the Czar, for which she was executed.

Gabrielle Petit

1893–1916; Belgium
A national heroine, Petit was a spy for the Allied armies during World War I, helping many soldiers to cross the border and conveying valuable information to the Allies. In 1916 she was executed for spying.

Augustina Saragossa

1786–1857; Spain
Augustina was a heroine in the defense of Saragossa against the invading French in 1808. She threw herself into the thick of the fighting, rescuing the wounded, ministering to the sick, and inspiring the people to withstand the French assault.

Hannah Senesh

1921–1944; Hungary
Heroine, spy, and freedom fighter, Senesh gave her life fighting the oppression of the Jews. Shortly after World War II broke out, she emigrated to Palestine. She joined a special group of Palestinian soldiers trained to help Jews escape from occupied countries, and, with her unit, she parachuted into Yugoslavia in 1944. Making her way behind the front lines in Hungary, she was captured, imprisoned, tortured, and executed by the Nazis.

Beatrice Webb

1862–1948; England
Webb was among the early members of the Fabian Society, an organization dedicated to social and labor reform. She collaborated with her husband on books on the history of trade unionism and Soviet Russia.

Vera Zasulich

1849–1919; Russia
Zasulich, a Russian radical and writer, taught reading and writing to workers. She was arrested in 1869, imprisoned, and then exiled, returning to Russia an even more dedicated revolutionary. In 1876 she moved to St. Petersburg, where she heard of the brutal beating of a political prisoner by the Chief of Police. Walking into his office, she shot him point-blank. Because the chief was widely hated, the jury sympathized with Zasulich and acquitted her, but the Czar ordered her arrest. She was smuggled out of the country and lived in Switzerland for some years, finally returning to Russia after the 1905 Revolution.

Clara Zetkin

1857–1933; Germany
Socialist leader, feminist, and editor, Zetkin formulated the socialist theory of women's emancipation in 1889, when she published *The Question of Women Workers* and *Women at the Present Time*. She was active in international socialism and in 1915 she organized the International Women's Conference Against the War; the conference did not have party approval, and Zetkin was arrested. The party repeatedly attempted to discredit her, and she finally moved to Moscow, where she spent the remainder of her life.

built a movement that was international.

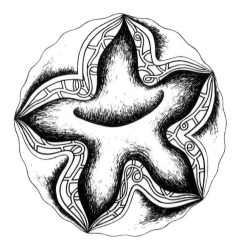

Natalie Barney

1876–1972

Natalie Barney's salon grew out of a long tradition in which, for centuries, women had exercised power and influence through their positions as salonières. But Barney's gatherings were different, as there the women's power was not derived from the status of their male visitors, although men were welcomed except on the all-female evenings. Until the nineteenth century, there was no concept of a person who was a homosexual, only the idea of a homosexual act – which was, of course, considered sinful. Homosexual communities were primarily centered around bars, restaurants, and clubs, all of which had an aura of secrecy. The openness with which Barney and her comrades lived provides a historic precedent for the efforts of contemporary lesbians to record their heritage and emerge from the hidden world to which they have been condemned by guilt, fear, social prejudice, and misunderstanding. Lesbianism is – in the context of those grouped around Barney – presented not only as a sexual preference, but also as a political choice, one which refutes the

heterosexual bias of the culture. Thus, in addition to avowed lesbians, other women in this section include those who chose women as companions, with or without a sexual relationship; women who refused to allow their identities to be submerged by the men with whom they were involved; and other women of the French salons.

Djuna Barnes

b. 1892; United States
Born and raised in New York and educated at home by her father, Barnes became a novelist, short-story writer, playwright, poet, reporter, theater columnist, illustrator, and painter. Her best known novel is *Nightwood* (1936), a surreal and poetic book that has influenced, among others, Anaïs Nin. Her less known works include: *Ryder* (1928), an illustrated novel; *Antiphone* (1958), a tragedy in blank verse; *Spillway* (1962), a collection of short stories; and another illustrated work, *The Ladies Almanack*, originally printed privately and anonymously and recently reissued. Based on Natalie Barney's social circle, this latter work is a highly original and somewhat outrageous satire on the lesbian community that revolved around Barney.

Anne Bonney

fl. 1700–1720;

Mary Read

d. 1720; England
Both Bonney and Read were pirates. When Bonney joined the crew of the ship on which Read sailed, Read – disguised as a man – had already become a pirate of renown, revealing her sexual identity only after she and Bonney were suspected of having a love affair. The two women fought side by side, encouraging and protecting one another until their life of adventure

ended in capture. Read died in prison, but Bonney, sentenced to hang, escaped and was never heard from again.

Romaine Brooks

1874–1970;
United States
Brooks, a painter best known for her portraits, was the lifelong companion of Natalie Barney and was part of the lesbian society that revolved around Barney's salon. Brooks' portraits recorded, directly or indirectly, her attachments and relationships with those involved in the overlapping worlds of high society, French arts and letters, and the homosexual elite of Paris, where Brooks established herself after she inherited her family's fortune. She had a one woman exhibition there in 1910, but, except for an exhibition of drawings in Chicago in 1935, her work was rarely shown. In 1971, a long-overdue retrospective of her work was presented at the National Gallery in Washington, D.C., one year after her death. Brooks' assembled work proved her to be a singular figure in the world of art and one of the first painters to deal with lesbian issues, both implicitly and explicitly.

204

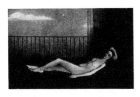

Weeping Venus, Romaine Brooks. (Photo courtesy National Collection of Fine Arts, Smithsonian Institution.)

The Weeping Venus

Laid out as dead in moonlight shroud
Beneath a derelict of cloud;
A double wreckage safe from flight,
High-caged as grief, in pris-
oned night –
Unseeing eyes whose clustering tears
Tell the pure crystal of her years
No crown of thorns, no wounded side,
Yet as the God-man crucified,
Her body expiates the sin
That love and life with her begin.

– N. Barney

Poems and Poèmes, au très alliances, by Natalie Clifford Barney. Paris: Émile-Paul, 1920.

Eleanor Butler
1745–1829
Sarah Ponsonby

1745–1831; Ireland
Both Butler and Ponsonby came from titled families. They met at a girls' school, and their relationship flourished for nearly a decade before Eleanor's mother tried to force her daughter into either a distasteful marriage or a convent. The two women, devastated by the possibility of being separated, attempted to elope, but were apprehended and brought back in disgrace. Sarah fell gravely ill and Eleanor was forbidden to see her. But they were determined not to remain apart, and as soon as Sarah recovered they staged a rebellion that finally wore down their families' resistance. The two

were given a small stipend on condition that they live far from home. They settled in Wales, where many of the greatest figures of the time visited them. Butler's journal recorded their day-to-day lives, documenting the deep and lasting bond which sustained them for a lifetime.

Radclyffe Hall

1886–1943; England
Hall's most notable work, *The Well of Loneliness,* was written in an effort to speak out on the then-taboo subject of lesbianism. Her book, published in 1928 with a foreword by Havelock Ellis, became a *cause célèbre* in the literary world. Judged obscene in England, copies of the book were confiscated and burned by Scotland Yard. *The Well of Loneliness* was condemned because Hall, an avowed homosexual, had treated lesbianism sympathetically and explicitly defended the lesbian experience. Eventually Hall's book was widely accepted, but its initial reception shocked and hurt the author, whose other work has remained relatively unknown. A member of the Barney circle, Hall lived openly with her lover, Lady Una Troubridge.

Mata Hari

1876–1917; Holland
Born in Holland, Gertrude Zelle went to Paris, was trained as a dancer, and changed her name to Mata Hari, claiming to be of Javanese descent. She became a celebrated, if somewhat notorious, exotic dancer who performed throughout Europe (most notably at Natalie Barney's all-female soireés). She met many government officials and, because she was intelligent and multilingual, was enlisted by the French government as a spy during World War I. In 1917 she was accused by France of aiding the Germans, but at

her trial she claimed to have passed only worthless information to the Germans; while there was no evidence to refute this claim, she was found guilty and executed for treason.

Louise Labé

1525–1566; France
A free-spirited, passionate feminist, Labé was one of the most important poets and cultural leaders of her epoch. At age 16, dressed as a man, she followed a soldier-lover into battle, demonstrating such military prowess that the army nicknamed her "La Capitaine Louise." She later married a wealthy merchant in Lyon, and her home became the center of cultural life there. Always an independent thinker, she wrote a volume of verse, dedicated to another woman poet, which was an appeal to women to strive for excellence in all areas, not only equaling men but surpassing them in achievement. Labé also wrote love poems which firmly established her as the most celebrated female poet of her day.

Lou Andreas Salomé

1861–1937; France
Salomé, one of the first female psychotherapists, struggled all her life to maintain her independence. Her achievements have been obscured by the double standard that informed most writing about her and the fact that she burned most of her letters. Known primarily as the inspirer of Nietzche, the confidante of Freud, and the lover of Rilke, Salomé was a writer as well as an analyst. Her books on Nietzche and Ibsen and her stories, novels, and essays made her extremely well-known during her lifetime. As Anaïs Nin wrote of her in the Preface to Salome's biography: "She demanded the freedom to change, to evolve, to grow.

She asserted her integrity against the sentimentality and hypocritical definitions of loyalties and duties. She is unique in the history of her time."

Marie Sallé

1707–1756; France
A lesbian and pioneer choreographer, Sallé made her stage debut at age nine. She performed with a touring company in France for eleven years, returning to London in 1927 as an accomplished dancer. She rejected the traditional costumes of the time, believing that they hampered freedom of movement. Instead she adoped a simple muslin dress draped in classical Greek style, wore slippers without heels, and let her hair fall free, which was considered shocking at the time. Nonetheless, Sallé triumphed as a dancer, a costume designer, and the first woman choreographer. She received a great deal of criticism, however, because she appeared in Handel's *Alcina* dressed as a boy and because she had a female lover.

Gertrude Stein

1874–1946; United States
Of her famous words "A rose is a rose is a rose," Stein said, "In that line, the rose is red for the first time in English literature in 100 years." One of the first to recognize the importance of the modern painters, Stein (with her brother) built a major art collection, and she herself created a literature comparable to the avant-garde trends in the visual arts. Several generations of male writers virtually sat at her feet, and her influence on them was a major force in shaping twentieth-century literature. Constantly rejected by publishers, she published many

of her early works herself. It was not until *The Autobiography of Alice B. Toklas* was released in 1933 that she received any kind of public recognition. This book, a memoir written by Stein in the persona of her lifelong companion, Toklas, was a bestseller and made Stein a celebrity in her American homeland. She toured the United States in the 1930's speaking, recording, and making radio broadcasts, and returned to France feeling that she had finally achieved the recognition she deserved. Stein's writing was largely concerned with formal rather than personal issues, but she did make an attempt in an early work, *Q.E.D.*, to describe lesbian relationships.

Cristina Trivulzio

1808–1871; Italy
A political and literary figure, Trivulzio left her marriage and from then on refused to have relationships with men. She went to Paris and wrote articles and pamphlets denouncing the political oppression in Italy, arguing in favor of unification of the country under a constitutional monarchy, a free press, and education for women and the poor. Returning to Milan, she fought in the "Five Days' Revolution" of 1848 and directed hospital services in Rome when it was under French siege. She founded several newspapers, through which she agitated for reform, and also wrote fiction, memoirs, and the four-volume *Essay on the Formation of Catholic Dogma*.

Renée Vivien

1877–1909; France
Vivien's elegant poetry, frankly lesbian and feminist, was profusely praised when it first ap-

peared. However, it has since become obscured and ignored. In 1899 she met Natalie Barney and began an affair with her which lasted until 1901 – an intense and volatile relationship nourished by their shared pride in lesbianism and feminism and their desire for the re-creation of a Sapphic tradition in literature. Vivien produced over twenty volumes of poetry which dealt with lesbianism and female mythology and created stories of Amazons, Biblical heroines, women who either refused to submit to men or preferred monsters to men, and women who clearly expressed their passion for women.

Many of the women associated with the salons were extremely knowledgeable and creative, but in the early salons women were usually told to "inspire but do not write." Nonetheless, continued contact with advanced intellectual, political, and artistic ideas gradually eroded not only sexual barriers but class discinctions as well. It came to be one's ability to think, not one's economic status or sex, that determined one's reputation. Revolutionary and feminist ideas thrived in the salons, which were, despite their limitations, ultimately encouraging to the development of women's talents.

Alice Pike Barney

1857–1931; United States
Alice Barney, the mother of Natalie, was an artist, play-

wright, patron, and philanthropist. Stifled by her marriage, she took her daughters to live in Paris, where she studied painting and exhibited at the Paris Salon. She also showed her work at the London Royal Academy. In 1903 she designed and built Studio House in Washington, D.C. – a cultural center that provided studio, performance, and exhibition space for artists. She established a similar environment on the west coast in the twenties, as well as organizing a small theater group that performed her plays.

Sophie de Condorcet

1765–1822; France
De Condorcet was one of the outstanding women who conducted salons during the period of the French Revolution. Initially devoted to intellectual and cultural pursuits, as the Revolution mounted her salon became the gathering place for Revolutionary Party members. Outspoken concerning her radical philosophies, De Condorcet was sent to prison but later released. Others of her circle died on the scaffold, and her husband committed suicide in prison. She struggled to make a living as a painter and died in obscurity.

Marie du Deffand

1697–1780; France
By age fifteen, Du Deffand knew that she did not want the same kind of life as most of the women she knew. She tried to build a life of personal independence, leaving her husband as soon as she could and establishing herself in Parisian society. Her salon provided an arena for the discussion and development of the political theories and philosophies embodied by the Revolution.

Ninon de L'Enclos

1615–1705; France
De L'Enclos' salon of the well-educated and intellectual was frequented by the most talented people of Paris. Although she never married, she did have numerous relationships and two children. She maintained her independence throughout her life and was a unique example of a woman who lived as she pleased despite social pressures.

Julie de Lespinasse

1732–1776; France
De Lespinasse entered the world of the salons as a companion of Marie du Deffand, one of the major salonists prior to the Revolution. De Lespinasse continued the salon traditions, and her own salon became the social and intellectual center for the Parisian nobility during the reign of Louis XV. Her letters, published in 1809, reveal her to be a fascinating woman and a strong supporter of a more democratic society.

Stephanie de Genlis

1746–1830; France
Author, musician, critic, salonière, and linguist, De Genlis is primarily known for her writings on education. She was extremely independent and was said to have dressed like a man and defied social convention by dancing with servants at balls and refusing to conform with other rules of social behavior that stressed class boundaries.

Marie Geoffrin

1669–1757; France
Geoffrin added a new dimension to the salon tradition when she brought authors and artists into direct contact with distinguished patrons, especially foreign patrons, thereby contributing greatly to the proliferation of French arts and letters.

Catherine de Rambouillet

1588–1665; France
De Rambouillet established the first literary salon in France and was responsible for the refinement of manners, the purification of the French language, and the birth of the modern art of conversation. Disgusted by the coarse and vulgar behavior she witnessed at the court of Henry IV, she created an environment in which chosen guests were encouraged to mingle, share their ideas, and express the best of themselves. She insisted on equality between the sexes in her salon. The Hotel de Rambouillet, a building actually designed by her, was the scene of France's most powerful social and literary forces for over thirty years.

Jeanne Recamier

1777/79–1850; France
It was said that Recamier's salon made her as influential as Napoleon. The emperor was enraged by what he saw as her subversive political gatherings, as well as by her close association with Germaine de Staël, one of his most vocal critics. Recamier, De Staël's protege, visited her mentor after she was exiled by Napoleon, and for this she was exiled for three years. After Napoleon's downfall she returned to Paris, where she resumed her position as a political and social leader.

Madeleine de Sable

1598–1678; France
The hostess of a literary salon in the De Rambouillet tradition, De Sable was also a gifted writer and influential literary stylist. The practice of condensing life's experiences into maxims and epigrams was introduced and made fashionable by De Sable.

Madeleine de Scudéry

1607–1701; France
De Scudéry, one of the most eminent literary women of the seventeenth century, created a complete and vivid picture of the social life of the period in her novels. She continued the tradition and spirit of the salon of De Rambouillet, and her circle included De Sable, De Sévigné, and De Lafayette. Discussions in her salon included such topics as the intellectual equality between the sexes.

Marie de Sévigné

1626–1696; France
De Sévigné was famous for the letters she wrote to her daughter over a period of thirty years – letters that present an accurate, lively characterization of the times and serve both as social history and as models of the literary style of seventeenth-century France. De Sévigné had the advantage of several viewpoints, since she could observe court life (to which she had been introduced at age fifteen) and could also record the development of the salons, which provided one of the few alternatives to the dreariness of formal court society.

Claudine de Tencin

1685–1749; France
De Tencin conducted one of the first salons in which the principles of monarchy were denounced in favor of a constitutional government. She encouraged freedom of thought and expression at a time when any criticism of the monarchy could result in arrest. De Tencin, like many of the other salonists, supported the French Revolution.

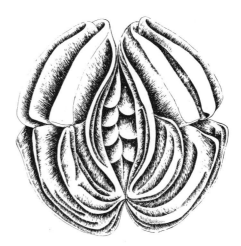

Virginia Woolf

1882–1941

The historical distinction between "masculine" and "feminine," as articulated by Virginia Woolf, is related to such traditional philosophical distinctions as those between spirit/flesh and rationality/intuition. These have always been conceived as opposites and one presumed superior to the other. Spirit is imagined to be purer than flesh, and rationality is regarded as a higher form of thought than intuition. Spirit and rationality are associated with the masculine and respected; flesh and intuition are identified with the feminine and devalued. This hierarchy of values has been projected on a worldwide scale. One race or culture perceives itself as civilized and others as "savage." Human beings see themselves as possessing higher intelligence than animals, whom they regard as lower forms of life. This entire structure of hierarchal thinking allows one group of people to dominate, oppress, exploit, and even exterminate another culture or species.

Challenging the assumptions of hierarchal thinking is the cornerstone of feminist theory. In addition to Woolf, many other women have suggested that the historic dichotomies can be reconciled. In fact, women have long been suggesting that these supposed polarities are the product of distorted male thought.

Spirit and flesh actually exist in one body, just as rationality and intuition reside in one mind. Women argue that there really is no fundamental distinction between the sexes – only that imposed by culture and society. Reconciling "masculine" and "feminine" values is not just a matter of equal rights; rather, the end of hierarchal thinking means the end of the catastrophic imbalances of the world.

Some writers recognized the imbalance in our social structures and addressed it by trying to introduce a female point of view that could counteract the predominant male view.

Simone de Beauvoir

b. 1908; France
A major twentieth-century author and philosopher, De Beauvoir was born into a bourgeois family in Paris. At fifteen she decided to become a writer, and in 1929 she received her degree in philosophy from the Sorbonne. She was second in her graduating class; first place was taken by Jean-Paul Sartre, who became her lifelong friend and companion. After the war De Beauvoir emerged as one of the leaders of the existentialist movement, and her ideas had a profound effect on the intellectual communities of Europe and America. *The Second Sex*, published in 1949, is an examination and indictment of Western civilization's treatment of women. It has been translated into nineteen languages and its impact felt around the world. In 1970, De Beauvoir published a thorough study of old age, Originally a socialist, she once looked to economic changes to bring about an alteration of women's status, but recently – discouraged by socialism's failure to create a true social revolution – she has become an avowed feminist.

Willa Cather

1873–1947; United States
Cather, raised in Nebraska and educated by her grandmothers, created some of the most memorable characterizations of frontier women in American literature. She left us a legacy of heroines who were powerful and independent, though usually punished for their strength by loneliness and isolation. As a teenager, Cather called herself William and dressed like a boy. While her lesbianism was never explicit in her work, she did have a lifelong female companion.

Anaïs Nin

1903–1977; United States
Born in Paris, Nin came to America as a child and was brought up in New York. She was bored with high school and quit at fifteen, burying herself in the public library, where she read from A to Z in the fiction section. She began writing at an early age; her first diary dates from the time she was eleven. In the 1920's she went to France and then traveled back and forth from Europe, working as an artist's model, studying dance, undergoing psychoanalysis with Otto Rank, and even becoming a therapist for awhile herself. She came to be known as a "patron of sorts," helping such struggling writers as Henry Miller and Lawrence Durrell.

Nin led a double life as an author. While writing surrealistic novels and playing multiple roles – wife, lover, protector, enigma – she confided her real self only to her diary, consisting of over 150 manuscript volumes. There Nin tore away the masks and artifices of her external life and recorded the slow, painstaking process of a woman emerging from a disguised identity into her authentic self. Despite the efforts of many men to tear her diary from her (including Rank, who believed it to be a symbol of her neurosis), Nin continued to record her isolated voyage, but until the 1960's her journey remained invisible to all but a few close friends. She did print limited editions of her own works on a press she purchased, passing them out to authors and critics in the hope of some response. The audience was so meager, however, that she herself began to doubt the value of her life. Once, while desperately ill and close to death, she had a terrible dream in which a voice told her that all she had experienced had been an illusion. She pleaded with the voice, arguing that it had all been real, but when she awoke she wasn't so sure.

Finally Nin's diary began to be published, but not because its value had been recognized. Rather, it was thought to be significant only because of the male writers she had known. When the diary sold out almost instantly, the publishers were puzzled. To Nin herself, the audience response to her books and then her public lectures was first surprising, then gratifying, and, finally, understandable. Her audience consisted largely of women, and they recognized in her solo flight the story of their own fledgling independence; they were not interested in stories of male heroes – they were interested in her. Her diaries, her novels, her letters were finally hailed as the expression of an original and brilliant literary figure. This recognition came almost at the end of Nin's life and was a fitting, if terribly belated, reward for a pioneer in the development of a female sensibility in literature. Nin herself stood as a unique symbol of the female creator of the future.

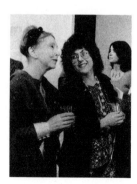

Anaïs Nin and Judy Chicago.

Colette

1873–1954; France
Colette's career began when her first husband locked her in her room, forced her to write, and published her work under his own name. Divorced in 1906, she had to sue to regain title to her work; she then became one of France's major writers and an international figure in the literary world. Colette's writing always centered on the personal, but she maintained an impartial view, observing what she saw and describing the continual struggle between women and men. Her interest was clearly focused on the lives of women, particularly her mother, of whom she wrote fondly.

Doris Lessing

b. 1919; England
Lessing is best known for *The Golden Notebook,* published in 1962. This book documented the intellectual, political, and personal life of a modern, emancipated woman – a theme that has recurred in Lessing's work. Her first novel, *The Grass Is Singing,* examined male/female relationships against a background of the destructive relationship between "the stupid and unimaginative" white colonizers and Africa's native inhabitants. In the five-volume *Children of Violence*, written and published over a seventeen-year period, Lessing chronicled Martha Quest's search for self-definition in a world which became increasingly terrifying and surreal. Lessing's view of life has become steadily more pessimistic; she has stated that she does not believe the human race will survive much longer.

Dorothy Richardson

1872–1957; England
The author of a thirteen-volume, semi-autobiographical novel, Richardson was an innovator in modern fiction. The term "stream of consciousness" was first applied to *Pilgrimage,* which took her twenty years to write, and in which she attempted to create "a feminine equivalent of the current masculine realism." This epic work is an account of a woman's search for self-discovery, freedom, and independence in a world dominated by men.

Olive Schreiner

1855–1920; South Africa
Schreiner's *Women and Labor* became a textbook for the early women's movement. From 1885 until her death, she worked on *From Man to Man*, a novel about sisterhood and motherhood that was published posthumously in 1926. An avowed socialist, feminist, and suffragist, Schreiner created at body of work that dealt with the position of women in society and their relationship to work, the family, and the class structure. In her books, short stories, allegories, and essays, she developed a powerful feminine symbology which influenced Woolf, Richardson, and Lessing.

Edith Wharton

1862–1937; United States
One of America's most distinguished writers, Wharton was born into a New York family of merchants, bankers, and lawyers whose biases against women and artists drove her abroad. She spent most of her life writing stories and novels that expressed her discontent with the constrained role of women and described the limited society from which she had fled. In *House of Mirth,* Lily Bart commits suicide rather than face the disgrace of not having acquired a suitable husband. In *Age of Innocence,* for which Wharton won the Pulitzer Prize, her male characters are vigorous only in their domination of women. She wrote about her own isolation in one of her letters: "I believe I know the only cure, which is to make one's center of life inside one's self…to decorate one's inner house so richly that one is content there…"

Adela Zamudio-Ribero

1854–1928; Bolivia
Zamudio-Ribero, feminist, poet, and educator, spoke out against the oppression of women in Bolivia. She argued for better education, more job opportunities, and the right to vote. In one of her famous satirical poems she complained that even the most ignorant and illiterate man could vote, while intelligent, educated women could not.

Other women chose not to directly confront patriarchal values or their situations as women, at least not in their work. Certainly, however, some of these writers made their position on women's issues obvious through their life-styles or provided role models for other women as a result of their achievements.

Isak Dinesen

1885–1962; Denmark
Dinesen was the pen name of Karen Blixen, a member of the Danish aristocracy. At age nineteen she published several short stories and a marionette comedy, but it was thrity years before she published again. She married a baron in 1914 and went to British East Africa, where they owned and managed a coffee plantation. The marriage ended after seven years, and she continued to operate the plantation alone until the drop in coffee prices forced her to give up her land in 1931. She then returned to Denmark and resumed her writing. Her best books, *Out of Africa* and *Shadows on the Grass*, are lyric evocations of her African experience.

Lorraine Hansberry

1930–1965; United States
Hansberry, an eloquent young author, wrote the first play by a black woman to be produced on Broadway. *A Raisin in the Sun* (1959), a milestone in the development of black literature, was also the first work by a black playwright to receive the New York Drama Critics Circle Award. Hansberry was commissioned to write a television play about slavery, but when network officials read it, they refused to produce it.

Selma Lagerlöf

1858–1940; Sweden
Lagerlöf was the first woman awarded the Nobel Prize for Literature (in 1909) and the first woman to become a member of the Swedish Academy. Beloved by the Swedes, her sagas and narratives are considered the finest of her country's literature.

Edna St. Vincent Millay

1892–1950; United States
A celebrated poet and dramatist, Millay began writing verses during her childhood. Her first volume of poetry was published in 1917, and in 1923 she was awarded the Pulitzer Prize for her poem *The Harp-Weaver.* One of a number of women writers who challenged the traditional image of the genteel lady poet, Millay created work that was usually impassioned and sometimes angry.

Gabriela Mistral

1889–1957; Chile
Mistral began her varied career as a primary and secondary school teacher. Because of her experience within the village schools of Chile, she was asked by the Mexican government to collaborate in the reorganization of that country's rural school system. She then became Chile's delegate to the United Nations and was appointed to the U.N. Subcommission on the Status of Women. Mistral was also a poet and is considered the founder of the modern poetry movement in Chile. She was awarded the Nobel Prize for Literature in 1945.

Emilia Pardo-Bazán

1852–1921; Spain
Pardo-Bazán has been called Spain's greatest nineteenth-century novelist. In 1879 she published the first of eighteen novels, thus beginning her career as one of the major naturalist writers of the period. In 1906 she became the first woman to chair the Literature Section of the Atheneum in Madrid. She was later named Advisor of Spain's Ministry of Education and appointed Professor of Romance Literature at the Central University of Madrid; the university faculty protested her appointment, however, and the male students boycotted her classes.

Nelly Sachs

1891–1970; Germany
Sachs was called the "Poet of the Holocaust" because she created a body of work that was a profound lamentation for the fate of the Jews. She was born in Berlin to a family of prosperous Jewish industrialists and received training in the arts and literature, but reading Selma Lagerlöf's books shaped her future as a writer. She began a correspondence with Lagerlöf that lasted for years. In 1940 Sachs and her mother were brought to Sweden by Lagerlöf, who presented a personal petition to the government to obtain their passage out of Germany. In 1966 Sachs received a Nobel Prize for her work, which created a universal metaphor from the tragedy of the Jews.

Vita Sackville-West

1892–1962; England
Sackville-West was a writer and a unique woman. Married to Harold Nicholson – a prominent member of the foreign service – for almost 50 years, she was the inspiration for Virginia Woolf's novel on androgyny, *Orlando*. Vita's marriage, chronicled by her son in *Portrait of a Marriage* (based on her unpublished memoirs), was one which challenged all conventional definitions. Both she and her husband had affairs with members of their own sex, and Vita's involvement with Virginia Woolf has been well chronicled. Unfortunately, this notoriety has obscured the fact that she was a highly gifted and successful writer of poems, novels, short stories, biographies, and literary criticism.

Edith Sitwell

1887–1964; England
Sitwell hated the dull and ordinary and devoted herself to "the avant-garde in literature and the eccentric in lifestyle." Sitwell, like her friend Gertrude Stein, was interested in the sound of words, once delivering a reading from behind a screen so that the personality of the poet would not impinge on the sound. On another occasion she read a work through a megaphone, and she often recited her poetry to music. Her later work was increasingly concerned with the human condition. Sitwell was also an astute critic, a prolific prose writer, and the author of several biographies.

Agnes Smedley

1894–1950; United States
A writer, radical journalist, and lecturer, Smedley grew up in poverty and hardship in rural Missouri and a series of small Colorado mining towns. She was deeply involved in left-wing politics and wrote about the Chinese Revolution, for which she was exiled from America and accused of being a spy. Smedley summed up her philosophy by saying: "I have had but one loyalty and one faith and that was to the liberation of the poor and oppressed."

Alfonsina Storni

1892–1938; Argentina
With the publication of her first volume of poems in 1916, Storni emerged as an important modern Argentinian writer. She wrote over a dozen poetic works and is considered the first poet in her country to write from a woman's point of view.

Sigrid Undset

1882–1949; Norway
A Norwegian novelist and the recipient of a Nobel Prize in 1928, Undset is best known for her novels depicting Scandinavian life in the Middle Ages. She had an unconventional early education; she was sent to the first coeducational school in Norway, run by an ardent feminist who later offered to send Undset to the university. She refused, taking a job as an office worker to support herself and her family instead.

Although she began to write in 1898, it wasn't until 1920 that her first successful novel was published.

Rebecca West

b. 1892; Ireland/England
West, a renowned journalist, novelist, and social critic, is admired and respected in both the United States and Great Britain. Her critical work was published in *The New Yorker*, and her feminist views appeared in political periodicals of the left-wing press. She examined Eastern European politics, culture, and history in *Black Lamb and Grey Falcon* and her astute reportage of the Nuremberg Trials was published as *A Train of Power* in 1955.

In the twentieth century a number of female theorists emerged. Some, like Diner and Harding, expanded our ideas of women's mythic and inner lives. Others, like Arendt, made inroads in philosophy but did not address themselves to feminist issues.

Hannah Arendt

1906–1975; United States
Arendt was a political philosopher, an author, and the first woman appointed to a full professorship at Princeton University. Born in Germany, she left in 1933, when Hitler came to power, and went to France, where she worked in Jewish relief organizations. She later sought refuge in the United States and served as research director of the Conference on Jewish Relations from 1944 to 1946. Actively concerned with the preservation and transmission of the Jewish heritage, Arendt translated and published a number of works by Jewish

writers. Her book *The Origins of Totalitarianism*, released in 1951, established her as a political theoretician of great stature.

Helen Diner

fl. 1929–1940; Germany

Diner – the pseudonym of Bertha Eckstein-Diener – was the author of *Mothers and Amazons*, the first feminine history of culture, as well as a number of other books. *Mothers and Amazons* has become a source for feminist theory concerning the matriarchal roots of society. Basing her work on the research of the Swiss anthropologist Bachofen and on the theories of Jung, Diner argued that primitive social organizations were matriarchal and that the patriarchal family was a comparatively recent social development. She therefore investigated matriarchal cultures with the intention of providing women with some understanding of their tradition.

Mary Esther Harding

fl. 1920's; United States

Harding, a Jungian psychologist and writer, was a forerunner of contemporary feminist therapists who are attempting to develop a female psychology. Her books *Women's Mysteries* and *The Way of All Women* are major works which interpret female history and experience from a Jungian perspective. In *Women's Mysteries*, she explored the relationship of goddess worship to the power women possessed in early civilizations.

Karen Horney

1885–1952; United States

In the 1920's Horney, a neo-Freudian analyst, offered her psychological theories as a direct challenge to the prevailing Freudian interpretation of female behavior. She

argued that social and cultural forces, not biology, shaped human personality and sexual identity, and she questioned Freud's notion of "penis envy," stating that women only envied men's privileged position in society. She even suggested that men may suffer from "womb envy" and are jealous of women's reproductive capabilities. In 1941 Horney founded the American Institute for Psychoanalysis, where she served as dean until she died.

Suzanne Langer

b. 1895; United States

One of the few women to achieve recognition in the heavily male-dominated field of philosophy, Langer was primarily interested in esthetics and the meaning of symbols. Her later works explored the nature of symbolism, poetic creativity, music, language, abstraction and the issue of emotion in art. In her book *Philosophy in a New Key*, arguing that life was barren without meaningful symbols, Langer sought a synthesis between the objective and the subjective – or, as she put it, form and feeling.

Simone Weil

1909–1943; France

Weil, a cult figure in France for several decades, was a scholar, philosopher, mystic writer, and revolutionary. She was known to identify so closely with the oppressed peoples of the world that existence was continual agony to her. During World War II, she became involved in the French Resistance and permitted herself to eat no more than the rations allowed her countrymen in occupied territory. Finally she refused to eat at all, as if, by denying her own body, she could deny the suffering of the world. She died of voluntary starvation, a symbol for many European intellectuals of her profound moral integrity.

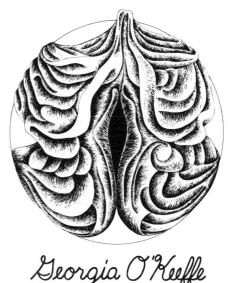

Georgia O'Keeffe

b. 1887

In the early part of the twentieth century, the barriers against training women in art had begun to be broken down and women entered the arts in large numbers, although they still faced formidable obstacles in getting their work shown, recognized, or supported. The same distinction between feminist and non-feminist work exists in the visual arts as in literature; some women worked within mainstream ideas, while others like O'Keeffe stood their ground as women and expressed their own points of view. The importance of the work of many women artists lies partly in their perception and representation of women's lives. This idea has not yet been incorporated into art values, however. The refusal by the art world to acknowledge and honor female subject matter reflects the larger society's denigration of women and women's experience. Moreover, women's art is still not evaluated within the context of women's history, and, because of this, the significant body of work that women artists have produced has remained essentially unacknowledged and unappreciated.

not by laws but by guilt and ignorance.

Marie Bashkirtsev
1860–1884; Russia
In 1877 Bashkirtsev enrolled in the women's art class at the Academie Julien in Paris. Ten years later her *Journals* were published, In the *Journals* she described her commitment to feminism, inveighed against the injustices faced by women artists, complained about the poor quality of instruction for women, and stated that women's lack of opportunities had a devastating effect on their art.

Rosa Bonheur
1822–1899; France
Bonheur, known primarily for her large-scale animal paintings, was one of the most celebrated and successful woman artists of the nineteenth century. Unable to study the nude because she was a woman, each day she dressed in men's clothing and went to the slaughterhouses and horse fairs to learn anatomy. Bonheur worked constantly making extensive preparations and sketches and working slowly (she would sometimes wait two years for the oils to dry before applying another layer of paint). Internationally acclaimed, she made enough money to buy an estate, which she filled with livestock and exotic animals. Bonheur and her companion of forty years, Natalie Micas, established an environment that was safe from the prejudices of the world.

Emily Carr
1871–1945; Canada
Little known outside of Canada, Carr was an unheralded genius. Accompanied only by her animals, she journeyed into the forests of northwest Canada to record the rituals, lives, and totems of the Northwest Coast Indians, by whom she was deeply loved. Her later paintings depict the raw Canadian wilderness, anthropomorphizing the untouched forest in feminine terms. Her final paintings were deeply spiritual – the forest transformed into a cathedral-like space, the images rich in symbolism. Carr did not have a one-woman exhibition until she was sixty-three, and she only exhibited five times in her life. She wrote, "How completely alone I've had to face the world, no booster, no artistic backing, no relatives interested, no bother taken by papers to advertise, just me and an empty flat and the pictures."

Mary Cassatt
1844–1926; United States
Cassatt, the most important woman artist of the nineteenth century and probably the best American artist of her generation, exhibited with the Impressionists in Paris, where she settled in the early 1870's. Fascinated by the Japanese prints that were then popular, she made a series of aquatints that are among the finest colored prints ever created. Her later work concentrated increasingly on the subject of mother and child; her approach to the theme was unique, generally unsentimental yet always expressive of a wide range of human interaction. She created a monumental mural for the Woman's Building at the 1892 – 1893 Chicago World's Fair. Entitled "Modern Woman," the mural consisted of a central panel called "Young Women Plucking the Fruits of Knowledge and Science," a left panel called "Young Girls Pursuing Fame," and a right panel devoted to women involved in music and dancing. Although this landmark work has been lost, Cassatt remains a powerful and important figure in art history and in the development of a female point of view in art.

Sonia Delaunay
b. 1885; France
A pioneer abstractionist and a co-founder – with her husband Robert – of Orphism, Delaunay has had a long and productive career in the arts. She tried to bring new energy to the decorative and applied arts, not only to earn money but also because she had strong feelings about the interaction among art, design, and democracy. She designed costumes, fabric, furniture, tapestries, and illustrated books and did interior decoration.

Natalia Goncharova
1881–1962; Russia
The painter Natalia Goncharova, with her companion Mikhail Larionov, led the movement that advanced Russian art in the early twentieth century. She traveled with the Ballet Russe, working with Diaghilev on decor and costumes.

Barbara Hepworth
1903–1975; England
By the time she was sixteen Hepworth had decided to become a sculptor, and she soon became a fellow student of Henry Moore. Hepworth began to pierce her sculptures, in 1931, a year before Moore, taking "the most intense pleasure" in modifying a form in accordance with her own biology. She always saw her abstract shapes as related to the earth, to the human figure in the landscape, and to her own experience as a woman. She believed that "There is a whole range of formal perception belonging to the feminine experience."

Hannah Höch
1889–1971; Germany
Höch and a male colleague invented photomontage, a medium she employed all her life. In collages, she utilized objects traditionally associated with women – lace, buttons, and bits of fabric – and often made strong and ironic images of feminine experience.

Harriet Hosmer
1830–1908; United States
In the mid-nineteenth century, Hosmer went to Rome to study and soon achieved considerable renown, not only for her neoclassical sculpture, but for her masculine attire, her midnight rides through the city, and her taste for ambitious projects. In her large studio, she employed as many as thirty assistants.

Frida Kahlo
1910–1954; Mexico
Because of her unique artistic vision and enormous personal courage, Kahlo has become a major heroine in the feminist art movement. Badly injured when she was fifteen, she faced her physical infirmity and continual, agonizing pain with grace and dignity, transforming the horror of her circumstances into haunting self-portraits. Her images are vividly infused with the warmth of native Mexican art – combining joy and pain, tragedy and humor, into a complex vision of one woman's universe.

Käthe Kollwitz
1867–1945; Germany
Kollwitz, a sculptor and a prolific graphic artist, identified herself with working-class people, saying; "When I really got to know about the want and misery of the working classes…I felt I had a duty to serve them through my art." Her work sustained her through the tragedies of her life: the death of her son Peter in World War I, the ban placed on her work by the Nazis, her evacuation from her home during the

war, and the death of her husband. She left a poignant record of a woman whose vision was heroic and whose art was drawn from the deepest wellsprings of feminine compassion.

Marie Laurencin

1885–1956; France

Laurencin was a painter and a member of the circle around Picasso in Paris during the early twentieth century. She also designed sets and costumes for the ballet and theater, illustrated a number of books, and produced lithographs, etchings, and woodcuts. Originally her work was critically acclaimed, but in later years it was ignored. Behind the artifice and perfumed sweetness of the women in Laurencin's paintings, there is an aura of sadness that speaks of containment and stifled rage.

Paula Modersohn-Becker

1876–1907; Germany

By the time she died at the age of thirty-one, Modersohn-Becker had produced almost four hundred paintings and studies and a thousand drawings. Her images of women are earthy, sensual, and celebratory. About one of her self-portraits she wrote: "And finally you saw yourself as fruit, lifted yourself out of your clothes and carried that self before the mirror, let it in up to your gaze…" Convinced by her husband to resume their marriage after she had separated from him in order to pursue her work, she became pregnant and, three weeks after the birth of her daughter, died of heart failure.

Berthe Morisot

1840–1895; France

Morisot was from an upper middle-class French family. She was trained in art, and, she continued to paint even after she married Eugene Manet, the younger brother of the artist Edouard. Because of its intimacy and its content (primarily women and children), her work has often been derisively labeled "feminine;" its gentle charm, however – though certainly "feminine" – combines with vigorous brushwork to make her paintings strong, but tender.

Gabriele Münter

1877–1962; Germany

Münter was closely associated with Wassily Kandinsky and the Blue Rider Group in Munich. After their relationship ended, and her work changed, and instead of brilliantly colored landscapes and portraits of her friends, Münter painted somewhat melancholy studies of women. Her last works are markedly introspective and, as always, are typified by an authentic and rich personal style.

Louise Nevelson

b. 1899; United States

Nevelson studied at the Art Student's League in New York. Dissatisfied with traditional materials and forms, she began to work in wood, gluing and nailing the disparate objects she had collected. Her earliest wood boxes were assembled in milk crates and painted in one tone to create an over-all unity of form. In the 1950's, after several decades of struggle and obscurity, Nevelson began to receive recognition for the sculptures, walls, and environments she had created. Finally her personal charisma and powerful art brought her the acclaim she deserved.

Elizabeth Ney

1833–1907; Germany

Ney, the first woman to attend the Munich Art Academy, was at first refused admittance because "There would be little work done by the male students with her to distract them"; she was finally admitted, but only because she promised to leave classes if other students' work suffered. She and her husband later emigrated to America, where she bore a son and for twenty years did little work. But in 1893, when she was commissioned to do a statue for the Columbian Exposition in Chicago, she resumed her career.

Augusta Savage

1900–1962; United States

Savage, one of America's most important black artists, attended Cooper Union in New York and then applied to art schools in Paris. Rejected without an explanation, she later discovered it was because of her race. From then on she worked on behalf of black artists, teaching art to black children, serving as president of the Harlem Artists Guild, and creating strong images of Blacks in all her works. Unfortunately, many of Savage's works have been damaged or destroyed because she lacked the money to have them cast in bronze. Most tragically, this was the fate of her largest and best known work, "Lift Ev'ry Voice and Sing." Commissioned for the New York World's Fair in 1939 – 1940, this monumental representation of black people's contribution to music was cast only in plaster and was bulldozed away at the closing of the fair.

Sophie Taëuber-Arp

1889–1943; Switzerland

Originally a weaver, an embroiderer, and a dancer,

Taëuber-Arp began to paint in 1916. Her work in the decorative arts perhaps led to her development of geometric abstraction. She worked secretivly, preferring the solitude of her small studio to the attention she might have received as a more visible artist.

Suzanne Valadon

1865–1938; France

Valadon, who had no formal training as an artist, began to draw in 1893 while working as an artist's model. **Bold** and intuitive, her work developed rapidly. Valadon produced strong, earthy, and unrelentingly honest art, bringing an uncompromising vision to the self-portraits that clearly documented the aging of a remarkable woman. Some of her most interesting work was done when she used her husband as a model and created images of the male nude from a distinctly feminine point of view.

Photography has only recently been hailed as an art form and incorporated into the art world. Early women photographers were very crucial in the development of still photography, and, though there are still many female photographers, the field is rapidly becoming dominated by men. Likewise, women were active in the early days of motion pictures, but as film grew into a major

213

rights had been won, and that their

industry women found it increasingly difficult to participate in anything but acting and editing.

Dorothy Arzner

b. 1900; United States
One of the few women to become a major director in Hollywood, Arzner began as a typist at Paramount. She became an editor and then wrote and helped shoot and edit *Old Ironsides* in 1925. She directed seventeen feature films and worked with the major female stars of the day, directing them all in roles which transcended the stereotypes perpetuated by Hollywood and explored many facets of the female personality.

Julia Cameron

1815–1879; England
Cameron, Virginia Woolf's aunt, picked up a camera for the first time when she was forty-eight years old and created some of the most expressive documents of the Victorian period. Cameron's work comprises over three thousand pictures, including portraits and religious, symbolical, and allegorical photographs.

Imogen Cunningham

1883–1976; United States
When Cunningham died at the age of ninty-three, she had just completed her last collection of photographs, *After Ninety*, portraits of "survivors" like herself. Impressed with the work of Gertrude Käsebier, she shot her first photograph in 1901. Her early work is allegorical and romantic in the soft-focus pictorial style. It was at this time that she photographed her husband naked on Mt. Ranier, probably the first time a woman

photographed a male nude, although the pictures were censored for years. She and her family moved to the San Francisco Bay area, and Cunningham was forced to spend more time at home raising children; she then discovered subject matter in her own backyard, and her enlarged, sharp-focus closeups of flower and plant forms are some of her finest work.

Gertrude Käsebier

1852–1934; United States
Käsebier had to wait until her three children were grown to begin expressing her lifelong desire to "make likenesses that are biographies." In 1897, Käsebier opened a portrait studio in New York. Her portraits were remarkable in that she used available light and natural settings, both departures from formal Victorian studio-portrait techniques. She also created a series of allegorical photos expressing different aspects of the concept of motherhood.

Maya Deren

1922–1961; United States
A major figure in avant-garde film, Deren was a pioneer in distributing her own films and championing the cause of independent filmmakers, urging them to "feed the imagination." Her major works included *Meshes of the Afternoon* (1943) and *Ritual in Transfigured Time* (1946). Her images, often heavily symbolic, offered striking examples of the possibilities of experimental film and revealed a unique and obviously feminine sensibility.

Dorothea Lange

1895–1965; United States
Lange is best remembered for her poignant photographs of migrant agricultural workers, pictures so eloquent that they served to arouse national sympathy

for the plight of these people. She began as a portrait photographer in San Francisco, but during the Depression she took her camera out of the studio and into the streets. She was sent by the Department of Agriculture to document the miserable conditions of agricultural workers and then photographed the dislocated Japanese who were being interred in concentration camps in California. In her last series, *The American Country Woman*, she attempted to depict an aspect of American womanhood that departed from the media image of "our well-advertised women of beauty and fashion." "These are women of the American soil," she said. "They are a hardy stock. They are the roots of our country."

Women have been more active as designers and craftspeople than as architects, primarily because the former fields, taken less seriously, were receptive to female participation, while the latter has been enormously resistant.

Eileen Gray

1879–1976; Ireland
Gray was a forerunner of the modern movement in design. She built several houses that expanded on the nineteenth-century concern with efficient employment of space. She also developed interior spaces and furniture that were rich, sensual, and personal. Interred as an enemy alien in France during World War II, she suffered the looting of her house and the destruction of much of her work. She was devastated by a lack of recognition during her lifetime, and by the events of the war, and lived in seclusion for the rest of her life.

Sophia Haydn

1868–1953; United States
The first female graduate in architecture from M.I.T., Haydn won the competition to design the Woman's Building at the Columbian Exposition in 1893 in Chicago. In an effort to draw attention to women's progress in entering previously all-male professions, the Board of Lady Managers established a $1,000 prize for a woman architect. Haydn, only 22 years old and just out of school when her proposal was chosen, went to Chicago to supervise construction. There she was confronted with constant interference, and when the building opened it was attacked as a student's creation and a "woman's work." Disheartened and depressed, Haydn never built another building.

Mary Louise McLaughlin

1847–1939; United States
McLaughlin, a pioneer American ceramicist, was fascinated by the European underglaze slip decoration she saw at the 1876 Centennial Exhibition. In 1879 she organized a group of women in Cincinnati to experiment in ceramics and china-painting and try to duplicate European quality. Her innovative work in the use of colored slip and underglaze painting became the basis for the Rookwood Pottery techniques. Rookwood, established by Marie Longworth Nichols, was one of the first important art potteries in America. McLaughlin's later experiments with porcelain resulted in her finest work, exquisite art nouveau pieces. A consummate craftswoman, she worked in wood-carving, stained glass, metalwork, jewelry-making, etching, needlework, sculpture, and painting. She also wrote two manuals on pottery decoration and one on oil painting.

Julia Morgan

1872–1957; United States
Morgan was the only woman student in the University of California School of Engineering when she received her degree in 1894. She was the first woman to study at the École des Beaux Arts in Paris and the first to obtain a degree there. Also the first licensed woman architect in California, she opened her own office in San Francisco in 1904. Morgan's buildings, whether brown shingle residences or Renaissance-style edifices, reflected her elegant sense of design, her concern with interior and exterior space, and her respect for materials and principles of construction. Her most famous building is Hearst's Castle at San Simeon, but she designed over a thousand others in a career that spanned fifty years.

Women have become a major force in the performing arts, primarily by interpreting roles written by men. Theater has never been shaped by women, and until recently playwriting has been almost exclusively a male field. The most significant breakthroughs in the performing arts have been in dance, which, at the early part of the century, was profoundly affected by women's creative efforts.

Sarah Bernhardt

1844–1923; France
Bernhardt was the most celebrated actress in French history. During her sixty-year career, the "Divine Sarah" became a legend throughout the world.

Among many other roles, she starred in *Queen Elizabeth,* the first full-length American feature film.

Isadora Duncan

1878–1927; United States
Barefoot, dressed only in a flowing white tunic, Duncan introduced a form of movement that revolutionized the dance world. She challenged the basic tenet of ballet and searched for a spiritual, rather than a physical, center of motion. Once felt, she said, motion became effortless. She believed that young children easily grasped this idea, but materialist society robbed them of their innate spiritual power and grace. Although enthusiastically accepted in Paris and Russia, Duncan's dancing and politics were too eccentric for American tastes, for she moved with an unconstrained, childlike freedom, as no woman before her had dared to do.

Eleanora Duse

1858–1924; Italy
Duse, one of the greatest actresses of her time, was praised for her naturalistic style. Her most famous role was Ibsen's *Hedda Gabler,* in which her interpretation was so profound that it terrified the playwright himself.

Edith Evans

1888–1976; England
One of England's foremost Shakespearean performers, Evans made her debut as Beatrice in *Much Ado About Nothing* in 1912. She first appeared on Broadway as Florence Nightingale in *The Lady With the Lamp* in 1931, and in the forties she began to appear in films as well. On November 20, 1950 – as England's first lady of the stage – Evans spoke the prologue at the reopening of the Old Vic Theater, which has been destroyed during the German attack on London in World War II. Evans

received numerous acting awards, as well as honorary doctorates from Cambridge and Oxford.

Martha Graham

b. 1894; United States
Graham created a new style of dance through which she explored and expressed "the emotions, the inner being." Her most forceful and vivid creations were her portrayals of heroic women, both real and legendary: Jocasta, Clytemnestra, Medea, Alcestis, Phaedra, Xochitl, Judith, Joan of Arc, Emily Dickinson. Graham's performing career spanned fifty years; by the time she retired from the stage in 1970, she had created 150 pieces and had taught and influenced generations of dancers the world over.

Katharine Hepburn

b. 1909; United States
Hepburn, the only woman to win an Oscar for Best Actress three times, has created some of the screen's most memorable portraits. The spirit and individuality which infuse her life and work were fostered in part by a feminist mother who was active in both the suffrage and birth-control movements. Her early performances were in light comedies, but over the years she has developed into a powerful tragedienne.

Ida Kaminska

b. 1899; Poland
A major force in Yiddish theater, Kaminska founded the Warsaw Jewish Art Theatre and then the Ida Kaminska Theatre, where she not only performed but worked as producer and director as well. Anti-Semitism forced her to New York, and she revived the Yiddish theater there. In 1965 she gave one of her most moving performances in the Polish film *The Shop on Main Street.*

Anna Pavlova

1885–1931; Russia
Pavlova, one of the century's greatest ballerinas, began her career with the Russian Imperial Ballet Company in 1899. She became the dazzling prima ballerina of the troupe, bringing new life to such classics as *Gisele.*

The question that remains unanswered, after surveying the lives of all these women of achievement, is why so many of their names are unfamiliar and their contributions obscured. To make people feel worthless, society robs them of their pride; this has happened to women. All the institutions of society tell us – through words, deeds, and, even worse, silence – that women are nothing. But our heritage is our power; we can know ourselves and our own capacities by seeing that other women have been strong. To reclaim our past and insist that it become a part of human history is the task that lies ahead. If that is left undone, all our gains will be lost once again. The future requires that women, as well as men, shape the world's destiny.

215

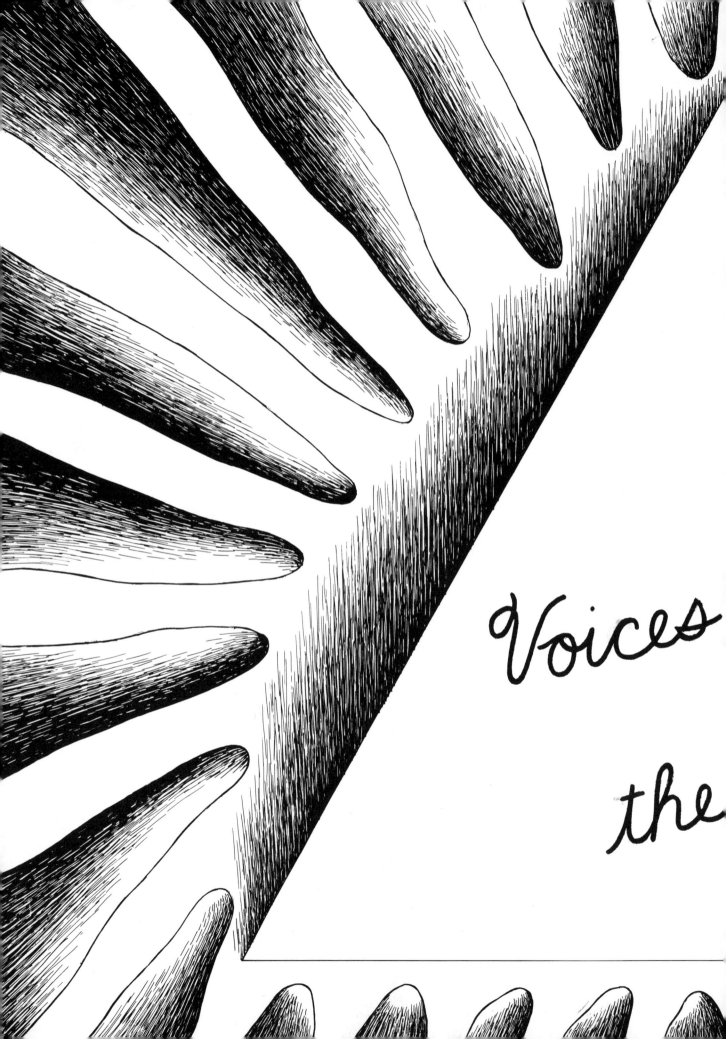

Voices

the

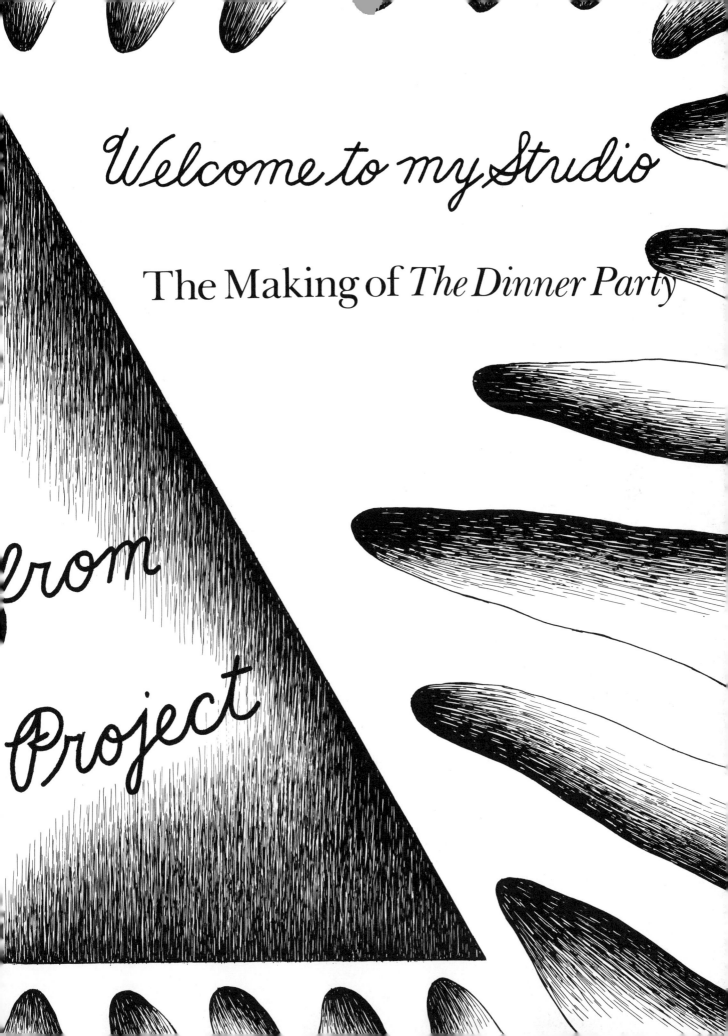

Welcome to my Studio

The Making of *The Dinner Party*

from

Project

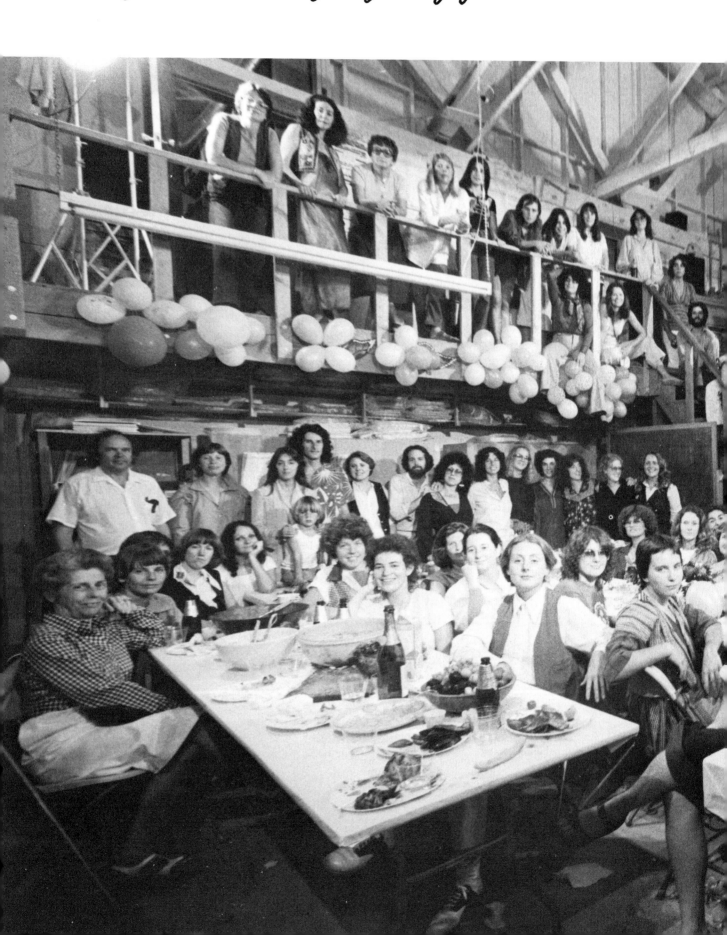

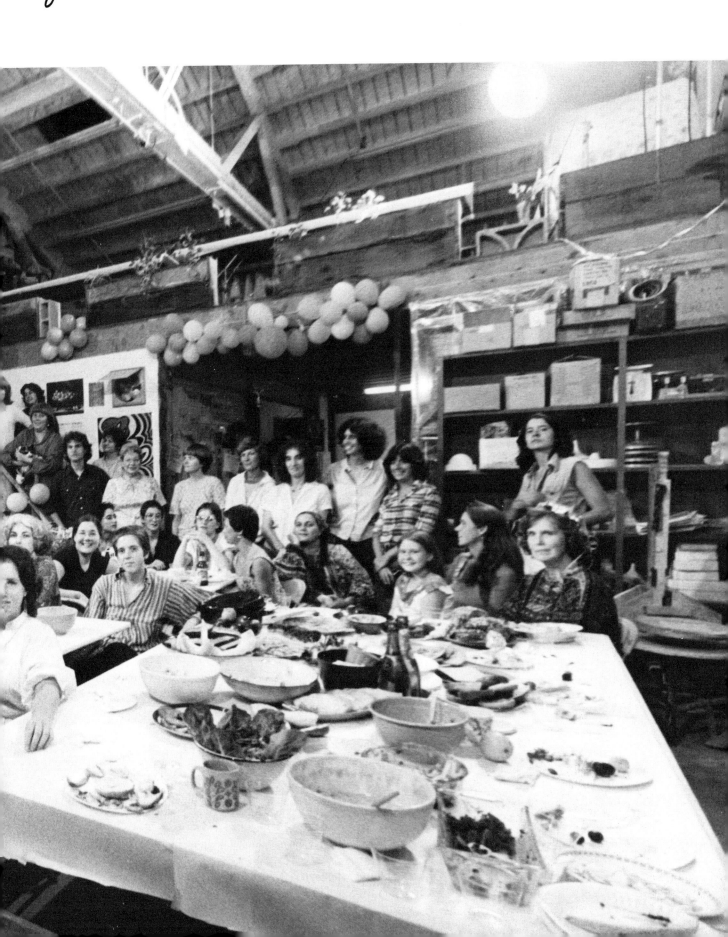

Chicago has taught me to hang in there and let the work speak for itself. I am learning.

—*Diane Gelon*

In the studio everyone had the opportunity to participate in the esthetic process and to take on more responsibility according to an increase in skill. We weren't equals because we didn't all have equal skills. Still, people with higher expertise were not inaccessible or unaccountable. There was a potential for downward as well as upward mobility in the studio operation which developed out of group interaction and cooperation.

Everyone contributed toward cleaning the workspace by giving either time, money, or supplies. We were expected to take turns emptying the trash, sweeping the floor, and answering the door. Some people did more routine work because they were less skilled, and maybe only one or two could actually do the complicated carving involved in ceramics. But even the most skilled workers did a share of the dull jobs.

—*Ann Isolde*

I got angry one night and said I didn't like the way the group was being run. "Well, what do you need from the group?" I was asked. I couldn't answer immediately but realized later that what I had wanted was to be led and taken care of. The first step for me was deciding to take care of myself.

—*Marguerite Clair*

It didn't feel different working with a lot of women, partly because I didn't notice it until somebody mentioned it. Mostly I wasn't aware of it at all.

—*Peter Fieweger*

The first time I talked in a consciousness-raising group, it was about my self-image, which wasn't all that great. I was overwhelmed and cried through most of my five minutes. I had never had to spend that much time saying out loud just what I thought of myself, who I thought I was. And I certainly had never had seven people listen without interrupting me.

—*L. A. Olson*

The studio is at once both wonderfully supportive and extremely demanding; the energy level of so many people working toward one goal can carry me and encourage me – or it can force me to go forward, using the deepest resources of my energy, confronting painful issues.

—*Susan Hill*

This project, and the decision to come, was a strong, almost spiritual experience for everyone. There was weeping in telling of the real need to create artistically – to make art – to let out something very deep and strong within them.

—*Dorothy K. Goodwill*

It's been quite a revelation to me that I could make the demands on myself and my family for making art without feeling guilty.

—*Stephanie G. Martin*

Preceding page: One of the more memorable *Dinner Party* potlucks – Judy Chicago's 39th birthday party.

Thursday nights gave a sense of community; people from all departments had a chance to exchange ideas that weren't based on the work we did. We could kid around, complain, tell anecdotes, occasionally embarrass or bore each other – but all the while a learning process was taking place. We were together for one reason: to work on *The Dinner Party*. I found we could trust each other, and the emphasis was on learning, growing, sharing, changing, creating new possibilities. If one had something to say it would be heard. It was difficult for me to talk in groups. I'm usually comfortable talking one-to-one or even two or three. With more people than that I'm unsure of myself. I don't do well at "thinking on my feet," and even if I can manage it I don't feel that I articulate well. My flickerings of self-confidence were mirrored in some of the other women – they said what I was thinking. I took delight in finding them; they reinforced the sometimes forgotten love that I have for myself.

—*Shannon Hogan*

I felt a great sense of personal satisfaction and role flexibility at the studio. It doesn't matter whether I'm a man or a woman. What does matter is whether I can come through. The content of the piece forced me to think about my life and my values all the time.

—*Ann Isolde*

One of the best things about being around Judy is that she is convinced that being an artist is truly an important occupation – second to none.

—*Shannon Hogan*

My biggest difficulty was trying to split myself up between the studio, husband, my children, school, my part-time job, and my household duties. I would try to get my life organized and go down to the studio. I enjoyed doing the embroidery and the calligraphy, and naturally I wanted to do my best, but I was put under so much pressure. I would see my hand shake when I picked up the pen or the needle. I had had previous full-time jobs and had worked as an accountant, but this was different. Not only was I completing a piece of work, but I was also working with other women for a cause I believed in.

—*Pamela Checkie*

I have always wanted to do something larger than life, something that would survive my lifespan. Without the project I would have been defeated.

—*Elfie Schwitkis*

I was kept honest by not being paid – my ego couldn't get in the way and allow me to think that my value grew out of how much I was making as opposed to what I was actually contributing.

—*Ken Gilliam*

Sometimes it was a heavy atmosphere for me. When I arrived I realized I could no longer conceal from myself concerns which required firm decisions and actions. In that sense it was sometimes frightening. The studio demanded honesty and responsibility.

—*Laure McKinnon*

Judy's drawings were the springboard for the ceramics team. We would congregate around the drawing and talk about our feeling toward the women represented and the imagery Judy had used. The large later drawings were most helpful because the image, the picture of the woman, and Judy's interpretation were all together. Then we started to address the problem of translating the drawing into a three-dimensional form from clay that would not only capture the sense of the drawing but also make it through a high-fire kiln. We had a lot of technical problems and disappointments. It was very difficult to remake a plate when four or five of its predecessors had failed in the kiln after weeks of work. There was always the question of whether I should put all my time and effort into something that had less of a chance of making it through the kiln than the one before. We tried everything technically that we knew to ensure a good result, and when we didn't know enough we sought out help. We got a lot of encouragement and even solutions at times, but mostly we had to solve the problems by ourselves.

—*Judye Keyes*

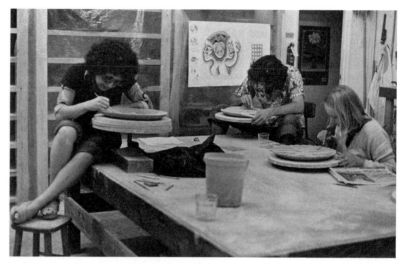

Chicago, Skuro, and Keyes carving plates.

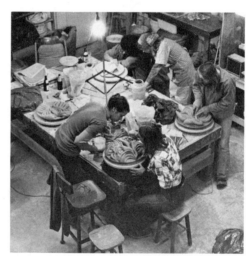

Clockwise: Chicago, Kathy Erteman, Daphne Ahlenius, Keyes, Meredith Horton.

One of the more memorable times occurred during a blitz of the ceramics team, which at the time was all women. We were working day and night for a solid two weeks in order to get the last images on the plates. We worked twelve-to-fourteen-hour days, beginning at 6:00 a.m. and often lasting late into the early morning. Thelma cooked for us and brought meals into the studio. We ate and then went back to work. The conversation revolved around the work we had done and the work at hand. The atmosphere was intensely focused on what we were to accomplish. It was a unique experience for me to work so cohesively with a group of women. There was a shared anxiety, love, and exhaustiveness that brought everyone onto the same plane – and the images were born.

—*Judye Keyes*

I spent much of the time working alone on the Project, since I had to solve problems before we could even begin. Everything was so difficult and I didn't know what I was doing. I had never built a jigger machine, never made fourteen-inch porcelain plates, and everyone told me I couldn't do it. We all know that didn't mean anything, but it doesn't help when you go to someone with a problem and they say, "Forget it, you're nuts." I had troubles with that when I was on my own. Then we set up the studio and Judy and I began to work together; she has a great discipline in work, and I got a lot out of this.

—*Leonard Skuro*

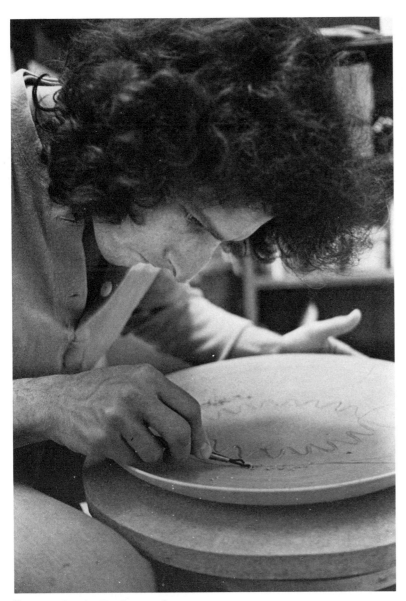

Skuro carving the Hatshepsut plate.

I was teaching with women at the same time as I worked on *The Dinner Party;* there I was the teacher, with a position of authority. Then I would go into the Project, where there was shared responsibility. It was a constant flopping for me, and sometimes I would blow it.
—*Leonard Skuro*

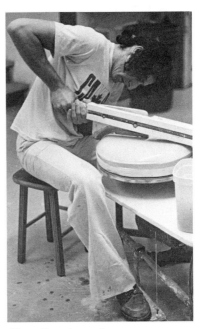

Skuro jiggering a plate.

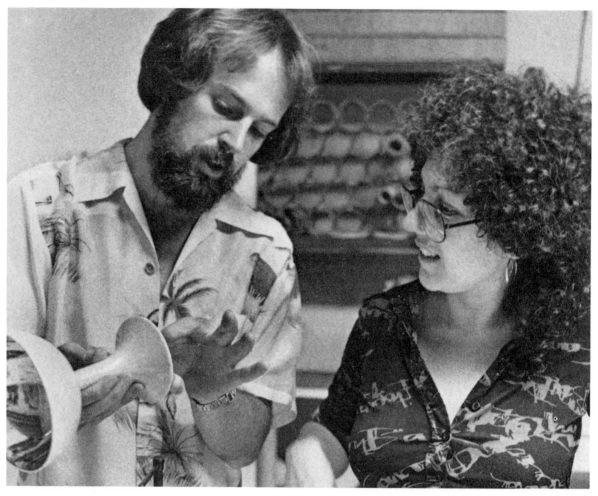

Ken Gilliam and Judy Chicago.

I think men operate in such a way that they avoid coming into contact with not knowing something, particularly when it's connected to oneself. Admitting my weakness or vulnerability, remaining open to input and criticism about my ability to operate with other people – this is what I've had the most difficulty with.

—*Ken Gilliam*

On Caroline Herschel's plate we did four prototypes and four for real. I laid in the wing which sets up the curve, and I did a lot of the carving. I remember putting the wing on and having a discussion of how to make the plate lift. "How do we make the wing look real and full of energy? What is the quality of a wing? What is the edge of a wing like? Is it blunt, is it sharp? How does this contrast with the lip, which has more mass?" There was real giving in that discussion. I felt very confident about making the curve visually correct. Judy was more concerned about the turning of a wing. In that place we would see very differently and yet see the same thing. Judy would be seeing it as an image, and I would be seeing it as a shape. This is my training. Sometimes we would just flop a wing on the table and play with it, saying, "That one is right, that one is wrong." The plate evolved, and we would talk about it and try to make this clay object, which has a limiting thickness, into something believable.

—*Leonard Skuro*

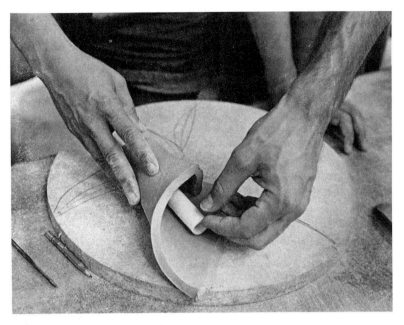

Working on the Caroline Herschel plate.

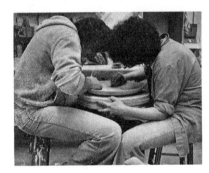

Skuro and Chicago.

Judy would do the curves because she had the patience. I would do undercuts and the flat areas because I could make the flat areas look very flat. Judy's areas were dependent on my areas, and my areas were dependent on Judy's. Nothing looks good unless what is next to it looks good.

—*Leonard Skuro*

We worked in silence. There was an energy, a body unison that came about. I shut out the world, bit by bit. I started by tuning out the loft, then tuned out the lower floor, and finally I tuned out everything except the plate and my hand working on the plate. At the same time I was trying to be in rhythm because Judy was on the other side, and it became a beautiful kind of dance or give-and-take because I couldn't move until she was ready to move. We would talk; I would say, "I'm scraping something flat and need to move half rotation, can you move?" If she was not ready, I would wait and allow her input to affect where I was going to work.

—*Leonard Skuro*

Judy's imagery is very easy to read, very blatant if you know something about the woman represented. The first plate I started working on was Theodora's. I had a lot of preconceived notions about how mosaics should be done. I researched different mosaic techniques which had been done by placing single stones side by side and grouting. But that wouldn't work in ceramics, so I had to devise a new way of working that was more applicable. I worked with templates and more or less laced the plate, expanded it outward and worked on sections at a time. I must have done about four or five test plates before getting something that I was satisfied with. It took four months to work it out and get one out of the kiln without cracking.

—*Judye Keyes*

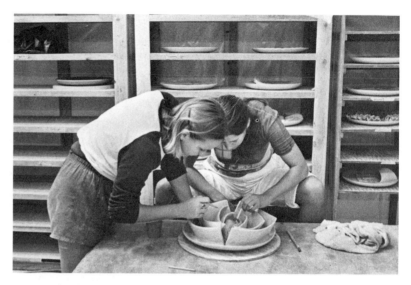
Keyes and Horton – Virginia Woolf's plate.

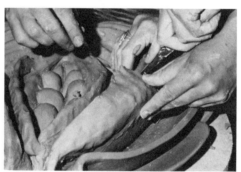
Building the Virginia Woolf plate.

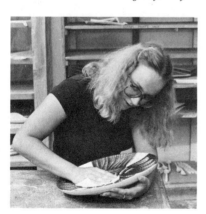
Keyes sanding Theodora's plate.

My confidence grew. Working day to day with Judy helped that, and as I got to know her better I felt more comfortable in making suggestions to extend the images. Working on the plates and listening to Judy's feelings toward the women, my own feelings came to be incorporated into the images. I remember making Margaret Sanger's plate and feeling very dissatisfied with the result. I read a biography and talked with Judy about what she wanted the image to convey. Then things just fell into place. She wanted an image that was strong and pushed itself up off the plate with a lot of tension. I would imagine myself on the plate and say, "Well, how would I push myself off? I'd grab onto the rim tightly and use every muscle."

—*Judye Keyes*

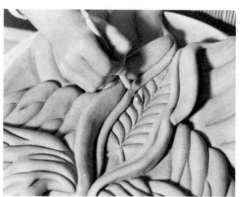
Finish-carving the Margaret Sanger plate.

June 16, 1978: What a terrific day in the china studio. I was struggling to paint the wings on one plate while Judy did the pen work on two others. I had been unclear as to what I thought Judy wanted to see, and I had been heavily and insensitively applying paint. After a few hours of work Judy picked up my plate, wiped off the bulk of the pigment, and began to paint. She talked about working with the underlying color and enhancing it rather than covering it up. She talked about building layers of wash and applying different colors over the existing color. When I went back to the plate I realized that I hadn't been painting – I had merely been laying on color. What I was learning while I painted those plates was to trust myself as an artist and to take risks. I watched Judy take on a strange color problem that she set up for herself. At that same moment she was asking herself whether or not to go for it. She said, "Sometimes I need to take an image when I have no idea where it is going and pursue it. When you do – you either hate it and dump it, or you go someplace entirely new with it, a place you could never have directed it."

—*Sharon Kagan*

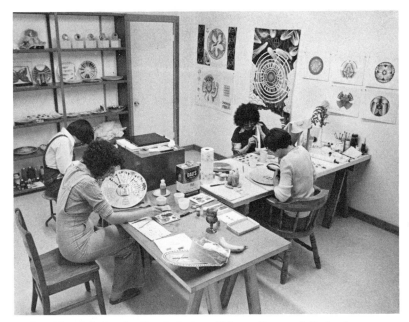

In the China-Painting Studio: clockwise – Chicago, Rosemarie Radmaker, Kagan, Margaret Thomas.

The plate that I expected the most difficulty with was Virginia Woolf's. The image incorporated ten slab pieces and a center form that had to be joined to the plate surface with grace and elegance and no surface cracks. We made a few test plates to see what our problems would be in executing the image technically. After we accomplished that, we approached the plate visually. Things would change and evolve around the image. This was a very different approach to ceramics than what I was taught – that the image would evolve around the technique. We had to make the clay do what we wanted, not be inhibited by preconceived notions of what it would do and what it would not. So we cut into the edge of the plate and created tensions and more stress on the body, but simultaneously added another dimension to the form.

—*Judye Keyes*

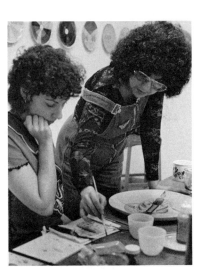

Kagan and Chicago.

When you look at the needlework of *The Dinner Party*, you are looking at thousands of hours of labor. Our runners have been worked carefully and patiently, thread by thread, for days and weeks and months in an effort to relate our history, to honor our tradition, and to build for ourselves an indisputable monument of proof that we can work together, sustain ourselves, be feminine and tough or masculine and soft, all at the same time. The needlework in *The Dinner Party* brings women's traditional way of operating into the main arena of society. It was all done by hand, by individuals who often came with no needlework skills into the feminist environment of the studio, and were taught to stitch and to operate as a support community. It was no mean feat. The enormity of the project itself and the concept of handmade runners was something far bigger than any of us had ever encountered. We made them stitch by stitch while we confronted problems of stained fabric and puckered fabric and thread that wasn't color-fast and expert advice that wasn't accurate and work that had to be taken out and continual money problems and feelings of insecurity and, as the years went by, physical and emotional exhaustion and arguments and tears and undisciplined work habits and constant interruptions and many misunderstandings and a great deal of joy and a sense of accomplishment and personal crises and an ever-changing roster of needleworkers.

—*Susan Hill*

Building a team in the loft was very much a part of my trying to grow in leadership. I did not really understand how to make a team, how to organize the information to hand out, how to allow people to function without my being controlling, how to delegate work and make it stick. I hated meetings. I did not understand the "feminist process." I talked on Thursday nights about how tired I was, or how I needed help to get the loft organized and functioning, or how people drained my energy when they could be taking the initiative. I kept trying; I watched Judy and Diane, and I learned how simple and clear and insistent you have to be.

—*Susan Hill*

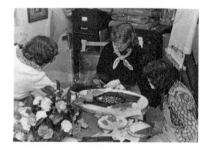

Von Briesen, Hill, Blecher – the Hildegarde runner.

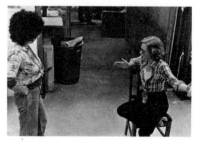

Chicago and Hill.

A lot of times in the studio there would be a very angry or tense moment. One happened between Judy and me during the design process. We were working one Saturday morning on something that should have been very easy. The tension mounted – we could just feel it – and then all of a sudden Judy opened up with what was bothering her. It was very true that she was operating as an accomplished artist; I do not have an art background, and she was making gestures in the fabric and with paint that I was ignoring. I was frustrating the hell out of her and she yelled at me. She couldn't work like this, she said, and asked me to leave. Being very stubborn, I wouldn't – I just held my ground. Despite the intense energy that was there, I said, "I need to supervise these runners; I need to be involved in this process." Basically, I wanted to be involved in the design with Judy. This was one of the real advantages of being in the project for me. So, because it was important that I have an understanding of the runners, she stopped. We talked about the gap that existed because she is an accomplished artist and I have no art school, no artmaking background. Judy slowed the process down and said, "Okay, stay included, it is important, I will slow down." Talking it out resolved the problem, and the work continued.
—*Susan Hill*

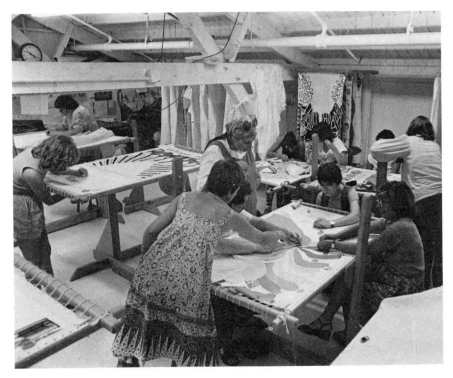

The Needlework Loft.

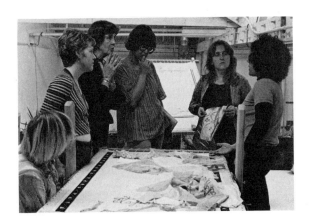

Discussing Aspasia's runner: Ruth Leverton, Hill, Connie von Briesen, Karen Valentine, Kathleen Schneider, Chicago.

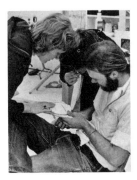

Hill, Blecher, Peter Fieweger.

their Goddess and their power.

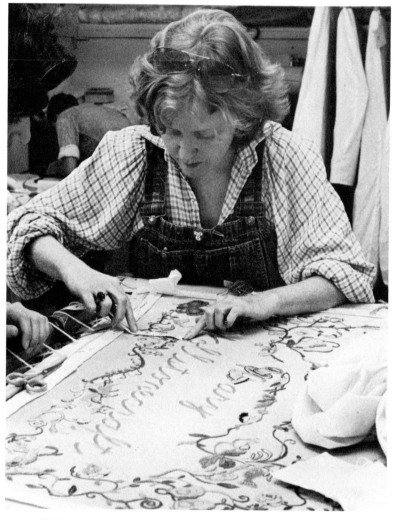

Susan Hill, Head of Needlework.

A work team did emerge. It was not built, but it formed as people came forward out of their own willingness to accept responsibility and their own desire to be visible. All the team members functioned best in different ways, so as the individuals changed over time, the team changed the way it functioned. Kathleen and I seemed to split the work down the middle without ever talking about it; she worked with some runners, and I worked with others. We made these choices out of instinct. We had a sense of what was happening with both the workers and the work. On really tense days, we would tell each other jokes under our breath, giggle, and keep going. In those very early days I did administration and supervision only; I answered questions and solved problems all the time. I needed Kathleen to help deal with the many artistic problems which I was too inexperienced and too insecure to handle. Kathleen left all the authority with me; I don't think she wanted it. When she left after a year of being there every day, it was to deal with some of the issues of authority and individuality that troubled her. While I understood and supported her move, it was very, very hard to see her go. An enormous burden settled back down on me, I felt trapped, and I suffered the loss of someone who could instinctively make me laugh, someone with whom I shared a special way of working.

—*Susan Hill*

230

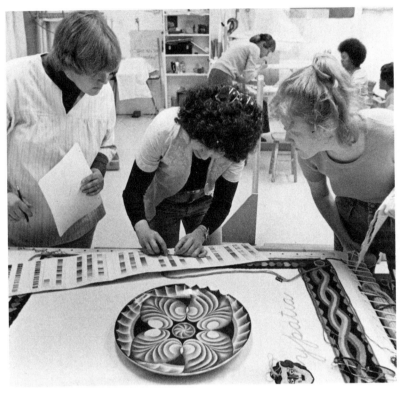

L. A. Olson, Chicago, and Hill – Hypatia's runner and plate.

There was so much work to do that anyone coming to the loft was welcome to take as much responsibility as they liked. Some people openly refused to take any. Some took responsibility as gradually as I did, and others consciously chose it.

—*L. A. Olson*

When we were designing some of the runners for the third wing of the table, everyone had different ideas and feelings. In the beginning of each design session everyone would be at odds with each other. It took most of the day and sometimes until late into the night to sort through all those different ideas and feelings and gain some clarity on what the image was supposed to represent. It was never easy, and it was hard to hold my own and assert my ideas even when they weren't popular.

—*Adrienne Weiss*

The new team grew slowly. Terry and Connie didn't like to administrate. They were great creatively, at problem solving, at giving technical help, but they didn't want to deal with people's work problems. Giving Connie and Terry space to work creatively, as hang-in-there stitchers, however, allowed them to function as role models. Adrienne Weiss functioned in much the same way. She was young, creative, articulate. She grew into responsibility in the project and had the sheer guts to outlast all our early criticisms of her work. L. A. Olson was very good at administration, and at stitching, and was often much clearer than I was in making work demands. L. A. and I learned to share power; that is, we both tried to operate at maximum potential, in the same area of work, with the same group of people. We talked openly about fears of competition, and about my previously ambivalent attitude toward letting go and sharing; we talked about how we could operate together so that one of us didn't feel invisible and the other like a martyr. We operated in a very fluid way – sometimes administrating simultaneously and, at other times, one concentrating on getting stitching done while the other concentrated on parceling out work on the loft.

—*Susan Hill*

The loft was set up to share work. The tools were laid out in specific places and had to be returned to their own places. Big schedules of work and goals were regularly posted for all to see. The runners were organized by team, with a "runner Mom" in charge and a team of people working with her until the runner was done.

—*Susan Hill*

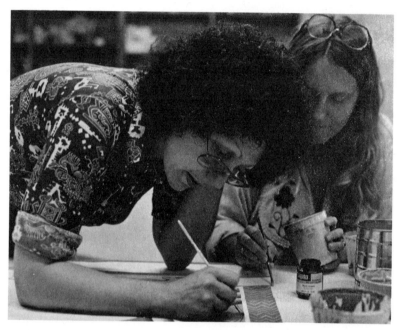

Chicago and Schneider.

Helping to design runners with Judy was always the high point of my work at the studio. It allowed me to use my painting and design skills – acquired over six years of schooling – and become involved in an immediate creative process. Working with Judy on this level, opening, exchanging ideas, mixing colors, and painting side by side, became a comfortable and stimulating experience.
—*Kathleen Schneider*

After most design meetings, I felt excited with the runner design and also frustrated with the group process and my place in it. On the one hand there was a wonderful energy of sharing ideas, and on the other hand I often let my insecurities stand in the way of taking authority and presenting my own ideas. In each meeting I felt that there was a beginning time when I was withdrawn – seeing where Judy's ideas started and left off and how (and if) I could extend them or add any valuable input. I often had trouble sensing her level of receptivity, and, because of my own personal "damage," I allowed her moods to keep me from offering input. As the artmaking process became more and more demystified for me and the people became less intimidating, I began to contribute more and become more confident. I found that my impulses and intuition were almost always headed in the right direction, and I even found that if I had mentioned my ideas, fears, or feelings about design decisions earlier, we could have gotten to our goals much quicker.

—*Terry Blecher*

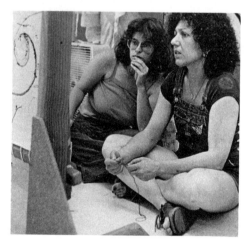

Blecher and Chicago.

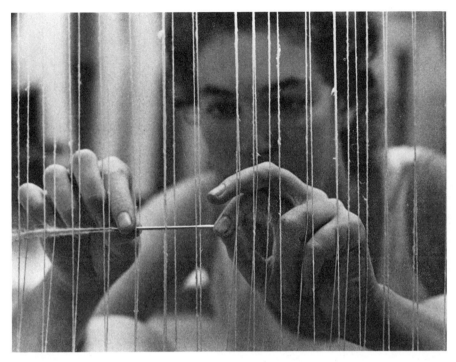

Adrienne Weiss.

When I first came to work at the studio I was seventeen (I had placed an ad in *Art Week* offering my services as an apprentice – I was in search of a "real" artist). For a while I felt like a bit of an outcast, since there was a lot of resistance from some of the people and they acted inhibited with me. I couldn't do certain jobs because I was "too young." I often felt angry and resentful; I saw myself as capable and aware while others did not. But I was fascinated by the piece, its scale, and how outrageous the whole concept was. I wanted to be connected with it and to "prove" myself. This experience opened my eyes to what working very intensely with others can be like.
—*Adrienne Weiss*

The Fertile Goddess runner was made primarily by Adrienne Weiss. Roughly woven, the runner is adorned with small clay fetishes, shells, coils, bone needles, and other objects reminiscent of early civilization.

I helped design and do research for the Boadaceia runner and did all the translation into needlework techniques. I felt deeply connected to the piece – as if I had been Celtic in a past life and Boadaceia's spirit was directing me. Because of this I was not always able to trust Judy's instincts without taking mine into close account. Judy's input was always valid; I listened and tried to understand her suggestions, and her way of spotting what was needed never ceased to amaze me, yet I also learned to listen to my own feelings and work with them.
—*Terry Blecher*

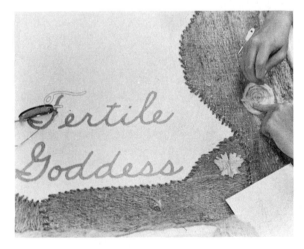

The Fertile Goddess runner.

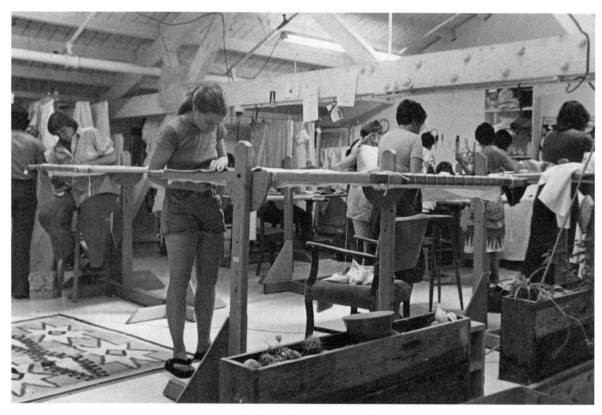

The Needlework Loft.

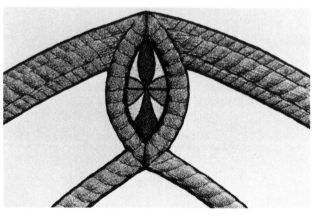

Stitched detail from the Hildegarde runner.

The studio environment transformed for me all that women do while waiting. It transformed the stitchery, the sewing, the chit-chatting, the aloneness – the waiting for the end of that dreadful aloneness – into something more tangible, something that added meaning to it all. The studio magnified a thousandfold one individual woman's pain, her loneliness, her waiting, her guilt, her confusions, her invalidity, her invisibility. Coming to that studio opened my eyes to the rainbow array of women who have experienced similar impositions, similar slow dyings, women who are no longer satisfied, no longer willing to be so imposed upon.

—*Elaine Ireland*

In working on Saint Bridget's runner, we ran into a disagreement about translating a Celtic cross on the back. My feelings were in favor of a pierced and carved wooden cross – using this medium would make a place for those intense religious feelings I'd had inside me all those years. Twelve years of Catholic schooling and my heavily religious childhood had almost been submerged until that day when, looking at symbols for the saints, it all came back. The wooden cross symbolized so much for me. After working on it the entire day, I was upset when Judy decided to change it because another woman said she could knit a cross instead. I felt that it was partly my design as well as Judy's, and I didn't want to give up easily; my artistic pride came to the surface. But in such cases Judy had the final say, and I conceded – although not without letting my feelings be known. (Eventually, however, we used the wooden cross.)

—*Kathleen Schneider*

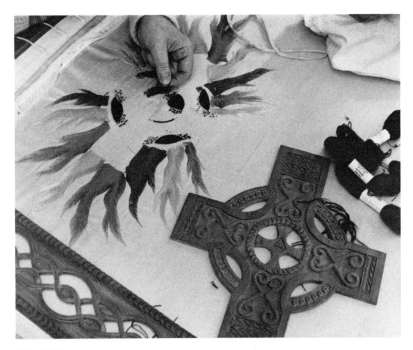
Saint Bridget's runner.

My only real difficulty at the studio was in acknowledging my own worth. When I started out I was sure Judy or someone would say, "Go home, you can't do anything." That never happened because it wasn't true, but it took me a long time to believe that other people's opinions might be more accurate than my self-image. While I'm still struggling with this, I'm better about expressing opinions and acknowledging my skills and worth. I'm not as panicky at the thought that the piece will be exhibited in a museum along with "real" artists' work, with crowds of people looking at it.

—*L. A. Olson*

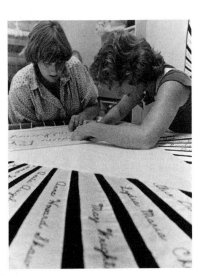
Olson and Hill stitching the Susan B. Anthony runner.

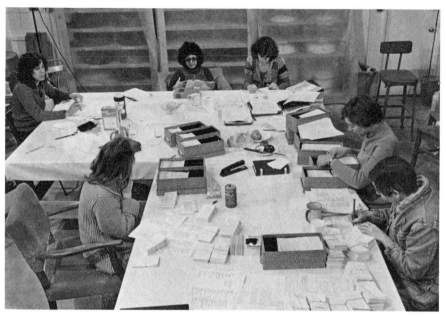

Choosing the 999 names: clockwise – Chicago, Isolde, Anne Marie Pois, Juliet Myers, Karen Schmidt, Diane Gelon.

We researched over three thousand women of achievement for the Heritage Floor. Information on each potential candidate for the floor was read aloud, discussed, and evaluated by the research team in successive, intense weekend sessions. Women were chosen on the basis of several criteria: If they had made a mark on history as we know it, they were considered and usually chosen. We also chose them if they had worked for the cause of women, something often disregarded in traditional history books. And they were chosen if their lives presented a role model for the future. But we had to reevaluate and reinterpret most of the available material and reread and rethink what had been written in order to redefine women's achievements from our own point of view. We then needed to place these women in a historical context which emphasized that each of them was not solitary and unique, but rather an inheritor as well as an originator of a long tradition of female achievement.
—Katie Amend

I'd been criticized by some people (men more often than women) for being "too serious" and working too hard. Ironically, in the studio I got messages to do more. So I had to come to terms with feminist values, to do a lot of reading and discussing, to fight a lot of resistance in myself from my earlier conditioning. Then for the first time in my life I felt really comfortable calling myself an artist. My whole attitude about history and women's place in it had changed immensely after two years of intense historical research. Now I can operate with the benefit of information about women rather than from a position of ignorance. I feel a lot of "invisible" but real support to achieve – it grows out of a deeper understanding of how and why women of the past did or did not achieve.
—Ann Isolde

The first fine point of discipline that I had to master was staying put in my chair – keeping my bottom affixed to the chair in which I was sitting.
—Juliet Myers

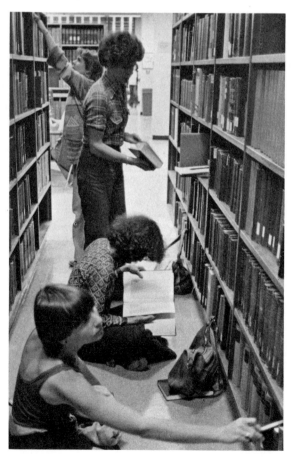

At the library: foreground – Myers, Isolde, Amend, Schmidt.

As soon as our card files (by profession/country/century) were set up and we had a certain amount of basic information accumulated, it was a matter of focusing our energy to fill in the gaps in each area. I organized a foreign language bibliography and also a regular book list on various countries. The task was overwhelming because that one book we needed, *Women in Western Civilization from a Female Perspective*, had never been written. We had to read tens and hundreds of books to collect all the fragments of information together. Most of the general survey books (which make up the majority of historical texts about women) don't deal adequately with a woman's relationship to her historical context. Women are represented like bonbons in a candy box, all beautifully wrapped and each one tasting different. The material is confusing because the women are not presented in any logical order or in terms of a fabric of historical events. I remember in college how history was presented according to events and the men who shaped those events. The women in some of the survey books don't seem to be connected with events in any active way at all. Often they appear as elaborately dressed yet isolated figures on a bare stage, struggling through their lines without the help of a supporting cast. Or else they are described more in terms of the men they are connected to than in terms

of their own achievements. Because of this, the research team had to develop a method of speed reading which concentrated only on hard facts. In addition, we had to start developing our own historical framework in order to relate individual women to each other and to some context of events.

—*Ann Isolde*

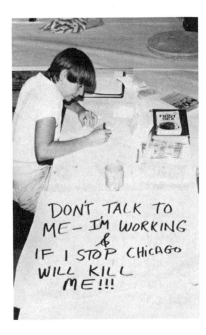

Juliet Myers.

My first task was to produce a chronology and outline of history for the women of ancient Greece. I remember Isolde showing me her work on Roman women. I was staggered by her thoroughness, organization, and attention to detail. Could I produce work of such quality? The question hammered at a brain slightly atrophied in the five years separating me from my thesis work and M.A. But I did do it! My fear of failure was immediately replaced by fear of success. I realized that once I'd produced, I must do it again and again, addressing ever more arduous tasks. As the months passed and our files filled with entries, I was overwhelmed by the volume, the variety, and the extent of women's contributions and achievements throughout history. And, frankly, I was puzzled as to how we as women could have allowed the obscurity, the trivialization, the belittlement to go on for such a long, long time.

—*Juliet Myers*

In *The Dinner Party*, we brought our knowledge and ability and interest together to work on creating a holistic, unified view of women's history. We were explorers, interpreters, and discoverers all in search of the same thing. We celebrated our discoveries by sharing them with one another. There was a continuity and a deliberateness to the research – a constant effort to reinterpret historical material, to revitalize it and discover parts of women's history that had been lost. Research was never done in isolation, for it contributed to piecing together a jigsaw puzzle more gigantic than we could ever have imagined.

—*Katie Amend*

Women's history needs to be unified and illuminated on a large scale at this time if our condition is to be understood. Only by better understanding our past will we be able to move realistically into the future.

—*Ann Isolde*

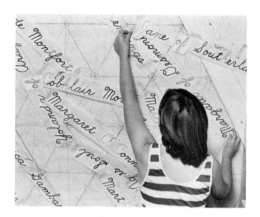

Martie Rotchford pasting up the Heritage Floor.

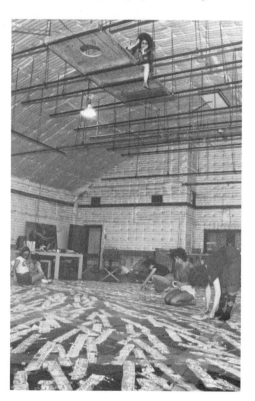

Laying out the Heritage Floor.

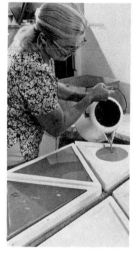

Evelyn Appelt.

To make the Heritage Floor, 2,500 twelve-inch triangular porcelain tiles were hand-cast and hand-sanded under the direction of Evelyn Appelt, owner of the China Boutique in Los Angeles. It took almost two years.

June 25, 1978: The design for the Heritage Floor was completed (basically) at 4:00 p.m. I felt absolutely wonderful! The image of women's history that finally emerged was simple, yet very organic and dynamic. It flowed like an energy field with channels in between. It reminded me of a pattern of metal filings created by a magnet or of an electron-microscope photograph of muscle tissue from the human body. It had been a month and a half since Judy, Ken, Martie, and I started the floor design project. When the last name was laid in, it was like cutting the umbilical cord, the life-support system. Now the design could be sustained by its own energy.

—*Ann Isolde*

My big necessity was finding a place for myself. I had no desire to volunteer my time and then stand around waiting for something to do. The floor names seemed to be the answer. Sandra Marvel was the only one working on names, and she came in twice a week. The names had been pasted up through the fourteenth century, but the whole process was running behind schedule. I was shown how to use the grid, the alphabet of Xeroxed letters, the correct slant to use when connecting them, the Palmer method reference booklet, the French curve, and how to slice the Scotch tape used for joining the letters. Once I'd mastered this (it took two or three weeks), I had found my niche. If the floor with its 999 names was ever to see the light of day, someone had to apply herself to pasting up the rest of the names. I took it as a personal challenge to see that these names were finished. I became very proficient at it, came in every day, and grew to like the almost mindlessness of it. Compared to the other concerns I had in my life (my husband, three children, painting and trying to promote my work to galleries, and a dollhouse booklet I was writing and publishing), this seemed lightweight. The only decision I made each day was whether to slice my tape in a straight line or on a diagonal! Sandra continued to come in, Martie – as head of graphics – was very busy but pasted names when she could, and after a couple of blitzes we finished – four

months later, far behind schedule, but not too late for the next process to begin. I could envision the floor and the names as a finished product and know that eventually what I was doing would be transformed into art.
—*Shannon Hogan*

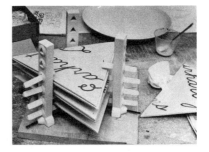
Preparing the tiles for firing.

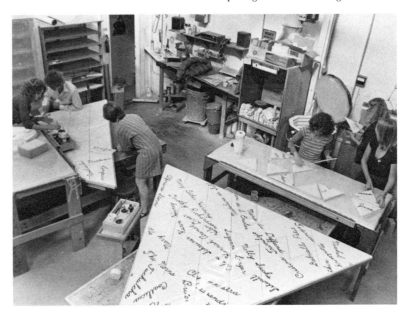
Golding and firing the Heritage Floor.

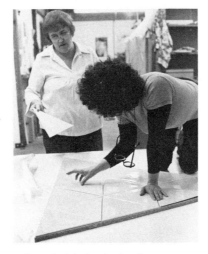
Helene Simich developing floor system with Chicago.

239

One night I came back to the studio around eight o'clock to work on the designs for the tapestries that would hang in the entryway to the piece. We were working on the one which comes between the reaching forms in the fourth design and the interlocked forms in the sixth and last design. The fifth tapestry is the one in which the forms begin to merge. We decided that the key word in the phrase, "And all that divided them merged" is *merged.* Judy said she'd been thinking of what to do, and she made a brief sketch. Then she got down on the floor on the graph paper and started out with a large gesture. She didn't ask me directly at that moment to help her with the drawing, although she had been asking Sharon Kagan and me to help on other designs all along. I knew I had the option to be involved if I wanted. I hesitated at first, and then I knew I had to get right down there on the paper too. I got the pencils, the markers, the eraser and went into the drawing with her. It was incredible! She started bringing in energy lines from one side, and I began bringing in lines from the other side. When the initial gesture was laid out with black markers, we picked up the drawing and laid it underneath the final graph paper which had the phrase written on it. Then, with pencil, we started to bring forms in around the words of the phrase. At first the forms reached toward each other without touching. Then one form reached out alone. Closer to the top the forms reached out again, and this time they touched. Then the last two reaching forms extended upward. The merging happened on many levels, incorporating varying degrees of touching as well as independence.
—*Ann Isolde*

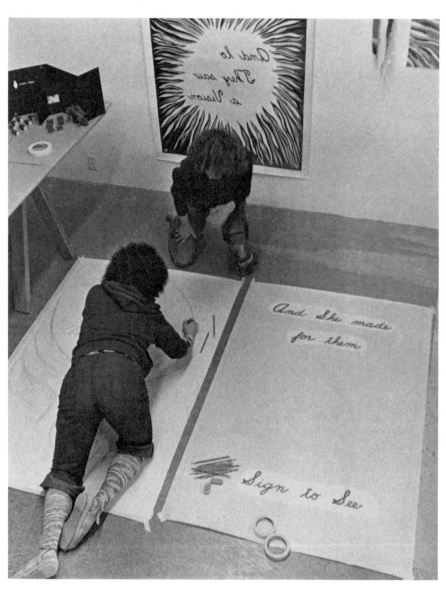

Chicago and Isolde laying out the tapestry cartoons.

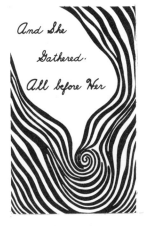

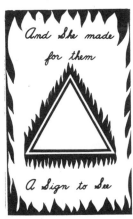

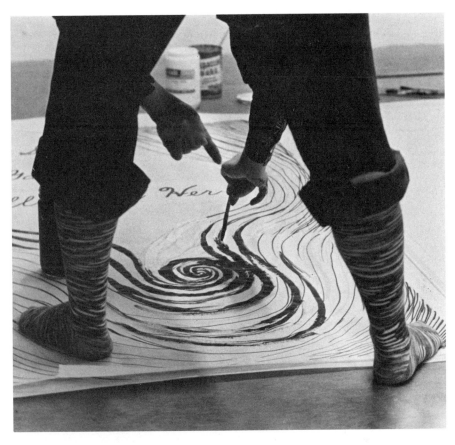

Chicago painting a tapestry cartoon.

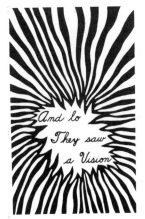

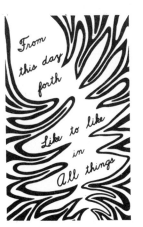

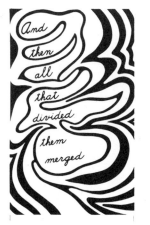

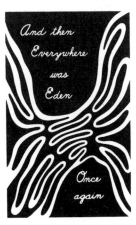

Tapestry cartoons.

1,038 women included in *The Dinner Party*

Most of my problems in taking responsibility had to do with my lack of experience – particularly because work in the Project had content and meaning and was not just skill-oriented. I've always been a responsible person, but not in relation to initiating things and then carrying through with what I initiated. I was trained in a relatively fragmented way, as most designers are. I came into the Project having no experience in really taking responsibility, with no one to turn to when I "finished my part."

—*Ken Gilliam*

The *Dinner Party* tapestries were woven at the San Francisco Tapestry Workshop, under the direction of Jean Pierre Larochette, on looms designed especially for the Project by Larochette.

I am still fighting the tendency to automatically accept a man's superior authority and to be intimidated into a position of deference just by his presence. When I accepted responsibility for coordinating the tapestry loom construction with Julie Leigh, I hit this difficulty head on. During a problem-solving session with Julie and Ken, Ken made some suggestions in a very authoritative manner. I rebelled violently against someone telling me what to do and how to do it. I felt my ideas had equal validity, but I lacked the self-confidence to express them with the same conviction. My back went up and we had quite a row. After much distressed discussion and a refereed dialogue, it became clear to all of us how much societal conditioning creates a man's authoritative demeanor, which Ken assumed as a cloak. Men do it whether they have the skill level for it or not.
—*Stephanie G. Martin*

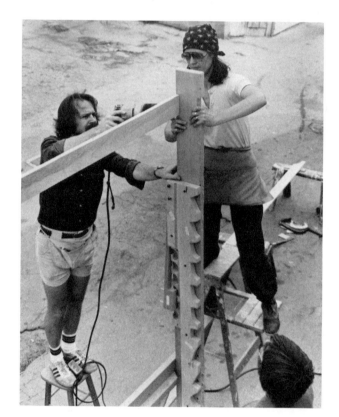

Gilliam and Martin assembling tapestry looms.

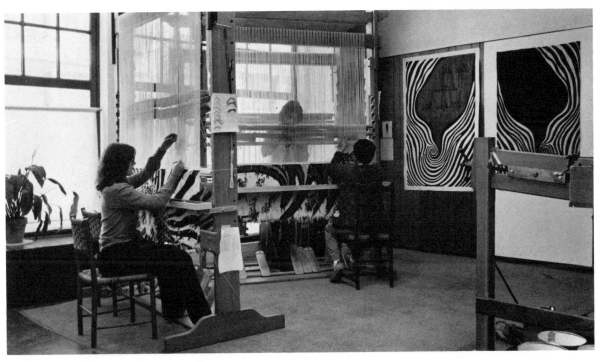

Ireland, Larochette, Barbara Kosman weaving the *Dinner Party* tapestries at the San Francisco Tapestry Workshop.

Being the fledgling facilitator of the tapestry workshop forced me to jump in and deal with power, powerlessness, and the illusion of power. In the past, I had usually allowed myself to let go of my self-esteem, my perseverance, my self-trust when the going got a little rough.

It was hard for me to make demands on others, especially those who resisted hearing and couldn't seem to understand why those issues should be addressed and examined anyway. I needed to share the reasons why one should make demands on oneself, push oneself, and not wallow in pure bitching or the personal problems that zap one's energy for the day. I was interested in getting past those gripes and pains.

—*Elaine Ireland*

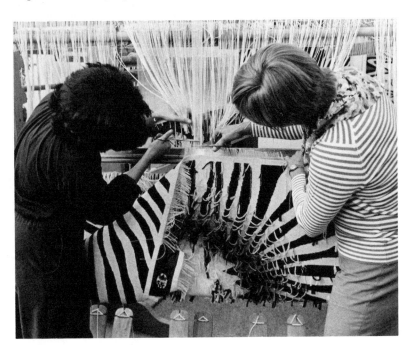

Linda Preuss and Mandy Haas cutting a tapestry off the loom.

243

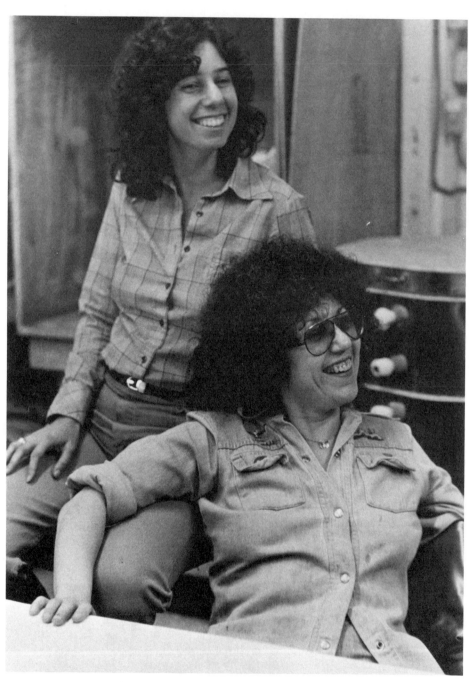

Diane Gelon and Judy Chicago.

worthless, society robs them of their pride; this

When I first came to Chicago's studio, only Susan Hill and Leonard Skuro were working with her. It had already become apparent to Judy that she would need a lot more help if the piece was going to get done. At that time, though, she thought she'd only need about a dozen people, and she had no idea how long the Project would take. Judy had built a large base of support among people around the country as a result of her work; there were a lot of people like me who believed that she was doing something important.

In order to support the studio, Judy lectured on *The Dinner Party*. When she talked about the Project, other people realized there was a way for them to join with her in what was a major effort to illuminate women's history. People started coming to the studio from around the country, and interest in the piece began to grow. Once there was more than a handful of people working, it became clear that we had to have some kind of organization so the studio could operate smoothly.

Judy and I had very similar values about creating an alternative structure. In her autobiography, *Through the Flower*, she had described how she set up earlier art programs. I began to implement her educational theories in the studio so that the work could get done. The artistic demands on the Project required Judy's constant attention, so I took on the administration, began to do most of the lecturing, and helped to bring in workers. I felt very strongly that Judy should not have to deal with ongoing studio problems. I knew from my studies in art history that almost all artists who had made an important contribution had someone who acted as a bridge between them and the outside world. Creative women have rarely had this kind of support, and I wanted to provide it.

Chicago had contributed all the initial money for the piece from sales of her work and lectures. She continued to support the studio financially, but I initiated a fundraising program so that the financial burden would not all be on her shoulders. The whole thing about raising money is that you have to take risks.

Monday
DECEMBER 5, 1977

My first day back in the studio was okay. I have lots of work to do just sorting out the last month – mostly letters to people I saw on the trip. Sometimes I wonder how the studio/Judy get along without me answering the phone. Took several calls this morning that I know no one else could have handled – arranging a lecture, appearing on cable TV in Santa Barbara to plug the D.P., spring workshops, and more. It's good to be back.

Judy's worrying about money again – so am I. We decided that the D.P. has been able to get this far on courage, talent, and vision. No one would ever have believed that we could get this far on so little money and such a lack of institutional support. We have come a long way in two years, but this last year – I hope it doesn't break us. But whoever said things are easy?

Yesterday I met for over an hour with a woman who is starting a foundation which would support women's projects. I really had to sell the Project. It's hard for people to understand Judy Chicago, how dynamic she is, how people will volunteer their time and move out to L.A. from all around the country... I'm not afraid anymore at all in terms of representing the Project. I do a good job. I'm very confident and as Judy says, "Try to let the images and photos speak for themselves."

Monday
APRIL 10, 1978

Sometimes it feels like all I do is spend time in airports and on airplanes. But I love it – all the traveling, being out in the world, lecturing, promoting the Project. I'm good at it and I enjoy it. Judy and I make a perfect team. She does the creative work and I do the P.R. and fund-raising. I have always had feelings about being a public person... but this transformation is often hard to integrate. I still think of myself as a little kid. But I am building confidence and am beginning to integrate all this into a new self-image. It's about time I changed – enough of the negativism... although it is easier to write about it than to do it!

When you start out you have no money, but you have to spend money to raise money – whether that's for phone calls, mailings, Xeroxing of proposals, or plane fares to get to where the foundations are. We paid for my trips by charging them on credit cards – first Judy's, then mine. We would pay them off with minimal monthly payments, and, by the time one would fill up, another would be paid off. We both applied for more credit cards. It was the only way we could do it.

I was often afraid to call someone on the phone; after all, who was I? I was only Diane Gelon. How could I call up somebody from the Rockefeller Foundation and say, "Hi, I'm Diane Gelon" – even if I did have the prestige of Judy Chicago behind me. I could always say I was Judy Chicago's assistant; that helped somewhat, but I was still me. It was a conflict – was I important enough to be able to meet with people I considered important? Did I have the guts to meet with them? I kept thinking, "I'm just this twenty-eight-year-old kid. Who am I to talk to Rockefeller?" I told all this to a New York publisher who said she felt the same way when she began; but she just did it: "You just get on the phone and remember they're all people." I did that, but I still got anxious.

The first thing I did was to research every foundation, finding out who gave money to the arts and to women's projects. That took several months. (I learned that you don't go to a foundation which sets up funds for disabled children and ask them to fund an art project.) Then I sent out letters of inquiry to those that seemed appropriate. Letter after letter came back saying, "Sorry, we're not interested." Getting all those rejections made me feel really crummy after all the work I had put in, but I knew somebody out there would support us eventually. I knew the Project was too good not to be supported. So I tried another approach: I went to New York, alone, with one contact – someone in P.R. and fundraising who said she'd help. I had gone to Washington with Judy once before to see the people at the National Endowment for the Arts (NEA), and I saw how Judy just laid it all out. She was very personal and honest with her feelings and was able to communicate the value of the Project. When I went to New York by myself I used those same methods. I started off with one contact, that person set up several appointments, and the next person set up several more. Most of the appointments didn't result in any money, but I was slowly building support – particularly among women of influence.

Our primary support came from the NEA, and, in addition to that, we received several foundation grants and a great many donations ranging from five to five thousand dollars. We probably received 5 percent of the grants we applied for; most of this grant support (outside of the NEA) came as a result of having a woman or women in a leadership capacity in a foundation. And the donations were almost entirely from women.

—*Diane Gelon*

Tuesday
MAY 16, 1978

I'm on the road again for another two weeks. Tonight in San Francisco for a talk at a Women's Caucus for Art meeting to facilitate local support when the piece opens. Then tomorrow I lecture at U.C. Santa Cruz. Then I go to Washington, D.C., for a D.P. benefit that the Washington Women's Art Center is doing. They expect about 200 people at $10.00 a person – to hear *me*! then I'll try one more time to raise money and see people in New York before the summer slowdown.

Everything is real clear today – it's beautiful looking out of the plane…

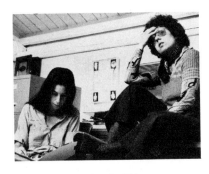

Diane Gelon and Judy Chicago, 1975.

and, even worse, silence – that we are

When I began working on *The Dinner Party*, my studio was a sanctuary. The only other person in the space was Lloyd Hamrol, to whom I was then married. His work took him away from both the studio and the city during a good part of each year, so I worked mostly alone in my four-thousand-square-foot studio in Santa Monica, as I had for many years. At first, my privacy was relatively undisturbed. Diane made sure that my concentration was not interrupted, but, by the summer of 1976, the studio was beginning to change its character. When Lloyd returned from his summer project, he was shocked at the number of people who had filled our formerly private space. My need to work with other people and his need for solitude led us to dissolve our marriage, although not our friendship.

I then faced the struggle of accommodating myself to a studio environment that was very different from what I thought a serious artist's space should be. Reared on modernist ideas of the isolated artist, I felt uncomfortable working with so many strangers. I had never before created images out in the open where everybody could see my process. In an effort to find support for my leap out of solitude, I turned, as I had so many times before, to history. There I found evidence of an earlier artistic tradition – several, in fact – which challenged the idea that artists had always worked alone. In the monasteries, the guilds, and the ateliers, artists (and artisans) worked and were trained together. I realized that it had been the Industrial Revolution which brought with it the notion of the isolated artist. For me, however, the psychic silence was not worth the pain.

At first I had a difficult time dealing with people being in my space, and I suppose I often reacted rather strangely. When I had been alone in the studio in the past, the rapid mood fluctuations that accompanied my creative process affected only me. Now all these people were witnesses to my constant changes. I learned a lot about myself by bringing others into the studio environment where I really lived. It was hard for me to accept that people could actually deal with me, as I was used to being told that I was too aggressive or too emotional or too defensive or just too much. The only way I had been able to preserve myself through the prior years of my professional life was to withdraw into the sanctum of my space.

Some people who came to work in the Project reacted to me as others had in the world outside my studio walls, and they often left because they couldn't deal with me. But some stayed and seemed to be able to interact with me honestly. This challenged my internalized beliefs that I really was too difficult to be around. I still have a long way to go, however, before I recover from the hurt I absorbed as a result of having a creative personality in a female body. I have come to understand that the outbursts of temperament allowed to creative men as a matter of course are simply not allowed to women. This, in addition to the lack of available support, is one of the reasons women have had such a hard time fully realizing our talents.

248

insignificant. But our heritage is our power;

We need to be able to be difficult, to be moody, to be preoccupied, to be upset – to be, in fact, human, with all that that means – in order to realize our dreams. I am grateful to the people who have come here, not only to work on *The Dinner Party,* but to help build an environment where women as well as men can be free.

—*Judy Chicago*

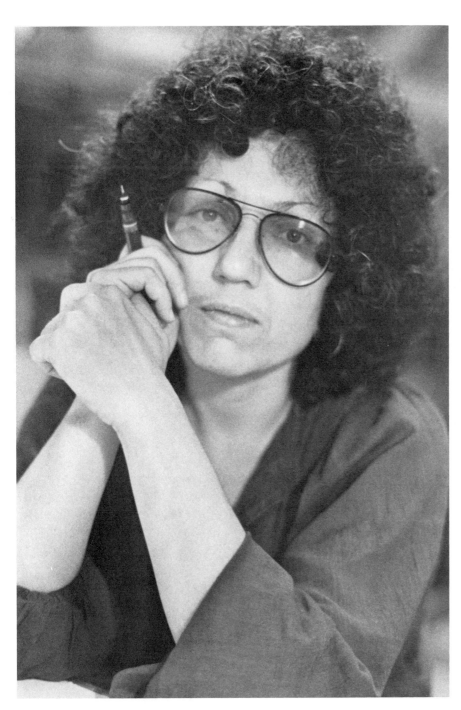

· Judy Chicago.

Acknowledgments

I wish to thank both Loretta Barrett and Angela Cox for their help and commitment; a special thanks to Katie Amend, who sustained both me and this book and to Diane Gelon; additional aid came from Mary Markovski, Peggy Kimball, Linda Norlen, and Martie Rotchford

I can never really thank Henry Hopkins enough for his support and friendship over these years, and I also wish to thank Alberta Mayo and the staff of the San Francisco Museum of Modern Art for their efforts. Additionally, I wish to express my appreciation to everyone who helped bring *The Dinner Party* and this book to fruition.

Included among the many contributors to the *Dinner Party* Project are the following:

Grants/Foundations

National Endowment for the Arts (NEA), Washington, D.C., a Federal agency:
Service to the Field Grant, awarded July 1977
Museum grant
to the San Francisco Museum of Modern Art, awarded July 1977
Museum grant
to the San Francisco Museum of Modern Art, awarded September 1978
Women's Fund, Joint Foundation Support
NOW Legal Defense and Education Fund – courtesy Bo-Tree Productions
Lucius and Eva Eastman Fund
Liberty Hill Foundation
The Ford Foundation

Corporate Donations

H. F. Coors Ceramics Company, Inc.
Earle & Jones, Inc., New York
Hanovia Hobby Products, Division of Engelhard Industries.
Philip Morris, Inc.
Warner Brothers Records.
Westland Graphics, Burbank.

Fund-raising Events Sponsored By:

Washington Women's Art Center.
Cleveland/Chicago Connection.
National Women's Political Caucus (NWPC) of Marin.

Individual Donors

Thelma Brenner.
Marny Elliott.
Doris C. Freedman.
Elyse and Stanley Grinstein.
Sandy and Bob Krasnow.
Tracey O'Kates.
Joan Palevsky.
Dr. Arlene Raven.
David Rockefeller Jr.
Kathleen Schneider.
Dr. Josephine Withers.

I wish to thank:

Margie Adam
Evelyn and Stan Appelt (China Boutique)
Anita Baron
Linda Bell (NEA)
Marjorie Biggs
Baird Bryant
Don Busteed
Anne H. Charles (Chair, NWPC of Marin)
Gail Counts
Robert and Lawrence Cowan
Janice Cox

Renato Danese (NEA)
Annette Del Zoppo
Johanna Demetrakas
Carlos Diniz
Ginger Eaton, Skip Paul and Chaffey Community College, Rex M. Wignall Gallery
Dextra Frankel
Dr. Paulette French (University of Maine)
Steve Gelon and Karin Joffe
Drue and Arthur Gensler
Mary Ann Glantz
David Greenberg, Century City Cultural Committee
Fran Griffin
Susan Grode
Walter Jankowski
Jean Pierre Larochette and San Francisco Tapestry Workshop
John McCone
Jane McMichaels (Director, NWPC)
Don Miller
Joan Mister and Washington Women's Art Center
Sandy Mullins (NWPC)
Pat Murphy and University of California, Santa Barbara (UCSB), Women's Center
Doreen Nelson
Kathleen Nolan
Neil Olson
Eugenie and Bill Osmun
Lyn Ostrow
Retha Ott (Chair., California Caucus, NWPC)
Rosemarie Radmaker
Adrian Sachs
Ruth S. Schaffner
Sue Severin (NWPC)
Manny Silverman
John Spencer (NEA)
Lael Stegall (Program Director, NWPC)
Ann Stewart
Deborah Sussman and Paul Prejze
Mary Ann Tighe (NEA)
Tom Tyson
June Wayne
Peri Winkler

250

by seeing that other women have been strong.

Color Photography

Don Miller
  Mary McNally
  With assistance from
  Robert Blakeman and
  Beth Thielen

Black-and-White Photography

Mary McNally
  Susan Einstein
  Diane Gelon
  A. Springer Hunt
  Lyn Jones
  Thea Litsios
  Amy Meadow
  Juliet Myers
  Linda Shelp
  Beth Thielen

Dinner Party Members:

Daphne Ahlenius
Marilyn Akers
Pat Akers
Katie Amend
Marilyn Anderson
Ruth Askey
Cynthia Betty
Marjorie Biggs
Terry Blecher
Sharon Bonnell
Susan Brenner
Thelma Brenner
Julie Brown
Frances Budden
Susan Chaires
Pamela Checkie
Adelth Spence Christy
Marguerite Clair
May Cohen
Audrey Cowan
Joyce Cowan
Ruth Crane
Laura Dahlkamp
Lynn Dale
Holly Davis
Michele Davis
Sandi Dawson
Ellen Dinerman
Jan Marie DuBois
Elizabeth Eakins

Laura Elkins
Marny Elliot
Kathy Erteman
Faye Evans
Peter Fieweger
Marianne Fowler
Cherié Frainé
Libby Frost
JoAnn Garcia
Diane Gelon
Sally Gilbert
Ken Gilliam
Dorothy Goodwill
Winifred Grant
Estelle Greenblatt
Amanda Haas
Judy Hartle
Arla Hesterman
Robin Hill
Susan Hill
Shannon Hogan
Meredith Horton
A. Springer Hunt
Elaine Ireland
Ann Isolde
Anita Johnson
Lyn Jones
Nancy Jones
Sharon Kagan
Bonnie Keller
Cathryn Keller
David Kessenich
Judye Keyes
Mary Helen Krehbiel
Jean Pierre Larochette
  and Staff
Sherri Lederman
Julie Leigh
Ruth Leverton
Virginia Levie
Thea Litsios
Mary Markovski
Shelly Mark
Stephanie G. Martin
Sandra Marvel
Judith Mathieson
Laurie McKinnon
C. Alec MacLean
Marie McMahon
Mary McNally

Susan McTigue
Amy Meadow
Chelsea Miller
Kathy Miller
Judy Mulford
Juliet Myers
Natalie Neith
Laura Nelson
L. A. Olson
Logan Palmer
Dorothy Polin
Anne Marie Pois
Linda Preuss
Betsy Quayle
Rosemarie Radmaker
Charlotte Ranke
Rudi Richardson
Martie Rotchford
Roberta Rothman
Bergin Ruse
Karen Schmidt
Kathleen Schneider
Mary Lee Schoenbrun
Elfi Schwitkis
Manya Shapiro
Linda Shelp
Dee Shkolnick
Helene Simich
Louise Simpson
Leonard Skuro
Sarah Starr
Millie Stein
Catherine Stifter
Leslie Stone
Gent Sturgeon
Beth Thielen
Margaret Thomas
Sally Torrance
Kacy Treadway
Sally Turner
Karen Valentine
Betty Van Atta
Constance von
Briesen
Audrey Wallace
Adrienne Weiss
Judith Wilson

And

Susan Andersen
Marian Banks
Mariona Barkus
Shirley Bierman
Virginia Birkenseer
Shirley C. Bess
Joann Brown
Nancy Catron
Alice Chew
Gloria Clark
Cleveland-Chicago
  Connection, research group
Dean Dresser
Lorna Eisner
Elizabeth Eldred
Lisa Feinstein
Jan Gandelman
Cynthia Gersch
Susan Goldstein
Holly Hampton
Janice Hansen
Margaret Herscher
Lynn Hickey
Sharon Hoffman
Sally Holstrom
Helen Hotchkin
Ann Marie Kennedy
Debra Knoppow
Michael Koester
Pearl Krause
Robyn Levinson
Margaret Litchfield
Susan Marcinkus
Beth Martin
Rayle Mozur
Maureen Murphy
Althea Olson
Elisa Ann Orozca
Ellen Perlmutter
Wendy Piuck
Michelle Posner
Lynda Prater
Karen Reed
Lana Rogers
Margaret Roumpf
Esther Rubin
Judy Schlecter
Nancy Schulman
Elizabeth Schwartz
Howard Schwitkis
Kent Schwitkis
Rachel Seamen
Tawny Sherill
Stephen Shotland
Bryna Skuro
Ráveli Soltes
Steve Stark
UCSB Women's Center,
  work group
University of Maine,
  research group
Kay Wiese
Peg Wood

251

Index

as well as men, shape the world's destiny.

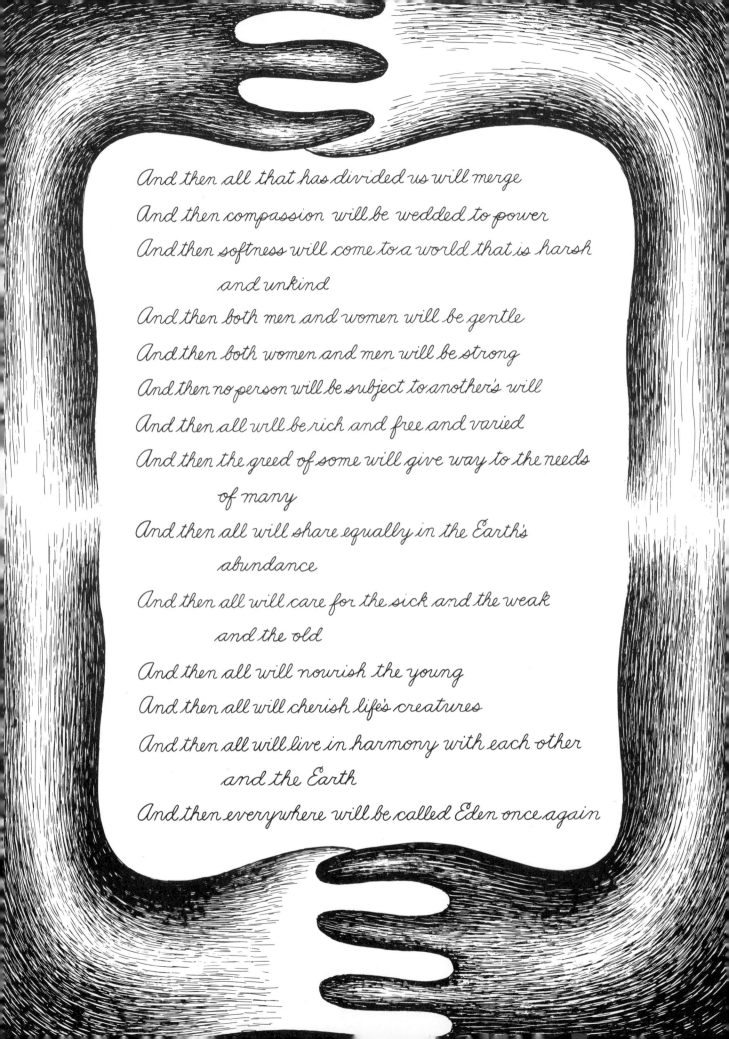

And then all that has divided us will merge

And then compassion will be wedded to power

And then softness will come to a world that is harsh
       and unkind

And then both men and women will be gentle

And then both women and men will be strong

And then no person will be subject to another's will

And then all will be rich and free and varied

And then the greed of some will give way to the needs
       of many

And then all will share equally in the Earth's
       abundance

And then all will care for the sick and the weak
       and the old

And then all will nourish the young

And then all will cherish life's creatures

And then all will live in harmony with each other
       and the Earth

And then everywhere will be called Eden once again

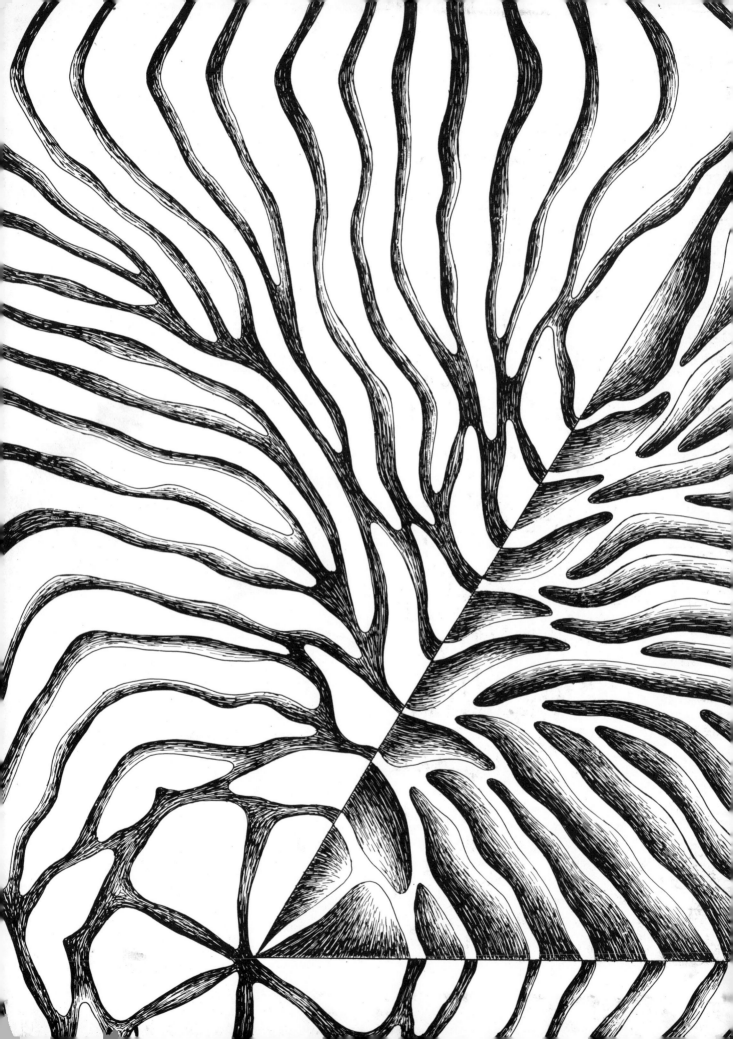